GENTLEMAN
AND PLAYER

GENTLEMAN
AND PLAYER

The Story of Colin Cowdrey,
Cricket's Most Elegant and
Charming Batsman

ANDREW MURTAGH

Foreword by Sir John Major

First published by Pitch Publishing, 2017

Pitch Publishing
A2 Yeoman Gate
Yeoman Way
Worthing
Sussex
BN13 3QZ
www.pitchpublishing.co.uk
info@pitchpublishing.co.uk

ISBN 978-1-78531-322-6

Typesetting and origination by Pitch Publishing

Printed in Great Britain by TJ International

Contents

This book is for my brother,
Dominic, who really was
Colin Cowdrey in those
interminable cricket
matches in the back garden

'Don Bradman was a great batsman.
Colin Cowdrey was a great man.'

Sir Garry Sobers on why he had chosen to attend
Cowdrey's memorial service and not Bradman's.

Foreword

Tribute to the Life of the Lord Cowdrey of
Tonbridge, CBE
By the Rt Hon John Major, CH, MP
Westminster Abbey
Friday 30 March, 2001

THERE is a moment, when someone dies, when raw emotion has a way of letting you know just how much they meant to you. When Michael Ancram phoned me with the news, I had a prickling in the eye that came unbidden and would not go away. No more Colin. Millions – some of whom had never met him – felt the same.

To those millions, Colin was one of the world's greatest cricketers. To those of us who knew him, he was one of the world's loveliest of men. That is why this Abbey could have been filled many times over.

Letters to the family came pouring in from all over the world:

From Australia:

'When one thinks of Colin Cowdrey, one thinks of grace, elegance – and England.'

From India:

'Sad to see you go, Mr Colin. We loved you in India.'

From Sydney came a prophecy, which I hope is true:

'Bowlers, beware! The great firm of Cowdrey and May are about to renew their partnership!'

There were many more such affectionate letters from all those whose lives Colin had touched.

It's not that Colin was a great cricketer – though that he was: the prodigious talent of the boy ripened, to make the man, the greatest pear-shaped batsman of our time. Although on a bad day he could have the cricketing equivalent of writer's block, most of his batting was pure poetry.

At Melbourne, aged 21, he scored a hundred for England that old men still babble about. I heard some of that innings over the static in the middle of the night – my ear pressed to the radio to avoid waking my parents who thought that a ten-year-old should be asleep. Lovely people, my parents – but they never did understand cricket.

Colin was a special man too. In the early 1990s he came to see me at Number 10 with some South African officials. As we sat in my study, beneath a portrait of W.G. Grace, he asked me to speak to some Commonwealth heads of government to help South Africa back into the world game. I did. They were admitted: but it was Colin's love of cricket that was the driving force.

He had a great affinity for the young. He helped me launch a sports initiative at a London stadium, following which we had an impromptu game of cricket with a veritable United Nations of children. An Indian boy bowled; I kept wicket; Colin batted and hit up a catch to a Jamaican girl. As she caught the ball, he cheered, 'Well played. Bravo! Well played' – an encouragement he used a thousand times a year. The girl skipped up and down, eyes shining and pigtails flying. Once again, Colin had used that extraordinary gift he had for making anyone in his company feel 100 feet tall. If I ever saw the joy of life, I saw it then. It was a very happy moment.

As Christopher has already said, Colin was a great writer of notes and a world-class user of the telephone. Whenever I faced political difficulty, Colin would be there. So we were in touch a lot.

The phone would ring and a voice would say, 'Morning, Skipper – Cowdrey here.' Or there'd be a note – many notes. They were always upbeat. 'Bravo! Well played. 100 not out,' he'd write – even if I had been bowled out for nought.

Sometimes if life was more than usually turbulent, he would phone those closest to me at Number 10 and ask if he could pop in for a drink.

For Colin, the answer was always yes. And when I walked into my flat above Number 10, late at night, he'd often be there – tumbler of whisky in hand – his gently smiling face and wise words bringing sanity and common sense to the frenetic world of politics. Colin never talked of this publicly – nor did I, before now. But it illustrates the kind of man he was: a friend in bad times as well as good. Truly a man for all seasons.

Colin's gift for letter-writing was no doubt hereditary. There is a letter written from Malabar, India, in October 1940, from Colin's mother, Molly, which paints a wonderful portrait of a happy cricket-mad boy 'enjoying himself' and loving cricket. 'And have you noticed his initials?' Molly wrote. 'MCC.' How proud she would have been of the extraordinary man her boy grew up to be.

But then family pride is a Cowdrey trait. Colin always spoke with such affection for Chris, Jeremy, Carol and Graham and his years with Penny. He was so proud of all their achievements – whether on or off the cricket field – with hundreds of stories which he would recount with an air of wonder that he and Penny should have produced such a talented crew.

And his joy over Anne and her horses bubbled over like uncorked champagne. He would phone me when a horse won. 'She's done it!' 'Done what?' 'Won.' 'Won what?' 'The race ... Anne's won.' And after a while even the horse got some credit too.

Colin is a loss to us all, but the greatest loss is to his family.

A modest man, blessed with the gift of friendship. A gentle man with a God-given talent. Kipling was right, 'If you can walk with crowds and keep your virtue, or walk with Kings – nor lose the common touch.'

Colin never lost it.

In life, said a lesser poet than Kipling, it matters not who wins or loses, but how the game is played. And how well Colin played it.

Captain of Kent and England; president of Kent and MCC; a Commander of the British Empire; a Knight of the British Empire; a Peer of the Realm. A man of Kent who left his mark on so many lives and had friends and admirers in every corner of the world.

And when Colin died, the England team wore black armbands for him and beat Pakistan in the gathering gloom in Karachi. As the unlikely victory neared, Colin's family and friends had returned from his funeral service and were gathered in his study at Angmering cheering them on. How he would have loved it. And how we missed him.

The day before he died, Colin was due to attend a meeting of the Master's Club, followed by lunch at The Oval – to honour Jack Hobbs – the man known universally in cricket as 'The Master'. He couldn't make it and sent a note, 'It is with great regret that I cannot be at The Oval today to celebrate The Master's Birthday.' He went on, 'What a magnificent season Surrey have had. Many, many congratulations.'

This was a characteristically gracious ending to a note that may well have been the last he wrote before the Young Master went off to join the Old Master, at a far Higher Table than The Oval.

It's hard to believe we will no longer hear his voice at the end of the phone. Nor be cheered by the notes he would send. But yet – Colin isn't gone. How can he be when he is in our mind, we can hear his voice and see his face? No man is gone while those who knew him – and the family who loved him – remember and talk of him. He left us too soon. For once, that immaculate timing was out – but it was a gem of an innings.

Colin played life as he played cricket: with a clear eye, a straight bat, and a cover drive from heaven. On the field and off it he was a true Corinthian. And when the Umpire of Life gave him out he went, without complaint and without rancour, to join so many of his old friends.

As for those he has left behind, we are blessed with an abundance of happy memories of the times we shared together. Well played, Colin. Bravo. Well played.

(Reproduced by kind permission of Sir John Major)

Introduction

MAY'S BOUNTY. Can there ever have been a more enchanting name for a cricket ground? It might just as easily have served as a title of a sonnet by Keats or the subject of a lyrical ballad by Wordsworth. But no, it is a cricket ground located in north Hampshire, donated by Lt Col John May, a member of a famous Basingstoke brewery family, to the local community for the purposes of sporting activity.

Cricket has been played there since the mid-17th century and it is currently home to Basingstoke and North Hants Cricket Club. From 1966 to 2000, Hampshire played a couple of their home games there every year.

A number of counties had similar festival weeks away from headquarters. Scarborough, Harrogate, Tunbridge Wells, Hastings, Eastbourne, Bournemouth, Bath, Cheltenham and Guildford were once as much of the first-class game as Lord's, Old Trafford and Trent Bridge but have now sadly fallen out of favour as being uneconomic.

Basingstoke Week was one such fixed point in the calendar, not greatly loved of the players, largely because of the cramped and spartan changing facilities, with a wooden floor that had more splinters than the gun deck of HMS *Victory* at the battle of Trafalgar. However, the post-match hospitality in the sponsor's tent was as generous as anywhere, it had to be admitted.

So why would I start a biography of Colin Cowdrey at a nondescript, albeit pretty, club ground which isn't even in his home county? The reasons are twofold. First, Cowdrey was no stranger to festival cricket. In fact, he loved playing at these outposts of the county game as much as he thrilled to the challenge and excitement of Test cricket at the great stadiums around the world. It was no great struggle for him to turn out for his beloved Kent the day after the conclusion of a Test match, no matter how modest and unexceptional the venue; county cricket was his bread and butter and he never turned up his nose at it.

Kent v Hampshire at Basingstoke was yet another fixture in a crowded season and he would have looked forward to playing. There was never an occasion when he did not look forward to buckling on his pads. He loved the game with a passion that never wavered from childhood to the day of his death.

Secondly, something happened at Basingstoke on 15 May 1974, which gave everybody who was there and many who were not cause for thought, throwing up an unusual but pertinent example of the enigma behind the public façade of Colin Cowdrey. By now, even in the earlier stages of the season, the name of Andy Roberts was making people, cricket lovers, journalists, players, selectors, sit up and take notice. Andy Roberts was fast all right, frighteningly so, and county cricketers up and down the land were now well aware of this. Including Cowdrey.

It hardly needs saying, but I shall say it nonetheless, that Cowdrey was as fine a player of fast bowling as there was in the game. His long Test career substantiates this. He faced all the fast bowlers of his era, from Lindwall and Miller, to Adcock, Heine and Pollock, to Meckiff, Rorke and McKenzie, to Watson, Hall and Griffith and to Lillee and Thomson. He knew how to survive and flourish against the very fastest. That is not to say that he relished it. Any batsman who says that he enjoys playing against fast bowling, I mean really fast, when you have only 0.4 of a second to react when the ball is rearing at you at 90-plus mph, is lying. Especially in those pre-helmet days.

So, when he went out to bat for Kent against Hampshire at Basingstoke in the early summer of 1974, Cowdrey would have heard of Andy Roberts and listened to the stories swirling around the county circuit about his fearsome pace but I doubt he would have felt intimidated. Admittedly the score was 21/4 and Roberts was steaming in down the slope but he had been here before, many times. For a few overs, he made it all look so easy, the mark of a good player. I had seen him at close quarters once or twice before and had always marvelled at the amount of time he seemed to have to play the ball. Many batsmen were hesitant, abrupt and sudden, often making an initial movement forwards or back before the ball was even bowled. Not Cowdrey. He was calm, unflustered, unhurried and economical with his foot movement and the ball seemed to glide off the bat. He was no different this day.

Then Roberts tested him with a bouncer. He did not attempt a hook; he let it go. But at the same time the old entertainer could not resist playing up to his audience. Theatrically, he made as if he hadn't seen it, ducking far too late and looking around as if to say, 'Good heavens, where did that go?' The crowd loved it, chuckling at the play-acting. But there was a collective intake of breath from the Hampshire players.

Up on the players' balcony, the Kent 12th man, David Nicholls, turned to James Graham-Brown and muttered, no doubt between mouthfuls of doughnut, 'Er, I don't think he should have done that.' Barry Richards, standing at first slip, observed out of the corner of his mouth to Bob Stephenson, Hampshire's wicketkeeper alongside, 'Uh-oh, red rag to a bull.' Richard Gilliat, the Hampshire captain, was fielding at mid-off. He told me, 'When I returned the ball to Andy at the end of his run, his face was expressionless, as it always was. We all knew what was coming.'

Indeed. Everybody in that Hampshire side was ready for it. Surely, it was inconceivable that Colin Cowdrey, who had faced more bouncers than pretty well anybody currently playing, was not expecting it too. The point was that Andy Roberts had two bouncers. We, his team-mates, had seen them both often enough and knew how devastating the second one was. The first was his slower bouncer, quick enough by anybody's standards but once evaded, it tended to induce a false sense of security in the batsman's mind. The second one, that bit quicker, was on the unfortunate batsman before he had time to react. Roberts hit more batsmen than anybody I have ever seen. And Cowdrey was not to be spared.

Richard Lewis, who was fielding at short-leg, said later, 'All I can remember was Colin falling like a sack of potatoes and in so doing he knocked over his stumps. He's out, I immediately thought, hit wicket!'

There is a wonderful series of shots, taken by the master of cricket photography, Patrick Eagar, which renders in almost cinematic form the moments before, during and after impact of ball on cheek, with Cowdrey's bat clearly rearranging his stumps. It was a horrible few minutes as concerned players gathered around the prone figure. A further picture of Eagar's, with Lewis kneeling down, one hand on Cowdrey's back and the other raised to summon help from the pavilion, is quite poignant. Sometimes, an image needs no words.

To everybody's relief, following a protracted period of medical assistance, Cowdrey pulled himself to his feet. We all expected him to make his way back to the pavilion, a little unsteady on his feet perhaps, with a severely bruised jaw and possibly missing one or two teeth, but thankfully upright and *compos mentis*. However, he had other ideas. He made as if to take guard again and resume his innings. Somewhat embarrassed, the Hampshire fielders pointed out to him that he was in fact out, hit wicket.

He turned to Gilliat to remonstrate. 'He said to me that he wasn't out and that he wanted to continue,' said Gilliat. *What did you say?* 'I just shrugged my shoulders and said, but Colin, you're out. Then David Constant, the umpire, bustled over and said, of course you're out Colin. And he had to go. He didn't want to, you know, and was muttering something about the spirit of the game.' Incidentally, Bob Woolmer, next man in, put it about in the Kent dressing room when he returned shortly afterwards, caught behind for three, that sawdust had to be thrown over the batting crease to soak up the blood. That was an exaggeration. I can confirm that there was no blood and no need for sawdust.

Three questions arise from this incident at Basingstoke, all of which we pondered over, at the time and subsequently. Even now, the answers, such as they are, intrigue me. First, why did Colin want to carry on batting? The answer to that probably lay hidden deep within his psyche. His pride. No batsman likes to admit to being hurt or discommoded by a bowler. A quick, surreptitious rub of the injury, with perhaps a wry little smile at your tormentor, is all you want to allow. Colin would have wanted to pick up his bat immediately, to show who was boss.

Secondly, he was more than likely, if not concussed, then not fully aware of what had happened. The man had just been struck a nasty blow on the jaw. Perhaps he had been unaware he had broken his wicket as he fell. Umpire David Constant was in no doubt. Colin had to go. He had to be dragged away but doesn't that say something about his bravery and his tenacity? Furthermore, the fact that he was immediately taken to hospital for treatment and took no further part in the match gives rise to the suspicion that he was not wholly in possession of his senses.

And the third is possibly the most perplexing. 'The strange thing was,' said Richard Gilliat when we talked about this many years later, 'Colin and I never really spoke to each other ever again after this incident, apart from casual greeting.' I was shocked. I had no idea. *Why was that?* 'I was never really sure. I think he believed that we had been unsporting, that we shouldn't have appealed and that he should have been allowed to continue.' *But there was no need to appeal, was there? It was out. End of story.* He wrinkled his nose, at a loss to explain it, as I was. 'I don't know. Perhaps he felt we could have withdrawn the appeal, not that we had made one. Connie had given him out, not us. In any case, I wasn't going to call him back. To me, the decision was correct and obvious.'

How very odd. Two of the true gentlemen of the game, two nicer men you could not wish to meet, Cowdrey and Gilliat, Tonbridge and Charterhouse, captains both of their school, their Oxford University side and their respective counties, having a spat that was never resolved. I had heard of historic quarrels between county captains that would fester over seasons, usually because one or other wouldn't declare, but between two scions of the cricket establishment, over a matter of principle, was, to say the least, unusual. Mystifying, even. I wondered what was going on in the Kent dressing room at the time. What was said when Colin returned, sat down and unbuckled his pads?

I asked an old friend and opponent, James Graham-Brown, who was on that balcony when David Nicholls made his remark. 'Colin was deeply upset, that much was clear,' he told me. 'He kept on shaking his head and muttering, "Bad form" or, "Unsportsmanlike behaviour." He felt that a line had been crossed.' But what was that line, I pondered. Surely it was not the fact that Roberts had bowled him a bouncer. He had been facing bouncers throughout his first-class career and none was better at playing them. Never had he suggested that the bouncer was anything other than a legitimate weapon in the fast bowler's armoury. So why had this one caused him so much disquiet, apart from the obvious fact that it had rearranged his jaw?

The answer – if answer it is – I unearthed many, many years later, during research for this book. He believed that Roberts had *thrown* it. This caught me by surprise; indeed, it would not be exaggerating to say that my jaw dropped when I heard the suggestion. I had played with Andy Roberts. I had faced him many times in the nets. Never did I believe there was anything dubious about his action. And neither did I hear the merest hint of a grumble from team-mates or opposing players, at the time or subsequently, that he was a 'chucker'.

However, since the advent of super slo-mo images, you do look at bowlers' action and sometimes wonder. Is it possible to bowl that quickly without a slight, almost indiscernible, straightening of the elbow? I remember seeing slow motion newsreel of Larwood bowling in the infamous Bodyline series and thinking to myself, hello, that was a bit jerky, wasn't it? As often happens, the advance in technology, far from making things clearer, has only served to muddy the waters.

Let us not forget that Cowdrey had been on that acrimonious tour of Australia in 1958/59, bedevilled by accusations of throwing, primarily by the Australians Meckiff, Rorke, Burke and Slater, though the Englishman, Tony Lock, was hardly above suspicion either. He had also faced Geoff Griffin of South Africa, and Charlie Griffith of West Indies, both of whom had suspect actions. So Colin knew all about throwing. If he had a suspicion that someone chucked, it was beholden on everybody to sit up and take note. But he never told anyone, other than his most trusted confidants. Why? We shall never know.

We can speculate. Perhaps he wasn't sure. Perhaps he did not want to cause a fuss, a furore even. He would have known that had he opened his mouth publicly, there would have been a storm of press interest. Roberts was just setting out on a long and distinguished career. Perhaps Colin felt he would not be believed, or, at the very most, accused of sophistry, inconsistency. He still had his pride. He could still play. He had not lost the urge to perform on the big stage. He would not have wanted to be accused of 'losing it' and blaming an illegal delivery for his misfortune. 'He set great store by sportsmanship, you know,' his son, Christopher, told me. I knew. He did.

It has been well documented that Colin Cowdrey believed that you should always carry yourself like a gentleman, both on and off the pitch, and that you should treat your opponent with respect. Benign, genial, chivalrous and kindly, he exuded a sort of generous, cheerful, even boyish delight in playing the game and he disapproved of the more abrasive, confrontational posturing that was beginning to take root towards the end of his career.

He wrote in his autobiography, 'I revere the manners and the customs of this country which are rather scornfully written off these days as old-fashioned and typically English.' He believed the virtues of the game of cricket were immutable and as good a frame of reference as any for a worthy life. He abhorred the coarse, the boorish and the ungentlemanly. It is entirely appropriate that the annual MCC Spirit of Cricket Lecture should be named in his honour, a past president of MCC himself. Together with Ted Dexter, he had been instrumental in incorporating a preamble to the laws of the game, *The Spirit of Cricket*. To him, cricket had to be played in the right spirit; otherwise, what is the point? It is a game, after all.

Ah, but there's the rub. Do we play cricket for fun or to win? Every games player worth his salt will tell you that it's much more fun when you win. And if you play it seriously, you must win, or else you lose your place in the draw or the competition or the rankings or the team, and ultimately your job, your livelihood. So more is at stake than pure personal enjoyment.

This is the dilemma facing all professional sportsmen and women. How far are you prepared to go to win? Where do you identify the point beyond which you will not set foot in your quest for the upper hand, because over there lies the murky territory of gamesmanship, sharp practice and cheating? As ever, it remains a matter of personal judgement. Opinions vary as much as human nature. One man's quick thinking is another man's chicanery. As often happens with these contentious disagreements, time lends distance and perspective. Looking back, it doesn't seem to matter very much now. It certainly didn't affect the result of the match. Hampshire won by an innings and 71 runs.

Andy Roberts took the county scene by storm in 1974, taking 119 first-class wickets at an average of 13.62, and went on to become one of the great West Indies fast bowlers of that generation. Colin Cowdrey quickly recovered from his mishap. Within a few weeks, he was playing as well as ever, so much so that his name was touted for the tour of Australia that winter. In the event, he was not selected. He was, as it happened, recalled to the national colours during that devastating series, to make his sixth tour of the country, but that dramatic story awaits us in a later chapter.

Colin Cowdrey came to represent this ethos of gentleman amateur but I am convinced he never set himself up as its ambassador. It was his nature to abhor shabby behaviour, on or off the field, and, as we shall see, it was a code of conduct buttressed by his upbringing and strong Christian faith. However, he was no apostle for courtliness at play; he never saw himself as an heir to Chaucer's *veray parfit gentil knight*.

It is true that he later did become a knight – of the realm – but others put him there. He did not seek the epithet nor the honour. He led his life according to his own lights. Others chose to behave differently. He did not, publicly at any rate, turn on those who had different values. He was no moral crusader. As he says in his biography, 'I am not the extrovert showman who happily wallows in the public eye. Indeed, I have always admired the unobtrusive touch.'

So, I think it would be true to say that he liked to do good, with a bat or a pen or a gin and tonic in his hand, by stealth, with no fuss, no fanfare. Anybody who saw his cover drive would understand what I mean. It was so well timed that it had just enough velocity to reach the boundary (I should know; I chased a few, convinced that I would catch them. But I never did). He was not one to crack the advertising boards. I believe he was a gentle man as well as a gentleman.

Yet it did surprise me how Cowdrey seemed to divide opinion. I was fully aware of the criticism occasionally levelled at him that he would sometimes go into his shell and allow bowlers to dictate to him.

I remember talking to Tom Graveney about Colin not long before Tom died. He was a huge admirer of Colin, as a player, as a person and as a captain. Colin's travails with the England captaincy, both when he had it and when he lost it, will concern us in a later chapter but Tom reckoned that his quiet authority brought the best out in his team, not least himself. So fond of Colin was he and so convinced of his moral probity and inherent decency, that he asked his friend to become godfather to his son, Tim. Tom was no fool; he recognised a good'un when he saw one. As for Colin's batting, he had this to say, 'He had the technique, the shots, the timing, everything. Sometimes he batted like a dream.' And then he gave a little sigh. 'If only he had had the ruthlessness of Peter May. There would have been none better.'

I wish I had had more time with him to explore exactly what he meant but alas, Tom's innings was shortly to be curtailed. Was he intimating that Colin lacked ruthlessness? As a captain, he was occasionally criticised for indecisiveness but according to Tom, in the Caribbean during the 1967/68 series, when he felt he had the full backing of the selectors and the team, 'Colin was a changed man – he cracked the whip, you know.' Or did he mean that sometimes an innings full of authority and thrilling strokeplay could be followed by one of scratchiness and diffidence?

Anyone who has played cricket for a living knows all about the vagaries of form; like a will o' the wisp, one day it is there and the next it has evaporated. Colin had a stockpile of talent and all the weapons to combat any attack yet his contemporaries wondered why he felt he had to retreat into his shell from time to time. Paradoxes abound about the man. It is what makes him an intriguing subject.

Listen to this observation of a young player just starting out on his county career for Kent as Colin's was coming to a close. 'I was playing in a second XI match against Surrey at Norbury in 1971,' James Graham-Brown told me, 'and I had scored 60, my first half-century for Kent. Colin phoned me – I had not even met him – to congratulate me. What a lovely thing to do. From that moment I was a Cowdrey man through and through.'

Here's another example. Bobby Parks was a young team-mate of mine at Hampshire, making his way in the game just as my time was drawing to a close. His father, Jim, had played many times with and against Colin over the years and they had been on several MCC tours together. 'Several days after my debut for Hampshire,' Bobby told me, 'Colin (I had never met him) sent me a note congratulating me on my first match. Apparently, he used to do this all the time. Later on, as I got to know him, he turned out to be probably the nicest man I've ever met.' This solicitude for others has been stressed time and time again by those whom I have interviewed for this book. Colin was undoubtedly a kind man.

He scored over 7,000 Test runs at an average of 44.06, so he can't have been quite so kind to opposing bowlers. You don't play 114 Test matches without having a steel rod for a backbone. I am reminded of the retort from David Gower, another one who has been unfairly castigated in some quarters for squandering his talents at the highest level, 'Well, I scored over 8,000 Test runs so I can't have been such a bad player, can I?' Indeed not. Incidentally, Gower's Test average of 44.25 compares very closely to Cowdrey's. And Peter May, generally regarded by many, Tom Graveney included, as one of the finest of post-war English batsmen? His Test average was 46.77. So, there was not much of a difference in record between the 'ruthless' May, the 'dilettante' Gower and the 'unassertive' Cowdrey. Public perception can be a capricious mistress. More anomalies to explore.

What intrigues me more than anything about the man is how he married his generous temperament with the inherently selfish business of scoring runs. 'It's nonsense to suggest that Colin had no ego,' Graham-Brown told me. 'Of course he had an ego. All the great performers possess an ego. Colin was no different. He knew how good he was, how blessed with God-given talent. But that ego was a fragile one. It occasionally fractured and, like Humpty Dumpty, it had to be put back together again. And do you know what – that made him an attractive man in my view. Somehow, his insecurity made him more endearing.'

Not everybody who played with him would agree, I expect. Sport at the highest level does not admit of weakness and certainly one or two found his vacillation infuriating. But the vast majority, I feel confident of saying, admired him for what he did achieve, in spite of these perceived weaknesses. Who doesn't warm to a person overcoming obstacles, particularly those placed there by his own nature, to reach the sunlit uplands of success?

Colin Cowdrey was born on a tea plantation in India and ended up in the House of Lords, being granted on his death a memorial service in Westminster Abbey. Only three sportsmen to have been so honoured, the others being Sir Frank Worrell and Bobby Moore. This is a life worth examining and, as Socrates once said, the unexamined life is not worth living.

Acknowledgements

'DO WE need *another* book on Colin Cowdrey?' pondered Jeremy Cowdrey. 'And why now?' demanded Christopher Cowdrey. So this is what it must have been like, summoned to appear before the Star Chamber in mediaeval times, my destiny, my head probably, resting on the answer I gave. We were not in the Palace of Westminster but in Jeremy's Surrey home and I had not been summoned. I had requested a meeting with the immediate Cowdrey family, represented by these two, Chris the eldest and Jeremy the next in line, in order to broach the plan I had of writing a book about their father. To proceed without their approval would be unimaginable. I took a deep breath. The next few minutes would be crucial.

'Your father was 67 when he died,' I answered. 'Same age as me.' Chris shot me an amused look. 'Well, yes, I know I'm not dead yet,' I babbled, 'but there seemed to be a certain synchronicity there.' Jeremy looked baffled, as well he might. I had no idea what I meant either. I decided on another tack. 'Look, I'm sure you guys used to play Test matches in the garden when you were young. Same with my brother and me. He was always Peter May and I was always Colin Cowdrey.' That was a lie, so God strike me down. It was the other way round. I was Peter May and my brother was Colin Cowdrey. And as he was – still is – younger than me, Peter May always had first knock. Strange that. If Dominic spills the beans, I inwardly vowed, I shall never declare and let him have a bat.

I am still unsure of the precise direction my petition took thereafter but at least the words flowed, gushed more accurately. Would they be enough to win the day and spare me having my head chopped off? I fled to the lavatory to allow the privy councillors to reach their verdict *in camera*. On my return, they were grinning. Chris always grins so that told me nothing. Jeremy was the spokesman. 'All right. We've decided to give the book the green light. Carry on...and good luck.' I jumped up on the sofa, punched the air, dashed out of the French windows, did a quick jig around the ornamental pond, kissed them both and roared off in my car down the drive.

That is another lie. I did no such thing. But I wanted to. This project was dear to my heart and any resistance from the family would have holed it beneath the water line even before it had sailed out of port. You see, Colin Cowdrey was dead and thus the prime source for material for a biography was not available to be interviewed. Thus I would have to rely on word of mouth evidence from others and none knew him better than his children.

Besides, I was a friend of Chris – we had played against each other on the county circuit – and I would not have wanted to go against his wishes. In fact, I would have found it impossible. Therefore, first and foremost in this list of acknowledgements, I wish to place on record my thanks and gratitude to the Cowdrey family, Chris, Jeremy, Graham and Carol. They have been a continued source of encouragement and information without, at any stage, seeking to interfere or influence. All I can say is that I hope I have repaid their faith in me and done their father justice.

Furthermore, I am indebted to Sir John Major for allowing me to reprint verbatim his inspirational address given at Colin's memorial service in Westminster Abbey. When you read it, you will understand how close was their friendship, forged in a mutually deep love of the game of cricket. Perhaps I am not the only one who has had this idle thought from time to time – I wonder what success Colin would have had in the world of politics, had he chosen that path. And how good a cricketer would Sir John have been were it not for that terrible injury to his leg?

The list of people who have helped me in the writing of this book is long. It could have been longer, much longer. For every person I spoke to, there were half a dozen others suggested during our meeting. And no doubt there would have been half a dozen more from them too, with the number of contributors increasing exponentially. For sanity's sake, I had to draw a line somewhere. Colin knew so many people. And so many people knew him and were more than willing to share their memories of him. To all of them, many of whom were unsparing with their time and assistance, I offer my sincerest thanks.

They are, in no order other than chronological:

Scyld Berry, Richard Gilliat, James Graham-Brown, Bobby Parks, John Hart, Ian MacLaurin (The Lord MacLaurin of Knebworth), David Kemp, Jeremy Eckersley, Jim Parks, Derek Underwood MBE, Charles Swallow, Howard Angus, David Makey, Alan Dowding, MJK Smith OBE, AC Smith, Mike Bushby, John Woodcock OBE, Graham Johnson, Geoff Arnold, Bob Willis MBE, Derek Ufton, Hubert Doggart OBE, Asif Iqbal, David Brown, John Inverarity, Rev Mike Vockins OBE, Hugh Carson, Ray Jepp, Roger Knight OBE.

I wish to pay special tribute to two people who have spent many a long hour poring over the manuscript, proofreading, correcting, improving, suggesting and generally fine-tuning the prose and the content.

The first is my wife, Lin. She is a marketing manager and knows what works and what doesn't in people's perceptions of what they read. The second is Ruth Sheppard. She is a professional editor and I call her 'Ruthless Ruth' for her uncanny ability to spot mistakes and uncover inadvertent solecism. The sobriquet 'ruthless' is entirely ironically bestowed; her surname is much more apt, for she 'leadeth me the quiet waters by'.

Furthermore, I should like to extend my grateful thanks to Paul Camillin, Jane Camillin, Dean Rockett, Duncan Olner and all at Pitch Publishing. Their continued loyalty and support of my writing career are much valued.

A Solitary Childhood

India, 1932–1939

*'Dear Master Cowdrey, I shall be watching your
career with great interest.'*

Letter from Jack Hobbs

OOTY sounds like a cheeky little bar in downtown New Orleans resonating to the foot-tapping, syncopated beat of traditional jazz during long, hot, summer nights. However, Ooty is to be found on another continent altogether, a different world, you might say.

To give it its full name, Ootacamund is situated in the Nilgiri Hills, the summer capital of the Madras presidency in India during British rule. It was one of 65 hill stations set up across India by the British to escape the searing summer heat. Ooty was considered to be one of the most beautiful, hidden among luxuriant forests and at over 7,000ft above sea level, its climate is pleasantly mild throughout the year.

The rolling hills are covered with trees, such as conifer, pine and wattle, with the scent of eucalyptus predominant. The green downs and lofty hills abound with exotic and colourful species of plant and flower; not for nothing was Ooty known as the 'queen of hill stations'. No wonder it was popular with the British. It reminded them a little of home.

Whatever else you might say about the British, who are notoriously lazy linguistically, they are remarkably accommodating with new words encountered on their travels. No language is more susceptible to borrowing words from another country than English and the British in India during the days of the East India Company and the Raj found a rich source of extending their vocabulary.

But being British, they made little attempt to spell or pronounce these words correctly, so they anglicised them. 'Blighty' comes from an Urdu word, meaning 'foreign'. 'Bungalow' loosely means 'belonging to Bengal'. And how about this? Deolati was a British camp near Bombay, where there was a sanatorium for soldiers affected by heat and stress. It soon came to be known as Doolally.

Ootacamund was no different; the popular contraction to Ooty was inevitable and typical. It was first set up as a place for soldiers to recuperate, but it soon became a home away from home for the colonial masters. Bungalows sprung up, with neat, tended gardens, a golf club, gymkhanas (another Indian word), churches and, as surely as night follows day, a club, the Ootacamund Club, founded in 1841. I suppose the recent TV series, *Indian Summers*, gives a reasonably accurate picture of what it was like back in the dying days of the Raj in the 1930s.

It was here that Colin Cowdrey was born, on Christmas Eve in 1932. In some official sources, his birthplace is given as Bangalore, some 200 miles away, but as he was cheerfully fond of pointing out, the distances in India are so vast that no one would quibble about a mere 200 miles or so.

It is an odd fact that, since the Second World War, about one third of England captains were born abroad. Apart from the obvious South African influence (Greig, Lamb, Strauss, Pietersen) and the pub quiz teasers such as Denness and Lewis (Scotland and Wales respectively), the list throws up some unusual countries of origin. Freddie Brown was born in Peru, Donald Carr in Germany, Ted Dexter in Italy and Colin Cowdrey in India.

One of the stories that swirl around Colin's early childhood was that his father immediately wrote to a friend in England requesting that the new arrival's name be put down for membership of MCC. Just over half a century later, that infant was to become MCC president.

Another legend that grew up with the boy was that his father had deliberately chosen the names Michael Colin Cowdrey, to give him the impressive and prescient initials MCC. Mind you, there are a number of Colin's army of fans in India who are convinced that MCC stands for Madras Cricket Club. And his father did play there.

For Ernest Arthur Cowdrey was a sports fanatic and cricket was his game of choice. He had ended up in India almost by accident. He was born in Sanderstead, a leafy enclave of Surrey, and after school, he worked in a bank. Good at games, he soon showed promise as a cricketer and for a time, as he moved up the age groups, he harboured dreams of playing professionally.

In such research into the early life of Ernest Cowdrey as has been possible, I was intrigued to discover that he first played for Beddington Cricket Club, where I too learned how to play the game as a schoolboy. He met Kathleen Mary Taylor there and later married her. From club cricket, Ernest graduated to Surrey Second XI and on to Minor Counties cricket with Berkshire but that was as far as his cricket career went – for the time being.

From the bank, he progressed to stockbroking in the City, buying and selling tea stocks. Quite what happened to provoke a sudden decision to sail off to India has been lost in the mists of time. He set himself up on a tea plantation high up in the Nilgiri Hills. Whether his wife approved of the move, we are none the wiser. According to Colin, she never betrayed any resentment but wives were expected to be loyal and dutiful and she played the part faultlessly. How much she enjoyed the gilded cage of life in a remote part of a far-distant land, he had little concept; he was too young and, in any case, parents were not wont to discuss their feelings with their offspring in those buttoned-up times.

For a gilded cage is what it must have been. The bungalow in which they lived, although hardly palatial, would have been nothing like a typical suburban bungalow in England; accommodation would have been spacious and comfortable. There was a tennis court in the garden and a golf course at the back, admittedly comprising only the single green, and half a dozen servants to cater for the needs of only three of them. And the views of tea plantations dotting the rolling green hills all around were indeed spectacular.

The climate was kind and one can be forgiven for thinking Colin's childhood was blessed and privileged. But it was an isolated existence. The nearest town was 66 miles away, Ernest was away all day supervising the 2,000-acre estate and whenever he could, he played cricket – never on his doorstep and sometimes in Madras, a good ten-hour drive away. There must have been times when Mrs Cowdrey felt very much alone.

Colin was an only child and in the way that an only child does, was very much thrown upon his own devices. He had no brothers or friends so he had to shift for himself. He immersed himself in his sport, no doubt making up the rules, terms of engagement and imaginary matches as he went along.

He was fortunate in two respects. It was an outdoor existence and few and far between were the times when he would have been driven indoors. He remembered the occasional violent thunderstorms that you get in a mountainous setting, the torrential rain adding to the green lushness of the terrain. But most of the time, he was either kicking or hitting a ball. And secondly, his father was quick to recognise the precocious talent of his young offspring.

Ernest was clearly no mean sportsman himself and his enthusiasm for ball games had in no way been diminished by his move to the subcontinent. This passion rubbed off on his son; you might say, percolated through his very pores. Before breakfast, it was golf on the pitch and putt hole (for the diminutive Colin, it was more of a par five).

There is a touching photograph of the boy Cowdrey – he must have been four or five at the time – teeing off on this single hole of theirs. Immediately, the trained eye in sporting talent would see that Colin was a perfect little player, even in the relaxed and balanced way he is addressing the ball. And standing behind him is the well-disposed but sternly critical figure of his father, no doubt about to make the odd tiny adjustment to grip and stance, looking so much as Colin would in later years, slightly portly, not tall, with the same kind, rounded features and a look of benevolent encouragement.

In the evening, when Ernest returned from work, it was cricket, cricket, cricket. He had his firm ideas about how to coach the budding batsman. Eschewing the slog to leg, the natural stroke of any untutored youngster, he placed Colin alongside the wire netting of the tennis court. If he hit to leg, his back would receive nasty abrasions. Thus the only strokes available to the young boy were on the off side, which endless hours of practice perfected.

It was a wonder in later years that he was ever able to play on the leg side at all. 'That's because everybody bowled an off stump line in those days,' laughed Christopher, his son, many years later. 'He didn't need to play much on the leg side, apart from the elegant whip off his legs over square leg.'

I'm not entirely sure about that; those who played against him can testify with total assurance that he was pretty adept on either side of the wicket. Colin always remembered the meticulous attention to detail of his father's coaching, frequently adjusting this, suggesting that, theorising about something else.

One wonders whether the seeds of Colin's obsession in later years with technique and execution – in some critical eyes, to his detriment – were sown in these early sessions. James Graham-Brown tells a surprising story when he once found himself, as a young pro, bowling to the experienced Test player and Kent captain, in the nets. Cannon fodder, we net bowlers used to call ourselves. But not a bit of it. After ten minutes or so, Colin stopped the bowler, advanced down the net and enquired of the tyro whether he felt that his, Colin's, top wrist was too far round on the handle. Graham-Brown was dumbfounded. He hadn't a clue, hadn't even noticed and in any case would have been hard-pressed to form a suitable respectful answer.

Great players are not easily pigeon-holed. Some just go out there and rely on their instincts and their eye. Others are forever tinkering with grip, stance, foot movement, head positioning, even weight and make of bat. Colin Cowdrey was a technician, who painstakingly analysed his own style and craft, as well as those of others, team-mates and opponents alike. Each to his own. It obviously worked for him, as his 7,624 Test runs amply attest.

Would it be too fanciful to speculate that Ernest Cowdrey, a competent club cricketer not quite good enough to make the grade professionally, lived his dream vicariously through his precociously talented son? What is beyond doubt is that he invested heavily in time and emotional support to make sure that the sapling was painstakingly cultivated. And once the eternal verities of batting technique had been firmly installed, he made sure that where Colin went to school took into account his cricket education. Some might say it was the sole driving force.

In fact, there is evidence to suggest that Ernest was rather more than a competent club cricketer. His own father reckoned he wasn't good enough to make the grade in the first-class game but on a level just below that, in Indian club or social or representative cricket or whatever you like to call it, he was more than a useful player. With the distances involved, the lack of formal structure, the absence of adequate practice facilities, the irregular nature of any fixture list, the long periods between matches, the matting pitches, the variable surfaces – all must have tested any batsman's technique, to say nothing of his enthusiasm.

Ernest must have been very keen to travel 300 miles to Madras for a game. Fancy getting a duck and facing a ten-hour drive back home, having spent most of your afternoon shuffling between third man and long leg. The first motorways, it is true, had been built by the time Colin was born but they were in Italy. India didn't catch on to the idea of expressways until 1990. The roads in and out of the Nilgiri Hills were single track, largely unpaved and frequently subject to landslides. Southampton to Scarborough was the longest and most arduous journey I ever made to play a game of cricket but I was paid to do it. Ernest made these gruelling trips because he loved the game with a passion; a passion, needless to say, inherited by his son.

It is a wonder that Ernest had time to play cricket at all. Despite the seductive image that life in colonial India might present to us in our mind's eye, all sun-dappled garden parties, tennis on the lawn, servants dispensing drinks, endless rounds of golf, tiger shoots and elephant rides, the reality on a large tea plantation between the wars must have been very different. He was responsible for a labour force numbering at various times between 500 and 600 men. There were no trade unions or organisation of labour; a strict class structure was still in place and the social divide between workers and managers, the whites and the Indians who served them, unbridgeable.

Running a plantation was a bit like running a mini city; the manager responsible for all his workers and their families, their welfare, their births, their deaths. The manager was very much the father figure, with all the responsibility that that entailed. Furthermore, the economic pressures must have been immense. The Great Depression of the 1930s hit the tea industry heavily, with wholesale prices dropping by 53 per cent in four years. During the war, conscription into the army deprived the owners of the younger English middle managers who supervised the tea planting. Beneath the apparent calm and stability of the British Raj was the seething undercurrent of political uncertainty and social unrest.

Nationalism was on the rise, the Indian independence movement was gathering force and the ethnic and religious tensions in the country were already at breaking point. Trouble was afoot. That much was evident even to the most purblind colonial master. And one assumes that Ernest was not blind.

The young Colin, perfecting his off drive, would have been blissfully oblivious of all this, of course. His days were spent with a teenage retainer of the household, by the name of Krishnan, whose sole occupation, it seems, was to play sport, hour after hour, with the little boy. If he found his role tedious, he never showed it, according to Colin; in fact he gave every sign that a day's activity of a combination of cricket, football and golf was all an energetic teenager could conceivably want. A bond was formed between the two of them, which survived well into their middle age.

It is interesting to speculate what ramifications such an unusual existence had on the young child. I have heard it argued that an only child, starved of the company of siblings or friends of the same age, necessarily becomes introspective, withdrawn, self-contained, egocentric even, slow to make friends, unsure of commitment and uneasy in relationships. Nonsense, cries my wife (an only child); you have the undivided love and attention of your parents, you have to fend for yourself and you make of life what you will. Besides, you have a bedroom all to yourself. And you don't have to share Christmas presents with anyone. So, I am not at all sure that we can confidently ascribe any trait of Colin's personality at this early stage of his life to his solitary Indian childhood.

More clues might emerge from his schooling back in England later but, for the time being, we have no reason to doubt his assertion that it was an 'idyllic' early boyhood. Endless games of cricket and football in the sunshine with a willing ball-boy certainly fits the bill, in my view.

I think we can take it as given that Ernest, on his return to the house every evening and following business/cricket trips away from home, would have engaged his son with tales of derring-do on the pitch. Whatever his wife thought of these frequent absences, history does not record but we know from her son's testimony that if she complained, it was quietly or in private.

Of Ernest's deeds with the bat, we know very little but there is record of him scoring a century for the Planters v Madras CC in their annual encounter. On the back of this, he was selected to play in a one-day match for the Madras Europeans against MCC (Marylebone Cricket Club, not Madras Cricket Club!) who were touring India during the winter of 1926/27, the first touring team to travel to the subcontinent to play first-class matches.

It was only a one-day game, but two odd facts emerge. First, the match was drawn. No such thing as a limitation on overs for a one-day fixture back then; the side batting first had to be bowled out or declare. And secondly, doesn't the very name of the local team, Madras Europeans, sound outdated, inappropriate and, frankly, a little racist to our more sensitive ears? So, all 22 players at the Chepauk Stadium that day would have been white. However, one's faith in human nature and the social glue that is cricket can be partially restored by a glance at the fixture list for that tour. MCC played against Muslims and Parsees XI, Hindus and Parsees XI, Hindus and Muslims XI, as well as the full Indian side (though it did not yet have Test status; that came a few years later, in 1932).

Enough of sociological musings and back to the match. MCC had brought out a strong side, led by Arthur Gilligan and including Maurice Tate, Maurice Leyland, Andy Sandham, Bob Wyatt, George Geary, George Brown and Ewart Astill. Their opponents may not have been of Test status but they were taking the Indians – or, in this case, the Europeans – seriously enough.

The Euros (if I can call them that) won the toss and batted first. They declared, nine down, for 201, after 66 overs. E.A. Cowdrey, opening the batting, top-scored with 48, 'batting with a vengeance' according to a contemporary report 'and taking a toll of the bowling', which comprised, let us remind ourselves, Tate, Geary, Mercer and Astill. In reply, MCC were 155/8, with only Maurice Tate with 53 bettering Cowdrey's score of 48. A moral victory for the home side, you could say, but a look at the scorecard reveals that MCC had only 36.2 overs to bat, before, one assumes, the light failed.

Later, Ernest did fulfil his lifetime's ambition to play first-class cricket. Only one match, it has to be said, but there it is in the record books, a three-day fixture between the Europeans and the Indians at the same Chepauk Stadium in Madras. He scored nine in the first innings and 27 not out in the second. He also bowled 11 overs for 48 runs but was wicketless. The match was drawn.

He continued to play regularly for Weynaad against Calicut in the annual Malibar series as well as touring teams from south India. He also played for Madras when he was in town and available. We are indebted to a local historian, W.K.M. Langley, for these words when writing an account of Planters cricket in 1953, 'It is needless to record Cowdrey's influence on Indian cricket, and indeed on most other games, as this is well known to everyone.'

By the end of the 1927/28 season, Cowdrey was described by Langley as a 'new star in the firmament' when he took the field for Wynaad against Calicut, 'so we knew what to expect and it is significant that thereafter I have not recorded which side won these matches!' Oh, that you had, Mr Langley, and furnished us with more than just an infuriatingly brief glimpse into the cricket career of one who must have been a considerable player in his own right.

But he did have this to add about Ernest, 'But his greatest achievement was yet to come in his early training of his now famous son. I believe this started on the level site of the old Chundale tea factory. We are all waiting with high hopes the full development of one of the three most promising cricketers in England.'

As this was written in 1953, it is interesting to speculate who were the other two 'most promising cricketers in England'. Peter May? Tom Graveney? David Sheppard? Fred Trueman?

And that, frustratingly, is pretty much all we know about the Cowdreys' time in India. Perhaps that doesn't really matter all that much. Colin was only six when he left for good – that is, putting aside the times when he later toured there with MCC – and how many of us remember much about our lives in those first half-dozen years?

All we have is a hazy recollection of one or two incidents and a general sense of whether we were happy or unhappy. Colin never wavered from his assertion that his childhood was blessed with love and affection and if he was on his own a lot, well, he wouldn't have known any different. He was content as long as he had endless hours of hitting, catching or kicking a ball, with the willing assistance of the faithful Krishnan, day after day, week after week, month after month, until the years merged into one another.

That is all that he could recall of his time in India, interspersed by the odd spectacular thunderstorm in the mountains and a village hunt for a leopard that had been worrying livestock and had killed a man. The leopard was cornered and ritually slaughtered. The head is probably still on display at the Ooty Club, where incidentally, the game of snooker was invented. It's true. There is prime source evidence, in the form of a framed letter from the game's inventor, Sir Neville Chamberlain (no, not that one, but a baronet of the same name), claiming that fact. It is not too fanciful to imagine Ernest Cowdrey excelling at that game too, whenever he visited the club.

Details of life on the Cowdrey plantation are sparse but one assumes that Ernest must have made a reasonably successful fist of the business. For when it was time to consider the schooling of the young Colin, in common with most expats in that part of the world, there was only one option – boarding at a public school back home in Blighty. And private education was no less expensive, comparatively speaking, than it is today. There was never any hint that Ernest would struggle to pay the fees. So Colin prepared himself for the journey back home. Quite where 'back home' was or what the very concept meant exactly, he was probably a bit vague. But it was an adventure.

On the long sea journey back to England, something happened that he remembered for the rest of his life. Having just emerged from the Suez Canal, their ship was steaming westwards across the Mediterranean Sea when Ernest sent for his son, safely tucked up in bed in his cabin, to join him on deck.

I leave the description of the scene to Colin himself, 'At the rails, he held me up in his arms for a better view of the SS *Strathmore* sliding into the gathering darkness. She was about three miles away but I can remember the scene vividly, with her lights pin-pricking her shape against the Mediterranean. What I can also recall most clearly is the change in my father's voice, for its tone, all at once, could hardly have been more reverent if he had been showing me the precise spot where Moses had delivered the tablets. He said, "Don Bradman is on board that ship. He's bringing the Australian team to try to beat England."'

Several interesting points emerge from this piece of description. First, what a turn of phrase the writer displays, a gift that remained with him all his days. It is often said that Colin Cowdrey neglected his studies, preferring the pursuit of cricketing to academic excellence.

On his own admission, this was probably true but let nobody assume that he wasn't bright, knowledgeable and articulate, as later evidence underlines. Note too the Biblical imagery; religion was to be an integral part of his life. As was Bradman.

The year was 1938. This was to be the last Ashes encounter between the old foes before war engulfed Europe and what a memorable series it was. Bradman's Test average for the season was 108.50, normal service, you might say. In the fifth Test at The Oval, where England squared the series with a mammoth win, Len Hutton broke Bradman's individual Test score of 334 by making 364. Bradman and Colin became firm friends. They died within two months of each other. There was another synchronicity in this passing of ships in the night to which I shall return later.

The destination of the travellers was England but the reason was schooling. Homefield School in Surrey, established in 1870 as 'a preparatory school for the sons of gentlemen', was not far from the family home in Sanderstead and seemed an eminently suitable choice, given that its headmaster, Charles Walford, was a keen games player, who had won a Blue at Cambridge for rugby. He was a cricket nut, so the fit would seem to have been a perfect one. And in some ways it was because by the time Colin moved on to Tonbridge, he was good enough to play for their first XI at the age of 13. The foundations of his cricket education, as Colin was the first to point out, were laid at Homefield, specifically at the feet of its headmaster.

However, what was good for his cricket might not have necessarily been best for him as a new boy at school. Colin joined Homefield in the summer term and all my schoolmastering instincts are troubled by this. Would it not have been better for him to start school at the same time – September – as the rest of his contemporaries, when they were all new boys together? By the time he arrived, at the start of the summer term, friendships would have been formed and he would have been the odd one out. Perhaps that matters less and less as you get older but at such a young age, all you want to do is fit in and be part of the gang. Most little boys hate to be 'different', set apart from their peers.

No doubt with his eagerness to please, he would have settled in quickly enough, especially when it became evident early on that he was good, outstanding even, at games. It does seem a strange decision, however. Unless of course, you take into consideration Ernest's burning ambition to further his son's cricket career. Because as we all know, the summer term is, in reality, the cricket term.

It is a fact of life, to some an uncomfortable one, to others a relief, that sporting prowess seems to smooth the path for a new boy at school. Perhaps it is because sport usually embraces the team ethos – you belong to a group – and as I have pointed out there is no one who yearns more ardently to belong to a group than a young boy. Perhaps being good at games hints at strength, vigour, manliness, in the same way that say, an expert bowman or horseman in the Middle Ages would have 1garnered respect.

Or maybe it was a sign of the times, where more value was put on external attitudes than internal character. Undoubtedly, his schooling had a lasting influence on the young Colin. In the latter years of his cricket career, his espousal of the tenets of good sportsmanship and comradeship became almost an article of faith.

If ever a man embodied the Latin adage, *'mens sana in corpore sano'*, it was Charles Walford. He believed, as did many others of his ilk and persuasion, in the importance of strong discipline and physical exercise, specifically the traditional team games, for the development of young boys and their spiritual and mental well-being.

It is a fact that John Rae, later a renowned headmaster of Westminster School in the 1970s, was a contemporary of Colin's at Homefield. There is no record of any later communication between them, nor indeed any evidence that they ever spoke to each other at school, but it would have been interesting to gain another insight into the character and personality of Walford. Sadly Rae is no longer with us but during his time at Westminster and in his frequent appearances and contributions in the national media, he was a strong advocate of tolerance and a sense of humour in the disciplining of his pupils.

One imagines therefore that his principles of education would have been at odds with his first headmaster's. Whether Rae was a bit of a rebel, even at that early age, we have no evidence but knowing his courting of controversy in his later career as an educator, I wouldn't have been half-surprised. Colin was no rebel. His avowed intent was to toe the line and not to cause trouble.

Charles Walford, for good or bad, was a martinet. Probably he would not have disapproved of the epithet, for a martinet was a drill officer in Louis XIV's army, and Walford was nothing if not a man of routine. The term has taken on a derogative meaning in modern times, which someone as fair-minded as Colin would not have really meant, because there were undoubtedly worthy aspects of Walford's influence on his pupils. But he was a hard taskmaster.

Privately, he led a spartan existence, following a rigid daily routine, which he expected his charges to emulate. He scorned frippery and worldly excess and attempted to instil a more spiritual disposition in his pupils. He was a fierce disciplinarian and beatings were frequent, though Colin avoided most, an instinct not to kick over the traces already firmly established in his personality. It is no surprise to learn that Walford taught mathematics, classics and scripture. Maths would have suited his predilection for order and method, classics would have supplied countless tales of morality and the virtuous life and scripture would have provided ample endorsement of the Christian faith.

None of this would have been lost on the impressionable boy. In Colin's own words, Walford demanded 'obedience, punctiliousness, truth, effort and conscientiousness'. Aristotle's famous saying, 'Give me the child until he is seven and I will show you the man' would have been familiar to anyone with Walford's classical education and is as good a way as any of understanding the essence of Colin's early schooling.

The headmaster encouraged academic endeavour – of course he did, he was a schoolmaster – but it was on the games field that his influence was mostly felt. He was as firm and unyielding in his cricket coaching as he was in the classroom. Nets were run with military precision; they commenced at 4pm on the dot. And woe betide any boy who was late.

He would stand, rigid and silent, behind the net and then come round every so often to correct a fault of technique. Colin called it a type of 'tyrannical tuition' but from it he really learned how to play. It was a tough environment; you either sank or swam. Colin was good enough to cope and believed the training had equipped him well for the battles he faced in Test cricket. Others, presumably, were not so fortunate. On reflection, from the perspective of adult life, Colin believed that Walford was 'too tough' and that sort of inculcation was not one that he would wish for his own children.

Colin can remember not a word of praise from his mentor but there was one episode that revealed a kinder aspect of Walford's temperament, one that Colin treasured for the rest of his life. It was the occasion of his first hundred. Nobody ever forgets his first hundred. Colin made 100 first-class centuries and even he could not remember all the others that were not recorded. But he remembered his first all right. Except that it wasn't. Not quite.

As a seven-year-old, he was playing in an under-11 match and he knew he was nearing triple figures. Excited commentary from his chums on the boundary kept him abreast of his score. Eventually, he made it and enthusiastic celebration among the young spectators ensued as Colin shyly raised his bat in acknowledgement. Soon afterwards, he got out. Then a recount of the score in the book revealed the awful truth. Cowdrey had been dismissed for 93, not 100. The poor scorer was not lynched but for a time his name was mud.

Colin was too generous to make much of the mistake but, unbeknownst to him, his headmaster wrote to Jack Hobbs about the incident. Several days later, Colin received a hand-written note from The Master, as Hobbs was universally known. 'Dear Master Cowdrey,' it said. 'I take great pleasure in sending you this little bat, which I have autographed. I shall be watching your career with great interest.'

Jack Hobbs died in 1963. Up to that point, he would have had a lot to keep him interested in Colin's career, for by then, it would have encompassed 67 Tests. And, following Hobbs's example, Colin became one of the great writers of letters and *billets-doux* in the cricket firmament.

In the autumn term of 1939 – Colin's second at Homefield – he was surprised that it was his grandmother, not his parents, who met him at the school gate. He was airily told that 'they had gone to work' and that was as far as the explanations went. In fact they had returned to India, which was always going to happen, with the boy left in England to continue his schooling. There had been no emotional preparation, no clarification, no farewell. One day they were there, the next day they were gone.

Perhaps, they felt it was for the best – no protracted goodbyes, no tears, no fuss. Besides, in those days, that was the way it was done. Colin's experience would not have been unusual in this regard. No doubt he missed his parents but prep school is a busy life, he had little time to ponder and, like most six-year-olds, he would have accepted the reality as the norm.

What nobody could have predicted, except perhaps Winston Churchill, was that the gathering storm clouds were about to burst over Europe and nothing was to be the same ever again. Colin did not see his parents for another seven years. Once war broke out, travel became next to impossible and the family was sundered. The emotional effect of the enforced separation can only be guessed at but it is as well to remember that dislocation of households, communities, societies, even races, became commonplace during the Second World War. And let us not forget that the war's duration – and thus the length of separation – was unknown, even to Churchill.

Colin's predicament would have been mirrored in tens of thousands of homes throughout the land. My sister was born at the same time as Colin, and she explained she had little recollection of our father before he went to war. Then suddenly, six years later, she discovered a strange man at home who immediately assumed the alpha male role in the family and started to lay down the law. It was a tense time of adaptation and familiarisation and she never, truly, established a close relationship with him.

It is no less easy to put ourselves in the shoes of the parents forced to abandon their children. When Ernest and Molly Cowdrey resumed their life in India, presumably they expected to see their son the following summer, when he would have travelled out from England during the long summer break. But war broke out and that was that. We do have a small window into the family's anxiety for their distant son. Among Colin's papers, I unearthed a solitary letter from Molly. It is addressed to Mrs Pickard, one of many acquaintances who were charged, together with grandmother, aunts and uncles, to look after the boy in their absence. It is dated 24 October 1940, when the situation in Europe was possibly at its grimmest. In the most beautiful handwriting, she profusely thanks Mrs Pickard for her many kindnesses shown to her 'little scamp' and assures her that it is a great relief that he is being cared for by such good friends.

She goes on to say that Colin is 'school mad' and that his life seems to be exclusively about having a good time. She is thankful that he is too young to comprehend fully the 'horrors of this ghastly war' and that he is in safe hands. Mind you, she continues, it helps that he is 'cricket mad, which pleases my husband very much for he is a cricket lunatic too'. The poignant bit comes at the end. 'Are not our RAF truly marvellous? Where should we be without them? To say nothing of our Silent Navy and the Dunkirk Heroes? All of them heroes, to whom we shall owe our lives and freedom, before long, we pray. God bless them. May 1941 bring us that much longed for Peace, Peace and still more Peace!' Little did she know that peace, in October 1940, was a long, long way off.

The tone of her letter is grateful, wistful, anxious but never self-pitying. We can only guess at how much she missed home once she was whisked off to India by her husband. We can sympathise with her at the desperately unfortunate circumstances that separated her from her son and we can admire her fortitude and constancy throughout these long years.

She must have been one hell of a woman? It was Jeremy who answered. 'Funnily enough, Dad never really spoke about his parents. But I remember Molly being a strong and feisty woman. She died in her 90s, you know. For 26 years, she worked as a volunteer at Bromley Hospital, pushing a trolley and looking after patients' needs. She saw that as her duty, giving back to the community. That was probably the same spirit that helped her survive in India.'

Molly Cowdrey was awarded the British Empire Medal, which is for 'meritorious civil or military service worthy of recognition by the Crown'. The certificate, but not, alas, the medal, was unearthed among Colin's effects. The familiar crest of the Greater London Council heads the citation, which was to be read by Mr R. F. Ashmole, chairman of the Bromley Health Authority, and in it lengthy and glowing tribute is made to her 26 years of dedicated service to the Red Cross. Furthermore, mention is made of her constant presence as a volunteer organiser and operator of the hospital trolley shop. She was an exceptional fundraiser for the hospital and this too is noted as well as her selfless devotion to the disabled. The citation concludes thus, 'It is fitting that Mrs Cowdrey's commitment, devotion and kindness are now recognised by the award to her of the British Empire Medal.' One would imagine that the applause was thunderous. Would it be unreasonable to speculate that it is obvious from what source Colin inherited his magnanimity and public spirit?

How did Colin cope as a lonely child? As he had been brought up to do, with stoicism and forbearance. He just got on with it. What else could he do? The psychological repercussions he would have to deal with later, when he was older and when he could understand what had happened to him. In the meantime, Charles Walford became his surrogate father, in all but name.

The question is whether this was a fortuitous or damaging twist of fate. Colin was measured and temperate in his own assessment. For a start, his extended separation from his parents was an inescapable turn of events. It was nobody's fault. Walford didn't ask for the job of nurturing the young boy, though he was quick to recognise the nascent talent and develop it. He was a headmaster and he had many other youngsters to take under his wing. Even though he could see, as plain as a pikestaff, that he had a potential genius on his hands, he showed Colin little favouritism. To spoil a child was just not in his nature.

At no stage could the young boy have got above himself. Modesty became a pillar of his personality. We have already seen that Walford instilled in his charges a strict moral code; wrongdoing brought its immediate and uncompromising consequences. Did this stifle any propensity for devilment, impetuosity, spontaneity? Probably.

I doubt that taking a gamble was greatly regarded at Homefield. Good manners were expected, demanded even, and Colin remained to his dying day the very acme of genteel behaviour. Courtesy, respect and civility underpinned all that he did. He disapproved of slackness, disorder and imprudence, all of which can be traced back to his early schooling. Shoddiness was not in his vocabulary; he could easily have quoted Evelyn Waugh's maxim, 'If a thing is worth doing at all, it's worth doing well.' And it is not at all fanciful to imagine Colin Cowdrey quoting Evelyn Waugh. Walford instilled in him, if not a love of learning per se, then definitely a desire to absorb.

However, even Colin accepted that a tough, at times harsh, regime left him, how shall we put this, a little short of self-confidence. This is a conundrum that stalked him throughout his life, something that left experienced onlookers scratching their heads in bewilderment. How can one so gifted and talented sometimes doubt his own ability? Sometimes the explanation is obvious. It was because nobody praised him when he was young. Certainly he got no praise from Charles Walford.

Colin's peripatetic early life meant that he became – and remained – the perfect guest. He was never in his own home, where he could let down his hair and behave with the boisterousness of youth. He was kindly fostered by a series of dutiful relatives but he was always conscious that he had to behave. In 1942, his grandmother died and the role of guardianship was taken on by various aunts and uncles. During term time, he boarded. During the holidays, he was thrown largely on to his own devices. He wasn't lonely, he always said, but he was alone. Mind you, if he had had the distractions of a full and raucous family life, he might not have spent those thousands of hours throwing a ball against a brick wall and practising his technique.

It reminds me of the story of Bradman's boyhood that the Don never tired of telling. He would throw a golf ball at the curved brick wall, which housed a water tank, in his back yard and attempt to hit the ball, which rebounded at speed and at different angles, with a cricket stump. He maintained that endless hours playing this form of solo cricket sharpened his reflexes.

In 1946, after the cessation of hostilities, Colin's parents managed to secure berths on a troopship home from India, which can have been no easy thing with an estimated five million men and women needing to be repatriated from all corners of the Empire. Eventually, the three of them were reunited.

It must have been a strange and strained meeting. Colin was now 13, on the cusp of adolescence. When he had last seen his parents, he was a little boy. Where on earth do you start? What do you say? How do you greet each other? How best to break the ice? Colin admitted that he found it all disconcerting and difficult.

In my experience, 13-year-old boys are not the most communicative of individuals at the best of times and we know that Colin was reserved and self-contained. It was a protracted and awkward period of readjustment. It says much for both mother and father that, slowly, a rapprochement and then a relationship of genuine affection was established between them and their son. Of course, especially with his father, there was the shared passion for sport that bound them.

The two of them, father and son, frequently speculated how fate might have dealt them a different hand altogether. What if Colin had been one year younger and the journey to England to go to school had been scheduled for May 1939, not 12 months earlier?

By then, war was imminent and Ernest might well have had second thoughts. Quite possibly, Colin would have stayed in India, attended one of the top schools in Bangalore or Madras, had the benefit of the best coaching in games (with the exception perhaps of rugby) and no doubt his precocious talent would have surfaced as readily under the Indian sun as it did under the cloudier skies of England. He would have played first-class cricket for Kanartaka and numbered as his team-mates, rather than opponents, Bhagwat Chandrasekhar, Erapalli Prasanna and Gundappa Viswanath. And who knows, Colin modestly deliberated, he might have played Test cricket for India.

Ernest Cowdrey had one final, significant decision to make in the cricketing apprenticeship of his son – where to send him to senior school. The choice rested upon another unconventional decision, much the same as had been made to send him to Homefield School. The original, favoured destination was Marlborough College in Wiltshire. But Ernest wanted Colin to start immediately, this being the cricket term and Marlborough had no spare places. Tonbridge School did, and so it was for Tonbridge that he packed his bags in April 1946.

Several points present themselves at this juncture. Did the registrar, or whoever was responsible for the enrolment of pupils at Marlborough, ever kick himself for missing out on a future England cricketer? And, once again, Ernest had sent his son to a new school at the wrong time, when he would be entering an environment as a stranger where friendships and alliances had already been made.

A senior school is not like a prep school either; it is bigger, harsher and more unforgiving, more like noisy kennels than a cosy spot on the hearth in a domestic home. Colin was no strapping, mature, sophisticated 13-year-old. That first term was going to be an unsparing test for him. Furthermore, he was leaving Homefield before his final cricket season, much to Charles Walford's chagrin. Whether Walford ever forgave Mr Cowdrey Snr is not recorded.

So Tonbridge it was. It turned out all right in the end. In fact, Colin developed a lasting affection for the place, recognising the enduring influence the school had on his upbringing, both on and off the field. The fact that he chose the name Lord Cowdrey of Tonbridge when he entered the House of Lords in 1997 says it all.

2

Tonbridge School
1946–51

'My last day at school will be one of misery.'

Colin Cowdrey

A FRIEND of mine, in fact the subject of my first book, was in
bed with flu sometime in 1965. As he was a former opening
bowler for Worcestershire, you will be unsurprised to hear
that George Chesterton's choice of reading while recovering was *The
Cricketer*. He turned the page and lighted upon a competition, the first
prize being a holiday for two in Corfu. Sending his wife to fetch the
relevant editions of *Wisden*, he set to work to answer the questions.
After an hour or so of the requisite research, he felt he had done as
well as he could, put the form in an envelope and sent it off to the
magazine's address.

A month or two later, he was astonished to learn by letter that
he had won the first prize. 'There were scores of people who came
second,' he told me, 'but all of them had got one question wrong.
I hadn't.' My curiosity knew no bounds. 'The question that had
flummoxed them all,' he continued, 'was which international
cricketer never watched a first XI game when he was at school?'
Colin Cowdrey. 'Wrong! It was D.J. Knight, who played for Surrey,
opening the batting with Jack Hobbs and who later played for

England. He never watched a first XI match at school because he was playing, even as a new boy.'

It has to be said, for this particular question, George had a bit of an unfair advantage. D.J. Knight went to Malvern College, where George had been educated too and where he had spent 32 years of his life as a teacher. *I thought it was Cowdrey.* 'So did everybody else. But Cowdrey wasn't picked for Tonbridge's first XI until the *second* game.' I ought to record as a postscript to this little story that Mr and Mrs Chesterton thoroughly enjoyed their holiday in Corfu.

Whether it was the first game or the second of Tonbridge's 1946 season mattered little for the school had already been tipped the wink before Colin had ever set foot in the place. Sometime during the early months of the year, his father had taken him for a coaching session at the famous Alf Gover Indoor School in Wandsworth, south London. My father had done much the same thing for me, and I remember being disappointed that it was not Peter May supervising my net but only Kenny Barrington. The presumptuousness of youth.

Supervising Colin's net that day was Andy Sandham, the same Andy Sandham who had played against Ernest Cowdrey for MCC v Europeans in Madras back in 1927. Somehow, I doubt the young Cowdrey engaged the old pro in airy conversation about their fixed point of historical connection as he effortlessly reeled off a succession of perfect cover drives. This was 1946, an altogether more deferential age. Besides, Colin was shy and had been brought up – strictly – to speak only when spoken to. However, he was aware of sudden interest and whispered comments from nearby onlookers as he played his shots.

The flurry of adult attention brought home to him, for the first time, that perhaps he was rather good at this game. Sandham's enthusiasm was so much aroused that he immediately contacted the professional at Tonbridge to keep an eye out for a youngster headed his way. And the name of the pro? None other than Ewart Astill, another of that MCC team who had played against Ernest some 20 years previously.

It is not difficult to imagine the scene. It was the first net session of the term and the new boy, drawn irresistibly to the practice area, would have been watching with a mixture of excitement and nervousness the older boys going through their paces. Suddenly, the cricket professional, resplendent in his MCC sweater, would have noticed the small, chubby lad watching closely from behind the nets. Probably, he had been looking out for him.

Calling him over, he asked the boy whether he fancied bowling an over or two. Yes and no would have been Colin's unspoken response. Yes, because he was desperate to get involved. No, because he was a junior and this was definitely not his place. He wasn't even changed; he was wearing his grey flannels and all the other boys were in whites. His fearfulness at appearing to overstep the mark would have turned to sheer terror as a Master in an adjoining net noticed him and loudly instructed him to clear off. Astill tried to intervene but in the hierarchical environment that obtained at the time, his explanations were brushed aside and the boy was duly banished.

Astill was not to be so easily denied however. Having served his apprenticeship – for all of one game – in the Colts, Colin found himself in the first XI for the match against the Free Foresters, a team of adults, it must be remembered. He was batting at ten, picked primarily, if not exclusively, as a bowler. For it was as a leg-spinner of some flight and prodigious turn that he was turning heads at this stage.

What is it about young leg-spinners with precocious talent who seem to fade with the onset of adolescence? It is a shame but in this country, few, all too few, survive in the world of professional cricket. It was the same with Colin. As he grew, his effectiveness diminished and he bowled less and less. However, he had another string to his bow. It seemed to knowledgeable onlookers that his batting was nothing short of heaven-sent. It was not long before another coach at the school, Maurice Tate, who, would you believe, had also been in that MCC team that had played against Ernest in Madras, was confidently predicting that he had unearthed a future England player.

But that was for the future. For the present, the young Colin was not at all assured that he would play against the Free Foresters, even though his name was down on the team sheet. In some of the public schools of the time, having a first year boy in the first XI was unconscionable. Peter May, in a similar position at Charterhouse, had been made to wait before being selected. At Malvern, there was a more pragmatic approach; if a boy was good enough, he was old enough. I point to the example of Ian (now Lord) MacLaurin – who knew Colin well, both on the cricket pitch and in the corridors of power – who played in the Malvern XI for five years and he was much the same size as Colin in his first year. The point was that his technique and temperament were up to scratch and he survived, prospered even. MacLaurin always said that he was desperate to play in the first XI. It meant he was excused fagging duties. Tonbridge took a similarly practical view. Colin, with the headmaster's approval, was cleared to play.

Mind you, he had a kindly housemaster looking out for him, as all good housemasters should. It is a fact that nobody who has been to boarding school ever forgets his housemaster, whether remembered fondly or with hostility, so significant is his influence at a formative stage of life. Colin remembered his with nothing but affection. Although he sensed that James McNeill, a rugby player of some repute himself, was 'on his side', he perhaps did not realise quite how much. Not until much later, that is. McNeill did good things by stealth.

We know this because we have first-hand testimony of one who was in that Tonbridge XI in 1946, barely one year older than Colin, who took the small boy under his wing and remained a loyal friend right up until Colin's death. David Kemp was opening the batting that day. He returned to Tonbridge as a teacher and remained there pretty much for the rest of his life and is regarded – fondly – as a sort of Mr Chips character. I prefer to think of him as 'Mr Tonbridge', assistant master, housemaster, second master, acting headmaster and president of the old boys' society. There is very little that he doesn't know about the school and that includes his years with Colin Cowdrey. His views on the development of the future England captain are insightful and invaluable.

Kemp believed that McNeill was very good for Colin. 'Colin's father had been, for one reason or another, largely absent from his childhood,' he told me. 'He had had a very good grounding at Homefield from Charles Walford but Walford was a tough taskmaster and a bit stern. On his own admission, when Colin came to Tonbridge, he had done all he could for him. There was nothing left he could teach him. That was why McNeill was so good for him now. Colin arrived, a small boy and very nervous and McNeill – a lovely man, very fatherly – was great with him. "Keep an eye on young Cowdrey," he told me.'

And did you? 'I certainly did,' grinned Kemp. 'I shaped his future! I'm joking, of course. In point of fact, Colin didn't need much in the way of protection. He was so modest and polite. Nobody had a bad word to say about him. He was never bullied or pushed around or anything. And everybody could see the potential in him, even though he was so small.'

Small he may have been but the stir he caused that day was anything but. He later confessed to nothing but acute embarrassment when, batting at ten, he was out for a duck and the crowd just melted away. In the side for his bowling, he was also wicketless and probably thought that was that; a swift return to the Colts awaited him. In the Free Foresters team, incidentally, was Gubby Allen, a former captain of England who had just finished his war service, retiring from the army as a lieutenant-colonel.

Allen, as a Test selector, would play an important role in Colin's fledgling international career not more than a few years later and their paths would cross at frequent intervals after that. It would have been interesting to speculate what he thought of the diminutive fellow playing on the opposing side and whether he had intimations of future greatness but there is no record of any comment he made at the time.

Despite his unpromising start in the school first XI, Colin was not dropped. His captain assured him he would be playing in the next game against Malvern and Colin rewarded him for his faith by scoring ten and taking four wickets. For the next five years, he remained a fixture. Slowly, he made his way up the order to three, where he stayed. 'In truth, we were not a very strong side,' admitted Kemp. 'We can't have been with a 13-year-old batting at three, no matter how promising he was. And I am proud to say,' he added with a smile, 'that I finished above the great Colin Cowdrey in both the batting and bowling averages. But only for one year!'

The climax of the season was the annual fixture against Clifton at Lord's. Kemp recalled that Clifton were particularly strong that year. He remembered their captain, Rodney Exton, a fine batsman and off-spinner, who later that summer made his first-class debut for Hampshire. Sadly, he contracted polio soon after, which put paid to his cricket career, but he went into the world of teaching, mainly at Eton, before becoming headmaster of Reed's School.

'He was a formidable schoolboy cricketer,' Kemp said, an opinion underlined by his performance in the Lord's match. Exton took 14 wickets in the two Tonbridge innings, which should have had him named as Man of the Match, had such vulgar traditions existed at the headquarters of cricket. That he was not so remembered was because a small, round boy of 13 stole the headlines. Literally.

For a start, Colin was the youngest player ever to appear at Lord's, a fact swiftly taken up by the press. Kemp remembered the game as if it were yesterday. 'We lost a wicket fairly early on and out came Colin at three and we managed to put on a decent stand. He played Exton as if he had been playing top-class off-spinners all his life. Then I got out, wickets started to tumble but Colin held the innings together.' Correct. Colin was last out, top-scoring with 75 out of a total of 156, Exton taking 6-64.

And then David Kemp started to laugh. 'Do you know what *The Times* wrote about him? They said it was like looking at Cyril Washbrook through the wrong end of a telescope!' As he made his way back to the pavilion after being dismissed, Colin looked up at the stands, well-populated for a school match, sighed with relief and knew, there and then, where the rest of his life was headed.

The match was a thriller. Tonbridge kept Clifton down to a manageable lead of 48, Colin taking three wickets, but when he and Kemp were dismissed, both scoring 44, the Tonbridge second innings collapsed, leaving Clifton a mere 117 runs to win. Kemp takes up the story, which is just as well for alarm and confusion reigned in the scorebox, judging by the gaps in the scorebook. Panic took over the Clifton batsmen when Colin came on to bowl. 'They were going well but when Colin came on, they went to pieces,' said Kemp. 'As they got closer and closer to the target, the question was whether we should keep Colin on. The decision was made by the captain to keep going, a shrewd move, so *The Times* said. Rubbish! Our captain was in a blind panic and did nothing. We bowled 'em out just two short! It was a thrilling match.' Colin had taken 5-59.

One of the many spectators that day was a keenly interested Brian Johnstone. In his book *Another Slice of Johnners,* he wrote, 'On the 30th July, I went to Lord's to sit in the sun and watch some schoolboy cricket. The previous day, in the Clifton v Tonbridge match, a 13-year old playing for Tonbridge had made 75 out of 156 and taken 3 wickets with teasing leg breaks. Michael Cowdrey the press called him and he was said to be the youngest player ever to play at Lord's. I thought I would have a look at this infant prodigy. I was rewarded by seeing him make 44 in his second innings and then win the match for Tonbridge by taking 5-59 with his highly tossed leg breaks. Three times he enticed the batsmen down the pitch and was rewarded with three stumpings. He was small but already had a slightly rotund figure.'

Of course, the press were eager to buttonhole this 'infant prodigy' after the match, feeling they had their story for the papers the following day. According to Kemp, Colin was horrified. 'He ran past them as fast as he could and escaped on the Tube.' He caught the train down to Cornwall for the summer holidays, staying with an aunt. Presumably, his parents had returned to India. In any case, he was now used to his peripatetic life. During the journey, he read about his exploits on the back page of the newspaper being read by a fellow passenger opposite. Much as he hated the fuss, the spotlight was now upon him and would bathe him in its harsh beam for the remainder of his days.

Much was expected of Colin the following season at Tonbridge but in fact it was, if not a torrid time, then certainly something of an anticlimax. He was despondent and felt that his cricket career, hitherto on a continuous upward trajectory, had somehow stalled. But perhaps this was no bad thing. Cricket is never an easy game, even for the most gifted, and once you allow yourself the luxury of believing it is, it will bite back.

Besides, let us not forget that the boy was still only 14. He maintained his place in the first XI but that, I suspect, owed more to the fact that the side was weak and there was nobody else pushing him aside. However, even though he struggled for runs and wickets, he would have been learning much, mixing and playing with older boys, and his enthusiasm and desire to improve never wavered.

But there was more to school than cricket. There were two other terms besides the summer one. Lessons had to be attended, work had to be done, exams had to be passed. And there was limitless opportunity to play games. 'He played them all, you know,' David Kemp told me. 'Rugby, hockey, tennis, squash, rackets, fives, even footie in the yard. He was good at all of them. He had a natural eye for the ball and was a shrewd tactician, a games player's brain, with keen anticipation. And beneath that affable exterior, he was a fierce competitor. He hated to lose – at anything.'

It surprised me to hear that Colin was a good rugby player. As a youngster, he was so small and when he grew, he never had the classical sportsman's physique, lean, strong and athletic. 'Ah, but he was surprisingly nimble on his feet,' said Kemp, 'He played fly-half for the first XV. His kicking was exceptionally accurate. He used to practise and practise his goal kicking.'

That Colin was good at games has always been a given in any account of his life. But I wanted to know how well he integrated into school life in all other respects. *What was he like academically?* Kemp smiled. 'Let no one say that Colin Cowdrey was a thick games player. He wasn't. He was intelligent, he was hard-working, he passed all his exams and he got into Oxford by right.'

That was unequivocal enough. I went back to the large plastic boxes handed over to me by Jeremy Cowdrey, full of his father's papers, and started to delve, burrow and excavate. One thing was immediately obvious. Colin Cowdrey wrote voluminously and kept *everything*. One box was filled with scores of old, blue, air mail letters, addressed to his parents in India, now faded and occasionally smudged, the tiny handwriting covering every nook and cranny of available space. Mention has already been made of Colin's predilection to put pen to paper.

Here was clear evidence that the habit was early ingrained. It would have needed an office staff of great patience and efficient magnifying glasses to decipher them. From what I could ascertain, much of the news being imparted by a breathless voice concerned the scores and details of countless cricket matches.

I decided to be more discriminating in my research. I lighted upon his school reports and read them eagerly, hoping to uncover one of those historic misjudgements of character as to be found in one of Winston Churchill's, 'He has no ambition.' Alas, no such bloomers were in evidence, no prediction that Cowdrey would never make a cricketer. In fact, Colin's teachers were pretty well switched-on in their assessments of him, particularly his housemaster.

David was quite right; McNeill *was* good for Colin. A perusal of his housemaster's reports reveal a wise, sympathetic and supportive man. What's more, he *praises*, so unlike Colin's earlier mentor, Charles Walford, without ever lapsing into sycophancy or cliché. Subject reports are meant to comment on a pupil's progress in the classroom; a housemaster should have the overall picture in mind, academically and pastorally. For example, would Colin's success on the games fields beget arrogance or a swollen head? It appears not. 'The excellence of his manners is not the least of his good qualities,' he writes. And again, 'His conduct in the House continues to be entirely excellent.'

This about a boy now in his teens, at an age when it is not unknown for mistakes to be made, trouble to be got into and traces to be kicked over. Son Christopher laughed when I read this to him. 'Like father, like son,' he observed, tongue in cheek. No, it seemed that Colin was not one to rock the boat. What impressed McNeill about the lad in his charge was not so much his athletic prowess and steady academic progress but his willingness to get involved in everything and always to give of his best. 'He has represented the school or house in some match every day for a fortnight.'

How Colin found the time to do any work is a marvel but work he did. His subject reports are crowded with phrases like, 'keen'; 'willing'; 'full of promise'; 'conscientious'; 'a hard worker'; 'pleasing progress'; 'always gives of his best'; 'interested and involved'. One or two of the comments made me laugh out loud. 'V so-so,' says his Latin teacher. 'Fair,' says his history teacher. Imagine spending large amounts of money (expensive even in those far-off days) to have your son educated at one of England's premier public schools and receiving that from a Master who couldn't be bothered to write any more.

And there was the odd, witty put-down, that if Ernest Cowdrey had had a sense of humour – which Colin always averred he did – would have brought a smile to his face. 'Some of his oral utterances,' observes another Latin teacher, 'would have been better unuttered.' And here is another remark that resonates with me down the years. I pick this out not only because I was an English teacher myself. 'It is impossible to place him fairly,' bemoans Colin's English teacher, 'as he has missed two-thirds of the periods playing cricket.' *Plus ca change, plus c'est la meme chose.*

I remember the same bitter complaints being made to me as a housemaster, that far too many Saturday periods were being missed because of cricket matches. He'll never pass his exams unless he gives up cricket, I was told. All I could say was that there must have been an inordinate amount of deeply inspiring lessons being taught throughout the school on a Saturday morning. 'Why does cricket have to last all day?' grumbled one Master to me. 'Why can't it be all over in 90 minutes, like football?' There are some conundrums in life that do not lend themselves to obvious answers.

McNeill seemed unconcerned by Colin's frequent absences away on active service. And neither was his headmaster, Mr E.E.A. Whitworth. Indeed, he appeared to be more exercised about when next he could spare the time to take on Colin at rackets. 'What an advance in two years!' was all he had to say about things beyond the rackets court.

However, it was not all good news. Hints emerge from time to time that Colin struggled sometimes with examinations. This can partly be ascribed to the fact that, as he made his way up the school, he also got promoted into higher forms, where I guess the standard of response expected was higher. But there was another reason, which McNeill, with characteristic shrewdness, puts his finger on. 'He is a plodder really,' he writes, 'and seems to get rattled if the continuity of his work is disturbed.'

The continuity of Colin's work was frequently disturbed, and not always by his sporting commitments, as we shall see shortly. The reports reveal someone who takes his work seriously and who worries about failing to understand and falling behind. Throughout his cricket career, mention was made of the fact that he sometimes – inexplicably – would go into his shell at the crease, becoming absorbed by the technical challenge and failing to dominate the bowling, as he was more than capable of doing. It was as if suddenly he doubted himself and his touch would desert him.

Was the charge of 'plodder' an early manifestation of a lack of self-confidence that he occasionally had to battle with later on in his life? By no stretch of the imagination could Colin Cowdrey be described as a 'plodder' with a bat in his hand but there were times when he appeared to plod.

Time to talk about rackets – the game – that Colin loved, was very good at and which he believed helped his cricket immeasurably. As the fastest ball game in the world, it takes enormously quick reactions and exceptionally developed hand-eye coordination even to lay a racket on the ball, so swiftly does it move.

Actually, what I have just claimed is not quite true. The fastest ball game in the world, so claim the scientists and technicians, is *pelota*. But *pelota* is only played in the Basque region and thus not well known. Neither is rackets I suppose, confined as it is to 14 public schools and a handful of clubs dotted around England, as well as one or two outposts in North America. Its exclusivity is a great pity for it truly is a wonderfully exciting game that demands a high level of skill and no little bravery.

Its history and development is an interesting story in itself. It was the game of choice of the inmates of debtors' prisons Fleet and King's Bench in London during the 18th century. They hit a hard ball against the prison wall with a racket. The game spread to the schools, first using walls then inside purpose-built, four-wall courts. The fact that only the public schools took up the game would seem to suggest that the debtors who first played it were of a higher class, it could be said.

Colin took to the game immediately and spent countless hours in the courts, that is, when he wasn't playing rugby or squash, which is incidentally derived from rackets, the courts being 'squashed' in size and the ball squashy, rather than hard. Daily, it seemed, he would be engaged in a practice foursome or involved in house matches and school fixtures, not forgetting the annual singles and doubles competitions held at the Queen's Club in West Kensington. Not only did his constant practice and match play improve his eye for the ball and his mobility around the court, it also gave his self-confidence a shot in the arm, because he became very good at it – and it is not an easy game to master – and what's more, very successful on the school circuit.

He won the under-16s singles competition at Queen's. Also at Queen's, partnered by J.F. Campbell, he reached the final of the public schools doubles, losing to Winchester by four games to two. He continued to play at Oxford and beyond, with some success, whenever his cricket commitments allowed, which wasn't very often. For the time being, he availed himself of ample opportunity to play during his time at Tonbridge. If there was a first XI cricket match at home, he would always go on court and hit a few balls before going in to bat. He believed it sharpened up his reflexes, made him watch the ball, loosened him up and mentally prepared him for his innings.

The year 1947 is remembered for some exceptionally severe weather. England was blanketed in snow for large parts of the months of January, February and March, with temperatures rarely rising above freezing. And then, later on that summer, the sun shone from cloudless blue skies as Compton and Edrich made hay in the county championship, scoring 3,816 and 3,539 runs respectively.

Almost casually, while on a salvage operation of his father's effects in the loft of his home, Jeremy Cowdrey handed me Colin's diary. A quick glance confirmed that the author had kept it assiduously, day by day, in that minuscule handwriting of his. 'I shouldn't get too excited,' Jeremy warned me. 'It's all a bit boring.' Maybe, but commonplace observations on daily life from even the most reserved and incurious diarist can shed light on a life. With closer inspection, so it proved.

First, I was struck by the slang and informal expressions of the day. Entries are littered with words such as 'ridiculous', 'wizard', 'rattlingly good' or 'rattlingly bad', 'dreadful', 'colossal', 'stinking', 'beat up', 'not brilliant', 'blow up', all used to describe a chapel, a lesson, an innings, an exam or even the weather. For example, one day in February 1947, 'Big freeze. No rugger yet. Played squash. Ridiculous Maths test. Won't get a mark. Corps cancelled much to everybody's delight. More snow. Tons of it. Feeling ill. Off exercise which is a blooming nuisance.'

Secondly, the entries are circumscribed by the narrow world in which he lived. The only reference to national events was this bland observation, 'Slack morning. Princess Elizabeth is engaged. My cricket bat is repaired. Do stinking Corps. Go to Grubber.' But you could hardly expect much else. Not many boys keep diaries. Fewer keep them up religiously. And life in a boarding school environment is all-consuming.

A busy boy – and Colin was fanatically busy – rarely raises his head above the parapet to observe and debate the metaphysical so it is no wonder that he simply recorded all the things he got up to, mainly sport and school work. Even within the confines of Tonbridge School, there is very little gossip or tittle-tattle on display. There is a vague reference to 'that shocking business' in another house but that is as far as it goes. He mentions 'a hell of a blow up with the coach' but does not identify the coach nor give us a clue as to the nature of the argument. He rarely talks about other boys, apart from the occasional observation, 'Kemp is playing well,' or 'Orchard has just about had it.'

I was alarmed at how many times he had to go to the 'Head', for that usually meant only one thing – trouble – before I put two and two together. The 'Head' was not the headmaster's study but the first XI cricket pitch. Of course he went there a lot. He practically lived over there. In any case, it would have been a shock to hear that he had been summoned by the head to have his fortune read. Colin was a good boy and rarely put a foot wrong. He does make this admission, but only once, 'Skipped a music lesson and got into trouble.' I almost cheered when I stumbled upon this entry. The boy is human after all.

Boring? He wasn't bored. He was having a whale of a time and I can imagine Ernest, hearing nothing but good about his son, would have considered that the fees was money well spent. Colin was happy, he was playing 'tons' of sport and he was working hard. What more could any reasonable parent want?

The weather may have been wizard that summer but Tonbridge's cricket, much to Colin's disgust, was anything but. 'Dreadful loss against Haileybury,' he says, immediately followed, as if it was divine punishment, by, 'Dreadful sermon.' He talks about the match against Bedford School, a four-innings affair, which gives a little insight into travel to away matches, always by train, before the days of motorways and luxury coaches. '7.40 Tonbridge 9.15 St Pancras 10.50 Bedford Play at 12.30. Lose match. Scores of 59 & 91 v 53 & 54. Unlucky. Dreadful pitch.' Hard to disagree with that report. The highest score on either side in both innings was David Kemp's 24. 'I may have been last man out,' mused Kemp, with a little twinkle in his eye.

Although Colin was excited to be back at Lord's for the annual Clifton match, one year after his triumphant debut, the whole experience was a disappointing let-down. 'Wonderful being at Lord's again but Tonbridge have a dreadful day.' He should say so. Clifton amassed 240 (Cowdrey 2-57) and Tonbridge were dismissed for 75 (Cowdrey 14). Before close of play, they faced the ignominy of following on and when stumps were drawn, they had lost another wicket for 39 runs. However, Kemp and Cowdrey were not out overnight and were ready to effect a heroic rescue act the next morning. Alas, no. 'They polished us off by an innings and 38. Worst defeat so far.' And that was that. The rest of the summer was spent on the sun-drenched beaches of Cornwall.

As he made his way from home to home of grandmother, uncle and aunts, it might be easy to assume that Colin led a rather comfortable and privileged existence. In many ways he did. There was lots of swimming and golf and tennis and squash as well as periodic trips into town to catch a show and dine at a nice restaurant.

But he also went up to Market Harborough in Leicestershire, where his uncle had a farm. Far from idling his time away, he was set to work doing jobs around the farm – potato planting, threshing oats, cutting hay, milking, driving the tractor, working the combine harvester, with a spot of hunting and shooting thrown in, and perhaps a goose for dinner – and from his comments, it would appear that he thoroughly enjoyed the experience.

How about this for a day full of incident down on the ranch, 'We have the bull out today and it goes for Joe – goes wild. We eventually get him to the cowshed.' I presume he is referring to the bull and not to Joe. He found time to go to watch Leicester Tigers and Leicester City and spent long evenings 'playing ping-pong'. It was a healthy environment and he was kept busy, with thoughts of the home that he didn't have and the parents who lived far away pushed to one side.

Farming's loss was cricket's gain and he returned to Tonbridge for the new school year much restored in body and mind. Rackets was beginning to take over from rugby as his game of choice and rarely did a day pass without a visit to the courts. His account of his triumph at Queen's in the under-16s singles competition is unconsciously amusing. 'I have an easy task against a Marlborough bloke.' Next round, 'I have a colossal tough fight against Coulman of Winchester. I beat him 3-0.' And to the final, 'I beat Thompson easily but I crack my fingers against the wall.' There is no self-congratulation, no crowing, no expressions of pride or pleasure, no description even of the awarding of the cup, just a bald statement of the facts, and no false modesty. Then back to school and, 'I do a lot of hard work.' He often wrote this. It must be true. His teachers agree. Occasionally, his self-discipline slips. 'I try to work all day but it completely fails so I play cricket in the changing room.' Which of us has not been there?

Confidence re-established, he had a much better time of it during the 1948 cricket season. Comments such as, 'I get 6-60, the best I've bowled for a long time' and 'I get 41 not out against MCC and batted the best for a long time' give credence to the widely held view that here was emerging a schoolboy of rare talent. Kent sniffed the breeze and made sure that the prodigy in their back yard was not going to waste the summer playing club cricket. They organised for him to play in their youth team (in those days they were called Young Amateurs; today they would be known as the Academy XI) and this is where he first made his mark, playing with and against the best of his age group.

There was first disappointment again at Lord's, Tonbridge suffering another thumping defeat, by 138 runs, at the hands of Clifton. I nearly missed it in my cursory glance at the scorecard but there, batting at seven for Tonbridge, was a J.H. Eckersley. Surely not. It couldn't be, could it? A swift telephone call confirmed that indeed the J.H. Eckersley was a friend of mine, Jeremy, who lives nearby and with whom, some years ago now, I used to play tennis and rackets. A respected orthopaedic surgeon, he is now retired and spends more time on the golf courses of Herefordshire these days than on any court.

Hotfoot, I crossed the Malvern Hills and sought him out. 'Yes, I remember Colin very well,' he said over coffee. 'We weren't close friends because he and I were in different age groups and different Houses. But we played in the same team and my impression was that he was a delightful and modest young man. A brilliant rackets player too, which was surprising really because he had flat feet, you know. But he had supreme timing. He never seemed to whack it, a cricket or rackets ball, but it flew.'

How was he regarded by others in the team? And in the school? 'He was two years younger than me but everybody looked up to him. Fortunately, he was not one to throw his weight around and we all liked him.' *Did you enjoy your time at Tonbridge?* 'Loved every minute of it.' *I get the impression from Colin's diary that he felt the same.* 'I'm not surprised. There was an excellent rapport between Masters and boys and it was significant that Tonbridgeans who went on to university seemed to be more mature and better equipped for adult life. And of course, there was all that sport.'

He was getting quite wistful. I pressed him for any memories of a particular Cowdrey innings. His brow furrowed. 'Oh dear, it was such a long time ago. I do remember a masterful century he scored against Lancing. Nobody else got runs. And then he bowled them out with his leggies. I also remember him hitting a six at Lord's, which was no mean feat.' *You lost, didn't you, in spite of that six.* 'Ah, but I wasn't playing. Never played at Lord's. I was 12th man, though.' *Yes you did! You scored four and three.* 'Did I? Not very memorable therefore, was it?'

The summer holidays followed a familiar pattern. From Cornwall, Colin moved up to the farm in Leicestershire and found himself playing a lot of club cricket. Though he was not very successful, playing in the same team as grown men added to his cricketing and personal development and he hugely enjoyed the experience. He was invited to play a few games for Kent Young Amateurs and herein lay a strange twist of fate.

The previous season, almost out of the blue, he had been asked to play a couple of matches for Surrey Young Amateurs. It was an experience he had not enjoyed. For the first time, he was playing with people he did not know and he was still a shy young boy. He felt out of place and inadequate. He failed with the bat and got hammered to all parts of The Oval when he bowled. Had he played well and caught the eye of the Surrey coaches, he might have played the rest of his career in a brown cap rather than blue. One can almost hear a horrified intake of breath by a generation of Kent supporters at the very thought. But it was Kent, not Surrey, who came calling.

He had a much better time of it this time round. Listen to the breathless excitement as he comments on one innings, 'Play Sussex YA. I am 97 not out at close of play. Will I?' Oh, the unbearable tension endured overnight. Next day, 'I complete my century and go on to make 159.'

Playing for Sussex was Jim Parks, whose cricket career ran pretty much parallel with Colin's, both in opposition and in the same England team. I know Jim. His son, Bobby, and I used to play together at Hampshire. Jim was a frequent supporter at matches, a cheerful presence without ever overdoing the role of fond father. One thing that struck us all about him was that he had an excellent memory.

I chanced my arm and rang him. 'Oh yes,' he laughed, 'I remember that innings very well. He made a big hundred against us.' *Was it obvious that he was a future Test batsman?* 'Well, let's just put it this way,' he replied with characteristic understatement. 'He looked a pretty good player to me.' He and Colin became the best of friends and remained so to the day Colin died. 'Do you know,' he said wistfully, 'one day he rang me up. It was in the morning and I was out. When I got back home, my wife asked me breathlessly whether I had heard the news. What news? It's been on the radio, she said, Colin Cowdrey had just died. So I never knew what he wanted to talk to me about. I often wonder.' Conversations with Jim about my subject were going to be fascinating and fruitful, I thought.

For the time being, Colin was in a rich vein of form. The following day's entry reads, '1st day's play at Oval v Surrey YA. Rain stops play when I'm 79 not out.' Will he? Sadly, no. 'Play called off before we can start.' Never mind. Although he was probably unaware of it, his card had been marked by onlookers on the Kent committee.

As he returned to Tonbridge for the new school year, he could have been forgiven for thinking that life was pretty good; all was set fair and a brisk following wind filled the sails of the good ship Cowdrey. However, reading the diary, it slowly becomes apparent, as it must have to Colin himself, that all was *not* well. Something was afoot, if you will pardon the pun.

For some time, he had been aware of a problem with his feet, specifically with his toe joints. Kicking a football became painful and a full toss on the foot left him hobbling for longer than it ought. But being a teenager who loved his sport, he ignored it, shaking off the discomfort, except when it became too bad and then not taking the medical advice when given. Here is a typical entry in the diary, 'I am off exercise because of the doctor but I very forgetfully play rackets.' Or, if there were other subterfuges to be engaged, he brought to bear all the time-honoured excuses, 'Corps and once again I get away with no uniform because it is at the cleaners.'

However, the condition worsened and it could no longer be ignored. 'See doctor and he says see specialist.' But that does not mean he's off games. Certainly not. 'Told I am to be playing in 1st XV. Oh dear! It's against Dulwich College and I am very nervous.' Despite his pre-match nerves, he plays well – at fly-half – and thoroughly enjoys the occasion. 'We win 16-3. Marvellous fun. 1,000 watching.' Imagine that. One thousand spectators at a school rugby match.

The specialist to whom he was referred, John Mayer, diagnosed a severe case of *hallus rigididus*, basically arthritis in the toe joints. Though a not uncommon condition in the elderly, the doctor was amazed to find it in one so young and was thus hesitant to operate and insert artificial joints, putting at risk a burgeoning cricket career. Hot wax foot baths, with electrical treatment, were prescribed, which meant regular visits to Pembury Hospital nearby. Colin found this tedious but at least he could carry on playing rugby and rackets.

He believes in his diary, rather fancifully perhaps, that the course of treatment is 'doing a little good' but more importantly 'I come back for rugger' but finds, to his chagrin, that in his absence, he has been dropped from the team. 'I am not wanted. Billy is playing. Oh dear. I am very disappointed.' Life was not all success and sunshine, even for one as gifted as he; it was a hard lesson but one that would stand him in good stead as he was soon to face a setback far more serious than being dropped from the XV. 'I'm told I am going to play v Uppingham tomorrow. Poor Billy is injured.' That concern for the feelings of others was fast becoming a noteworthy feature of his personality. His last hurrah before the delivery of the bad news was the following day's match, the last of the term. 'We just lose 11-15. What a game!'

His next appointment with Mr Mayer is described thus, 'Have to go to Pembury to show my toes to orthopaedic surgeon. They really are in a shocking state. I have got to have them operated on and probably in bed for 12 weeks next term.'

The dismay can be well imagined. For an active boy to be bed-ridden for any length of time is purgatory; for one whose life is defined by his sport, the news must have been a hammer blow. But Colin being Colin, he decided that no time was to be wasted and, seeing as the operation was not scheduled until after Christmas and the New Year, there was absolutely no reason why he should miss the Public Schools Rackets Singles Handicap competition for which he had been entered. He nearly won it too, losing in the final 3-2 'to a nice bloke from Eton'.

On his return to school in January 1949, he was straightaway informed that he had been appointed captain of cricket. It was an obvious choice really but he was hugely honoured and even more determined, if that were possible, to recover quickly from the operation in order to be fit for the forthcoming season. Perhaps it was just as well that he was ignorant of the fact that it was by no means certain that the surgical procedure would permit that. Mr Mayer kept his private doubts away from his patient. He wasn't even certain that Colin would recover sufficiently to play cricket again – ever. It was that tricky. But how about this for a touch of equanimity in the face of adversity? 'I am told I have to go to Pembury Hospital tomorrow. I play rackets v Jennings.' Sir Francis Drake would have been proud of the boy's insouciance in the teeth of impending crisis.

There is something intrinsically odd about walking into a hospital, climbing the stairs to your ward, being told to undress and put on a surgical gown and put to bed when you feel perfectly well. It is not as if you have been in a car accident or suffered a heart attack, when you are clearly very ill and hospital is where you want to be. Presumably, you have every hope and expectation that you will feel much better when you leave than when you came in.

For an operation like Colin's, in keeping with many sporting injuries requiring surgery, you feel fine but know that shortly you will feel anything but. Colin was put to bed at 10am and his operation was not scheduled until the next day. Unsurprisingly, he was bored. 'But I do learn all about the hospital lift,' he observes, before adding a little cryptically, 'Awful!'

All he could remember about the events of the following day was that he was 'wheeled into the theatre in the presence of a howling baby.' Either his pre-op medication was working too well or the porters had taken him to the wrong theatre. He was awoken at 4.30am 'and a full English breakfast at 7.15. Very boring indeed. I've got plaster on both legs and it is very uncomfortable indeed.'

Uncomfortable and bored, he was to remain for the next three months. To his relief, he was soon moved from hospital back to the school sanatorium, closer to friends and staff, but there was no hurrying the healing process. He had a steady stream of visitors and some work was brought for him to do, but the tedium was unalleviated. There were no reports written on him for this term; there was little point, for he was only able to have a distant relationship with the syllabus.

In his diary, he did his best to keep up his spirits but there is little to report except the dull routine of the day. You can sense his frustration and impatience as life at Tonbridge, especially on the playing fields, seems to be slipping past him. There are moments of unconscious humour, 'Valentine's Day. Matron comes to see me. She is very nice.'

At last the moment of truth dawns. It is the last day of March, 'My D Day. A very good result. Mr Mayer decides to take off the plaster. I have a walking iron on.' Colin was not the only one nervous of what he would find when the plaster was removed. But Mr Mayer professed himself satisfied with his handiwork and the process of rehabilitation commenced for his patient.

Colin was taken back to Ferox Hall but his movements were strictly limited. No stealing away for an unauthorised game of rackets. It would have been impossible anyway. His feet swelled alarmingly just as he was about to go home for the Easter holidays, though where home was at this time, he does not record. He had to go for daily physiotherapy at Pembury, so Mr and Mrs McNeill, with unwonted kindness and generosity – something Colin never forgot – looked after him and treated him as one of their own during the holidays. Even when the school reopened for the summer term, he was nowhere near fit.

He was the captain and he was resolved to set a good example, in the nets and at fielding practice, so much so that he had to be warned to take it easy. The support of a special type of shoe, which he wore for the rest of his playing career, helped as did the best healer of all – time – so when the first match of the season came along, against Lancing College in mid-May, he felt fit and ready for the fray, albeit confessing to some pre-match nerves. He need not have worried. 'A grand win to us,' he writes. 'I got my maiden century, 119 run out, and 5-28.'

Jeremy Eckersley, who was playing in that match, remembers the innings vividly. 'It was a tremendous knock. Nobody else scored very many. I think it was out of a total of 200 odd. He had all the shots and his timing was immaculate.' And this performance from a young man who had spent most of the previous three months in bed. That he was tired afterwards was no surprise. 'I have a complete rest from cricket,' he mentions the following day but adds, once again with complete lack of irony, 'but I do some Colts coaching.'

And so ends the saga of the feet, if for the time being. He may have been forgiven for believing that the worst was behind him but it wasn't. The feet stood up well enough to the rigours of continual first-class and Test cricket but the ramifications were going to dog him in years to come.

A sportsman's body occasionally lets him down. And if this sportsman is a household name then that particular part of the body becomes newsworthy. Think of Ollie Milburn's eye, Henry Cooper's eyebrows, Shane Warne's shoulder, Michael Atherton's back, Denis Compton's knee, David Beckham's metatarsal. To this list can be added Colin Cowdrey's feet and Colin, an intensely shy man in his youth, found the press interest and the opprobrium it stirred, profoundly upsetting. All that lay in the future.

In my years as a housemaster, I was closely associated with boys who had to, for one reason or another, deal with personal and physical misfortune and I was always in admiration of their resilience and cheerfulness in the face of adversity. Colin was no different. His housemaster and headmaster recognised as such and made comment of it in their reports. 'I am sure he will face with his usual balance and wisdom the bad luck that has come his way,' wrote McNeill. 'He has the sympathy of us all during this period of inactivity which he must now face,' said his headmaster, before adding, typically, 'And how I shall miss him on the rackets court next term.'

It would have been good if these observations from people in positions of authority had been released into the public domain when the controversy over 'Cowdrey's feet' was stirred five years later but of course that would have been impossible; they were private. In the meantime, all Colin had to think about was long summer days on the Head.

It was as if the shackles, both mental and physical, had been cast off. He scored over 800 runs for the school and continued to take wickets, 49 of them, with his leg breaks. He broke a 40-year-old Tonbridge record for an individual score with 181 not out against the Buccaneers, 123 against Haileybury, 140 against the Old Boys and 72 not out against Dulwich, not forgetting the century against Lancing earlier that summer. Fair stood the wind for Lord's and the annual fixture against Clifton but once again Old Father Time witnessed a Tonbridge capitulation. 'Lord's. Clifton 248, 119 (28) and 8-1. A tragic day!' he writes in his diary. The second day was no better. 'More tragic than ever! We lose by an innings and 17.'

Disappointment may well have been acute but it was not the end of his season, for representative matches were to follow, of a more testing standard and he was not to be found wanting. But as he reflected on the term's cricket, he was satisfied with his personal performances and had thoroughly enjoyed the responsibilities of captaincy. He was beginning to immerse himself in the technicalities of the game and the challenges of leadership.

Frequently, he discusses in his letters and diary the pros and cons of batting first or second on a this pitch or that, the conundrums of selection, whether to press on for victory or to shut up shop, the setting of fields and the changes of bowling – all these tactical facets of the game fascinated him. Dealing with people, getting the best out of his team, how to read personality and character and everything that went with being captain of a cricket team, he found intellectually rewarding. In short, he was beginning to grow up.

There was no fleeing on the Tube away from Lord's for a holiday in Cornwall; the rest of the summer stretched out in front of him and it was to be filled exclusively with cricket. He was playing almost every day now and loving it. Selection for the Southern Schools versus The Rest swiftly followed. Team-mates were Mike Bushby, Dennis Silk and Robin Marlar, all of whom he was going to encounter later in Varsity matches. Colin top-scored in the first innings with 85 and took 4-44 in the Rest's second innings. He was eight not out when his team completed a seven-wicket victory. He was a shoo-in for the Public Schools against the Combined Services. He did not set the world alight in this two-day match but one interesting statistic screams from the scorecard: P.B.H. May c&b Cowdrey 12. Fast forward seven years and picture the scene as Colin and his best man, Peter May, exchange nervous pleasantries in the church before the arrival of the bride:

'Peter?'

'Yes, Colin.'

'Have you remembered the ring?'

'Yes, Colin.'

'Do you remember 9 August 1949 at Lord's?'

'Yes, Colin.'

'P.B.H. May c&b Cowdrey 12?'

'Hmm.'

'Fancy getting out like that to a *schoolboy!*'

'If I were you, Colin, I'd shut up about that. Remember, the best man's speech is yet to come.'

'Peter?'

'Yes, Colin.'

'She will turn up, won't she?'

'If I know her father, she will.'

The step up from school cricket, let alone club, to professional level is hefty and much more challenging than is often imagined. I have seen many a gaudily coloured school cap, proudly worn by some *ingénue*, ruthlessly targeted by a county fast bowler. All right, this was in the days before helmets, but I am sure that a school first XI sweater has the same energising effect. Some sink without trace. Others learn to survive. It is a bit of a bear pit but it does separate the boys from the men, so to speak.

Colin survived. For that he was grateful for he still, inexplicably in many people's opinion, suffered from a lack of self-confidence, not at all sure that he belonged at this level. Take the game against Norfolk, for example. Colin scored 35, no mean feat against experienced bowling of that class. The highest score in the innings was 62. He was perhaps overawed by an innings of 170 not out by one of the famous Edrich brothers, Eric, who struck the ball far and wide. Imagine Colin's wide-eyed wonderment as he sat with his pads on, slated to come in at five against Wiltshire, while the first-wicket pair put on 158 and the second 257, before the captain declared. So for most of the first of a two-day game, Colin did nothing except watch other people bat. Such things just did not happen in schoolboy cricket.

But it was to school that he returned that September. The usual routine was re-established and life proceeded gently and agreeably. There was a great deal of rackets and squash, he was playing rugby for the first XV and his feet were fine. He was working hard too, as witnessed by the comments of his teachers in his reports, 'He has written a number of exceptionally interesting things in his essays'; 'The examination paper was a remarkable achievement of accurate translation; he must have put in an enormous amount of work'; 'His application has been commendable'. The comments of his housemaster tell a familiar tale but are worth repeating for all that, 'His work is going ahead rapidly. He also finds time – I don't know how – to coach juniors in the House for which they and I are extremely grateful.'

There was now a new headmaster at the school, Rev. L.H. Waddy, and, as is often the case, he was a completely different kettle of fish to his predecessor. According to David Kemp and Jeremy Eckersley, Mr E.E.A. Whitworth was popular with the boys. 'A splendid chap,' said Kemp. 'Oh, a lovely man,' agreed Eckersley. You will remember that his headmaster's reports on Colin had been totally complimentary. Waddy's first impressions of Colin are more heedful and reflective, 'It is hard to know where to start writing of so many-sided a boy so I shall only say that it is a very great thing for the school when a boy much in the public eye is so unselfish and sincere in all that he does, and he does a wonderful amount.'

There is a telling little entry in Colin's diary at this time. At an annual dinner of the Buccaneers Cricket Club, he met a number of eminent figures from the world of cricket. 'Superb result! GO Allen, RWV Robins, John Arlott, Neville Cardus!!' The double exclamation mark says it all. In later years, Colin became a by-word for social networking. Some saw this as a great strength, especially in view of the inherent shyness he had to overcome; others saw it, perhaps jealously, as social climbing. The debate will concern us later. But the point is that, as he happened to be there, he made the effort to chat to them. They cannot have been unimpressed with his amiability and courtesy. Everybody who met him, even at this tender age, thought so too.

Though there is little evidence in his letters, diaries and school reports that Colin was ever naughty or rebelled or overindulged socially – indeed, in his biography, he wrote, 'My whole life was a narrow corridor surrounded by cricket. My needs were few. I did not smoke, drank little and had no hankering after new clothes and pop records' – I do not think it would be fair to label him a 'hearty', as games players of limited intelligence were called. Colin was no narrow-minded hearty: he had a hinterland. He interested himself in music, art and drama, albeit not terribly successfully, and he was mindful of the rich variety of experiences he was exposed to at Tonbridge.

His love was always cricket, however; it was what defined him and his pulse quickened as the 1950 season came round. Now a senior at school and captain of cricket, he was ready to step on to the stage and take ownership of it. His unspoken ambition was to score 1,000 runs in the term, a tall order but not an impossible one for one of his hunger and talent. No team is a one-man band, no matter what Brian Lara may have thought, for someone has to bat at the other end, someone has to share the bowling duties and others have to catch the catches and field the ball.

Tonbridge without Cowdrey were a very limited team; with him, they could take on all-comers. It was a successful season and Colin was in such a rich vein of form that he seemed to score runs whenever he walked to the wicket. He scored his perennial century against Lancing, 175 not out against Christ's Hospital, 109 not out against the Old Boys, 95 against Dulwich, and 116 against Band of Brothers, as well as other useful scores.

Morale and confidence were rocketing and characteristically, Colin lays the credit for this firmly at the door of their new cricket professional, Maurice Tate. In the 1920s and 1930s, Tate had been England's stalwart all-rounder, who single-handedly, it seemed, led the bowling attack before the arrival of Larwood and Voce, a tireless seam bowler, perhaps the first of its kind. After a sudden and bitter departure from his home county Sussex, he took up as a pub landlord, with the odd coaching duties, such as this at Tonbridge, to augment his meagre income.

He died in straitened circumstances, largely forgotten and ignored. Colin and all the boys who came under his wing at Tonbridge would have been shocked at this; there was no one more popular at the school and his cheerful grin and infectious good humour did much to make the cricket term so much fun. He was in his element among the boys, Colin would later say, for he was no more than an overgrown schoolboy himself. There is a good story about Tate that I unearthed among Colin's papers. It was net practice. Tate asked the senior boys, 'Who is that chap with curly hair in the far net? He looks a seriously good bowler.' Colin's mirth chortles down the years. 'It was our new headmaster, Rev. L.H. Waddy!'

And so to Lord's, for the fifth and, as it transpired, the final time – as a schoolboy. Colin's form with the toss had been in inverse proportion to that with the bat and predictably he lost it, with Clifton taking first strike. The total of 201 was handy (Cowdrey 4-59) but by no means unassailable. However, the curse of Lord's resurfaced and Tonbridge were dismissed for a meagre 128, Cowdrey top-scoring with 31. The next day, it all changed as Tonbridge fought back well, bowling Clifton out for 102 (Cowdrey 3-28), which left them a target of 176 to win.

There were two motives driving the captain on as he took guard after a wicket had fallen in the second over: to win the game and finish off the season in fine style, which he publicly espoused, and to reach his personal milestone of 1,000 runs for the season, which he kept to himself. He knew the magic number was 63 but he did not know that everybody else knew too. When he passed 63, he puffed out his cheeks in silent thanks and was flabbergasted when a great roar went up from the Tonbridge contingent of the crowd. He was moved when the Clifton fielders, once they knew what was going on, came up to congratulate him and to shake his hand.

All that was to do now was to complete his century and finish the game. Alas, he was bowled for 97 trying to hit the four to win. The difference between 97 and 100 is only three runs but to a batsman it is the difference between raising your bat to acknowledge the applause and smashing it through the dressing room window. Colin of course was far too restrained to have done that, though some have, even at Lord's, but his annoyance would have been acute. No matter. Tonbridge secured their victory soon after, by four wickets.

A single entry in the diary offers a frustratingly brief suggestion of what it all meant for him, 'PARTY!!' His statistics for the season, incidentally, were 1,033 runs at 79.00 and 49 wickets at 14.00. A one-man band? Almost. He would never have said it but others did. Dennis Silk, an opponent both at school (Christ's Hospital) and at university (Cambridge) and later a much-respected Warden of Radley College, said this about his old friend, 'The whole idea was to get Colin out. If we did that early, we won. If we didn't, we may just as well have given up.'

Selection for the Southern Schools against the Rest a few days later was a formality; being asked to captain the side was not. Captaining a team of handpicked representatives from other schools is not like being in charge of your mates. He would have recognised faces from opposing teams or from previous years but it is difficult to forge a team spirit in two days. But he seemed to take it in his stride, as he did when asked to captain the full Public Schools XI against the Combined Services.

It certainly did not affect his batting. He scored 126 not out and 55. He said later that these innings put him on the map, so to speak. This was not a century against schoolboys but battle-hardened men, county pros on National Service some of them, and those MCC members sitting in the pavilion watched, took note and nodded their heads in approval.

Two of Colin's team caught my eye. John May was the Charterhouse captain and a glittering career was predicted for him along much the same lines as his elder brother, Peter. These predictions were not entirely wrong for he made his name as a liquidator in the City, though he had by no means an undistinguished career as a minor county player for Berkshire. Micky Stewart, from Alleyns School in south London, needs no introduction. His and Colin's careers ran side by side for pretty well all of their playing days, one for Surrey, one for Kent, though they did share the same dressing room on half a dozen occasions for England.

It is not unheard of for a cricketer to make his first-class debut while still at school but it is still something of a rarity and a notable talking point, especially for the local newspaper. *The Kentish Gazette* took more than a passing interest in the 'young prodigy' when it was announced that the 17-year-old schoolboy, Colin Cowdrey, was going to make his debut for Kent against Derbyshire later on in that August of 1950. In truth, had Colin been at any one of the bigger and more successful clubs, such as Yorkshire, Surrey, Lancashire, Warwickshire or Middlesex, he would have had to wait considerably longer to break into the first team but Kent, at that time, were a struggling side. Many had had their careers curtailed by the war and probably their best years were behind them.

Their captain was the legendary Les Ames but he was now 45, having made his debut for the county way back in 1926. Imagine how the young lad must have felt as he took a look around his team-mates, some of whom he had never met, and searched for an inconspicuous place to lay down his bag. He was spared this ordeal because he was immediately shown into the amateurs' dressing room, which proved to be even more of an embarrassment. He was the only amateur in the team. He had no idea that such distinctions existed.

To spare his blushes, Ames picked up his bag and moved in with him. It was obvious that the senior man was intent on looking after the debutant. He had already dined with him the night before. Just as well too; Colin had to ask him about the their opponents' opening bowlers, the feared pair of Gladwin and Jackson. Not how to play them but which was which.

Colin did settle down to watch Ames bat – he would have been a fool not to for Ames was the foremost wicketkeeper-batsman of the pre-war era and was enjoying something of an Indian summer in 1950. But no sooner had Colin settled down to watch the great man bat than he was swiftly up again, in both innings. Ames bagged a pair. When his captain returned to the pavilion after his second dismissal, Colin made his first acquaintance with the sort of tomfoolery that went on in county dressing rooms the length and breadth of the country. One of the team donned a giant pair of spectacles to welcome their returning hero, to general amusement, including, it has to be said, the object of their fun, who was not averse to a bit of leg-pulling himself.

Colin's diary entry rather blandly gives a brief summary – 'Lost toss and they get 300. I get my first wicket and first maiden' – but he later confessed to considerable nerves. Not surprising really – who isn't nervous on his fast-class debut? But oddly he was more worried about his fielding than his batting. He was petrified that he would drop a catch and let down the bowler and the team. In fact, he had little need to worry. He missed nothing and even caught Charlie Elliott (whom he came to know well when Elliott became an umpire), a swirling steepler off the bowling of the leg-spinner, Doug Wright. And his first victim? Paul Vaulkhard, the Derbyshire captain. No, I have never heard of him either but he was a regular for Nottinghamshire before the war.

Like other counties in the post-war period, Derbyshire struggled to find an amateur prepared to commit to the captaincy full-time so Vaulkhard accepted the offer and apparently did a reasonable job. They came fifth in the county championship that year. Mind you, with an attack of Gladwin and Jackson, augmented with the leg spin of Dusty Rhodes, Derbyshire would have been formidable opponents with a Frenchman in charge.

Colin felt that he acquitted himself reasonably well with the bat, making 15 (out of 96) and 26 (out of 151), hardly exceptional scores but on both occasions, only one Kent batsman bettered them. He was dismissed twice by Gladwin but it was Les Jackson who left the more lasting impression. Colin was surprised by a bouncer. Now, in school cricket and club games, there is no such thing as a bouncer. Not a real bouncer. Some bowlers might be able to bang it in short and make the ball balloon harmlessly over the batsman's head but a true bouncer, a vicious delivery that rears at the throat off not that short of a length, can only be delivered by a bowler with genuine pace. Jackson certainly had that. He was hostile, especially on uncovered pitches, and could have considered himself unlucky to play in the same era as Trueman, Statham and Tyson, otherwise he would surely have exceeded his two caps for England. His first had been gained the year before, in

1949. Oddly, he was to wait until 1961 for his second, at the age of 40, probably well past his best.

That he should have tested the young Cowdrey with a short ball would have come as no surprise to anybody who knew him. It certainly came as a surprise to Colin, who was forced to jerk his head backwards, out of harm's way. Hmm, he pondered, I'm going to have to learn how to play this short stuff if I am going to survive at this level. That he did, by adapting his back foot play, is the stuff of legend. Kent lost by an innings and 98 runs, a fair thumping in anybody's book. In Colin's book, it was described as 'a hopeless mess'.

Dover to Derby – 215 miles. Derby to Dover the next day – still 215 miles. Such were the vagaries of the fixture list that both teams had to pack their bags and travel down to the south coast side by side, or in crocodile line for all I know, for the return fixture on the following day. Nowadays, when such a bewildering Horlicks of the championship schedule is uncovered, blame is put squarely on the computer. In 1950 computers were in their infancy and were certainly not in evidence in any office of MCC. So one can only assume that the person organising the itinerary must have had a mordant sense of humour. No motorways, let us not forget.

But at least the weather was on Kent's side, or else the groundsman deliberately on purpose had left the hose on, for the wicket was wet and favoured their spinners more than the Derbyshire seamers and Kent had their revenge by nine wickets. Colin scored four. He fared better against Nottinghamshire in the following game, also at Dover, scoring 27 and two. Batting cannot have been easy on this pitch either. Only two batsmen from either side exceeded 50 in both innings. Twice, he was dismissed by Arthur Jepson, another future umpire on the county circuit. In later years, Colin must have got sick and tired of umpires reminding him that they had played against him when they were a lot younger. And got him out on one or two occasions, they might have added.

As August slipped into September, the West Indians were in town, with a side including Roy Marshall, Clyde Walcott, Everton Weekes and Alf Valentine. Once again, Colin looked the part without building an innings of substance but to be fair to the young man – and there were those in the know at Kent who were trying to be very fair – there were not many others in the team pulling up trees either.

At least he had youth on his side, and class, which would surely tell in the end, they no doubt told each other, nodding their heads. For Colin's part, he recognised how much he needed to improve to cut the mustard as a county player. Representing England must have been a pipe dream.

Understandably, his diary falls silent during this summer. The life of a first-class cricketer, playing every day, is a full-on existence. The routine is relentless. There may be periods of *longueur* during the match itself – rather more than you would wish for if you are a batsman and going through a bad patch – but there is very little time to relax and it would be a brave man, certainly one more brave than a 17-year-old schoolboy, to bring out his diary to start scribbling down his impressions of the day's play and the personal habits of his teammates round about.

But the diary resumes once the season has finished. On 22 September, 'Daddy takes me back to school. Mother has a tooth out.' As if to underline the familiar routine of life back at Tonbridge, he notes on the following day, 'Read the lesson in the first service of the term.' David Kemp said that Colin was religious at school and became increasingly so when he went to Oxford. 'Christianity was important to Colin,' he said. 'He even flirted with the idea of going into the Church at one stage but was convinced that he could do a better job in its service by being a good man and a principled example to others in his role as an international cricketer. He read the Sunday lesson in whatever church he found himself on his travels.' That is certainly true. He took guard in as many pulpits as cricket grounds. And this commitment took root at Tonbridge.

Sometimes a diary tells you more by what it doesn't say than what it does. Nowhere can I find reference to the fact that Colin had been appointed head boy. It was an honour no doubt fully deserved and one that he was mighty proud to accept so it could be expected that he would have made mention of it in his private ruminations. But no. We have no idea when he was told, what was his initial reaction and what, if any, were the misgivings he had about accepting such a privileged position. For head boy in a boarding school is no sinecure.

Later, he likened it to the role of a chairman of the board and you can take it as read that he took his responsibilities, as he did everything else in his life, very seriously indeed. It helped form his philosophy on captaincy. Man management it would be called today. He was firmly of the school that believed in a collegiate style of leadership, quite at odds with the more autocratic approach of someone like, say, Raymond Illingworth.

With a career in cricket beckoning, he was loath to play rugby this term, worried that his feet would not stand up to the pummelling. But his surgeon, Mr Mayer, convinced him that as he had withstood the rigours of a full season of cricket, there was no reason not to go ahead and play. So he did and was promptly made captain of the first XV. 'He was a tactical stand-off,' David Kemp told me. 'He was a very good kicker and could read a game well.'

That Colin enjoyed the mental tussles is undisputed but he relished the physical struggle as well, which surprised me a little. Not being a rugby player myself, I was always of the uninformed opinion that fly-halves kept themselves well away from trouble. Clearly, Colin did not spare himself. 'Get really tired,' he writes and 'deadbeat at the end of it' and the day after, 'have a day of rest' or 'my leg is really stiff after the game yesterday.'

My faith in my judgement of the ball-playing backs is restored by a comment, 'Play whole rugger game with forwards against the backs. It was really miserable.' No doubt because they were playing with 'a filthy wet ball'. His observations on, not so much the quality of the opposition, but their manners and behaviour, made me hoot with laughter. Haileybury, admittedly in the rain, was 'a miserable place'. Another school that met with his disapproval was Sevenoaks. 'We win 27-9. They have dreadful manners at tea!' Harrow is 'a grand place – very good food'.

I searched in vain for any suggestion that he had a social life in the sense that we would understand today. As he said himself, his needs were few and he was busy enough immersing himself in the routine of the school day. There is a certain wry touch to his comment, 'I go to summer dance – as gatekeeper!' but that is as far as it goes with any reference to the fairer sex, other than sisters of friends and cousins, with whom he usually played tennis or went bathing. I suppose we should not be greatly surprised. It was a more protected and innocent age and he was still at school and the concept of co-educational boarding schools was in its infancy. And public schools in the 1940s, whatever else they were, could not be classified as progressive. It is likely that the only women the boys at Tonbridge encountered were housemasters' wives and matrons.

Another smile was evinced by his references to a certain Master. With this one exception, Colin's comments about adults were uniformly respectful. 'Slimey' did not get away so easily, 'Slimey is away so we have a double free'; 'Busy doing Slimey's essay'; 'Slimey does a very amusing sermon.'

Who was Slimey and why was he so called? I sought clarification from my two inside sources and both Jeremy Eckersley and David Kemp answered with a simultaneous guffaw, even though they live at different ends of the country. 'Slimey Somerville!' they cried. 'A Tonbridge legend.' *I wonder if you could be a bit more specific.* 'Slimey was a lovely chap, a real character,' said Eckersley. Kemp agreed. 'He was a brilliant teacher, a most erudite man who knew an enormous amount about his subject, history. But he was what you might call a true eccentric. If he didn't feel like teaching you, he'd tell you to get on with some work and then just sit there at his desk reading the paper. But he got away with it because he was so charismatic.'

So why was he called 'Slimey'? 'Because he sort of...slithered around the place,' said Eckersley, after giving the matter some thought. 'He was tall and thin,' Kemp assented, 'and he did walk in a sort of...odd manner.' *So the sobriquet was sympathetically bestowed?* Both were in total accord. 'Absolutely.' Do not forget that public schools practically invented the nickname. It would have been the mark of blandness and insipidity *not* to have one.

Colin's diary is full of snow, if you see what I mean. 'It did seem to snow a lot more in those days,' said Kemp. 'Sometimes it was a foot deep. Jolly cold too.' *Played havoc with the games programme.* 'The rackets courts were often covered in it,' remembered Eckersley, 'and as the roof was glass and there was no lighting, it would be pitch black in there with no natural light. Play would be impossible so we went off and played squash. Which Colin was very good at,' he reminded me. 'Funny really, because he wasn't terribly quick around the court because of the problems with his feet but he didn't need to be. He always seemed to be there even before you hit it. Anticipation, I suppose, a quick brain.'

If Colin were alive, he would love to hear you say that. Both agreed that during the two winter terms, before and after Christmas, there were days and days when it snowed heavily. 'Tons of it,' wrote Colin. 'Heaps of it.'

Exactly when the discussions took place about the next stage of Colin's education is not clear but what is certain is that he seemed to be heading for Oxford as he was entered for a scholarship – and missed it. But the point is that he was entered at all. The school must have thought his going for it was worth the gamble, even if it failed. He may have missed the scholarship but he was good enough to fulfil the entry requirements.

As Kemp took pains to stress, Colin was no mug academically and he worked hard. Once he was awarded the Heath Harrison Exhibition to Brasenose College, his immediate future was settled. It should be pointed out that an exhibition is an award in the gift of the college and is usually granted to someone with potential, not necessarily but neither exclusively, outside the lecture halls. This was still an age when sporting prowess was not seen as an obstacle to entry into Oxbridge. Times were changing, it has to be said, from the generations when excellence at games was almost a key to the front gate of a college but in 1950 it cannot have done Colin's chances any harm.

And now Ernest Cowdrey makes another, crucial appearance on the stage. Over once more from India, he persuaded his son, no doubt with a wink and a nod from the powers-that-be at Kent, that he should leave Tonbridge at Easter 1951 and spend the summer playing county cricket before going up to Oxford. So once again, Ernest wrong-footed the school authorities and robbed them of their star player for one last triumphant season. It had happened at Homefield and now he did it to Tonbridge.

What Colin thought of the idea is not recorded. No doubt he was torn; it would have been nice to remain and smash all school records but on the other hand, to play county cricket was all that he had dreamed about. It was a dilemma and when the decision was made, it was a wrench to leave. But before we judge Papa Cowdrey too harshly, it is well to consider his reasoning. He thought that the extra term at Homefield would do Colin's cricket no good, and in this he was probably right.

The same rationale lay at the heart of this decision. Probably Colin *would* score buckets of runs but would his cricket improve? He believed it was time for him to move on and face the challenges of learning the game at first-class level. And who was to say he was not right on this occasion too?

In a letter to his father, Colin expresses no resentment for the decision; in fact he gives every indication that he agrees. He even starts to consider his career at Tonbridge in terms of a *valete*:

'And so I feel I ought to take this opportunity to thank you *very very* much for sending me to Tonbridge, for at no other school would I have had such (not only enjoyment) a great time in every way...But it is not the games I enjoy so much but the grand, friendly atmosphere and it makes one feel honoured that one day one will be an OT. *And so I thank you* for what you have done for me. My last day at school will be a day of misery.

'Now, about what I am going to do. If they really think me good enough to play for Kent then I would like to spend a lot of time between 20 and 30 playing seriously, and as a schoolmaster NO CAN DO.

'I must add a brief account of my plans and I want to hear your views and criticisms:

1. Fail the army
2. Pass Higher Cert
3. Take another Jupp Scholarship in Feb 1951
4. Stay on for summer '51
5. Go to BNC (*Brasenose College*) in Oct '51
6. Read a subject on which to schoolmaster
7. Hope a good job comes my way leaving me plenty of time so that I can play whole of season
8. Have a degree and ability to start teaching at 30 when July, August, September cricket will be quite sufficient probably.'

We have no need to imagine Ernest's advice. In fact we know it. 'Play cricket, son, for as long as you can.' Which he did.

The die was cast and Colin departed Tonbridge quietly, without any fuss or fanfare, at the end of the Easter term. His last appearance as a pupil on the school's playing fields was somewhat incongruously at sports day. His departure may have been low-key but he had been captain of cricket, captain of rugby and head of school and his housemaster paid this tribute to him in his final report. 'I have been very proud of his achievements as Captain of Cricket and his success as Head Boy.'

His headmaster was even more fulsome and his wise and generous farewell is worth quoting in full:

'Things that seem small to other people matter to him and this thoughtfulness, as well as his success, make him a much-loved leader, which is better than pearls or rubies, or even centuries and scholarships.'

Colin may have been wistful as he boarded the train from Tonbridge station to London but he cannot have been downcast with those words ringing in his ears. He makes no mention of his feelings in his diary but we can read between the lines. There is a single, bare entry:

'THE END'

And there the diary, together with his childhood, comes to a close.

3

From Brasenose to Brisbane

Oxford 1951–54

*'Cricket at Oxford will always be perfectly embalmed
in my mind.....Warm days in the sun, net practices
that were never a chore, good wickets, good
fellowship – a simple, uncomplicated life.'*

Colin Cowdrey

W HEN I discovered that Colin Cowdrey had been
awarded the Heath Harrison Exhibition to Brasenose
College, Oxford, I laughed out loud. The coincidence
was preposterous. George Chesterton, the subject of my first book,
had been awarded the same exhibition for Brasenose half a dozen
years earlier – for pretty much the same reasons. Both had passed the
entrance exam, both were talented sportsmen, both would have been
expected to gain Blues at cricket (which they did), both had all-round
careers at school and had been enthusiastically recommended by
their headmasters and both were considered to be 'excellent chaps'
who would no doubt bring credit to the college. And to be fair, both
did.

The reason I laughed was that George once told me that he was delighted to have 'won' the exhibition until he realised that he had been selected from a shortlist of one. I wonder if Colin had been up against equally fierce competition. No matter. The stipend of £20 per term was more than useful in making ends meet and considering Colin's status in the game already, I have no doubt that Brasenose considered it money well spent. He was a little embarrassed by the award, with its suggestion of pocket money for a bone-headed sportsman; he was no dilettante, he would knuckle down, work hard, pass his exams and score hundreds of runs in The Parks.

Before books could be opened, there were balls to be hit. Not that Colin had much success in making contact with the ball early on in his first season for Kent. He could have been flaying it to all parts on the Head at Tonbridge. Not surprisingly, Colin struggled. He won't have been the first, or the last, to find the step-up to county cricket problematic, and I am including here players of undoubted ability and class.

Just three years earlier, Tom Graveney began to doubt that his decision to forsake a promising career in the army to play for Gloucestershire was such a good one as he struggled to make any impact during the early months of the 1948 season. But they stuck with him, he eventually found his form and he was away. The same with Colin. He was so perturbed by his initial run of low scores that he intimated he should be dropped. Nobody listened to him. He scored two against Nottinghamshire and four and nought against Hampshire and was in despair. The swing and movement of Hampshire's opening pair, Shackleton and Cannings, had punctured his confidence. He simply had no answer and felt he was floundering. But he was patient, he watched and he learned and a better match against Northamptonshire (27 and 47) restored some of his confidence. He had the strokes, of that he was sure, but he still felt he had much to learn about playing the moving ball.

In early June, he had played for the Free Foresters against Oxford University in The Parks and scored 143, thus laying down a marker with many of his future team-mates at the university, but he still wondered whether he had the technique to cope with the higher demands of the county game. The match was deemed first-class (thereby his century was counted as the first of the eventual 107 of his career) but it was a cut below the exacting standards of the county championship and he realised he would need to sharpen up.

Slowly his scores improved, including 54 against Leicestershire and 51 against Lancashire. But it is worth pointing out that of his first 17 innings, six were ducks, and we can include two other scores of four and four in that total. What does that hint at? That he was a nervous starter? This is one criticism that was occasionally aimed at him during his career but I would dispute it. Who is not a nervous starter? If you're not nervous when you go out to bat, then you don't care. It is how you control the butterflies that counts.

Colin's weight of runs in a lengthy career is evidence enough that he was never paralysed by nerves. It is true that he rarely came out with all guns blazing; he was raised in a more cautious era and in any case, he relied on touch and feel and he needed a few overs to get the pace of the wicket and the measure of the bowlers. But these quick dismissals did underline a weakness that he knew he had to eradicate. It was fast bowling that was the problem, not so much extreme speed but movement through the air and off the pitch at a pace to which he was not accustomed.

He was by nature a technician, always intrigued by the mechanics of batting, and he set about adjusting his technique to counter the moving ball. As an exemplar to study and emulate, there was none better than the man who was often batting down the other end from him, the Kent opener Arthur Fagg. At one time, before the war, Fagg had been compared favourably with Len Hutton, almost an exact contemporary, but poor health and the six years of his career lost to war meant that he had never quite fulfilled his early promise. By now, he was nearing the end of his career but he was still a fine player. Watching Fagg adjust to the moving ball, Colin realised that he needed to take that extra split second before committing himself to the stroke and adapted his style accordingly. He later said, 'During that summer, Arthur Fagg taught me the value of playing late.'

Fagg subsequently became another of those umpires whom Colin would meet regularly on the count circuit. He is perhaps best remembered as an umpire in the 1973 Test at Edgbaston when he became so upset at the behaviour of the West Indians after he had turned down an appeal for a catch that he refused to take the field the next morning. Alan Oakman deputised but only for one over, by which time a placated Fagg resumed his station. Fagg was also officiating in the Headingley Ashes Test in 1975 when the pitch was dug up by vandals.

Let us not forget that pitches were not vandalised very often by protesters but they were by the weather. In the days of uncovered pitches, the medium-pacers thrived. You only have to think back down the ages to recall a noble line of them, from Sydney Barnes to Maurice Tate to Alec Bedser to Tom Cartwright but their effectiveness declined once wickets were covered. The twin bugbears of Colin's first full season, Derek Shackleton and Vic Cannings of Hampshire, were two such wily campaigners, allying nagging accuracy with little variations of pace, swing and cut, able to strangle the scoring rate when conditions were favourable for batting and quick to exploit a damp pitch when they were not. It is no wonder that Colin struggled initially. Many of his more experienced colleagues fared little better.

At which point an old problem reared its head. He had to rest his feet. They were giving him trouble and he was out for three weeks. Although he would not have admitted it at the time – he confessed to being worried and depressed by his lack of form – the enforced break probably did him good. The pressure was off and he could reflect at leisure on what he needed to do to improve. When he returned to action, it was with a slightly modified technique and mindset – play the ball late and eschew the risky shot until well set.

It seemed to work. By the time of the return fixture against Hampshire, he was in an altogether better frame of mind and top scored with 90 out of a total of 263. Cannings and Shackleton took four wickets apiece and were never easy to play but he felt he could cope. Evidently that view was shared by his captain, David Clark, for during the tourist match against the visiting South Africans at the end of the season, he awarded Colin his county cap.

The ceremony of a captain handing over a cap to a player in his team is a very special moment in anyone's career, none more so than for Colin. It signifies acceptance by your peers, recognition that you are now an integral part of the team – in short, you have *arrived*. Colin never forgot the importance of the occasion and always made a fuss of the recipient when he was captain. Derek Underwood told me the delightful story of when he was capped by Colin, his captain. 'It was in 1964,' he said, 'against the Australians at Canterbury. Suddenly, Mike

Denness, who was 12th man, came on to the field and handed Colin a cap. Play was held up as he presented it to me. Norman O'Neill was the second person to shake my hand after Colin. Apparently, Colin had rung up my parents the night before and suggested that it would not be a good idea to miss the following day's play, so they were there to see it all. That was typical of Colin. I never forgot that gesture.'

How different from the experience of Tom Graveney. At the end of the final match of the 1948 season, Tom was unbuckling his pads in the dressing room when he was hit on the head by a flying cap. It was his captain, B.O. Allen, who had casually flicked his county cap in his direction. The contrast between Allen's off-handedness and Colin's considerateness could not have been more marked.

Gentlemen v Players, the Scarborough Festival at the season's conclusion, tables, white linen and tea brought out on to the middle while the band played; all symbols of a bygone age. I remember playing at the famous seaside ground of North Marine Road and staying in the (not so) Grand Hotel. I was surprised by the crowd drifting off from 5.30pm onwards. 'That's because tea in the boarding houses is at six o'clock 'oop 'ere,' a team-mate explained.

The atmosphere was different, quirky even, but let no one say that the cricket was nonchalant and light-hearted. Yorkshire folk don't do frivolous. It was an unexpected honour for Colin to be invited to represent the Gentlemen against the Players in the annual end-of-season bash at county cricket's northernmost outpost but he would have been forewarned that the professionals would be taking no prisoners. As an 18-year-old amateur, he would have been right in their sights.

On a damp morning, the Gents batted first and it immediately became obvious that the opening bowlers for the Players, Tom Pritchard, Warwickshire's New Zealander, and Alec Bedser, who needs no introduction, were not in the business of frivolity either. They were 84/4, with Reg Simpson, Bill Edrich, Peter May and Hubert Doggart sent on their way, and it was the young Cowdrey standing between them and a complete breakthrough. He struggled at first and often that is the mark of a great innings, the fact that it has not come easy. The pitch dried out, greater fluency in his strokes came to the fore and in due course, his second first-class hundred was achieved.

Looking on with admiration no doubt hidden behind those guarded eyes was the Players' captain, Len Hutton. One can almost envisage him making a mental note of the undoubted class and supreme timing of the youthful prodigy. As we shall see, Hutton was to have a crucial impact on Colin's early career. After a while, he clearly had seen enough. He brought himself on to bowl with his occasional leg breaks and had Colin stumped for 106, taking 4-20 as the rest of the innings folded for 318.

Praise was generous afterwards from all quarters, press included. Colin knew that he had made a name for himself but was unaware until later how much of an impression he had made on the England captain. Hutton said later that it was not this innings that had convinced him that in Colin he saw a future England star but he was distinctly impressed. And Len Hutton was not easily impressed.

It is a far cry, both in distance and culture, from the windy seaside of Scarborough to the dreaming spires of Oxford. No doubt too it was quite a change to shift from the set routine of a county cricketer to the more *laissez-faire* world of the undergraduate. For all of his life, in India, at Homefield, at Tonbridge and with Kent, Colin would have had to rise in the morning at a set time for a day's activity that had been pretty well predetermined. Now, nobody would have bothered had he not surfaced all day, though I doubt he was a natural slug-a-bed.

For the next three years, he was to rejoin Kent only after the summer term at university had finished. Sadly, that is not a state of affairs that exists anymore. Counties seem to want to get their hands on a promising young player and tie him down to a contract without allowing him unfettered access to further education, an attitude that betrays a lack of understanding of what a university education is all about, even for aspiring cricketers. This was a debate that Colin himself pondered, at the time and later, when he had to make some hard decisions about his future.

Did he gain intellectually from his study of geography, his chosen subject? Well, he put the subject to good use by learning how to navigate his way around the country, from cricket ground to cricket ground, once he had got his own car. As for the more esoteric aspects of the course, he admitted he pursued his studies 'with some interest but no great zeal'. He won't have been the first student to have similarly scraped by.

His cricket was not greatly enhanced by the university experience. He had already been exposed widely to the first-class game so playing for Oxford would not have been a step up in standard. For most undergraduates straight out of school, university provides untold opportunities to forge new friendships, bonds, affiliations, even romantic attachments but Colin had already joined his tribe. Cricket, and cricketers, henceforth circumscribed his world.

For all that, he enjoyed his time at Oxford and felt that it had broadened his hinterland and opened up his mind to a variety of activities, interests and influences. Dominant among these was obviously sport but there was another facet of the academic community that intrigued him, one that had lain dormant, occasionally stirring from time to time when he was at school, but which now he felt free to explore and debate.

David Kemp judged that Colin was God-fearing at school; he remembers his being hugely impressed by a sermon from the Bishop of Croydon during one Sunday chapel. As we have discovered, Colin's was no uncritical ear. His diary is punctuated with less than flattering comments about the weekly sermons given by a variety of visiting preachers. I particularly enjoyed this tart assessment one Sunday, 'Dreadful sermon by Vicar of Tonbridge.' Another reference to '29 minutes of supper sermon' could possibly, I suppose, be describing the meal given to the speaker by a grateful headmaster but was probably a spelling mistake.

In any event, Colin kept in touch with Cuthbert Bardsley, Bishop of Croydon, and they continued to communicate after he went up to Oxford. According to Kemp, who was also at Brasenose at the same time as Colin, the relationship went much further than desultory exchanges about the latest Test score. In fact, it was David's opinion that Colin was seriously probing the strength and depth of his faith. I wasn't altogether surprised. Oxford at this time was something of a hotbed of religious fervour, dialectic and contemplation. Those dreaming spires were prompting thoughts of the hereafter as much as today.

George Chesterton, who preceded Colin in the Oxford side by just three years, told me that most of his team were extremely religious, 'It was the time when Moral Re-Armament was very strong in the university. Dedicating your whole life to God.' Moral Re-Armament was popular at Oxford from the mid-1920s onwards and gradually became known as the Oxford Group. The movement had Christianity at its core but based itself on the four absolutes – absolute honesty, absolute purity, absolute selflessness and absolute love. Changing the world could only begin by changing oneself. 'The trouble was,' admitted George ruefully, 'I was absolutely *none* of those things!' He went on to say that he came back to his hotel room one evening on tour, hoping for a quiet drink and a natter about the day's play with his room-mate only to find him on his knees at prayer. 'And he was there for a good hour or so,' he added. The name of his devout team-mate was Brian Boobyer.

The scorecard for Colin's first Varsity match, in 1952, records that opening the batting for Oxford was B. Boobyer. In Colin's words, he was a 'solid, determined batsman' and in George's opinion 'a bit stodgy' but he was in the Oxford side for four years and scored 1,970 runs. His obituary in *The Daily Telegraph* described him as 'a doughty rather than spectacular cricketer'. The same could not be said of his rugby. He won nine caps for England, playing at centre, and was named as possibly the most inventive back of his era. But it was not his sporting prowess that defined his life. While at Oxford, he had become increasingly attached to the Moral Re-Armament movement and at the age of 24, having come down from university, he turned his back on all sport and other superficial pursuits and devoted the rest of his life to the challenge of his Christian commitment.

Boobyer was at Brasenose with Colin and may well have influenced him. Yet Colin resisted the siren calls of Moral Re-Armament and its total subjugation to its doctrine – after all, his fledgling cricket career would have been its first victim – but he was not immune to the notion of taking orders. 'We were both enticed by the idea,' said Kemp, 'and discussed it a lot. I think the Moral Re-Armers went in a bit strong – sportsmen seemed to be their main target – and that was clearly not the answer to our spiritual quest. But becoming a priest certainly had its attractions for both of us.'

But neither of you took that step? 'No. We both decided against it. I felt that schoolmastering was probably where I should go.' *And Colin?* 'It was the bishop, Cuthbert Bardsley, who dissuaded him. No, Colin, he told him, you'll disappear without trace if you take up holy orders. Play your cricket and do good that way.' *Thus the cricket world owed the wise bishop a debt of gratitude. Though I bet the clergy cricket team were disappointed.* David gave a little smile and nodded.

There were two classic exemplars of religious conviction whom Colin got to know well and who both, in their different ways, had a profound effect on him, one a Dark Blue and the other a Light Blue. Peter Blake was Colin's captain in the Oxford side. He took holy orders, became a parish priest in Leeds and then devoted the rest of his life to missionary work. Colin kept in touch. The captain of the opposing Cambridge team was David Sheppard, who needs no introduction and who will make regular appearances in this book. He and Colin remained close, long after both cricketing careers had finished.

I suppose that with friends like these, it is no surprise that Colin was no playboy libertine when he was at university. He worked hard enough, he soaked up the sociological and philosophical character of contemporary Oxford, he explored his own religious convictions, he made friends and started to widen his social circle, and he played a lot of sport.

There was no more rugby, much as he would have liked to play. His feet would not stand the pummelling. But he was once or twice prevailed upon to play football for his college in the Cuppers. 'He scored a hat-trick and won the game for them,' announced David, with enthusiasm, 'even though he had not played before. He was surprisingly quick on his feet for one who was not naturally athletic. And he had superb anticipation.'

Rackets was his main winter game, however. In fact, he gained his rackets Blue before cricket, if only by virtue of its seasonal nature. The university courts had fallen into disrepair during the war and had not yet been restored so a lot of their practice matches took place at nearby Radley College. There he encountered the 16-year-old Ted Dexter and it was clear to him even then that here was a massively gifted games player.

It is interesting to record that in the three years that Colin was in the first pair, Oxford had considerably more success in the annual encounter with Cambridge at Queen's than they did at Lord's. Records reveal that in 1952, M.C. Cowdrey and E.N.C. Oliver (Oxf) beat A.H. Swift and W.S.S. Maclay (Cam) 4-0; in 1953, M.C. Cowdrey and E.N.C. Oliver (Oxf) beat C.H.W. Robson and J.M.M. Barron

(Cam) 4-0 and in 1954 M.C. Cowdrey and M.R. Coulman (Oxf) beat C.H.W. Robson and J.M.M. Barron (Cam) 4-0. Almost as impressive as the scorelines is the number of initials on display.

Contemporaries of Colin on the rackets courts at Oxford are now thin on the ground and, sadly, memories even thinner. However, I managed to track down a few people who played with him. Charles Swallow played in successful pairs against Cambridge several years later in 1959, 1960 and 1961. He was runner-up in the final of the Amateur Championships in the 1960s and later became chairman of the Tennis and Rackets Association (T&RA), which ran the game.

He does not remember playing against Colin but played in a number of the same tournaments. He particularly recalls one rather eccentric foursome with Colin at a private court belonging to Lord Buckhurst, built to commemorate the centenary of the lifting of the siege of Sebastopol in 1854 during the Crimean War. 'The T&RA,' said Swallow, 'were hoping that Buckhurst's sons, who were at Eton, would become passionate about the game but they never did. I don't know whether the court is still in existence.' He went on to say, 'Colin was a natural hitter of the ball and despite his bulk was a very quick mover. He tended to play a defensive rather than an attacking game,' and he added, 'Behind his genial and courteous exterior, there was always a strip of steel on court.'

For further information, I contacted Howard Angus, former Queen's professional and world champion, whose knowledge of the history of the game is second to none. He had this to say, 'Colin was a fine rackets player but by the time I started playing, in 1957, he was only an occasional player owing to his cricket commitments. Perhaps his best performance on a rackets court was when he got through to the final of the Amateur Singles in 1952, when he was at Oxford, losing to Geoffrey Atkins, who two years later, became world champion. Colin and John Thompson of Tonbridge won the Noel Bruce Cup for Old Boys Doubles in 1953, 1956 and 1957. I watched him play in the same competition a year or two later but by that time he had put on a few pounds and was not quite so mobile around the court.'

For the record, he added, as did so many people to whom I spoke about Colin, 'It was always a pleasure to see and chat to him whenever he came to Queen's – one of nature's gentlemen.'

I am indebted to David Kemp for his account of that unexpected and remarkable run of Colin's to the final of the Amateur Singles. 'The championships at Queen's coincided with pre-season nets at Oxford. It was 1952 and Peter Blake was the captain. He was persuaded by Colin to allow him to miss the first day to play his rackets match in London. "I've got no chance of winning," he said, "I'm playing Hubert Doggart. I'll be back tomorrow." He beat Doggart 3-2, having been 0-2 down. That meant another day in London, another day's nets missed.'

And so it went on? 'And so it went on. Next up was John Thompson, a fellow Tonbridgean, whom Colin knew well. Once again, he did not expect to beat him but he did, 3-0, and John was a very good player. Embarrassed, Colin had to phone Blake that evening to explain his absence from nets again the next day. "Don't worry," he said, "I'll definitely be back. I won't progress further than the semi-final." He wasn't expected to either. His opponent was David Milford.'

I remembered the name. He was more famous as a hockey player. Christopher Martin-Jenkins, of treasured memory, in one of his books described Milford as 'a shy man with a genius for games and revered as one of England's finest hockey players.' He was no mean exponent of the game of rackets too but Colin polished him off. 'He was in the final, for heaven's sake,' cried Kemp, 'but he had to call up his captain – again – and offer his profound apologies. Blake was not best pleased but there was nothing he could do about it.'

The fairytale came to a juddering halt in the final, unsurprisingly really, as he was up against a future world champion, Geoffrey Atkins, who claimed that title in 1954 and did not relinquish it until an astonishing 18 years later. Colin lost 3-0 but it was no disgrace. It was a triumph to get that far. 'And you know what?' Kemp added. 'He genuinely believed he had no chance of winning any of those earlier rounds. His promises to Blake to be back the next day were utterly genuine. He was like that, Colin, so modest despite his huge talent.'

Possibly the last word on Colin's rackets is a touching one really. David Makey is the rackets professional at Tonbridge and remembers Colin coming into the courts when he was around, watching his sons play. 'I played rackets with him several times,' Makey told me, 'and the way he hit the rackets ball was different from anyone else I have ever played with. Extraordinary timing and feel. Can't describe it but something was special and it was an awesome experience for me.'

And if you think Makey is being a little fulsome here, you don't know rackets professionals. They are normally a critical lot. His description of Colin's timing of the ball reminds me of a story told to me by Jonathan Smith, former English master at Tonbridge, successful author, father of Ed (Middlesex and Kent), who taught Colin's sons. He was walking around the Head one day, chatting to an American acquaintance. Colin was batting at the time, probably in a Cricketer Cup match. Colin hit a four. The American, who knew nothing of cricket, turned to Smith and remarked, 'That's amazing! He hardly hit the ball and look, no one can catch it.' And that, said Smith, is as good a definition of timing as there is.

It should be no great surprise that Colin was multi-talented at ball games. Many good sportsmen are. The game of cricket is littered with famous names who excelled at another sport. Two shining lights from cricket's Golden Age were C.B. Fry, an England international at both football and cricket, as well as holding the world long jump record, and R.E. Foster, who uniquely captained England at both sports. Moving forward to Colin's era, two contemporaries of his, Willie Watson and Arthur Milton, were double internationals and others such as Denis Compton, Brian Close, Ken Taylor, Micky Stewart, Derek Ufton, Mike Barnard and Don Bennet all combined a first-class cricket career with one in professional football.

From my own era, there were a number of cricketers who would play for Football League clubs in the winter: Chris Balderstone, Graham Cross, Jim Cumbes, Ted Hemsley, Phil Neale, Jim Standen and Alistair Hignell, who played rugby. I have already mentioned Brian Boobyer, Colin's contemporary at Oxford. In 1954, perhaps the most famous of the double internationals, certainly the last alive, joined him in the Oxford side. M.J.K. Smith played fly-half for England against Wales in 1956 and later successfully captained England at cricket for several series. More of him later, too. Nowadays, the full-on nature of careers in all sports makes doubling up impossible but there are surely members of the England team who could play other sports to a high standard.

Colin's observations on the all-round games player are typically interesting. When he was at Tonbridge, he played a lot of golf. That much is obvious from only a brief look at his diary. While staying in Sutton, he spent many an hour in Harry Weetman's shop in Croydon. Weetman was a formidable golfer in his day, a frequent winner on the PGA circuit and a regular Ryder Cup player. He took the young Colin out on the course and tried to persuade him to give up cricket and take up golf, promising him he would turn him into a Ryder Cup player before he was 25. Golf's loss was cricket's gain.

But Colin was not alone in being adept at both sports. In his opinion the best cricketer-golfers in his era were Arthur Milton, Tom Graveney and Ted Dexter, all of whom, he believed, could have made a living out of hitting a small white ball into a hole in the ground. Although Colin did not gain a Blue at golf, he played several times for the university and developed a passion for the game that he never relinquished.

In the days before the advent of the Sunday League, legions of professional cricketers would take to the golf courses on their day off. Colin was always wary of grooving his swing too much; he believed that the two games are not complementary on a technical level. Among his papers I discovered several pages of typewritten notes, obviously groundwork for an article or longer piece that was never completed, which explain his reasoning.

'Cricket is not a natural game,' he avers. 'The bowling action is clumsy and awkward. It is much more natural to throw the ball. Batting looks more natural when players are slogging, as they might do in baseball or rounders. To play with a straight bat demands a sideways-on position and stiffening of the arms at vital moments. Tennis and squash are natural games. There is nothing more natural than hitting a golf ball, even if it requires learning quite complicated techniques if you want to hit the ball consistently straight and well.'

Unnatural as the game is, he goes on to say, most cricketers are good games players. In his time, nearly all his fellow cricketers would have played football in the winter months and be handy with a tennis racket or a golf club. He calculated that in 1952, in his first full year of first-class cricket, out of 200 or so professional cricketers, at least 60 played top-class football. I could not help but wonder if the base of the pyramid in English football would be stiffened by the assimilation of these 60 cricketer-footballers instead of all those barely recognisable foreign players. 'Bluidy sight cheaper too,' Brian Close would have pronounced.

But I digress. Geography and rackets aside, the real reason Colin was at Oxford, it has to be acknowledged, was to play in The Parks. For those who have played there, and even those who went only to watch, the cricket ground occupies a cherished corner of the heart. Idyllic memories of the long, lazy days of university life can be beguilingly delusionary but most people who visit The Parks, particularly when there is a match in progress, are of the opinion that it is a most agreeable place to while away an hour or two.

Colin fell under its spell at once. He found his early months at Oxford trying, probably because he had to knuckle down and pass his preliminary exams. He was no natural or confident examinee. But once the season hove into view and net practice commenced, he felt utterly at home. In his own words, 'Cricket at Oxford will always be perfectly embalmed in my mind...Warm days in the sun, net practices that were never a chore, good wickets, good fellowship – a simple, uncomplicated life.' The more I unearth about the character of Colin Cowdrey, the more I am convinced that this is what he really yearned for in his life, peace and tranquillity while playing the game that he loved. Unfortunately, he was so good at it that it was always an impossible dream. He became public property when he would have preferred the pleasant anonymity of the club's third XI.

If he felt his batting stagnated during his three years at Oxford, he might have said the same thing about Dark Blue cricket in general. While he was there, Oxford failed to win a single first-class match. It has to be admitted that they were not a very good side. In comparison, the 1949 team, in which his friend George Chesterton played, included three future Test captains, Donald Carr (England), Abdul Kardar (Pakistan) and Clive van Ryneveld (South Africa). That team beat the touring New Zealanders. 'It was a bit of a shock,' Chesterton told me, 'but not *that* much of a shock. We were a pretty good side, you know.'

The 1952–54 teams contained no stars save Colin (except perhaps J.P. Fellows-Smith, who did play much later for South Africa), that is until the arrival of M.J.K. Smith in Colin's final year, and it was only in the Varsity match that year that he came to realise how good a player Smith was. Adequate batting and enthusiastic fielding failed to compensate for lack of penetration in the bowling department and, more often than not, county batsmen filled their boots on the perfect Parks surfaces.

Colin did not fill his boots in 1952 but he made a few decent scores and whenever he batted for any length of time, his opponents were never less than impressed with his style and technique. A county batsman of the future? He already was a county player. A future Test player? It is unlikely at this stage that anybody could have confidently predicted that. He scored 80 against Lancashire, 83 not out against the Free Foresters, 56 against his team-mates at Kent and 79 and 92 against Sussex before being brought down to earth by bagging a pair against MCC.

The match against India held particular sentiment for him, bearing in mind his background. He always loved playing against the Indians, home or away, and felt he had a special affinity with the country and its inhabitants. He batted well in both innings (92 and 54) but he remembered two other innings with greater clarity. Surprisingly, Oxford had their opponents at 32/3 before Umrigar and Hazare restored normality with an unbroken stand of 300 before the declaration came. Colin watched and admired. 'I loved Polly Umrigar and his forceful batting,' he wrote later in his unpublished reminiscences and he 'marvelled at the artistry of Vijay Hazare, an effortless, leisurely strokemaker, a right-hander in the mould of David Gower'.

Lord's. For Colin, it was becoming as much of an annual pilgrimage as Ascot is for the Queen and chimneys for Father Christmas. The Varsity match, dating back to 1827, is the oldest first-class fixture in existence and remained, even in these post-war years, a major social and sporting occasion, attracting large crowds and widespread press coverage. Given his association with the place, Colin could well have been a bit blasé as he carried his cricket bag through the Grace Gates but not a bit of it.

He always felt a thrill of anticipation when he made his way down the pavilion steps, through the small, white, wooden gates and on to the famously sloping outfield. Oxford came to the climax of their season on the back of some poor results and were obvious underdogs. A quick look at the Cambridge side highlights the gulf in class. It included David Sheppard (captain), Peter May, Mike Stevenson, Raman Subba Row, Gerry Alexander, John Warr, Robin Marlar and

Cuan McCarthy. Sheppard, May, Warr and Alexander were all future Test players; McCarthy already was. On paper, it was a mismatch. That Oxford came away with a draw and were pleased with the result says it all.

On his own admission, Colin was not at his fluent best as Oxford batted first. He made 55 out of a total of 272 but in his defence, and that of his whole team, it has to be said that they were up against one of the fastest, and most controversial, bowlers of the day. In his native South Africa, Cuan McCarthy had already made a name for himself as the quickest and most hostile bowler seen in that country for two generations. In 1948, he was picked for the first of his 15 Tests, against the visiting Englishmen, taking 21 wickets in the series.

He came on tour to England in 1951 but fared not so well in the Tests. Although nothing was said, or done, officially, there were rumblings of discontent from his opponents about the legality of his action. In 1952, he took up a one-year scholarship at Cambridge and he bowled with conspicuous success for the university that season, taking 44 wickets. However, he had been involved in two unfavourable incidents before the Lord's match. He had hit Jim Langridge of Sussex a nasty blow on the head and he had been called for throwing on five separate occasions when he bowled at Worcester, the first bowler to be no-balled for that offence in English first-class cricket since 1908. You can bet your bottom dollar then that the Oxford team were out in force on the players' balcony watching closely whenever McCarthy bowled.

Colin, in later comments, remained diplomatic about McCarthy's action, only admitting that he suffered a few bruises and that he found his bowling 'suspect'. The contentious issue of throwing was to stalk McCarthy throughout his career.

Cambridge piled on the runs in their innings, with Sheppard scoring 127, his seventh century of the season, before declaring at 408/8. Oxford were soon in trouble at 50/5, with Cowdrey stumped by the future West Indian captain and wicketkeeper Alexander for seven, 'off his pads', he later ruefully complained. The game was all but up at 135/8 and at 174/9 but an extraordinarily unorthodox and undefeated innings of 43 from tail-ender A.J. Coxon, during which he inexplicably charged the fast bowlers Warr and McCarthy, saved the day. In his book *Oxford and Cambridge Cricket*, co-written by George Chesterton, Hubert Doggart wrote, 'I watched Oxford's rearguard action and recall A.J. Coxon, Oxford's number nine, heading a short-pitched ball from McCarthy with remarkable insouciance to cover point.'

Oxford's unlikely escape owed much to a fine innings of 52 by Alan Dowding, an Australian, in England on a Rhodes scholarship. He is still alive, much to his wife's surprise, having survived a recent fall downstairs, and I managed to track him down in their delightful cottage in the Cotswolds. Shoulder broken, arm in a sling but with memory unimpaired, he shared with me some fascinating detail of this game, and subsequent university matches (he was Oxford's captain the following year), as well as his impressions of Colin, as a player and as a young undergraduate.

Did McCarthy chuck it? You would be hard-pressed to recognise Dowding was Australian from his beautifully enunciated and well-modulated reply. 'Well, I have been in this country a very long time,' he smiled. 'Now, in answer to your question...We knew that McCarthy had been called before but when I faced him – he was fast, accurate and pitched it full, with only the occasional bouncer – I think I can say that I detected no illegality. Perhaps he only threw occasionally, when instructed by his...' He tailed off. *His captain?* 'Hmm, I wouldn't put it past his captain. It was David Sheppard, you know.'

I knew. Sheppard was undoubtedly a hard and cussed competitor. Dowding then went on to tell me about the 'somewhat discourteous' behaviour by the Cambridge team at the denouement of the match. 'Shortly before stumps, when it was clear that there was now no possibility of Cambridge winning, with Oxford nine wickets down and 43 runs ahead, without so much as a by your leave, Sheppard, apparently disgruntled at his failure to win the match, led his team from the field. As far as I know, there had been no handshake, no agreement to call time by the captains. Ours was in the pavilion anyway.'

So you won! 'I beg your pardon?' *Of course, I am not being serious about claiming the match. But that is not the correct procedure to agree a draw, not the way things are done, is it?* 'Precisely. It left a sour taste in the mouth. We had battled hard to save the match, one that we looked like losing, and Cambridge spoiled it with their less than gracious behaviour. It rather coloured what was to happen the following year.'

Now, about Colin the player? 'We used to call him Master. Which he was. His talent was there for all to see. Being an Aussie, who learnt his cricket on concrete pitches without a mat, who favoured the hook and the cut, I particularly admired his strokeplay square of the wicket on either side, as well as the more traditional English shots in front of the wicket. That cover drive of his....' My interviewee was lost for a moment in pleasant reverie.

And Cowdrey the young man? 'Do you know what?' he seemed to be asking himself, his brow furrowed at the incongruity of it, 'I never heard Colin offer a word in the dressing room. He would answer if asked but he never initiated discussion. He was always sort of...over there but never to the forefront. Same away from the dressing room. He was never, how shall I call it, one of the lads. Some of us would wind down after play with a few pints in the pub. Colin would disappear. Not that he was stand-offish or unsociable. I just think that chatting over a pint wasn't his thing.'

What about tactically? Did he have any interesting theories or ideas? 'That's the strange thing. He never offered an opinion on how the game was going. When I became captain, I'm sure I made lots of mistakes, some that he must have spotted, but he never uttered a word.'

Shyness? 'Perhaps. I'm not sure. I don't think I ever really got to know him, not *really*. None of us did. That's not a criticism, just an observation. He was a super chap, much liked and greatly respected, but he was a quiet, reserved, slightly apart figure.'

I found this intriguing, puzzling even. Captain at Tonbridge, future captain of Oxford, Kent and England, and he had no opinions about the game? Extraordinary. Indeed, one might be tempted to say – and I have not been alone in saying this – that sometimes he seemed to drown in theory. *Still waters run deep.* 'Indeed. Same with his religious convictions. There was a lot of converting going on at Oxford at the time. Forever you were being asked, "Have you given your life to Christ?" There were a few around, even in the dressing rooms. Don't get me wrong. There was a lot of converting going on at Oxford at the time, what with Moral Re-Armament and the like. There was no problem. We all got on fine, no...tension or anything. But I was aware Colin was quite religious.

'As it happened, both captains in this match, Sheppard and Blake, became priests.'

Colin toyed with the idea of taking holy orders but was persuaded against it. 'Was that so? That wouldn't surprise me. He was certainly in that bracket of team-mates. Never a hell raiser!' Dowding's regard for Colin has remained undimmed, even in the twilight of his life. 'Throughout his career, both at home and abroad,' he said, 'Colin was a shining example of kindness and courtesy.' He then recounted a story which underlines this solicitude for other people, 'a hallmark of Colin's personality' as he called it. Knowing that Dowding's mother lived in Adelaide, Colin made a point of visiting her every time he was on tour and staying in that city. 'It meant a great deal to her,' he said, 'and I have never forgotten it. That was the sort of man he was.'

After a short rest – a summer term spent playing cricket can be *so* exhausting – Colin returned to Kent. They had need of him. These were lean times for the hop county and though he did not set the world on fire with his performances in July and August, there was never any doubt that he would be in the team.

By now a staunch man of Kent, as he remained for the rest of his days, it is an odd fact that throughout his long career, he never played a full season for the county, that is, he was never able to play in all their games. For the time being he was up at Oxford for the first half of the season. Thereafter, England commitments took him away on a regular basis. Up until 1956, he played no more than ten matches for Kent a season and even after he took over the captaincy in 1957, his appearances were always curtailed to more or less two-thirds of the full itinerary.

As it had been for Oxford, his form for Kent in 1952 was patchy. But significantly, he found his touch when most it mattered, and when prominent eyes were upon him. At Canterbury, against the touring Indians for the second time that summer, he batted beautifully and this time he made no mistake by converting his 90 into a hundred, his only one of the season, it turned out. If the Indians were impressed by his strokeplay – his style, all touch and timing, would have been familiar to batsmen from the subcontinent – he was again in awe of Polly Umrigar's batsmanship. He had plenty of time to study him; Umrigar scored 204.

Kent's next match was against Yorkshire, also at Canterbury. Colin scored 85 not out and single-handedly held the Kent innings together. Watching from first slip, growing more appreciative by the minute, was the England captain, Len Hutton. The mutual admiration society was strengthened when Colin observed at close quarters Hutton himself give a master-class in the art of batting with an innings of 120.

After the match had finished, which Yorkshire predictably won by an innings and 51 runs, Colin took a fateful car journey. He, somewhat to his surprise, had been selected to play for MCC against Yorkshire in the end-of-season festival at Scarborough. His team-mate, Godfrey Evans, had been similarly honoured. Hutton, of Yorkshire, also had to make the long journey north. Evans and Hutton knew each other of old so Evans invited his England captain to join him in his Bentley as navigator and companion. 'Come with us,' he cheerily told Colin. 'Plenty of room for the three of us.'

With two cricket bags already in the boot, Colin squeezed himself into the back of the Bentley and made himself as comfortable as he could with his own bag for company and off they sped. Speed was the operative word. Evans did nothing slowly. It was a drive that Colin never forgot.

But it wasn't the white-knuckle ride that made such an impression upon him. It certainly wasn't the discussion about what music should be tuned into on the radio. There has never been a car journey with two or more county cricketers in attendance without an argument about which radio station to listen to. I played cricket once or twice with Godfrey Evans, admittedly in his bewhiskered dotage and only in charity matches, and I can attest to his uninhibited, clubbable personality. Len Hutton I never met but Tom Graveney assured me that beneath the dour Yorkshire exterior dwelt a surprisingly warm and witty personality. You can imagine the conversation.

'What roobbish is this, Godfrey?'

'Brazilian salsa, old boy. Ever heard of Carmen Miranda?'

'Carmen who? Carmina Burana – now, that's more like it. Love me light opera, I do. Give me a bit of Gilbert 'n' Sullivan any day. Not this banshee wailing.'

'What's your taste, young Colin?'

'Er... well, to be truthful, Godfrey, I, er–'

'Look where you're bluidy well going, Godfrey. Have you passed your test?'

'Missed by a mile, captain. Didn't even get a nick.'

'Anyroad, as I were saying about these Australians coming next year....'

Throughout, Colin was engrossed as the conversation ranged widely over the technical and mental strengths and weaknesses of countless contemporary players. He began to understand that not only was Hutton a great player but he was also a great student of the game and its intricacies, especially the art of batting. In Hutton he discovered a fellow theorist and listened with rapt attention as Hutton opened up. In that unbeaten 85 which Colin had just made against Yorkshire, he had batted for four hours and it had been a struggle throughout. Not that he was batting poorly and was fumbling around for some semblance of form; no, it was the quality of the bowling and the perilous situation of the Kent innings that had made the preservation of his wicket so crucial.

Like all the top players, Colin always took into consideration the level of difficulty when judging an innings. The fact that he had had to fight to survive would have been right up Hutton's street. He was, after all, the first professional to captain England. He was a flinty and uncompromising opponent, as hard as nails on the pitch, and he eschewed frippery. That innings of Colin's would have appealed to him. That is how Test match cricket is played, he might well have thought; this young lad sitting in the back may be a public schoolboy and an Oxford undergraduate but he's no soft southerner and he can *play*. He resolved to keep an eye on Colin's development.

It is worth noting how large the figure of Len Hutton loomed in the minds of English cricket followers of this generation. By all accounts, he was never quite the same player after the war as he was before, not only because of the lost six years of the conflict but also because of an accident he had suffered in 1941, working as an army PT instructor. It necessitated several operations on his wrist, leaving him with a left arm two inches shorter than his right. Nonetheless, he returned to play Test cricket and all that could be said about his post-war exploits with a bat in his hand was that if he was a great player with one arm shorter than the other, he must have been a magnificent one when he was at his peak.

Wisden tells us so. They lauded him as one of the greatest batsmen in the history of the game. Few disagreed. Certainly not Colin. As he developed into a fine player himself and took more and more interest in the technical side of batsmanship, what better model for him was there than Hutton? He listened intently to Hutton during that car journey and he watched intently over the next three days at Scarborough as Hutton batted...and batted.

He had hero-worshipped Hutton from a young age, as many of that generation did, but he was now able to study the great man's technique at close quarters as Hutton helped himself to a century in each of the Yorkshire innings against MCC. According to Colin, in both innings, he did not play a single false stroke. In his autobiography, he refers to Hutton's perfect balance at the crease and says, without a hint of bashfulness, 'I became a total disciple of the way he played.'

Hutton's style was orthodox and conventional, as was Colin's. Hutton had all the shots and could demolish the bowling with forceful strokeplay when the situation demanded. But he was an opening batsman and a Yorkshireman to boot and his natural instinct was defence first, attack second. And that was probably true of Colin too. Hutton was a cautious fellow. Colin was no gambler either. Hammond the Cavalier; Hutton the Roundhead? Dexter the Cavalier; Cowdrey the Roundhead? Cliches are easily dismissed but sometimes they contain more than a germ of truth.

In that match at Scarborough against Yorkshire, Colin did not bat so badly himself. For the second time against the same opponents, he scored 85 not out, but he would be the first to admit that he was upstaged by another one of a gifted, some might say gilded, generation of young English batsmen, Peter May. Like his predecessor as captain of his country – he succeeded Hutton in that role in 1955 – May scored two centuries in the match, 174 and an exact unbeaten 100. It is interesting to note the season's final batting averages for this year; if the young guns were blazing, the veteran was enjoying an Indian (literally) summer:

1st David Sheppard (University of Cambridge and Sussex) 64.62

2nd Peter May (University of Cambridge and Surrey) 62.45

3rd Len Hutton (University of Life and Yorkshire) 61.11

All three scored over 2,000 runs in the course of the season. Colin only managed 1,189 at 33.02, not a poor season, by any means – remember he was still only 19 – but it told him that he still had a fair way to go before he could be mentioned in the same breath as May and Sheppard, even though he had played one or two exceptional innings.

It was not an exceptional innings that saw off Colin's season but an exceptional piece of fielding. He was not yet a regular slip fielder; in this company he was well down the pecking order for that coveted role. He found himself in the covers playing for the Gentlemen against the Players, the finale to the Scarborough Festival. Hutton, as usual, was batting serenely. He moved comfortably through the 90s, his eye set on his fourth successive hundred, not a unique feat but a considerable one nonetheless.

On 99, he pushed the ball into the covers and called for a single, only to be inexplicably sent back by the non-striker, Johnny Wardle. Hutton slipped, Cowdrey gathered the ball and with only one stump to aim at, hit the wicket before Hutton could regain his ground. Colin said he felt guilty about that...but only a bit. He was ever a gentleman on the field but never a soft touch.

As Hutton was leading England to a famous, and long-awaited, Ashes series win in 1953, Colin was helping Oxford to a winless season, culminating in a loss to Cambridge at Lord's, and Kent to 16th place, just avoiding the wooden spoon, in the county championship. Those are the bald facts but they hide a considerable truth; Colin's form throughout the season was greatly improved and he played some wonderful innings, one or two of which were significant for his career. It is difficult to relax, play your shots and shine when all around you appears to be crumbling and that is how it must have seemed to him.

Oxford and Kent were both weak sides. He knew that his wicket was the one his opponents prized and that puts pressure on any batsman, even the best. He scored two hundreds against county opposition before the Lord's showdown, 127 against Lancashire and 154 against Surrey. Both were important in different ways. Harry Altham, a big hitter at MCC, was present in The Parks when Colin made his century against Lancashire and could not have failed to be impressed. Whether he made a mental note at the time is unclear but he certainly remembered the innings when he was made chairman of selectors the following year, charged with picking the MCC touring team to Australia that winter.

At The Oval, never an easy place to visit in the 1950s, Colin played what he considered to be his best innings to date. His 154 was out of a total of 270 and perhaps just as pertinent, his second innings score of 34 was out of a total of only 63, Jim Laker doing to the undergraduates what he did to Test players when conditions were favourable – he ran amok.

There was also an interesting and telling encounter with the Australians. Colin was bowled by Keith Miller for three in the first innings and by Richie Benaud for five in the second. First blood to the Aussies, you might say. He could put that one down to experience for the true focal point of the season was the Varsity match. Cambridge were not so strong this year and Colin believed that his side, though short of class, were better equipped to put up more of a decent show than the year before. And for all but the final afternoon, his confidence was fully borne out.

Once again, I rely on Hubert Doggart for a summary of proceedings, 'Oxford's 312, made in good time on the first day, owed most to M.C. Cowdrey, who gave a masterly display of strokeplay for 116. The Cambridge captain [Robin Marlar] who captured his wicket in both innings, was the only bowler to trouble him.' Having bowled Cambridge out for only 191, the Dark Blues were reasonably confident of securing their first victory for two years but Marlar had other ideas. He skittled them for 116 'with fine command of flight and spin', taking 7-49, bringing his match tally to 12-143.

Notwithstanding, the victory target of 236 for Cambridge seemed unlikely, particularly when Oxford bowled with accuracy and control. But with cricket, you just never know. 'Do you want me to describe what happened, first-hand, as it were?' Alan Dowding asked. I proffered the plate of biscuits, he selected a chocolate digestive and settled back comfortably to tell me the inside story.

Cambridge, at no stage in their second innings, looked likely to reach the required total, that is until an extraordinary passage of events ensued. 'Dennis Silk, in his inelegant but effective way, had been defying us, largely strokeless, for four and a half hours. He was on about 70 not out, as I recall. A wicket fell and out came Robin Marlar. Or at least out Robin Marlar did *not* come. They were eight down and we could smell victory. We were all standing around impatiently, wondering what on earth was going on. Where was he? Eventually – it must have been a good five minutes – he made an appearance.'

You were the captain. Did you not invoke the two-minute rule and appeal? 'To be honest, I wasn't quite sure of the law. Not that I would have appealed. But still, it was all a bit odd. I went up to the umpire, Frank Chester, and sort of raised an eyebrow but, as was his way when he didn't want to answer a difficult question, he turned away. At last, Marlar arrived on the pitch. It took him another five minutes to take guard, tie and re-tie his bootlaces, adjust the straps of his pad, take another guard, walk down the pitch, prod it, look around the field, before he was ready. In all, he had wasted...well, I guess, conservatively, eight minutes.' *Why?* 'Making sure of the draw, I suppose.'

Marlar survived the two remaining balls of the over. Silk, who had been impassively watching all this from the other end, then promptly hit the first ball of the next over for four. And the next one. So began an extraordinary, and wholly unexpected, assault on the Oxford bowling that saw Cambridge secure an improbable victory with three minutes to spare, Silk carrying his bat for 116. Cambridge were cock-a-hoop. Oxford were in despair.

Come on, Alan, what happened? Why did Dennis Silk change tack? He smiled enigmatically. 'It's surprising but true. To this day, Dennis and I, and don't forget he was my headmaster at Radley College for over 20 years when I was teaching there, never spoke about it. But my hidden conviction is that he did not really approve of Robin Marlar's blatant time-wasting, and thought to himself, right, it's hell or high water. We're either going to win this or lose it but it's not going to be a draw.'

In common with the rest of his team-mates and captain, Colin confessed to acute feelings of disappointment after the match, even when he reflected upon it many years later. During his long career, he experienced many highs and lows but there is something special, something deeply emotional, about a Varsity match. Unlike a Test series or a one-day final (which is the culmination of victory in several rounds), this is a one-off encounter and dominates all thought and attention for those concerned throughout the whole season. For some, a whole career. A Blue, forget not, is only awarded for playing at Lord's; if a player is incapacitated or injured and cannot play, even if he has been a regular member of the team, he does not get his Blue. It means that much.

George Chesterton once tried to explain to me what it felt like to lose to the 'enemy', something he suffered back in 1949. 'The dressing room was like a morgue,' he said. 'Quietly, with barely a word, we dispersed. And that team, that had been through so much together, never met up again.' You can imagine Colin's disappointment. For all that, his team behaved impeccably, as the last rites to the game were administered.

'Regrets there must almost always be,' wrote E.W. Swanton in his match report, 'but if there were any, Oxford kept them to themselves as they shook Silk warmly by the hand and clapped him all the way back to the pavilion.' That is how the game should be played, Colin believed, and he never wavered from this article of faith.

The epithet 'enemy' was not used offhandedly. Whatever alluring image I had of our two ancient universities coming together in manly and sporting contest in the oldest fixture of them all, on the historic playing field of St John's Wood, I was disabused by the comments of several who played in those games around that time. 'No quarter given, none asked,' said Chesterton. 'We were out there to *win*,' said Mike (M.J.K.) Smith. 'Not a vicar's tea party,' said Alan (A.C.) Smith. Perhaps the most telling observation came from David Kemp, 'The atmosphere between the two sides was not good, frosty at best, sometimes downright acrimonious.'

That would not have suited Colin's approach to the game and as we shall see the following year, together with his opposite number as captain, he made efforts to change the unfriendly atmosphere of the fixture, with only limited success it has to be said.

Before that, there was the rest of the season with Kent to negotiate. He was more confident now, with runs under his belt and the ball pinging off the bat nicely. He felt that he had become a little too bogged down with theory and technique, so he relaxed, trusted his eye and judgement and everything seemed to click into place. Ah...form, so elusive but so rewarding when it comes calling. When present, it feels it will never yield and then, like a will o' the wisp, it has gone.

Colin's form remained pretty constant throughout 1953, though his scores for Kent rarely reached the peaks; he did not score a hundred. But once again, it is necessary to study the scorecards and to try and interpret what was going on. Of the nine county matches he played that summer, Kent won two, lost four and drew the rest, though in one of these draws they were 47/7 in their second innings before time saved them. In all four losses, they were heavily defeated. Frequently, Colin played well and scored runs but in a losing cause. They were bowled out for 43 against Middlesex, after he had underpinned their first innings with 64 (out of 175). Against Yorkshire, he carried his bat for 24 as his side were bowled out and defeated by 152 runs. Again, he carried his bat for 52 out of 163 in the return fixture against Middlesex but to no avail as they went down by 99 runs. He top-scored with 81 in Kent's second innings only for his side to lose to Leicestershire by seven wickets.

It has to be conceded that it is very difficult to compose a century when you are left high and dry by the rest of your fellow batsmen. Who knows how many times he perished in the quest for runs as partners were falling away and a more measured approach would normally have resulted in three figures. Kent were far from a one-man band but they heavily relied upon him to make runs and he never seemed to have the luxury of steady players around him to enable him to make big scores. He would never have grumbled about this; Kent was his county. But one does wonder how many more runs he would have scored had he played for a stronger county, such as Surrey, like his compatriot and friend, Peter May.

Was it chance or was it the fact that he was playing for a stronger team that he flourished in the end-of-season festivals, as he had the previous year? For the Gentlemen against the Australians, he scored 50 and 57 and said he could not have played better against a formidable attack of Lindwall, Johnston, Archer, Ring and Benaud. And for the Gentlemen against the Players, he made exactly 100, in the company of May, who made 157. To onlookers, including Hutton, it must have seemed the future of England's batting was unfolding in front of their eyes. Later, Hutton denied that there and then, he decided to take a punt on the young Cowdrey and take him to Australia 12 months hence but Colin always believed that the selectors, of whom Hutton was only one, had their attention caught by that innings.

Following these traditional epilogues to the season, Hutton took his MCC team off for an acrimonious tour of the Caribbean, the run-of-the-mill county pros found winter employment where they could and Colin returned to his studies at Oxford. He was elected captain of the university side for 1954 and as his attention wandered from his books and he started to plan for the forthcoming campaign, he felt he had reasonable cause for confidence. Most of the old Blues remained and the arrival of M.J.K. Smith would give the batting a more solid look. His confidence seemed in no way misplaced, as the season got under way. He had a good look, a very good look, at the new boy, Mike Smith, as they shared a profitable fourth-wicket stand against Gloucestershire in the first match, Cowdrey 78 and Smith unbeaten on 104. Colin was even able to declare. All right, nine wickets were down but it wasn't often that the university were in such a happy position.

At the time, although he was impressed by a freshman making an unbeaten century on his debut, he was not fully aware how good a player Smith was. That is until Smith firmly swept any residual doubts from his captain's mind with his astonishing innings in the forthcoming Varsity match. He had already made his mark at the university that winter as a rugby player, having played in the 6-6 drawn Varsity match at Twickenham. Colin remembers watching him play. He reminded him of another double rugby and cricket international, Clive van Ryneveld, who had been at Oxford a couple of years before him. He had 'the same long-ranging stride but not so angular', both possessing 'good vision of the game in front of them'.

Even in these early stages of their acquaintance which was to flourish as England team-mates over the years, he was struck with Smith's imperturbability, 'master of the deadpan expression', he called it. I always believed that the distracted, professorial, Smith manner had a lot to do with the fact that he wore glasses, which tended to shield the bright blue eyes behind. That air of casualness and laid-back manner proved a deceptive mask in his career.

Colin scored two hundreds in the matches against the counties in the weeks leading up to Lord's. The first was against Kent. One can imagine the mutterings of his opponents as he raised his bat to acknowledge The Parks faithful as they too, politely, joined in the applause, 'Hell's bells, he can do it for them but not for us.' If so, that would have been a bit harsh but county cricketers are, by nature, a pretty hard-nosed lot. Besides, he was going to rectify that omission soon enough, in the same season in fact. The other hundred was against Sussex, a match in which Hubert Doggart made two centuries of his own.

Doggart became a regular opponent on the county circuit and later, a much-respected and dear friend in the corridors and committee rooms of MCC.

Colin played a most satisfying innings against the champions, Surrey, slap bang in the middle of their decade of dominance in the domestic game. Nor did they rest their best bowlers, as some counties were wont to do, not that it would have made much difference if they had, they were that strong. Against an attack comprising Alec Bedser, Peter Loader, Tony Lock and Eric Bedser, he steered his side to safety with an innings of 79, thus avoiding defeat by two wickets.

Defeat was not on Colin's mind in the following match, the last before Lord's. Oxford came within a whisker of beating Warwickshire, which would have brought to an end the long saga of never winning a match against the counties while he was at university. He really believed he had the pros on the run – they all did – but in the end, they were unable to take the final wicket and Warwickshire wriggled free. Disappointment was acute but by now he was beginning to get familiar with the bitter-sweet taste of cricket's vicissitudes.

Regret was not to last long. Lord's once more and as he made his way through the Grace Gates and into the now-familiar inner sanctum of the pavilion, he believed his team were in good shape for the challenge ahead. Oxford had not won a match leading up to the big one but they had given a good account of themselves and Cambridge, without May, Subba Row, Alexander and Marlar, were not the force they were. The two captains, both in their third year of this fixture, knew each other, of course, from previous encounters but not well. It was Mike Bushby who made the first tentative approach to his opposite number to discuss the forthcoming match, its significance and the bad press that recently it had been getting.

Bushby, still very much alive and kicking, was most forthcoming with his opinions about this and the match itself. He felt that the stories about bad blood between the two sides had been exaggerated. Perhaps it had something to do with the fact that one or two players in both teams were also rugby Blues and the Varsity matches at Twickenham *were* hotly contested, with no holds barred. He believed that the tension that attended the cricket match – which rarely spilled over into poor behaviour or bad sportsmanship – had more to do with the singular nature of the contest. It was a one-off, with everything riding on the result. There was no second chance. If you lost, the acrid taste of defeat remained with you for the rest of your days. So, inevitably, the matches were laced with pressure, nerves and caution.

That is why, he surmised, E.W. Swanton wrote a piece in *Wisden* or *The Cricketer* or perhaps for his newspaper, *The Daily Telegraph* – Bushby cannot remember which – bemoaning the negative attitude that seemed to prevail in the university matches, especially in recent years. Swanton quoted the words of Robin Marlar, the previous Cambridge captain, in which he said that he wished both teams would come to some sort of agreement 'to banish this grimness from the game'.

Easier said than done. As an illustration, let me draw a comparison with another historic Lord's institution, the annual Eton v Harrow match, which actually predates the Varsity match, regularly played at HQ since 1822, as opposed to the first Varsity match there in 1827. When I was master at Malvern (including cricket), I remember speaking to my opposite number at Harrow, Bill Snowden, during a lull in proceedings in one of our games. I was envious of his yearly trip to Lord's with his team to take on Eton, with a large and boisterous crowd in attendance. 'Yes, it's a great privilege,' he agreed, 'but it's a bit of a poisoned chalice as well. It's all the boys think about for the whole of the season, as if the rest of the cricket they play is not important. If you think that is disproportionate, you have no idea what importance the Old Boys place on the fixture. If you lose, that is all you hear about for the next 12 months. I've even feared for my job once or twice. All of which makes for a nervous, cagey game. Avoid defeat at all costs. Not ideal circumstances to encourage positive cricket.'

Not long afterwards, I noticed that the match had changed its format from a declaration to a limited-overs format. Still not necessarily a blueprint for a pulsating game of cricket but at least it was no longer possible to play for a draw.

I imagine that the lack of enterprise and willingness to embrace risk, what Marlar referred to as 'this grimness', similarly bedevilled some of the Varsity encounters, and this was what Bushby was anxious to banish. Cowdrey was receptive to his views, he said, and together they resolved to make a decent game of it. 'And I think we succeeded,' Bushby told me. 'It went to the wire, it was a most pleasant game and we all have good memories of it. Even Swanton commented on that fact in his article the following day,' he added with a laugh.

To this end, the two captains organised a cocktail party for the teams at the conclusion of the first day's play. *I imagine Oxford enjoyed it more than Cambridge.* Bushby grimaced. 'We only had three bowlers,' he announced, by way of explanation for Oxford's score of 401/3. 'Mike Morgan, our opening bowler, broke down after eight overs. Gami Goonesena and Colin Smith bowled all day.' Well, not quite, but so it must have seemed. They shared 69 overs between them.

Why did you go in with just a four-pronged attack? 'It had worked fine all season,' Bushby replied. 'Besides, if you can't bowl 'em out with four bowlers, rarely can you with five. It was just bad luck that Morgan got injured.'

I should say so. Oxford made hay. By the end of the day, Mike Smith was on 201 not out, only the third double centurion in the history of the Varsity match. Colin, in his autobiography, called it the most astonishing exhibition of batting he had ever seen. 'We were playing slightly on the Tavern side of centre, which suited Mike well, as he was able to give anything bowled at him from the Pavilion End the full range of his on-side strokes. I stood fascinated as balls pitched far outside the off stump were flashed past midwicket.' When Colin stated that he stood fascinated, he meant at the non-striker's end. He and Smith shared in a third-wicket stand of 180 in two hours, pretty good going for that era. Grim it certainly wasn't.

Mike Smith is very much alive too, a sprightly 83-year-old, now living in Warwick. I paid him a visit and as he bustled about, making coffee and excusing the debris of his desk worktop in his search for relevant pieces of paper he used as *aides memoire*, he chatted cheerfully and at length about Colin Cowdrey.

'We met long before we played county cricket,' he said, 'even before we overlapped up at Oxford. When he was a boy, he used to stay with relatives in Leicestershire. I lived in the next village. I always remember two of the mainstays of the Leicestershire attack in the pre-war years, George Geary and Ewart Astill, who became coaches at Charterhouse and Tonbridge, saying that they had unearthed two of the best cricketers they had ever seen. They were...?' He waited for my reply. *May and Cowdrey?* 'Correct. P.B.H. and M.C.C.' He seemed moderately impressed with my grasp of cricket history.

'Now, when I went up to Oxford, I didn't have any serious thoughts about playing county cricket. I'd played a few games for Leicestershire in the holidays but I was *hopeless!* I was never coached. D'you know who was the greatest influence on my batting career?' This time he didn't wait for an answer. 'Colin Cowdrey. We batted a lot together, you see, in that summer for Oxford in 1954.' *How did he influence you?* 'If you've got half a brain, you watched and copied the best. And there was no finer technique than Colin's.'

Tell me about this innings at Lord's. 'I was dropped first ball!' he guffawed. I knew that. It was not a case of my secure grasp of the finer details of cricket history on this occasion; Mike Bushby had told me a week or so before and the anguish in his voice was tangible, even 60-odd years after the event. He wouldn't name the culprit but went on to praise Smith's temperament. 'What I always admired about Mike was that he was so phlegmatic about things. He just blinked, put it out of his mind, set himself again and never looked like getting out. Classy.' I returned to quizzing my subject. 'I got off the mark with a nick between the wicketkeeper and first slip,' Smith said.4 'It was an absolute dolly. Neither moved as it went past the two of them. Dennis Silk was at first slip.'

Ah, now I know the culprit. 'Wasn't really his catch, to be fair. Then I got my head down.' *Not what Colin wrote. He said he's never seen hitting like it.* 'That was later, when we were well set and I could go for it.' *What about the view that you were a predominantly on-side player?* 'I played on the leg side because there were no bloody fielders on the leg side in those days,' he grinned. 'I did it to mess up the bowlers' line. Hit the ball where there aren't any fielders, that was my motto.'

And Colin? How did he play it? 'He just stroked it. He could play all the shots on both sides of the wicket. He was the best timer of the ball I've ever seen. He had the perfect technique. He was so good he could do anything with a bat. But it was an orthodox technique. I watched and learned and became a better player as a result.' *The cocktail party that evening? I expect you sank a few.* 'Too knackered,' he quickly interrupted.

Declaring overnight with 401 on the board, Colin's plan would have been to bowl Cambridge out and seize hold of the game. But once again, they were thwarted by the obdurate figure of Dennis Silk, who made his second century in successive Varsity matches. True to his word about trying to inject urgency into the fixture, Mike Bushby declared at the end of the day 57 runs behind.

Off went Oxford when play was resumed the next morning in pursuit of quick runs in order to declare themselves, with enough time to bowl Cambridge out. But valour conquered discretion, wickets tumbled to a range of injudicious strokes and Colin was left with more of a thorny problem in trying to gauge the timing of his declaration than he would have wished. But like Bushby, he was conscious of his obligation not to kill the game so he declared with Oxford at 148/9. The target of 206 in two hours and 25 minutes was 'a fair one', Bushby said.

Cambridge went for it but the loss of early wickets hampered their progress, they fell behind the clock, Oxford pressed for victory but the wicket eased and they lacked the wherewithal to apply the *coup de grace*. At the close, Cambridge were eight down. The match was drawn but it had been anything but a 'grim' draw. Both captains were satisfied that their team had given their all and that the fixture had regained some of its lost lustre.

Never mind, he must have thought as he packed his bag, there's always next year. Soon he would have turned his attention to Kent and the remainder of the county season. He had not completed all of his exams – one can only assume that cricket had got in the way of his finals – and he expected to return to Oxford that autumn for another year. But on 27 July, at the completion of the match against Surrey at Blackheath, everything changed.

4

Bookends of a Test career

Australia 1954/55
Australia 1974/75

*'If I could watch one innings again, it would
be Cowdrey's first hundred at Melbourne, on
Hutton's tour.'*

John Woodcock

T HE inclusion of the young Colin Cowdrey, straight out of
university, for the MCC tour to Australia in 1954/55 was not the
most contentious decision by the national selectors, surprising
though it was.

In truth, controversy about the choice of captain and the
composition of the party had been rumbling on for most of the
summer. Len Hutton was the first professional to be appointed
captain of England and that in itself was a break with tradition which
had not met with wholehearted approval. But he had wrestled the
Ashes back from Australia the previous summer for the first time since
the infamous Bodyline series 20 years before and thus his position as
captain was secure – or so you would have thought.

However, after a tour of the West Indies that had its fractious
moments that winter, in which the England players, it was alleged,

had presented a less than flattering image of their country to their hosts, the grumbles about a professional leading the side had started to resurface. Furthermore, Hutton, never the most physically robust person, had declared himself unfit for the second and third Tests that summer, against the Pakistanis.

The anti-Hutton cabal at Lord's had seized their moment and appointed the amateur, David Sheppard, as captain in his place. Sheppard was already well advanced on the clerical career that would see him eventually becoming Bishop of Liverpool, but he had taken temporary leave of his episcopal duties to put himself in the frame to lead the side to Australia. He had been asked to make himself available so he did. But Hutton was a Yorkshireman and he was not going to be as easily sidelined as that. He had been injured, not sacked, and the job of England captain was still his. Public opinion was on his side and eventually the Sheppard apostles admitted defeat and withdrew.

Hutton was the general of his army and he knew what soldiers he was going to take with him. It was a popular opinion at the time that one of these favoured warriors of Hutton's was Colin Cowdrey. He had been so impressed with the young man's batting on the occasions that he had seen him play, mostly in opposition, that he had insisted on his name being put forward. Not so, he said later. He may have been taken with Colin's technique and temperament but he was not at all convinced that an Oxford undergraduate was physically and mentally ready for the heat of battle Down Under.

He had to be persuaded and it was the other members of the selection panel, principally Harry Altham, who did the persuading. Perhaps Hutton gave way and acceded to their petitions because he had already got what he wanted.

Like any good general, he had reconnoitred the terrain, he had assessed the strengths and weaknesses of the enemy forces, he had handpicked his troops, and he had a plan. Pace was the key. Actually, there was nothing particularly radical about that. Australian pitches favoured fast bowling and he was as aware of that as anyone, having suffered at the hands of Lindwall and Miller often enough.

But on this occasion, he had an ace up his sleeve, a secret weapon, if you like, and his name was Frank Tyson. Although a bit of an unknown quantity nationally, Tyson's reputation for extreme pace was already a talking point among his opponents on the county circuit. Earlier that summer, he had performed the extraordinary feat of hitting the sightscreen at Old Trafford on the full as a short ball sailed over the wicketkeeper's head. Colin had faced him at Maidstone only weeks before and could testify to the genuine hostility of the Northamptonshire speed merchant. No, Hutton knew exactly what he was after. To him, the selection of Tyson was no gamble.

As it happened, David Sheppard did not tour. If he was not required to captain, he wasn't interested in going and thus resumed his ministry. As for the young, untested Colin Cowdrey, there were one or two voices raised for his inclusion 'for the future' but as Colin himself wrote, 'Realistically, I had no chance.'

His form for Kent had been patchy – he had still not scored a hundred for his county – and if he ever thought he was on anybody's team sheet of 'possibles', he would have convinced himself that he was well down the list. However, as he was making his way across the car park at Blackheath at the conclusion of the match against Surrey in late July to pack his bag in the boot for the trip to Northampton, he was aware that the touring party for Australia was about to be announced on the 6pm news. He was interested, of course, but his interest was no more than academic.

In his unpublished notes, this is how he described what happened next, 'At the end of the introductory headlines I heard, "There are several surprises in the MCC touring party to Australia under the captaincy of Len Hutton." By chance the Surrey team had arrived en masse to listen to the announcement and I saw Peter May and Alec Bedser getting into a car. They were certainties. This was confirmed in the next few moments. As was other staggering news. I had been selected.

'I did not know where to look, where to hide. Feeling hugely embarrassed, I hopped into the back of Arthur Phebey's car. I could not wait for us to get moving as the other selections were beginning to sink in. Standing in the car park, just a few yards away, were Tony Lock and Jim Laker. Both had been sensationally omitted...There was no room either for Arthur McIntyre, who everybody had expected to go as Godfrey Evans's deputy. He was another one in that Blackheath car park that fateful day.'

As he headed north, with Phebey at the wheel and Derk Ufton alongside, conversation inevitably swirled around those contentious omissions. It was a while before they realised that Fred Trueman had been left out too. 'My brain was in a whirl,' Colin wrote. 'Australia! How extraordinary that they should want me to go to Australia.' Over the coming days and weeks, he was not the only one who expressed surprise. In fact, there was something of a press storm and not for the last time, Colin was right in the middle of it.

In one of my conversations with Jim Parks, Colin's old friend, the following reference to the selection of this touring party caught me on the hop. 'Of course, you know it was between me and Colin,' Jim suddenly announced. I put down my mug of coffee. *What do you mean, Jim?* 'The batting place on that tour. I'd been picked for the third Test that summer against Pakistan. I was dropped, Colin got in for the fourth Test and he was on the boat.'

There are two observations I should like to make about this. First, I did not know that Jim had made his Test debut way back in 1954. Only one match, mind you. He had to wait until 1960 before he got his second, against the West Indies. He marked the occasion by scoring an undefeated 101. Secondly, he made this reference to Colin's selection ahead of him without the slightest hint of rancour. 'Well, it could hardly be said they made the wrong choice,' he grinned. *But to be dropped after only one match – that was a bit harsh, wasn't it?* He gave a shrug and a little smile. There was no need for him to add anything; that was the way things were done in those days.

A quick glance at their respective figures for 1954 would suggest that he might have had a point. Parks scored 1,649 runs for the season at 36.64; Cowdrey scored 513 at 28.50. But the selectors were adamant that he was the right choice – 'When in doubt, one must back class,' one of them, Gubby Allen, remarked – and Hutton, initially sceptical, had been persuaded. Alan Ross, *The Observer*'s cricket correspondent, wrote of Cowdrey's selection, 'Anyone who saw him could hardly doubt he is a vintage player, mature beyond his years...Jim Parks was the probable alternative but Cowdrey is to him as burgundy to a sparkling hock and for a tour of this kind, body is preferable to fizz.'

A trifle hard on my friend opposite me, sipping his coffee, but as we shall see, Jim would have his time in the sun at a later date. Now was Colin's moment and he was resolved to seize it.

In fact, Jim's memory had let him down slightly. Colin was not picked for the fourth Test that summer; he was 12th man. The touring party had been announced on 27 July, which seems extraordinarily early, seeing as the team was not scheduled to leave England until mid-September, with a large chunk of the season still to go, to say nothing of the final Test of the Pakistan series. This was at The Oval and as Laker and Lock had been overlooked for the tour to Australia, they were both omitted from the team to play in this deciding match of the rubber. To go into a Test match in England without Laker and Lock – and on their home ground – seems perplexing to say the least but this was a season of surprises. Pakistan won the match – their first Test victory in England – to square the series. Any comment the Surrey spin twins may have made about that remains unrecorded.

Although Colin was not going to play, it was felt that it would be a good idea for him to act as 12th man to get a feel of what it was like to be involved in a Test match. As it happened, he was given little opportunity to savour the atmosphere. He suffered a reaction to the injections he had just been given for the Australian tour and spent most of the game in bed. Why am I not wholly surprised by that? Somehow, I can't picture Colin carrying the drinks.

So, once the last rites of an unusual season were concluded, instead of greeting the head porter at The Lodge of Brasenose College at the start of a new term, Colin shook hands with the captain of SS *Orsova* who welcomed the MCC team aboard at the start of their voyage to Australia. Coincidentally, the span of this brand new ocean liner's seafaring service was to run exactly parallel to Colin's Test career. It had only recently made its maiden voyage. This was Colin's first in the colours of MCC. SS *Orsova* was decommissioned and broken up in 1974. Colin was not broken up in 1974, I am pleased to report, but it was the last time he played for England.

There was another accidental connection on that voyage, which we will come to shortly. Colin's parents had come to Tilbury to see their son off. While they were saying their goodbyes, Len Hutton took Ernest Cowdrey aside and talked earnestly to him, if you will forgive the pun, for 20 minutes or so. It was only later that Colin found out what was being said. With a kindness and solicitude that belied his plain-speaking persona, Hutton was assuring Ernest that he would keep an eye on his son and do his best to look after him.

Those who knew Hutton and played under him would not have been surprised. He was as hard as nails on the pitch but he had a soft side to him and could be surprisingly emotional. Colin had cause to be grateful for his captain's thoughtfulness much sooner than he anticipated.

Among the dignitaries and well-wishers thronging the dockside as the MCC team embarked was a middle-aged man, spare of frame and prominent of nose. He was seen to engage the young Cowdrey in deep and urgent conversation. Part of what he said was overheard by some of Colin's team-mates. 'When you get to Australia, just remember one thing, Cowdrey – hate the bastards!' Who was that, Colin demanded later, to be informed it was Douglas Jardine.

If he had any doubt of the magnitude of the task ahead, the presence there of the last man to captain an Ashes-winning team in Australia 20 years previously, albeit in highly controversial circumstances, would have dispelled it. Apparently, he had come down to Tilbury for the specific purpose of seeing Colin off. 'The least I could do for a fellow Oxford man,' he said. He gave the young man further advice, 'Don't aim to hook too early. Not only does the ball skid through, it hits you on the foot – play it wide of mid-on.' At which point, the bells sounded throughout the ship and those not sailing were urged to go ashore. It did not escape the attention of several of the travelling press corps that Tilbury was the scene of Elizabeth I's famous speech to her troops before the expected invasion by the Spanish Armada ('I know I have the body of a weak, feeble woman but I have the heart and stomach of a king, and a king of England too').

Was Hutton about to employ the same rallying call to his troops? It seemed not. His style was quite different but no less effective. Colin, among others, came to appreciate his dry sense of humour, his tactical acumen, his absolute dedication to the cause and his peerless – and courageous – batsmanship. But he was not one for grand speeches.

Life on board SS *Orsova* was far from the boot camp favoured by modern sides as preparation for an arduous series. Colin described it as a 'comfortable, even luxurious voyage' though he admitted to a certain amount of bashfulness in the company of so many well-known players. Time, of which there was a lot on such a journey, slowly broke down the barriers. From when anchor was weighed in the Thames Estuary to the eve of first Test in Australia, it would be 71 days.

On board was John Woodcock, a cub reporter for *The Times*, entrusted with his first major assignment overseas with MCC as cricket correspondent. He told me, when I made a pilgrimage down to his delightful cottage in Longparish in Hampshire, that Hutton, as a professional captain, made sure that co-existence with the amateurs in the party, of whom there were five, Cowdrey included, was seamless. As it should be, he added. And thereafter, as long as the distinction survived, it always was.

In a piece written for *The Cricketer* in 2005 celebrating the 50th anniversary of that famous tour, Woodcock remembered the long, leisurely days aboard ship, 'It was more a rest after the relentless English season, and for the chance to talk cricket, than as a bonding exercise, that the voyage was beneficial. It was tedious at times but incredibly spoiling: comforts galore, the stirrings of romance and the journalistic bliss of an unexpected office.'

Slowly, Colin relaxed. Inevitably, though unconsciously, the two rookies were drawn to each other to form a friendship that was to last Colin's lifetime. 'I got to know him well,' said Woodcock. 'I became very fond of him. That didn't mean I couldn't criticise him sometimes, which I did. I was critical of him in India, for example, in the 1963/64 series, when he seemed to bat without ambition. It was surprising really, because from the start of his career to the end, he had so much ability that he *could* play anything. But sometimes, through inclination, he didn't.'

Tell me about the relationship the accompanying press corps had with the players. 'Not the same as it is these days. We became friends really, sometimes close friends. On board, and later, travelling around the country, it was almost as if we were one big family on a great adventure. Did that mean we became too close? Possibly. But there was a certain amount of trust between the two sides, which sadly seems to have been lost nowadays. We felt free to pass comment on the cricket, bad or good, but the...hah, how shall we call it, the extra-curricular activities were off limits.'

That is not the first time I've heard such sentiments uttered about journalists from a bygone era. Tom Graveney told me that the press on those trips comprised cricket reporters, not newshounds. He was unsure quite when the balance shifted from pure cricket reporting to the pursuit of gossip and scandal but once it happened, the relationship between player and reporter changed forever.

It was my good fortune that during one of Jeremy Cowdrey's periodic rummages in his loft through his father's personal effects, he unearthed Colin's diary of this trip. It is written on pages that you only find in those old school exercise books, bound and held together with string. Much like his school diary, it is full of commonplace record and observation but it occasionally yields snippets of information that are pure gold dust.

For a start, Colin has manifestly grown up. His comments reveal a maturity that is perforce lacking in the commentary of his school life. Furthermore, there are flashes of humour, heralding the masterful light touch as a witty public speaker for which he became renowned. He notes down jokes that he has heard, nothing to do with the tour or the players necessarily, almost as if he is putting them in safe keeping, to be wheeled out at a later date. One such example is a story of a previous MCC tour to the West Indies. At the bottom of a menu at the team's hotel was printed this reassuring guarantee: *The water has been passed by the manager.*

The diary is more lively, too, in its tone; he seems more aware of his audience, that is if he had any idea that one day it might see the light of day. Crucially, for my purposes, it offers a fascinating glimpse into life on board and on the road, at a time when travel was slower and more leisurely. Plainly, there was time to kill during the long sea voyage, which means that a disproportionate amount of the diary's contents are concerned with what happened before they reached Australia. Thereafter, it becomes more rushed and few details emerge of the actual Tests, other than scores and brief summaries of the day's play. But that is all right. I can look up *Wisden* for the scorecards but I cannot, except through Colin's eyes, get an impression of his team-mates and what they did away from the cricket. And it is often here with no more than a hint or a suggestion, the value of his diary lies.

The Bay of Biscay, as is its wont, tested the sea legs of the party. All were at one stage or another afflicted by seasickness. All that is except Colin. 'PBH spends all day in bed. Evans better. He's off that banana diet the ship's doctor prescribed. Spots attractive twins and he's off!' When Evans was in bed, ill, you understand, Reg Simpson went to visit him in his cabin. He was ticked off by a steward, 'Give the cricketers a break.' Colin was wryly amused by the others' assessment of their fellow Yorkshireman, Bob Appleyard, 'There's only one 'ead bigger than Applecart's and that's Birken'ead!'

Hutton was always taking individual members of his team aside for a private chat. The young Cowdrey was no exception. 'Advice from Len,' he writes. 'You want to make up your mind how you're going to play. Set your mind to it with the utmost confidence and don't interfere with it much. Listening to people's advice on wickets etc only gets you more confused. I used to do that, asking all sorts of people, Jack Hobbs, Patsy Hendren etc and it was disrupting.'

Let no one say that Colin did not listen to, and act on, his captain's words. It was clear that Hutton, while the rest of his team were relaxing and enjoying the entertainment and activities on board, was restlessly planning for the campaign ahead.

Colin may have set great store by the received wisdom of Hutton but he did not neglect the spiritual guidance to which he had become disposed. He was a regular participant at religious services on board, often 'accompanied by EWS'. Jim Swanton, *The Daily Telegraph* cricket correspondent, a fellow man of Kent, was to become a devotee of Colin's, never failing to sing his praises or fight his corner. Quite what Colin thought of this patronage he never said. Embarrassed would be my guess. He always passes comment on the service, just as he did when he was at school. 'Lovely church service taken by the Captain,' he writes. And then he adds a droll comment. 'Attendance was sparse. Everybody suffering from Press party last night.'

The warmth and the calmer seas of the Mediterranean came as a welcome change from the storms in the Bay of Biscay. 'Awoke to a terrible stench coming through the portholes – Naples!' See Naples and die, goes the old saying. For one poor passenger, this was tragically prescient. 'Terrible drivers the Italians. Indeed one of our passengers was killed and the wretched Captain had to cable the terrible news to his wife and small child.'

There was time amid the hurly-burly of their short stay ashore for a bit of peaceful reflection. 'Len took a party of Yorkshiremen to pay homage at Hedley Verity's grave.' Verity, one of the game's finest slow left-arm bowlers before the war, was a captain in the Green Howards when he was hit in the chest by shrapnel in the Sicily campaign. Taken prisoner, he was moved to hospital in Naples, where he died of his wounds. Hutton was close to Verity and respected him as a man as well as a cricketer. He ensured that they laid a wreath, a single white rose and a Yorkshire scarf at the grave.

As was the custom, MCC stopped off en route in Ceylon, now Sri Lanka, to play what Woodcock called a 'picnic' game in Colombo. Colin thought it no picnic – he found it disconcerting to play a game of cricket so soon after disembarking after a long sea voyage, 'The ground seemed to be swaying under my feet,' he writes. 'Peter May holes out to a long-hop and lets me in three balls before lunch. I just survive, 0 not out. Have a healthy lunch but not so many mangoes as Bill Edrich. After lunch, in good form until Peter declares with me on 65.' In fact it was 66, but who's quibbling about one run?

Unless of course you are on 99. This happened to Reg Simpson later on in the tour, as Colin recounts. It was in one of the state games and just as Simpson was about to complete his century, Hutton took them off because it was drizzling with rain. On the resumption of play, Simpson was immediately out without adding to his total. 'Furious row in the dressing room,' Colin records, and leaves it at that.

They packed their bags and set sail again that evening. Colin was happy that he had got a few runs under his belt. It may have been a bit of a 'picnic' match but at least he had shown one or two of his fellow tourists who had never seen him play that he could bat. The significance of the innings was lost on him at the time but later he was to discover the poignancy of its association, one that he would never forget.

His own words describe it best, 'Back at home that evening, my father was sitting listening to the radio and on hearing the good news, hurried upstairs to fetch a pencil and paper to make a note of the scores. He came down again but a few minutes later when my uncle sitting opposite looked up from his paper, he saw my father had died in his chair.'

Ernest Cowdrey, who had suffered from a bad heart for many years, was 54. Colin too died from a heart attack aged only 67.

The news of course did not reach him immediately. It was not until the SS *Orsova* docked at Fremantle that he finally learned what had happened. It cannot have escaped his mind that there was a sad irony in all this. The last time he was on the high seas, his father had dragged him from his cabin to watch a passing ship carrying Don Bradman and the 1938 Australian team on their way to England. As his father was drawing his last breath, Colin was on a ship going the other way, with the MCC team to tour Australia.

Blissfully ignorant for the time being of the tragic event back home, Colin continued to enjoy life on board. On one occasion, he was invited by the team manager, Geoffrey Howard, to be his guest at the staff commander's cocktail party. 'I then meet a chap on deck,' Colin records, 'who invites me to drinks that same evening. I apologise and say I cannot come because I'm having drinks with the staff commander. "That's me, old chap!"'

As they steadily approached Fremantle, as if to call a halt to all the entertaining, socialising and deck games, Hutton summoned a team meeting, to remind them of what was ahead. His message was uncompromising. Colin's words, 'Len – "Graft away. Stay there long enough and the runs will come."' Thus spake a true Yorkshireman. But there was one final party, thrown by the captain – of the ship, not MCC. 'He gave a speech to the England team and remembered the last time he had sailed with English cricketers. Except on this occasion, they were women.'

The speech obviously made a big impression on our tourist because he recounts it in detail. There was prize giving. To his dismay, the captain could see they were one prize short so he whispered to his purser to nip along to his cabin and select any item as a notional prize and bring it back. The purser duly hurried off and returned, breathless, to hand the captain a tankard, just in time.

'The recipient was a rather Amazonian figure. He shook her hand and presented the tankard, with which he got a tremendous crack across the head. On the tankard was inscribed, Best Behaved Bitch at the Show. Len responded brilliantly.'

News of his father's death filtered through gradually on the ship's cable. First of all, his mother sent word that he was ill. 'Ominous,' he writes, 'because Mother would not have wired had he been ordinarily ill.' Soon, his worst fears were realised. We can only guess at his feelings because he remained tight-lipped, as he had learnt to do throughout his childhood. He says only this, 'The thrill of embarking on Australian soil was sobered by the tragic news of Daddy's passing. We have a meal with all the team together.'

On the face of it, that is an extraordinary non sequitur. The two pieces of news, his father's death and a team meal, are separated only by a full stop. Not even a new paragraph. What do we make of that? Perhaps not as much as our cod psychoanalysis would have us believe.

He was born into an age when things like that were not readily and openly discussed. Yet the death of one's father is always a difficult thing, whatever the circumstances.

It is tricky at this distance to gauge the true nature of their relationship. Colin was ever the dutiful son, respectful of his father's influence on his cricket career and grateful to him for smoothing his path for future success at every turn, even if he had been, as fate would have it, a distant figure. For the time being, stuck at the other end of the world, there was the dilemma of what to do next; should he return home or remain with the party?

Obviously upset and with conflicting emotions swirling around his head, he sought advice from his shipmate and future ally and best friend in cricket, Peter May. What was to be gained by going home, May told him. He would be too late for the funeral and, in any case, his father would surely have wished for him to stay. After all, that was his lifetime's ambition, to see his son play for England; to abandon the tour now would have been the last thing that Ernest would have wanted. So the decision was made. Colin would stay and no doubt the MCC captain and management heaved a deep sigh of relief.

That is not to say that his team-mates were in any way unsympathetic to his plight. In fact, Colin remained forever hugely grateful to Len Hutton and the calm and kindly influence that he exerted on his young protege during these difficult weeks. Hutton had assured Ernest Cowdrey on the dockside at Tilbury that he would look after his son and that he did, without fuss, as was his way, but genuinely enough. And what better way was there to take his mind off his loss than to make sure he was fully occupied in doing what they had set out on this journey for – to play cricket?

For all that, there was no evidence that Hutton had it in mind that the 21-year-old uncapped undergraduate from Oxford would be an integral part of his master plan to take on the Aussies. In fact, Colin's surprise selection had prompted Hutton to add an 18th member, Vic Wilson, to a touring party that customarily only numbered 17. Wilson was another batsman so Colin had no reason to believe anything other than that he would be well down the pecking order for a place in the Test side. All that was to change during the warm-up games against the state sides. First up were Western Australia and to his surprise, he found himself in the XI.

'It was a great experience for me to bat with Len Hutton,' is his breathless comment. 'We put on 127 together, batting for two and a half hours. He retires with a strained groin after running a shortish single.' I didn't know Colin was in the habit of scampering singles but we mustn't forget he was still a young man. And when your captain calls, you go. 'We nearly collided in the middle of the wicket. He gets his 100 just on lunch and it's a nightmare in case I run him out.' He did not and did his cause for further selection no harm either.

That cause was strengthened against a strong New South Wales team, captained by Keith Miller and including Alan Davidson, Arthur Morris, Jim Burke, Richie Benaud and Bobby Simpson. According to Woodcock, in this game, 'Cowdrey touched the heights with a century in each innings, batting at number six in the first and opening for the first time in his life in the second.' The innings caught the eyes of his team-mates too. This is how Frank Tyson, in his diary of the tour, described it, 'It was an outstanding knock. He is a natural timer of the ball and seems barely to touch the ball for it to speed to the boundary.' His second innings was every bit as good. Tyson again, 'A month short of his 22nd birthday, the baby of our side, Colin Cowdrey today scored his second hundred of the NSW game, against an attack that was the equal of anything Australia can throw at him. It was a superb response to the team's needs and a wonderful display of temperament, well in advance of his tender years.'

Note that Tyson was more impressed by his mettle than his skill. Colin's observation was merely this, 'It was a softish wicket, helpful to the bowlers. Have to buy the boys some hock in the evening.'

It must have become increasingly obvious to Colin during the course of the match that far from being well down the pecking order he had climbed up, one might say, to the very top. The top of the order. The request from his captain to open the innings, which he agreed to without demur, for a request from Hutton was not one that ordinarily was refused, surprised him, and concerned him.

He had never fancied the role; it is, after all, a specialised position. He had never considered himself an opener and he never would, despite the number of times he was asked to do it. He always agreed, against his natural inclinations and better judgement, because the team came first, but he never liked it. On this occasion and for the rest of this tour, he was spared the predicament because Reg Simpson rediscovered his form and he opened in the first Test match with Hutton. But the opening bugbear was to raise its head from time to time throughout Colin's career.

The burgeoning relationship between Colin and Len Hutton is an interesting one and sheds surprising light upon both of them, particularly the elder man. 'Len thought the world of Colin,' John Woodcock told me. 'He wasn't a fan originally, unsure about the maturity and resilience of one so young, no matter how impeccable his technique. But Colin won him over.'

No doubt it was that maiden Test hundred at Melbourne that convinced him? Not so, averred the distinguished journalist. He believed it was during their first innings partnership of 163 in that match against New South Wales that his mind was made up. 'Len took him under his wing,' he said, 'and thereafter, they became firm friends.'

Quite clearly, something about Colin's batting that day took root in the Yorkshireman's mind and convinced him that here, despite his youth, privileged upbringing and fine manners, was a cricketer tougher than he looked. Tough enough to take on the Aussies in their back yard? Time would tell but Hutton's envisaged Test team was slowly undergoing some modification. Not that he would have let on. 'Len was a bit funny like that,' Tom Graveney told me. 'Nobody was quite sure what was going on in his mind. I got on all right with him but one or two of the others found him a bit stiff and uncommunicative.'

John Woodcock agreed. 'An essentially private person, Hutton gave few clues to his thinking,' he wrote. 'He was introspective yet endearing, single-minded yet unassertive.' Even Frank Tyson, who flogged himself into the hard-baked Australian ground for his captain, in much the same way that Larwood had done for Jardine 20 years earlier, recognised that Hutton 'was not everybody's cup of tea'. According to his account, Hutton forfeited the sympathy and respect of some of the senior members of the team for one or two quite separate reasons, but there was no denying his tactical acumen and single-minded determination to get one over the old enemy.

Having suffered enough at the hands of Lindwall and Miller, he resolved that the only way to beat them was to fight fire with fire. In this regard, he was lucky enough, some might say far-sighted enough, to have two outstanding fast bowlers at his disposal and in the prime of life and the form of their careers, Tyson and Statham. 'No, four!'

Woodcock insisted. 'Peter Loader didn't play in the Tests but he was a mighty fine bowler and cut a swathe through the state sides. And don't forget, we had left Fred Trueman at home.'

It is a truism that bowlers win matches but as Geoffrey Boycott never tires of pointing out, aye, but it's the batsmen's job to put enough runs on the board for the bowlers to get to work. In this respect, Hutton would have been the first to admit that without the contributions of two young men, May and Cowdrey, who were to provide the backbone of England's batting for the next decade, the Ashes would never have been won. May was his vice-captain and already an experienced Test player. Colin was the surprise package. No longer was he M.C. Cowdrey, Tonbridge and Oxford, but Cowdrey of Kent and England, and Hutton's acceptance of him as a bona fide member of the England team was important for both of them.

Dare one advance the theory that Hutton had become something of a father figure for the young man? Colin had to rely on figures in authority to fulfil that role throughout his early life, predominant among them Charles Walford, James McNeill and Rev. Lawrence Waddy, all men of culture, intelligence and standing. Is it too fanciful to imagine that Len Hutton had the same sort of influence? Certainly Colin's admiration for the man was unstinting. He wrote these words about his captain on his return from Australia, 'I remember his kindness to me upon hearing of the death of my father and his impeccable behaviour that Monday morning in Melbourne after the watering of the wicket. To me, his was a great achievement.'

The watering of the pitch we shall come to shortly but it was Hutton's sportsmanlike response to it – not something normally associated with the obdurate northerner – which impressed Colin. Cricket was a tough business but it was not warfare. And his respect for Hutton as a cricketer knew no bounds, 'His technical ability, his immense concentration, his fine cricket brain assure his place among the masters as long as the game is played.'

There was another, surprising element to their relationship – a shared sense of humour. The image of Hutton as an austere, saturnine northerner is incorrect. He was not the team joker, like Godfrey Evans or the life and soul of the party, like Bill Edrich but as Frank Tyson observed, he had a 'dry, enigmatic wit' and John Woodcock wrote, 'The Hutton twinkle was easily lit.'

Colin told two good stories about him on this trip. During the course of their partnership against NSW, Colin noticed that his partner, hitherto untroubled by the bowling, suddenly seemed to struggle. It was a turning wicket but Hutton was used to batting on them and had been dealing with the turning ball with his usual skill and *elan*. Between overs, the truth was revealed.

Alan Davidson, the peerless left-arm seamer, was experimenting with a brand of orthodox spin and Hutton rather fancied him in this new mode. 'Much easier than his usual stuff,' he told the junior player. 'Let's see if we can keep 'im on.' And that is what he proceeded to do. 'Hutton's imitation of a great batsman in trouble was a classic...worthy of an Oscar,' wrote Colin. Anybody who has tried to bat badly and get out not too obviously in a benefit, exhibition, Fathers v Sons or any non-serious match will know exactly what he meant.

Later, as Colin recalls in his diary, he went up to Hutton and remarked, 'Hard work, skipper.' The reply was pure Hutton. 'Aye, it is when you're not paid for it!' The reference to his amateur status would not have been lost on the junior partner.

Colin was slowly relaxing and able to let his sense of fun bubble to the surface. At the conclusion of the match, with NSW left just 75 minutes to score an improbable 198, a challenge they declined, Colin entertained everybody during the closing overs with some expert impressions of the bowling actions of their adversaries – Miller, Lindwall, Benaud et al. 'Kipper was an accomplished mimic,' stated Tyson.

Note the use of the nickname 'Kipper'. This is the first time in my study of Colin's life that I have encountered it. It was the name that was to stick with him, used by friends and opponents alike throughout his career and beyond. It is sometimes – erroneously – ascribed to his flat feet; in fact it derived solely from his propensity to take a nap in the dressing room, not an uncommon habit among cricketers.

The 'baby' of the touring party had been given a nickname; he was now one of the lads. This talent to entertain was not reserved exclusively for his batting. One is put in mind of his habit of pouching a catch in the slips, quickly pocketing the ball and turning to point to third man.

It amazed me how often the crowd were fooled. But they loved it. In the same way, ill-advisedly on this occasion as it turned out, he pretended not to see one of Andy Roberts's bouncers. The urge to have a bit of fun was never far away from a man who had an almost boyish enthusiasm for the game.

Fun was to be had a-plenty during down time on tour. There was a great deal of golf, tennis, real tennis, squash and swimming. There was also a fair smattering of social engagements, some of which were official but others that were informal and enjoyable, to say nothing of visits to the cinema and theatre. It really was a different world then, a complete contrast to present-day tours where one senses that the players rarely venture forth from their hotels, unless it is to go to the ground, and as for getting out of their tracksuits and donning a dinner jacket.

Here are a couple of examples of Colin's convivial invitations, 'Had dinner with Oxford Rhodes Scholars at Public Schools and make a speech.' And how about this for a spot of name-dropping? 'Lord Mayor's Dinner. On my table Don Bradman, Bill Woodfull, Geoffrey Howard and the Archbishop of Melbourne.' Clearly, he was making a name for himself Down Under. But with fame goes press intrusion, something he was never able to reconcile in his life. In Brisbane, he read with horror a newspaper headline, 'Colin's in love but nobody knows the score!'

Fun was brutally curtailed at the Gabba in Brisbane, the venue of his Test debut. A more inauspicious match for the tourists is hard to imagine. Pretty well everything that could go wrong did go wrong. First, Hutton completely misjudged the pitch, put the Australians in and paid the price. True to his conviction that pace would hold the key, he went in with four seamers, Tyson, Statham, Bedser and Bailey, and no spinner!

E.W. Swanton, before even a ball had been bowled, made the acerbic observation that, at that time, England had played 314 Test matches, and in 313 of them there had always been at least one spinner in the team. Truly, it was a gamble, and as soon as Australia started to bat Hutton saw that the pitch was a beauty, 'full of runs', said Colin, and knew his gamble had misfired.

'Just a minute!' my *Times* correspondent interjected here. 'Not *that* much of a gamble. In the previous match against Queensland, Hutton had taken note of the fact that of all the wickets to fall, not one had been taken by a spinner. So leaving out Appleyard and Wardle and playing four seamers seemed a reasonable decision under the circumstances.'

Reading a pitch is never a precise science and can make fools of us all. Furthermore, Godfrey Evans had fallen ill on the morning of the match and had to be replaced by the untested Keith Andrew.

Once he won the toss, Hutton obviously thought 'in for a penny, in for a pound', and, hoping that if there was something, *anything* in this pitch it would likely show itself in the first hour, he elected to bowl. Thus, he condemned his team to two days in the field in searing heat as the Australians piled on the runs.

To add injury to insult, Denis Compton broke his hand in the first hour, catching it on the white picket fence of the boundary as he went to field the ball. England were immediately one batsman short. To compound their woes, they fielded like drains. A conservative estimate among onlookers was that in total a dozen catches were dropped. If Hutton believed he had a plan to take on the Aussies, it lay, smudged and torn, beneath the rubble at the Gabba. 'We were hammered,' is Colin's terse description.

Australia amassed 601/8 declared and all of the England seamers came away with the dreaded hundred to their name; Bedser 1-131, Statham 2-123, Tyson 1-160, Bailey 3-140. The jitters in the field afflicted everyone, even the safest of catchers. Colin was not faultless either; he dropped three, of varying difficulty. When he finally caught one at second slip, Arthur Morris off Bailey for 153, he had his stomach to thank more than his hands. Hutton, beside him at first slip, looked at him and sardonically enquired, 'Do you catch 'em all like that?'

Hutton's dark mood was perhaps understandable. It was all his fault, he believed, and now his best-laid plans had turned to dust. 'Hutton was unapproachable,' Colin wrote. 'He communicated with no one.'

As England set out on the almost impossible task of trying to save the match, he became even more depressed as his side were bowled out for 190 and forced to follow on. This was Colin's lament about his first Test innings, 'Trevor and I stay until I am given out caught off my boot at twenty nine and a half minutes past five.' He had scored 40. Swanton reported, 'Cowdrey's innings was the one bright gleam of light in a dreary day for England.'

The batsmen made a better fist of it in the second innings but the result was never in doubt. They were eventually dismissed for 257, thus suffering a catastrophic defeat by an innings and 154 runs.

The England skipper was a tortured man. The pain etched on his face was plain for all to see. 'Depression in the camp,' reports Colin. 'Len presents me with a stump as a memory of the match. I tell him that it will only bring back the unhappiest memories of five galling days in my first Test match.'

But as is the way with young men, the disappointment swiftly subsided, champagne was drunk that night and everybody went about telling each other that the next Test would be different. 'The experience,' wrote Tyson in his diary, 'shows me quite clearly that when we take our catches – and when we have just a modicum of luck – we can beat this Aussie side.'

Even Hutton's mood lightened, reassuring his team that the Ashes were not yet lost. His sense of humour was restored too. Colin tells of an amusing incident in the hotel foyer a day or two afterwards. E.W. Swanton was present. 'Hey, Skipper,' cried out one wag from the assembled group, 'have you read what the *Telegraph* said about you?' 'No,' was Hutton's disingenuous reply. Whereupon, he strode across the marble floor, removed the folded *Telegraph* from that paper's correspondent's arm, spread it out and sat down to read. Taking his time, as he always did, Hutton eventually stood up, refolded the paper and replaced it in Swanton's grasp. 'I have now,' he announced, deadpan.

The Englishmen approached the second Test in Sydney by no means downcast but aware that this would be the vital match of the series. As Swanton had reported in that article in the *Telegraph*, 'In brutal truth, the game had been bungled by England from start to finish.' They were determined not to do so again.

Controversy raised its head again before a ball had been bowled. Alec Bedser, a stalwart of the side since the war, was dropped. This in itself, though sad, was by no means indefensible. Bedser by now was 36, he had been suffering from shingles and he had not been at his best. Perhaps his friend and greatest champion, Len Hutton, sensed that this was the end of the road for the lion-hearted seam bowler and made the decision in the team's best interests, putting his faith in speed and youth, namely Tyson and Statham. And subsequent events bore him out.

But he never told Bedser! The first Bedser knew that he was not playing was when the team-sheet was pinned to the dressing room board 15 minutes before the start of play. He was upset and felt aggrieved, understandably so. Colin tried to make sense of what had happened, the decision and the manner of its implementation. 'It was an understandable but tragic omission,' he wrote.

The truth was that Bedser had not been bowling well but the handling of his omission was insensitive, he believed, something he resolved never to do whenever, if ever, he captained his country. The trouble was, and this afflicts all captains who are opening batsmen, there is precious little time to compose yourself for batting after the toss has taken place and your team is taking first knock. For Hutton, concentration was all.

'On his batting days,' Colin observed, 'Hutton retired into a world of his own. He neither spoke to anyone nor appeared to hear if anyone spoke to him.' Bedser was the victim of this cocoon of self-absorption. He was deeply hurt, no doubt reflecting that this was probably the end of his Test career. The whole thing, Colin felt, could have been done more sympathetically.

One of the unassailable requisites of a great match, I have always believed, is that the result should be in doubt until the very end. Great deeds can be performed, great skill and bravery may be present in abundance, but there has to be an element of nail-biting tension for it to go down in the annals as a magnificent contest. The Sydney Test had it all.

Once again, England were disappointing in the first innings, bowled out for 154. 'We get an awful slating from the press,' Colin informs us. That boozy party with the press on board SS *Orsova* must have seemed a long time ago. But Australia were able to take only modest advantage in replying with 228. Tyson and Bailey were the two main destroyers, taking four wickets apiece. Frank Tyson was particularly hostile and it was here, in this innings, that he seemed to assert a dominance over the Australian batsmen that he did not relinquish for the rest of the series.

Up until now he had been fast, *very* fast, but a bit woolly and erratic in his control. The change had been his run-up. 'Frank had a long run, about 38 paces,' Tom Graveney said. 'It seemed too long, especially in the heat. And, don't forget, we had eight-ball overs in Australia then.' According to Colin, it was taking him about 11 minutes to bowl an over.

Alf Gover, the former England fast bowler and noted coach, was covering the tour for one of the English newspapers, and he was aware that Tyson, in the nets, particularly in his famous indoor school in Wandsworth, south-west London, employed a much shorter run, without a discernible lessening of pace. He advised his protege to use that shortened run, to conserve energy and at the same time maintaining forward momentum. The result was electrifying.

'Tyson's bowling was sheer blind speed,' said an admiring Colin, no doubt thankful, as you always are, that the nasty fast bowler was on his side. The Australian batsmen's discomfort was plain to see. No doubt Hutton was jubilant. He had gambled on Tyson and it was working. And he had gambled on leaving out Bedser and that was working too. Furthermore, he would not have been human if he had not felt a touch of *schadenfreude*: after all, he had been suffering at the hands of Lindwall and Miller for long enough. By the way, our young tourist had been suffering in the heat. 'Feel a bit crook,' he says, deliciously unconscious of plagiarising the Australian language.

In their second innings, England were swiftly reduced to 55/3, still 74 in arrears, and it seemed that they had thrown away any advantage that Tyson and Bailey had wrested back, and with it probably the Ashes. I shall leave it to the *Telegraph*'s correspondent to describe what happened next, 'Thus arrived the youthful Cowdrey once again to plug a hole, this time a yawning hole.'

Colin joined Peter May and both knew that the series would be over if either had got out; the stakes were that high. 'If the grace belonged to May, Cowdrey supplied an equal calm certainty of judgement and common sense,' continued our scribe. Together, they put on 116 priceless runs in what was turning out to be a low-scoring game.

Swanton was not the only one to wax lyrical about their batting. Back in the dressing room, Tyson spoke for them all, though more articulately than most. 'What marvellous young batsmen are these two from the universities of Cambridge and Oxford. As one watched their afternoon dominance of the Aussie bowlers, one sensed that here before our very own eyes, we were watching the arrival of a fresh young generation of future England batsmen.'

May's was a peerless innings, John Woodcock told me, 'particularly savage on anything short, which was immediately despatched to the midwicket boundary'. Tyson again, 'Kipper's brooding concentration sat heavily on his shoulders but did not inhibit his natural penchant for playing strokes. He hid his intensity behind a bland impassive expression.'

Eventually, that concentration was snapped, Benaud luring him into a mistimed lofted off-drive and he departed for 54. Tyson gives a moving account of the scene when Colin returned to the dressing room. 'Colin came back utterly despondent and immediately burst into floods of tears. "I've just thrown away the Test match, Frank." I replied, "Not if I can help it." He and I have the same depth of feeling about certain issues.' If Tyson wore his heart on his sleeve, the buttoned-down Cowdrey certainly did not. He merely reports in his diary thus, 'I hole out off a massive shot and am in tears.' No mention of the fact that he had scored a crucial half-century.

Depth of feeling can be expressed in different ways. Colin was always of the undemonstrative breed. To him actions spoke louder than words. Tyson was a fast bowler and by nature they are more bellicose. They have to be. It takes it out of you, fast bowling, and though the spirit is always willing, the flesh tires and sometimes flags. Every so often, something other than pure cricketing motivation is required to stir the blood.

On this occasion, Tyson got cross and the Australian batsmen took the brunt. The following day, Peter May completed a memorable hundred but the England lead of 223 was precarious. Most of the sensible money was on an Australian victory. In the previous Test, Ray Lindwall had batted very well, scoring 64, adding weight to the view that he was a genuine all-rounder. In fact, Australia were blessed with four of these multi-talented cricketers – Benaud, Archer, Miller and Lindwall, with Alan Davidson waiting in the wings.

In view of Lindwall's status as a batsman, the runs he had scored and the understandable frustration of the England bowlers at Brisbane, Tyson now decided to put aside the age-old custom of a fast bowler not giving a bouncer to another of the brotherhood, and let him have one. The look that Lindwall gave his tormentor did not bode well for the Englishman's well-being when it came to have his turn to bat. Lindwall had his opportunity now. He repaid the compliment.

Tyson lost sight of the ball, turned away and was hit a sickening blow on the back of the head.

For a while, he was unconscious, as concerned players gathered around. 'My God, Lindy,' his batting partner, Bill Edrich cried, 'you've killed him!' Lindwall hadn't but still, Tyson was carted off to hospital for X-rays. Fortunately, the skull remained intact and he was left with nothing more than a sore head. Oh, and a burning sense of resentment. 'I was very, very angry with Ray Lindwall,' he later said, 'and the whole of the Aussie team knew it.'

I guess the situation was not a lot different to The Oval in 1994, when England were playing South Africa. Devon Malcolm, the England fast bowler and tail-ender, was hit on the head in similar fashion. Incensed, he turned to the South African fielders and uttered the famous remark, 'You guys are history!' He then took 9-58.

Tyson didn't put it quite like that but the fury that was aroused in him was similar, with the same result. He took 6-85 and his ten wickets in the match 'were the reward for as fine a display of sustained speed and stamina I have ever seen in a fast bowler', wrote Swanton.

'I was fielding at first slip,' Graveney described to me. 'There was a gale blowing down the ground and I was standing 40 yards back. And still the snicks were flying over my head. It was frightening.' Trevor Bailey believed that he had not seen anybody, or thought it was *possible* for anyone, to bowl as fast as Tyson that day. Don Bradman always maintained that Tyson, on this tour, was the fastest he had ever seen. And he had faced Harold Larwood in the Bodyline series. Australia were blown away for 184 and England had secured a famous and vital victory.

Despite Tyson's heroics, they almost didn't get there. While wickets were tumbling at the other end, Neil Harvey was playing serenely, as if engaged in a completely different contest. At 145/9, he was joined by the last man, Bill Johnston. Harvey expertly manoeuvred the strike, Johnston swung away merrily, Tyson was tiring and the score mounted. Suddenly, an unlikely Australian victory seemed possible before Tyson summoned up one last burst of energy to have Johnston caught behind by the acrobatic Godfrey Evans for England to scrape home by 38 runs. Harvey was left stranded on 92 not out and 'his innings was the best I have ever seen him play', said an admiring Cowdrey later.

'And don't forget George!' said Tom Graveney, much later. *George? Who was George?* 'George was our nickname for Brian Statham.' Colin agreed with Graveney's assessment. 'Typhoon bowls magnificently with Brian Statham giving splendid support, with great accuracy and heart.' That was true. He bowled 19 overs (of eight balls) for 45 and took three wickets. He gave Hutton control at one end while Tyson wreaked havoc at the other.

By general consent, Hutton's tactics throughout had been faultless. In his writing, Colin gives an insight into a great captain on top of his game. His placement of the field, his changing of the bowling, his knowledge of the opposition and their strengths and weaknesses, were outstanding. And he was a master of psychological pressure. Colin gave an example. Whenever Benaud came to the wicket, Hutton would stop whoever was bowling the next over just before he had started his run. 'Hold on a second,' he would say, raising up his hand at slip, and then walking slowly up to the middle, 'Where's Frank?' while looking all around the ground, unable to locate his fast bowler.

Of course he knew exactly where Tyson was but Benaud had shown fallibility against him in the past and this was Hutton's way of ratcheting up the pressure a notch or two. Jardine had done the same with Bradman during the Bodyline series, affecting to scan the horizon unsuccessfully for Larwood. Another ploy was to wait until Tyson was about to bowl. Hutton knew his man was tired, blowing a bit. Once again, he would hold up his hand, march slowly all the way from first slip to where Tyson was waiting at the end of his run, and ask, 'Are you all right, Frank?' 'Fine, Skip,' Tyson assured him. Hutton would then walk slowly back to his place. Tyson had had his little rest.

Christmas in a hot country just doesn't feel right. There is something incongruous, phoney even, about fairy lights, sleds on cotton wool and Father Christmas sweating heavily in the heat, ringing a bell outside supermarkets and department stores as shoppers pass by in shorts and flip-flops. And turkey with all the trimmings in the evening, when the heat of the day has barely diminished, is an uncomfortable experience.

For all that, the MCC team did their best to try and replicate the traditional cheer of the occasion in their hotel, always difficult when separated from family and friends. But they were in good spirits, having a victory to celebrate, secure in the knowledge that they were back in the series and, who knows, in with a very good chance of winning it. While most of the players took the opportunity of a bit of a lie-in on Christmas Day, Frank Tyson noted one early riser.

'Kipper was off to church early.' In his diary, Colin makes other comments about the church services he attended, usually with a brief appraisal of the sermon. 'What a fine individual he is! A true Christian who practises and preaches,' Tyson concluded. One can only assume that the practice he refers to has more to do with doctrine than nets, because there was no Test on Boxing Day, as is now the custom in Australia. Colin adds a tart little comment about Boxing Day in Melbourne, 'Shambles! We are turfed out of our hotel. Team split up to alternative accommodation.' Notwithstanding, they all had a few welcome days off and most of them, including Colin, opted to watch the Davis Cup Final between Australia and the USA in Sydney.

It did not appear to Colin and others that Hutton had been able to relax in the short holiday break over Christmas. 'Meet Len at the tennis,' says Colin, 'who is bored stiff and hopes the Aussies lose!' They did. But it was the fate of the Ashes, not the Davis Cup, which occupied Hutton's every waking moment. It would define his legacy as an England captain.

In fact, he was teetering on the brink of what can only be described as a nervous breakdown. He looked wretched, his fibrositis had flared up again, he wasn't sleeping and the pressure was clearly getting to him. Privately, Colin wondered what it was that had triggered this state of affairs. It wasn't that Hutton lacked courage or mental resilience. He had been carrying the England batting, almost single-handedly at times, for years. What's more, he was an opening batsman and been taking the brunt of the new ball since before the war.

So why did he hide in his room on the morning of the Melbourne Test, unwilling to emerge and claiming he could not play? *Could not play?* The very idea was unthinkable. England had got the Aussies on the ropes, they had every intention of delivering a knockout blow, and they needed their leader. Perhaps, mused Colin, the explanation for Hutton's cold sweat – he could not call it stage fright, for Hutton was used to the grand stage, even one as big as the impressive MCG – was the burden of captaincy, not the fear of failure. Hutton had never captained before his elevation to the England job, not even with his native Yorkshire. He was then 36. Inexperienced then. Not as a player, of course – he had played 56 Tests before being appointed – but as a leader. If he had been made a captain much earlier in his career, which of course was impossible in those days, on account of his being a professional, he might have been better able to cope, Colin believed. However, he kept these thoughts to himself; though established in the team, he was still the baby of the party.

Fortunately, older heads than his were thinking along the same lines. A group of senior players and management went to Hutton's room and managed to persuade him to play even if he was feeling below par. He donned his blazer, went out to toss, won it and chose to bat. After Brisbane, he could hardly have done anything else. Soon, he probably wished he had stayed in bed. Edrich and May fell almost before Colin had buckled on his pads. Out he wandered, yet again in the middle of a crisis. If Swanton referred to the state of the England batting at Sydney as a 'yawning hole', then this moment of truth was more like a gaping chasm.

In Jack Bannister's excellent book, *The Innings Of My Life*, Colin describes how he felt and what he was up against, 'All I could do was to fight for my life but things seemed to get even tougher when I watched Keith Miller bowl to Len two of the greatest maiden overs I ever saw. It was a privilege to be at the non-striker's end and watch two great cricketers in opposition. Keith bowled out of his skin but Len somehow coped...And there was me, an undergraduate, wondering what on earth I was doing there.'

Perhaps it is easy to forget, those of us having been brought up in later eras of wonderful all-rounders – Sobers, Procter, Imran, Botham, Hadlee, Kapil Dev – just what a magnificent cricketer Keith Miller was. Here he was, ripping the England batting to shreds and a quick look at the Australian batting order will tell you that he was scheduled to bat at three. It was not long before he snared his prey, Hutton caught in the slips for 12. He set his sights next on his old friend, Denis Compton.

Colin continues, 'Miller roared in and the first ball nipped back and hit Denis. "Morning, Mr Compton," from Keith, who then ran in and bowled the equivalent of a lightning leg break which lifted as well. Not too surprisingly, Denis never got within several inches of what was a brute of a delivery.'

Two of the most recognisable and charismatic cricketers of their era were going at it, hammer and tongs. This was the opening session of a pivotal Test match, with the series and Ashes in the balance. But there were no histrionics, no snarling, no pointing, no swearing, no abuse. It was a Test match, played in front of a packed, raucous New Year crowd at the MCG but tempers did not flare and nobody squared up to anybody.

This was cricket as it should be played and Colin never wavered from his belief that, at the end of the day, both literally and metaphorically, it was a game, not war. His career straddled several generations and the later practice of sledging and aggressive behaviour never sat comfortably with him.

For the time being, he concentrated on survival. Miller had his tail up and like all fast bowlers with the scent of blood in his nostrils, he went in for the kill.

'I swallowed hard and watched and listened. Nothing was said but as Keith came back past me, he winked and smiled and said, "I don't know, Col – I've played against Compo since 1946 and he still doesn't get any better!"'

Eventually, Miller had his man. Compton was caught by Harvey and England were in the perilous position of 41/4, with Cowdrey as the last top-order batsman left. It wasn't even lunch. Not that Hutton would have fancied eating anything. He could see the game, and the Ashes, slipping away through his fingers before it had barely started. Few sides come back to win a series having gone 2-1 down. At the break, Miller went in with the extraordinary figures of nine overs, eight maidens, five runs, three wickets. And don't forget, they were eight-ball overs. He had bowled unchanged throughout the session, a spell that Colin described as 'as near unplayable as I have ever seen'. The five runs he conceded all morning were three from Compton past cover and two off the back foot from Cowdrey, also past cover.

Lunch provided some respite and a chance to take stock. On the resumption, Colin played what John Woodcock always believed was 'the first, and to mind, the finest of his 21 Test hundreds... His 102 out of a total of 191 was the pivotal innings of the whole tour.' It was this display of fearless batsmanship that earned Hutton's undying respect and admiration. Quite simply, without it, England were sunk.

As it was, they hung on for Tyson to wreak his havoc in the last innings. Together with Bailey, then Evans, Colin batted flawlessly, 'getting his body behind short, rising balls, which Lindwall and Miller were able to bowl almost at will', reported *Wisden*, 'Cowdrey specialised in perfectly timed drives, both straight and to cover and he forced the ball skilfully off his legs.' Ernest Cowdrey, watching the game from his armchair up above, would have purred with pleasure at his son's off-side play but must have puckered his brow in surprise at his leg-side shots.

Like all batsmen in prime form, Colin was aware that he was in the groove. 'The ball was never far from the middle of my bat...The moisture in the pitch started to dry and things seemed easier.' For him, that might have appeared so. It certainly wasn't the case for anyone else. For a while, he became becalmed on 64, the way it sometimes happens. He kept on losing the strike and balls to hit seemed to dry up. He got a fearful barracking from the crowd and it was here that he made his only error of judgement.

In an effort to throw off the shackles, he had a go at one and was narrowly missed being caught at mid-on. Fortunately, the ball went wide and, having berated himself, he resumed concentration and the strokes flowed once more. He effortlessly moved towards his hundred.

'I hit Archer through the covers to go from 93 to 97 and I was so close.... Sometimes players get stuck in that position through no fault of their own. The bowling stays tight, the fielding becomes keener, with the opposing captain understandably trying to play on nerves, but this time I had no problem. Archer dug one in short and I played the Peter May trademark shot – wide of mid-on. I knew I'd got a chance of three and so did the crowd. They had given me the treatment earlier when I got stuck in the 60s but now the cheering rose to a crescendo. It was generous and I found it touching, because they knew what it meant to me over and above the match situation (my father having died only a few weeks earlier).'

One could say that there and then was forged a lifetime's love of Australia and its people.

He had every intention of carrying on in the same manner but a combination of Johnston and Johnson did for him. In some ways it was a bit of a freakish dismissal, a sure sign that the gremlins had not left this pitch and never would for the duration of the match. Johnson pitched one in the rough outside his leg stump, footmarks created by the left-handed Johnston when he had been bowling from that end. It turned quickly, evading his front pad and passed through his legs to bowl him. 'It hit the edge of one of the cracks,' observed Evans.

'Colin was icily superb,' wrote Tyson. 'For four hours his concentration never wavered...Shooters became more frequent but Colin dug them out... He is a superb striker of the ball and is completely unflappable. He exudes a complete dedication to cricket and to his side.'

He was out for 102 and just one statistic, among so many, underlines how important an innings it was. He made his runs out of the lowest total (191) to contain a century, to share that record with Don Bradman, who scored 103 not out from a total of 191 in the 1932/33 Bodyline series.

Statistics rarely troubled the Cowdrey mind. What was more important was the quality of the innings. If we accept that all the ingredients of a great innings were here – top-class opposition, a tense match situation, a difficult pitch – then this one was truly great.

In his own words again, 'What was so satisfying was that I did not give a chance and I hardly played a loose stroke....It was a day that had everything for me: Miller's marvellous spell, the interplay between him and Compton, and then the two vital partnerships with Trevor and Godfrey. And all in my third Test in front of the biggest crowd I have ever seen.'

Cricket is a strange sport, a team game incorporating a composite of individual performances. Colin may well have gone to bed that night thrilled at his maiden Test hundred, but there was a match to be won and England were still in a perilous position. Thanks to his innings, it wasn't a hopeless position but his team needed to bowl out Australia cheaply, or at least keep the lead down to manageable proportions. At the close of play on the second day, their score was 188/8.

The game was very much in the balance. The next day was a rest day and the temperature soared. 104 degrees Fahrenheit was recorded in Melbourne and the England team, relaxing in the shade of the hotel, fully expected the fierce sun to widen those cracks in the pitch even more. 'The heat was incredible,' Woodcock said.[1] 'There was a hot wind blowing from the north, the interior.' So hot, Colin tells us, 'Bush fires were breaking out all over the place.'

It being a Sunday, Colin sought temporary shelter in the cool sanctuary of St Paul's Cathedral before somehow persuading the prime minister of Australia, Robert Menzies, to perform a favour. Already, even at the age of 22, he was 'persuading' people, often influential people, to do him a good turn. The prime minister! Almost casually, Colin records the nature of the request, 'Mr Menzies fixes a call through to my mother. The night is so hot, I didn't sleep much.'

Once again, we may well be nonplussed by the non sequitur. For the moment, how else can we explain it other than he was young, he was not in the habit of talking through his emotions, he was in the middle of a Test match and he was drained after playing one of the great Ashes innings? And it was *hot*.

Hot and dry. There had been no relieving thunderstorm. The team's surprise, therefore, soon turning to bewilderment, then to anger, knew no bounds as they arrived at the ground on the Monday morning to find the pitch wet and the cracks closed up. Foul play or a groundsman's mistake? It depends whether you are inclined to conspiracy theories or more prepared to accept the official explanation. 'I wouldn't like to say!' is Colin's wink and a nudge.

Actually, there never was a satisfactory explanation given by the ground authorities and the England players sat and fumed. 'It wasn't malpractice,' Woodcock insisted. 'It was a genuine mistake. One of the groundstaff had panicked and thinking the pitch would not last – which it didn't anyway – he had watered it in an attempt to bind up the cracks.'

It appeared that England would be put at a disadvantage by this strange turn of events. Australia, batting last on a pitch with cracks widening into fissures, would not have fancied their chances. It was at this point that Hutton revealed the full extent of his leadership qualities, thus underlining why his senior players were so anxious to rouse him from his sick bed on that first morning. Bitterness, recrimination and, most important of all, loss of focus could have affected his team and turned their attention away from what they were there for – to win the match.

'Len said nothing,' Colin wrote, 'and to his eternal credit... appeared to be only interested in getting on with the game. I do not think he has ever been given full credit for his extraordinary restraint on this occasion.' As it happened, Woodcock insisted, the watering of the pitch helped rather than hindered England but that takes nothing away from Hutton's composure at a decisive moment.

Australia were dismissed with a lead of only 40. England saw off the arrears while the dampened pitch slumbered but it was not long before the cracks re-appeared and batting became hazardous again. This time it was the other young star in the firmament, Peter May, who saved his team. 'Peter went on to make a brilliant 91,' Colin wrote, and he was not the only one in the England dressing room to be very disappointed that May did not reach the hundred he richly deserved. For once it is not the purple prose of E.W. Swanton that illuminated these two innings by the young Englishmen during the match but Alan Ross of *The Observer*, 'May split the air with the noise of his strokes, Cowdrey the field with the ease of his timing.' Somehow, England scraped together 279. Australia needed 240 to win and it was anybody's game.

Well, it could have been were it not for that man Tyson...again. Within five overs, the game was, to all intents and purposes, over. Harvey, Benaud and Miller were summarily despatched and the Australian innings was in ruins. They were bowled out for 111 before lunch. Tyson had taken 7-27 and England had their victory by 128 runs.

'But I couldn't have done it without George,' Tyson announced in a generous and honest nod of appreciation to his fellow fast bowler, Brian Statham. As ever, Statham had toiled away at the other end, providing no respite for shell-shocked batsmen with his accuracy and pace. Colin observes, 'Brian bowls like a dingbat!'

To be fair to the Australian batsmen, it has to be said that facing Tyson and Statham on a good wicket would have been no picnic; to combat them on a wicket that was always tricky and had now deteriorated sharply was beyond them. To put it into context, Cowdrey with his 102 and May with his 91, were the only batsmen from either side in both innings to score a fifty. England, having been 1-0 down, were now 2-1 up and 'in tremendous spirit and form', Colin tells us.

When I read Colin's diary, I hoped to uncover morsels of information of life on the road for an MCC touring team. I did not expect this, 'I hold Ned Kelly's gun that was his when he was shot.' Ned Kelly was an Australian bushranger and notorious outlaw, famous for his homemade metal suit of armour, eventually overcome after a killing spree and hanged for his crimes. The mental picture of

Colin Cowdrey flourishing a pistol at an alarmed museum curator is difficult to put down. 'Hasn't this Pommie done us enough damage?' one can imagine him thinking. Colin was back on more familiar territory in Adelaide. 'Meet Hoad and Rosewall. Splendid evening with Don Bradman.'

Adelaide, the venue for the fourth Test, is known as the City of Churches. Colin therefore had a very wide choice, 529 to be precise, for a place of worship but opted to attend matins and read the sermon at St Peter's Cathedral. 'He is the most virtuous of the touring party,' remarked Tyson, without a hint of irony or disdain. To seek the cool and cloistered atmosphere of a cathedral was probably a sensible call in view of the heatwave that had engulfed the city in mid-January.

There was no such respite on the first morning as the captains went out to toss in the match that would decide the destiny of the Ashes. As the holders, England had only to secure a draw to retain the urn but a draw was not on Hutton's radar. He wanted to beat the old enemy in their back yard. Australia won the toss and with the temperature nudging into triple figures, unsurprisingly elected to bat.

It was a day of turgid cricket. Scores of 51/0 at lunch, 119/3 at tea and 161/4 at stumps hardly sound like riveting fare for the punters and from the perspective of modern-day crash, bang, wallop batting, even in Test matches, it seems like an unconscionably slow run rate. But one must take into account the low level of confidence and the caution of the Australian batsmen, especially after their drubbing at Melbourne, the slowness of the pitch and the excellence of the England bowlers, all of whom kept a tight grip on proceedings on an unhelpful surface. It may have been tedious but it was tense.

After the day's play, Hutton came in for some pointed criticism for the slow over rate. Even John Woodcock agreed that it was 'awful'. He went on to write, 'It was, I am afraid, a deliberate ploy, aimed at upsetting the Australians.' Colin was more forgiving; he ascribed it to the searing heat and the eight-ball overs. Both of them had a point but it was no defensive tactic from the England captain. Those spectators who believed that he was playing for a draw did not know their man.

Frank Tyson understood him better than most. 'I sense that Len is still pursued by his own personal demons,' he wrote on the eve of the game. 'He will never be content until the series has been won and he has exorcised his two personal tormentors, Lindwall and Miller.' The slow over rate was intended to strangle the Australians and nurse his bowlers in short spells through a day of the most intense heat. Whatever it takes was his motto.

Colin was less concerned about the over rate than the closeness to the bat at short-leg he was expected to stand when Appleyard was bowling. 'Twas ever thus. That is where the young shavers of any team are put. Colin had not yet secured for himself a regular spot in the slips, which, once occupied, he never relinquished until he retired. His apprehension was not without foundation, as we shall see.

The following day, the Australians ground away without much purpose but the tail wagged and they felt reasonably content with their total of 323. For once, England did not get off to a disastrous start in their reply, posting the first 50 opening partnership of the series. On the morning of the third day, that bubble of security was punctured by the swift loss of two wickets and yet again it was Cowdrey who steadied the ship, together with his captain.

They had put on 99 runs before Hutton was deprived of his hundred – it would have been his first of the series – by a freak piece of bad luck. Johnston served up a juicy long-hop, Hutton latched on to it eagerly, only for his full-blooded pull shot to disappear into Davidson's midriff at short leg. Somehow, the fielder clung on to the ball as he doubled up in pain. Partnered now by Denis Compton, Colin hung on.

It was hard going. If ever confirmation were required that a slow pitch produces slow scoring, then here was it, two of England's finest stroke-makers reduced to passivity. In Colin's words, 'The wicket was slow, the Australians were bowling defensively and runs were hard to come by.' The barracking got to him. 'The 42,000 crowd gave me some stick.'

He flashed at a few balls, intent on breaking the deadlock. He was then surprised to see the arrival of England's 12th man, Vic Wilson, resplendent in his tour blazer, making his way to the middle. Usually, the excuse is a change of batting gloves, always accompanied of course by a few words of advice from the dressing room. Wilson produced no gloves. Instead, he flourished two bananas. 'Skipper thought you might be a bit hungry,' he announced cryptically. That was typical Hutton. With an oblique reference to Colin's already hearty appetite, he made his meaning clear. Now was not the time to get out. Colin took the hint and knuckled down.

His five-hour vigil came to an end having scored 79 painstaking runs, hardly the fluent batting of his century in the previous Test but crucial in terms of this England innings and the outcome of the match. In the side's total of 341, only Hutton with 80 had outscored him. With little separating the two sides as Australia started their second innings, once again a game was in the balance. Oh no, it wasn't. Tyson and Statham, aided and abetted on this occasion by Appleyard, bowled them out for 111. England needed only 94 to win, wrap up the series, retain the urn and attain immortality.

The scene in the dressing room was far from the confident, expectant headquarters of a general on the cusp of his most famous victory. It was as if Hutton could not quite believe it. Surely there would be a sting in the tail yet. There always was with the Australians, bitter experience had taught him. Colin, while fielding in the gully, had been struck a nasty blow on the nose. 'I'm carried off,' he informs us. 'Go to Calvary Hospital for X-ray and find that the bridge of my nose is broken. It is swollen and painful.'

The following morning, 'breakfast is sent up to me in bed and my face is still swollen and sore'. He did not expect to be batting but Hutton was a tough nut and when asked by Peter May, the vice-captain, with a sideways look at Colin's two black eyes, who was going to bat in his place, he answered, 'No one.' Hutton's foreboding and May's forewarning were borne out by an extraordinary spell of bowling from Keith Miller – who else? – which, for a few wobbly moments, threatened catastrophe.

In 20 balls, Miller dismissed Edrich, Hutton and Cowdrey, the score was 18/3 and all was a-jitter back in the England dressing room. 'Len was sitting down, not even unbuckling his pads,' said Graveney. 'He kept on saying, "The booger's done for us!" Denis hadn't even gone out. "Hang on," he said, "I haven't batted yet." And he went out there and knocked off the runs. Only then was the tension released and a great cheer went up as he saw us home.' Colin noted with grim satisfaction, 'The Aussie crowd are streaming mournfully out of the ground before the closing scenes.'

England had won and the celebrations commenced. Colin noted that there were tears in Hutton's eyes as he said, 'I wish Lord Hawke was here now.' His Lordship captained both Yorkshire (for 28 years) and England, was a noted administrator in the game and became the father figure of Yorkshire cricket. Despite being an amateur, he was a staunch supporter of the professionals. Hutton would have appreciated that.

It was rumoured the team got through 56 bottles of champagne that evening. Who paid? 'I have got to pay the bill,' notes Colin ruefully, 'and it amounts to $60!' Graveney told me that at one stage Bill Edrich, God knows how, shinned up one of the marble pillars of the hotel ballroom and gave a stentorian rendition of 'Ginger', holding on with one arm while the other was cradling one of those bottles. 'Somebody asked him to extinguish his cigarette,' said Tom. 'He did so by jumping fully clothed into the swimming pool.'

Where was Colin while all this carousing was taking place? 'Off to bed early because my nose is a bit rough.' He was also sickening for something. Within days, it had developed into full-blown influenza. So 'rough' was he that a stay in hospital was ordered and there he remained for five days.

The final Test of the rubber at Sydney was a damp squib, in every sense. It rained. And rained. Play did not start until after lunch on the fourth day. For the umpteenth time on the tour, Hutton kept his plans close to his chest. Even when he went out to toss, nobody was entirely sure who was playing.

Colin had only just come out of hospital and certainly wasn't expecting to have to get changed. Had the match started on time, somebody would have had to fetch him from his hospital but now, three days later, without practice or even a warm-up, he was informed by his captain that he most certainly *was* playing.

Bill Edrich was exhausted. After a long and illustrious career in the service of his country, he had finally shot his bolt. But who was going to open with Hutton? The captain returned from the toss, looked around the dressing room, his eyes lighted upon Tom Graveney and he said, 'Pad up, Tom. You're opening with me.' Graveney was astonished. He was not an opener, had never done it and, frankly, it was not a job he relished. But like Colin earlier on in the tour, when asked to fulfil a similar role, he didn't argue and walked out of the green-roofed and ornately designed pavilion at the SCG with Hutton to open the innings. He scored 111, his first (and only) hundred against the Australians.

Everybody contributed to a score of 371/7 declared, with the exception of Hutton himself, snared by his old nemesis Lindwall for eight, and Colin. 'I sit with my pads on while 180 is scored and then get a very quick 0, first ball to Ian Johnson. Everybody expected us to declare but Len decides to go on batting. They put us in and they had better bowl us out.' They didn't. Hutton did eventually declare but not before he had well and truly rubbed his opponents' noses in it.

There was time for England to force the follow-on but that was about it. The final act of the series had a touch of farce about it. Benaud had a wild heave against, would you believe, Hutton, who had brought himself on to indicate that, as far as he was concerned, the match was over, and was bowled. Immediately afterwards, the players shook hands and the game, and the series, really was over.

And how did our hero celebrate? 'I have a terrific haircut. I SMOKE MY SECOND CIGAR AND DO A CHURCHILL!' The capitals are his.

The tour, however, was not over. In those days, a two-Test series against New Zealand was tacked on to the end of the Australian leg. It is odd to hear the modern international cricketer complaining about the amount of time spent away from home. Although no one can deny that the schedule is punishing and the physical toll onerous, nothing can compare, surely, with six months continuously on the road. Or rail. Or sea.

It would be interesting to unearth what the players thought about a further month's cricket in New Zealand after the pressures and rigours of an Ashes series. They had achieved what they had set out to do. Now, they must have been tired and getting sick of each other's company. Colin believed that the party was more or less equally split in their feelings about the New Zealand leg. The older ones, married and with families, were not unnaturally keen to get home. The younger ones, with no family ties, especially those whose roles in Australia had been largely restricted to walk-on parts, were more sanguine. Colin only saw opportunity. 'All I wanted to do was play cricket,' he wrote.

In fact, the cricket was as dull as the country was beautiful and the inhabitants hospitable. The pitches were slow and low, the balls were of an inferior type and the opposition, frankly, second-rate. Colin preferred the ball to come on to the bat and was at his best when the heat was on. He did top score with 42 in a low-scoring first Test, in which Tyson took seven wickets, and England won comfortably by eight wickets.

The second game in the series provided an interesting footnote in Test match history. Tom Graveney told me the story. It featured Hutton. Of course it featured Hutton. Most of what had happened on this tour had featured Hutton. But on this occasion, he is seen at his wryly humorous best. 'Typical Len, really,' Graveney chuckled. 'New Zealand scored 200. We got 266. As he led us out to field, he announced, "Reet, lads, we've got a lead of 46. Just enough to beat 'em by an innings." And we did! We bowled them out for 26! It was all over in one and a half hours.' To this day, it remains the lowest total ever recorded in a Test match. It was also the final team talk of England's leader. He was mentally and physically exhausted and that was his last appearance on a Test match ground. He retired not long after.

By now, Colin had been informed that his mother was gravely ill, news that had been kept from him until the completion of the match. In view of the death of his father at the start of the tour, the very sensible decision was taken to send him home on the next available plane, with Graveney as his travelling companion.

On their circuitous journey back to England, via Fiji, Honolulu, San Francisco and New York, the two of them struck up a firm friendship that was to take in long careers in the game, often side-by-side, lasting up until the time of Colin's death. They were actually cut from the same cloth, though the tall, spare frame with the rubicund face that was Graveney's did not much resemble the fuller figure of Cowdrey. One came from the Dark Blue of Oxford, the other from the khaki of the army. But they both had a charm and ease of manner, they were both adored by cricket lovers the world over, they were both hero-worshipped in their home counties (Graveney had two) and they were both stylists with a bat in their hand.

Their Test records were remarkably similar. Graveney's average was 44.38 and Cowdrey's 44.06. They were both still playing Test cricket in their forties and their first-class careers were equally enduring; Graveney played for 24 years and Cowdrey for 26. They both, let us not forget, bowled a filthy brand of leg-spinners, which in Graveney's case snaffled 80 first-class victims and in Cowdrey's case, 65. In their retirement, they both assumed the highest position at Lord's, president of MCC. And both, surprisingly, shared an occasional crisis of confidence in their ability during their playing career.

'Were we great players?' mused Tom, during one such reminisce. 'Probably not. But we both played great innings.' Of the tour to Australia they had just undergone, they had time to look back and assess as they flew across half the globe. 'I hadn't had a great tour,' Tom confessed, 'but there, neither did other more experienced players, Bedser, Compton, Edrich, Len himself with the bat. It was clear that it was the youngsters who had won it for us, May and Cowdrey with the bat and Tyson and Statham with the ball. It was the changing of the guard really.'

Both felt that they were very much part of that future. But ironically, much as they loved Australia and its people, both were to be ultimately disappointed in their encounters with the old enemy on the field of play. Graveney's record against Australia was patchy, in direct contrast to the way his career flourished against other countries. And Colin's sadness at never leading an England team to Australia is an undercurrent that runs through this book.

* * * * *

Together with the rest of the cricket-loving supporters in England, Colin listened to the announcement of the MCC touring party to Australia and New Zealand for the winter of 1974/75 with more than passing interest. It had been three years since he had had any personal involvement in the list of names but he was still playing first-class cricket, he knew all the players involved – among whom he believed there would be a large Kent contingent – and he would have had his own opinions on the make-up of the team.

Did he harbour hidden hopes that, against all expectations, he would be called up again? After all, the selectors had surprised him once before, 20 years ago. Could lightning strike twice? He had been on five tours of Australia, one short of the record set by Johnny Briggs, who toured six times in the late 1800s. Should he not be satisfied with that doughty achievement and put his feet up in front of the fire for a well-deserved winter's rest? After all, he was 41 and county cricket, though still enjoyable, was taking a toll on his stamina.

But still something rankled in his heart, a feeling of being unfulfilled, a sense of a job not yet done. His fifth, and no doubt final, tour Down Under had been a deeply unhappy time. All his life, he had dreamed of leading England to Australia, a place he loved and where he was loved. It had never happened and once he had been passed over as captain for the 1970/71 tour in favour of Raymond Illingworth, he recognised that now he probably never would. He had lost form, he had been dropped and thereafter he remained a sad and peripheral figure among the tourists, past his sell-by date. He had not been selected for England again. It was the end.

Or was it? No player of the ability and stature of Colin Cowdrey ever really believes the game is up. There is always another innings, one last, glorious swansong, one final triumphant walk back to the pavilion, cap doffed and bat raised to the cheering crowd. So had he listened to the announcement of the touring party on the radio with just a slight twinge of hope, a vague fluttering of the heart? After all, he had been batting pretty well that summer. Not quite with the fluency and weight of runs of his heyday but he flattered himself that he could still cut the mustard at the highest level and nobody else, let's be fair, shared his experience and know-how of Australian conditions and Australian wickets.

Earlier in the season, he had been hit on the jaw and knocked out by a fearsome bouncer from Andy Roberts, something that had never happened to him before. For a few days afterwards, while recuperating, he had reflected upon this and asked himself, seriously, whether he was still up to facing the quickest of bowling. As we know, Colin and self-doubt were not entirely strangers. This is ridiculous, he told himself; it's time to get a grip. I can still do this.

He missed Kent's next game at The Oval but played the following week against Somerset. In both innings, he was done for by Hallam Moseley, another West Indian quick, and his confidence was at a low ebb. The next match was at Tunbridge Wells, against Hampshire, as fate would have it, and Roberts had Colin in his sights, the way fast bowlers do. You might say normal service was resumed. After softening him up with a few rapid bouncers, he had his prey snared at short leg, fending off another rib-cruncher.

Graham Johnson, Kent's all-rounder, told me much later, 'Colin was as white as a sheet when he came back into the dressing room. "I was nearly killed out there," he muttered. We said nothing because it wasn't far from the truth.'

I have the account of James Graham-Brown, a young lad on the Kent staff at the time, to describe what happened next. 'I lived quite near him; he used to pick me up in his car to go to matches. I was surprised to get a call from him to come over to his house. Of course, I did as I was asked. He said that he wasn't happy about his technique at facing bouncers and wanted me to throw balls at him from 15 yards, to sharpen up his reactions and to practise playing the short ball.

'I was astonished that someone as famous and as talented as he would admit to such doubts but admired his determination to climb back on the horse, so to speak. I threw balls at him until my arm ached, hoping I was doing him some good.'

Evidently he did because on his return to first team duty at Tunbridge Wells against Sussex, with John Snow at his most hostile, Colin made 107 out of a total of 282. For good measure, there was another masterful hundred, undefeated this time, against Gloucestershire, with Mike Procter bowling at full pelt. Nerve was restored and he was now firmly back in the saddle.

So, had the call come from the selectors, he believed he was ready. But of course, it never did. Alec Bedser, the chairman of selectors, was asked by a journalist whether they had considered Cowdrey for the touring party. 'Yes we did,' answered Bedser at his diplomatic best, 'but not for long.' The talking point among press and pub critics was the omission of John Snow and Geoff Boycott, both linchpins in Illingworth's successful tour in 1970/71. Boycott was on his self-imposed sabbatical; Snow's exclusion was less easily understood. Nobody was seriously thinking about Cowdrey. Refusing to admit to even a touch of disappointment, Colin lit the fire, put up his feet and watched the highlights on television.

Even he, used to horror stories in Brisbane for the first Test of an Ashes series, must have winced at the events that unfolded at the Gabba in early December 1974. A tornado blew into town and, as tornadoes do, it left a trail of devastation in its wake. The tornado's name was Thomson. There had been no blip on the radar, no severe weather warning, no prior battening down of hatches and boarding up of windows.

The England team had heard of Jeff Thomson but rather like Michael Fish on the BBC, they had discounted any possibility of a storm heading their way. Furthermore, Dennis Lillee had recently undergone surgery on a stress fracture of the back and was not thought to be anywhere near match fit. They were brutally disabused of both presumptions in an assault by the Australian fast bowlers that Christopher Martin-Jenkins, the BBC cricket correspondent covering the tour, described as 'so fearsome that even hardened campaigners in the press box were seen to blanch'.

In a nutshell, England were blown away, losing the Test by 166 runs. But it was the ferocious manner in which Lillee and Thomson hunted down their prey which sent shock waves through the England batsmen, an experience from which they did not recover, not until perhaps the Ashes had long since been lost. For some of them, it was a traumatic chapter from which they *never* recovered. Martin-Jenkins described Thomson's bowling at Brisbane thus, 'He bowled with stinging speed and got the ball to bounce from a good length with truly frightening malignity. Dennis Lillee, the fastest bowler in the world when last he had played against England, was made to look second best.'

That may have been so but as the series progressed and Lillee became more and more confident of his back, he bowled faster and faster. *Wisden* reported, 'Watching these two in action, it was easy to believe that they were the fastest pair ever to have coincided in a cricket team.'

Ironically, it was the Englishmen who had started the bouncer war. In Willis, Lever and Greig, they had the firepower to deliver short balls of pace, bounce and menace. Indeed, it could be said that the first person to drive a coach and horses through the unwritten law that tail-enders should be spared the short stuff was Tony Greig. That would hardly surprise those who knew and had been at the sharp end of the native South African's combative attitude on the field of play. He had dismissed Lillee with a bouncer in the first innings of the series and the mouthed response from the Australian as he quit the scene left no one in any doubt that the Poms could expect ample payback. Which is precisely what they got, tenfold.

The psychological effect of the fast bowling barrage on the England team was immediate. And it wasn't only their spirit that had been bruised. Bones too had been battered, some broken. Two front-line batsmen, Amiss and Edrich, had suffered fractures and were ruled out of the second Test at Perth, an even quicker and bouncier wicket than Brisbane. A replacement batsman was needed immediately. The management were in a quandary. The problem was not how but who. In these days of jet travel, a replacement could be flown out and be with them in 48 hours. In 1954/55, it would have taken three and a half weeks by sea.

No, the discussion centred on who could best cope with exceptional pace, such as few contemporary English batsmen had ever faced. Several names were put forward, Frank Hayes, John Jameson, Mike Harris and Barry Wood, who had all outscored Cowdrey in the recent English county season. But making runs on relatively benign English pitches was no preparedness for the blitzkrieg that lay in wait in Australia. Several of the senior members of the team put their heads together. In the words of Martin-Jenkins, 'In their hour of need, MCC turned to a man who for 20 years had played against the greatest fast bowlers in the world, one of the magical names of cricket, Michael Colin Cowdrey.'

So, why Cowdrey? Or, to put it another way, yes, of course Cowdrey, but why now, when he was 41? Nobody is the same player at 41 as he was at 21, or even 31. For an answer, I sought the views of several players who were on that tour. Derek Underwood said that, even at this late stage of his career, 'He was considered to be the best at playing the quicks.' Geoff Arnold remembered discussions among the team as to who would be the best bet. 'Kipper was as fine a player of fast bowling as there was,' he said, 'and to be honest, there were not many options.' Bob Willis made this observation, 'Here were Lillee and Thommo peppering our batsmen and we needed someone with experience who could counter them. I don't remember being consulted personally. It seemed the decision was made by the management, not the selectors back home. But I do know that Denness rated him very highly.'

There was the large Kent contingent in the party, he reminded me, all of whom knew Colin well and would have been firmly in his corner. For the record, the Kent group comprised the captain himself, Denness, Underwood, Knott and Luckhurst. Furthermore, battle-hardened warriors such as Amiss, Edrich, Fletcher, Greig and Titmus had been team-mates of his in England sides in the recent past and knew his pedigree. As Willis said, it was a *fait accompli*. It was not the press that shouted his name. It was not the management that chose him. It was not MCC back at Lord's that made the decision. It was not public opinion that clamoured for his recall. No, it was the players' initiative. And there is no greater accolade than a vote of confidence from your peers.

According to son Christopher, his father really did have his feet up in front of the fire but was actually listening to the Test on the radio when the call came, not watching it on the television. As Thomson and Lillee were running amok, Colin was uttering involuntary oohs and aahs as the England batsmen sparred, missed and ducked. One of the commentators remarked that what England needed was someone with experience and skill to take on this Australian attack, an old-fashioned player, someone like Cowdrey, for example. 'Quite so,' agreed Colin. At which point, Mike Denness, 10,000 miles away in Brisbane, picked up the phone and dialled Colin's home number. Would Colin be prepared to fly out and lend a hand to the beleaguered team was the question. Colin's reply was immediate. 'I'd love to.'

His family and friends thought he was mad. 'Dad,' Christopher reminded him, 'you're 41. Why on earth would you want to put yourself through all *that*?' The response was pure Colin. 'I think it will be rather fun.' He was, in cricketing terms, practically a pensioner, he hadn't picked up a bat since the conclusion of the previous season, he had everything to lose and little to gain by accepting and of course there was the real possibility of his getting injured, perhaps seriously, as other, younger batsmen on the tour had already discovered to their cost. But he was undaunted.

If his country came calling, who was he to refuse? After all, this was *Australia*, practically his second home. He packed his coffin, and after a quick net indoors at Sevenoaks, he boarded a Boeing 727 for Perth. The flight was not exactly uneventful. Following some engine trouble, the plane was diverted to Bombay, where there was a frustrating 22-hour delay while the technical hitch was fixed. Eventually, after a journey of 47 hours, rapid enough when compared to the voyage on SS *Orsova* 20 years previously, he landed in Perth.

A.C. Smith was the assistant manager of the MCC touring party and remembers driving to the airport to pick him up to take him to the team hotel. *How was he when you met him?* 'Oh, typically Colin,' A.C. smiled. 'There was a huge scrum of reporters and cameramen because everybody in the country was intrigued by England sending for an old man – a sure sign of desperation on our part – but he charmed everybody, smiling and chatting, not at all put out by all the hassle. He was asked what he felt about facing two of the most terrifying fast bowlers in the history of the game and he grinned and said something like, what have I got to worry about – after all, I have faced McDonald and Gregory in my time.' For the record, Jack Gregory and Ted McDonald had destroyed England in the Ashes series of 1921.

After a much-needed night's sleep, he was in the nets early the next day. He was fortunate, and grateful, that two former sparring partners, Tony Lock, currently coaching in Perth, and Graham McKenzie, still a regular in the Western Australian side, bowled and bowled to him in the hot Perth sunshine. Colin was keen that McKenzie, who had lost little of his pace even at a late stage of his career, should not hold back. McKenzie, a surprisingly gentle soul for a fast bowler, did not but he could not stop himself warning Colin when he was going to send down a bouncer.

As a start, it had seemed to go well but Colin was perfectly aware that a couple of net practices was no adequate preparation for playing in a Test match. He needed time in the middle. And that was precisely what he was not going to get. For all that, Woodcock observed, 'Cowdrey could have done no more to cram two months' practice into three days,' and Martin-Jenkins wrote, 'He went through his preparation with all the calm dignity of a bishop, with time, a word and a smile for everyone.'

It would be interesting to pick Colin's brains about his feelings as he embarked on his sixth tour of Australia, whether he was excited, apprehensive, intimidated by the prospect of putting his reputation, to say nothing of his creaking body, on the line in the service of his country when a cosy fire, with a drink to hand, might well have seemed the more attractive proposition. Alas, he is no longer with us to ask. He would not have confided in friends and team-mates. Not really. What top-class sportsman ever admits publicly to doubts and misgivings?

But here, at this juncture, I stumbled upon some gold dust among his papers. In his unpublished book, which he only had time to jot down in draft form before he died, I discovered a whole chapter on fast bowling and how to play it. His comments on coping with Lillee and Thomson are illuminating.

On the long flight from the UK, he did give the matter some thought. Plenty of it apparently. Analytical as always about his cricket, he pondered how best to combat what he called 'two of the most hostile bowlers that have ever been'. Was he scared, he asked himself. Nobody enjoys facing fast bowling; if he says different, he is a bluffer. Colin was no exception. In the back of every batsman's mind is the worry of getting hit. He averred, 'More players are more scared of getting hit on the head than they would like to admit.'

But he felt 'relaxed' about the battle that lay ahead, for three reasons. First, he had been facing fast bowlers for 20 years and believed that he had 'learnt a few tricks along the way'. Above all, he was confident of his technique. Secondly, he reckoned he was 'a better player under hot sunshine, good light and faster pitches'. And thirdly, he was sure that he would be able to watch and observe Lillee and Thomson from the dressing room while he acclimatised.

On the first two counts, he was proved right. On the third, his optimism was greatly misplaced. 'It never crossed my mind that I would be playing in the Test match at Perth,' he wrote. The injury crisis, one that Alec Bedser described as the like of which he could not remember in all his years in cricket, was worse than Colin realised. The touring party was down to 11 fit men on the morning of the match and he was in. England won the toss, elected to bat and back came Denness from the middle to inform Colin he was batting at number three. At the very least, he had expected to be tucked away somewhere in the middle order but no, prime position it was to be. The best batsman in the side normally takes the number three slot so it was with that characteristic ironic little smile that he padded up.

Tony Greig watched him closely. 'As Colin released the lock of his cricket case,' he later wrote, 'it sprang open as if alive. Then gradually, like bread rising in an oven, a mountain of foam rubber rose from the interior. This was Cowdrey's protection and he had obviously been well briefed. He padded almost every part of his body but nobody laughed. We had seen enough to convince ourselves he was right.' And then Colin took his place in a seat to watch the opening overs. Not for nothing was the seat known as The Condemned Man's Chair.

I wasn't being strictly accurate when I said he was unable to watch the Australian opening attack from the sidelines; in point of fact he had one hour in that chair before the first wicket fell and up he stood, putting on his gloves and cap, to go out and meet his Maker, as some of the team dryly put it. I leave it to Martin-Jenkins to describe the scene, 'It was the signal for tears to prick the eyes of all but the stony-hearted. For out of the pavilion, rotund beneath his MCC sweater, blue England cap proudly worn, stepped Colin Cowdrey in his 110th Test match and his first for three and a half years. A great crescendo of applause greeted him as, with his old familiar walk, stooping slightly forwards as he moved, he strode out to face the music.' Who ever said that Australians were an unsentimental lot?

That is with the exception perhaps of captain Ian Chappell and the twin spearhead of his attack. The exchange between Colin and Jeff Thomson, once he had gained the middle, has gone down in cricket folklore. That has more to do with Thomson, because it takes the form of his *piece de resistance* in interviews, cabaret acts and after-dinner speeches at which he is invited to reminisce.

Colin would have thought the little chit chat hardly out of the ordinary, merely a snippet of polite, everyday intercourse. Thomson always says that he will remember the scene to his dying day, 'This 41-year-old man, with a teardrop figure, walking up the wicket, past the umpire to where I was ready to bowl, all revved up to kill someone and this bloke comes up to me and says, "Mr Thomson, I believe. It's good to meet you."' Thomson's alleged riposte tends to differ depending on the composition of his audience. It is either, 'Piss off, fatso, that's not gonna help you,' or, 'Good luck if you think that's gonna be any help.'

I will leave you to decide which is the more likely. All I shall say is that the greeting was a world away from Keith Miller's on Colin's first appearance in the middle at a Test match, 'G'day, young Cowdrey.' Mind you, he did follow up that cheery greeting with a bouncer first ball.

'There was a strong wind blowing down the ground,' noted Colin, 'and Thomson and Lillee took it in turns to bowl downwind, with Max Walker, a fine bowler in his own right, with an economical action, upwind.' How did he cope? More than one onlooker feared he might not. Derek Underwood thought he looked old and feared he was past it. John Woodcock, by now a firm friend of Colin's, said that he felt as shaky as if his own son were facing and had to take himself off to the bar to calm his nerves.

He was sure that Colin got away with a confident LBW shout first ball and then watched in admiration as 'the old boy got stuck in'. Bob Willis knew what a fine player Colin had been but privately wondered whether 'this Falstaffian figure, now 41, still had it in him'. Geoff Arnold and others in the dressing room 'marvelled at the old fella's courage but doubted that he should ever have been put in this position'.

How did 'the old fella' manage? In his own words, 'What I did was to give myself a strong talking to between balls. It went like this – no backlift, right fingers on splice, move back early, stand motionless, head and eyes still.'

Those who have faced fast bowling might say that there is nothing revolutionary in all this. It makes sense. Easy to say, of course, not so easy to implement. Discipline was paramount, according to Colin's model, deciding which balls to play and which to leave. 'Anything wide or higher than the stumps, leave alone. Then, when the eye is in, certain shots come into play, the defensive push for one, or the odd stroke for four. All the rest can wait until later in the innings.'

This simple but effective technique had been developed over years of trial and error. His mind went back 14 years, to a torrid time in the West Indies, when he had been thrown in at the deep end and forced to 'learn a hard lesson'. Not for the first time, and certainly not for the last, he had been asked to open. Together with Geoff Pullar, he had gone out in Trinidad to take on the might of a triumvirate of West Indian fast bowlers, Wes Hall, Charlie Griffith and Chester Watson, and had found the experience overwhelming. He had been dismissed for 18 and five and he retired to his hotel room in a gloomy frame of mind. 'Clearly, they were too quick for me. I had to adapt my technique.' Pretty successfully, it transpired. In the next Test, he made 114 and 97 and thereafter, with a great deal of practice in the nets, he perfected his craft.

The crucial factor was stillness at the crease. 'A clear photograph needs a still head. Therefore, must move back and across before delivery. But don't put weight on back foot and get stuck there. Balance on ball of foot, ready to spring into action for any shot (or evasive action). It's amazing how many balls can actually be left alone.' In the end, he said, the repetition of movement became a sort of jingle in his head, 'Move early. Stop still. Ready to pounce or leave alone.'

Derek Randall used to sing 'God Save the Queen' as Dennis Lillee ran in to bowl. Marcus Trescothick's favoured refrain at the crease was by Eminem. Michael Clark would hum 'When The Saints Go Marching In'. *Chacun a son gout.*

And what about the ball which rears up from just short of a length and is impossible to avoid, 'getting big on you' as they say nowadays? This was Colin's method of self-preservation, 'In pre-helmet days, I used to use the left shoulder as a defensive buffer, as a last resort to shield the head, particularly in those awful moments when you lose sight of the ball as it comes off the pitch.'

Thankfully, he did not lose sight of it as came off the lightning-fast Perth track. He took a few blows but for the most part, it was gritty and resolute defence. Between overs, he wandered down the pitch to chat to his batting partner, David Lloyd. He did not know Lloyd well. There had been no leisurely six weeks aboard ship to get to know each other; the two of them had not even shared a flight. Lloyd has recounted the story many times. 'This is fun, isn't it?' Colin remarked. Lloyd's reply was pure Lancashire. 'Ah can think of foonier places than this!'

At length, after 125 minutes of what Martin-Jenkins described as 'a splendid and courageous example to less plucky team-mates', Colin was bowled leg stump, perhaps shuffling across too far this time, for 22. In the second innings, who emerged from the dressing room to open with Lloyd instead of the injured Brian Luckhurst but the comfortable figure of Colin Cowdrey?

Once again, he had been pressed into service, unwillingly but uncomplainingly, at the top of the order. He was there, looking on horrified at the other end when Lloyd was struck amidships by a thunderbolt from Thomson, another old chestnut that Lloyd has delighted his audiences with over the years. It was of course no laughing matter at the time.

It begs the question, how fast was Thomson? He was once measured by a speed gun as bowling at 98mph but Thommo being Thommo, he always said that the experiment had been carried out in the nets, it was a cold day and he had not even taken his sweater off. 'Aw look mate, I was only in fourth gear,' he claimed. 'I had another gear to go.' Those speed guns were notoriously unreliable anyway and have now disappeared from Test match grounds. Was he faster than Tyson? Larwood? Shoaib Akhtar was once timed at 100mph but Bob

His father gave him the name Michael Colin Cowdrey. The initials was no blunder.

Under the watchful eye of the faithful family retainer, Krishnan.

Colin's father, Ernest, was a keen sportsman himself, when able to take time away from his tea plantation in the Nilgiri Hills in India. The young Colin already knew how to handle a golf club.

Colin became the youngest player ever to appear at Lord's as a 13-year-old as a member of the Tonbridge School XI.

Colin made his first-class debut for Kent v West Indies in 1950, aged 17 and still at school.

Colin scored his maiden Test century against Australia at Melbourne on the 1954/55 tour. Here he is playing his favourite shot, the cover drive.

Len Hutton's MCC team to Australia 1954/55. Colin (middle row, second from right) was only 21 and still an Oxford undergraduate.

In that majestical first Test century of 102, out of a total of 191 – crucial in the context of the match – Colin played as well as he ever did. Keith Miller, at first slip, would seem to agree. Not much is coming my way, his pose seems to be suggesting.

In 1956, Colin married Penny Chiesman. Rev. David Sheppard took the service and Peter May was best man, both England team-mates.

Colin was a fine exponent of
the game of rackets. In 1952,
he was runner-up to world
champion, Geoffrey Atkins,
in the Amateur Singles at
Queen's.

That stand! Peter May and Colin Cowdrey
acknowledge the crowd's applause at Edgbaston
during their record stand of 411 v West Indies in 1957.

The full-blooded sweep shot, down on one knee, was never in Colin's repertoire. He
preferred the 'paddle', here executed against Australia.

Colin was always a man of Kent, and remained loyal to his county all his life. Here he clips the ball through midwicket against Yorkshire at Gravesend in 1963.

Touring was not all cricket. Colin discusses field placing with Princess Margaret and Anthony Armstrong-Jones during one of his visits to the Caribbean.

England v South Africa at Lord's 1960. Top l to rt: Jim Parks, Ray Illingworth, Peter Walker, Alan Moss, Mike Smith, Ken Barrington. Seated l to rt: Ted Dexter, Raman Subba Row, Colin Cowdrey (c), Brian Statham, Fred Trueman.

England tour of Australia 1962/63. England's captain, Ted Dexter, in discussion with Tom Graveney and Colin Cowdrey.

England v West Indies at Lord's 1966. The two captains, Colin Cowdrey and Garry Sobers, toss for innings. Both were knighted, incidentally.

It is often overlooked what a fine slip fielder Colin was. Here he catches Bill Lawry off the bowling of David Allen at Melbourne on the 1965/66 tour of Australia. It was Allen's first Test wicket.

That cover drive! You will never see a more beautiful stroke. Body balanced, head over the ball, leading with the top hand, showing the maker's name (Slazenger, always!).

England v Australia at The Oval, 1968. The moment of victory.

In 1970, their centenary year, Kent won the county championship. For Colin (captain, centre) and Les Ames (manager, on Colin's left), the campaign had been a lifetime's crusade.

Benson and Hedges final at Lord's, 1973.

On 4 July, 1974, at Maidstone against Surrey, Colin completed his 100th first-class century. Asif Iqbal was batting with him at the time.

Ouch! Colin suffers a blow to the ribs, hit by Jeff Thomson on the 1974/75 tour of Australia.

In 1970, following Kent's triumph in the county championship, Prime Minister Ted Heath, MP for Bexley in Kent, invited Colin and the team to a celebratory party in 10 Downing Street.

Colin Cowdrey was chairman of the International Cricket Council from 1989–93, during which time he was largely instrumental in engineering South Africa's return to international cricket.

Colin is greeted by Nelson Mandela on one of his diplomatic missions as chairman of the ICC.

John Major, a lifelong lover of cricket, was a close friend of Colin's. Frequently, they would chat over a whisky in 10 Downing Street at the end of a day of political turmoil.

In 1997, Colin was created a peer, Baron Cowdrey of Tonbridge, by the prime minister, John Major, with the specific purpose of bringing a voice to the House of Lords to extend sporting opportunities for the young.

This picture was taken one week before Colin had his stroke, which in turn was six months before he died. He was playing for President's XI v Leatherhead CC, along with his three sons. This is probably the last photo taken of him.

AFRICAN NATIONAL CONGRESS

25th September 1991

Mr Collin Cowdrey
Chairman
ICC Lordes Cricket Ground
St. John's Wood
London NW8 SQN
UK

Dear Mr Cowdrey,

The United Cricket Board of South Africa is making an application to participate in the World Cricket Cup Competition due to take place in Australia and New Zealand in February, 1992.

In this regard the ANC wishes to inform the International Cricket Council that the ANC fully supports the application of the United South African Cricket Board. We would gratefully appreciate it if permission was granted for their participation in that competition.

The United South African Cricket Board is a non-racial, democratic body and it has cricket development programmes which it is implementing throughout South Africa. Further, their participation in that competition will enhance the process of unity in sport as well as the spirit of reconciliation generally in my country.

With warmest regards

Nelson R Mandela
President

As soon as Colin received this letter from Nelson Mandela, he knew his quest to get South Africa re-admitted to international cricket after its exile would succeed.

Portrait of Colin Cowdrey in the Long Room at Lord's.

Willis told me that was with 'the advantage of a bent arm more than the legal 15 per cent'. He went on to say that it was undeniably true that 'Thommo was the quickest I have ever played with or against, and that includes all those West Indian pacemen of the 1970s.'

Geoff Arnold told me that he did not believe it was possible for anyone to bowl faster. But it wasn't so much the sheer speed that undid the England batsmen, it was the fierce lift he got, together with the unusual slinging action, that surprised them, then hit them, then demoralised them. I remember talking to the Kent boys during the summer following this tour. They told me that Luckhurst went white whenever talk of the tour surfaced; he was so shell-shocked. He was not alone. It did for the international careers of quite a few of that team. Or as John Edrich wryly observed to his batting partner, Fred Titmus, during one particularly brutal onslaught, 'One tour too many, Fred.'

Through it all, Colin was batting with a calmness that was extraordinary. Once again, 'he set an example', wrote Martin-Jenkins, 'to team-mates that ought to have been shamed by the way he was withstanding two of the fastest bowlers in the world after only five days' practice.' The coveted three-figure score that even the partisan Perth crowd would not have begrudged was not to be; he was LBW to Thomson for 41. Some might say that 41, on that pitch, against that attack, in that situation would have been worth a hundred at other times in other parts of the world. It was all in vain though. England were routed by nine wickets. Colin felt he had done himself justice. His tried and tested technique had withstood the most searching of examinations and he was happy with that. Alec Bedser agreed, 'He has done far more than we could possibly have asked of him.'

By now, England were a beaten team. The Ashes were finally surrendered at Sydney in the fourth Test but the result had been a foregone conclusion long before that. Even if the Grand Old Man, as Colin had been dubbed, had been able to summon up the heroics of yesteryear, it is doubtful it would have made much of a difference. It is doubtful that *any* batting side in world cricket would have been able to withstand the onslaught from Lillee and Thomson, which bordered on the savage at times.

Everybody I have spoken to who faced them on that tour is adamant that there were times when life and limb were at risk. 'Thommo hit me on the elbow before I'd even picked my bat up,' Arnold said. 'And

Lillee towards the end was bowling just as quick. He bowled a ball at me that flew past my nose, over Marsh's head and disappeared one bounce into the crowd. They all said I didn't see it and I could have been killed. Dunno about that. I saw it go past me but I couldn't do very much about it.' Let's not forget that tail-enders had to bat as well and there was no let-up in the ferocity of the barrage. To put the travails of the England side into context, it is as well to have it in mind that the West Indies, with a batting line-up comprising Fredericks, Greenidge, Rowe, Kallicharan, Richards and Lloyd, fared no better the following season in Australia. England lost the series 4-1. The West Indies lost 5-1.

Colin made no significant score in the remaining Tests but constant references to his courage were made on both sides of the press divide, as he seemed to be the one continually taking the brunt of the Thomson-Lillee assault. Several times, he settled in, content to take the sting out of the fast bowlers, but failed to go on to make the large score that none would have begrudged. 'His defence was flawless,' wrote Martin-Jenkins, 'but his attacking shots in front of the wicket were no longer at his beck and call.'

For all that, I sense it was a happy farewell to his Test career. 'Far happier than his previous tour to Australia,' Willis told me. 'On that tour, 1970/71, which seemed at the time to be the end for him, he cut a sad, disconsolate figure, for reasons that are well documented. But on this tour, he felt at home and enjoyed himself.'

Was he part of the team? By that I mean, did he socialise and integrate or was he a bit distant once play had ended for the day? 'Well, he wasn't one who propped up the bar in the evenings. That wasn't his style. But he was very much part of the team and was a helpful and encouraging presence in the dressing room. He had been on six tours there, don't forget, so he had loads of friends all over the place and would go out to dinner with them. He'd invite one or two of us along sometimes, if he felt we'd be interested. He was an amateur really, although amateurs no longer officially existed. That was the era in which he grew up so it was no surprise that he knew all these important people all over the country. He was fine, a real gentleman, in the old-fashioned sense.'

Arnold was in complete agreement. 'Kipper was a good lad, one of the team. I didn't know him well beforehand but I found him to be a really nice chap. An utter gent.'

How was team spirit? It must have taken a bit of a hammering. There must have been times when everybody wished it could just finish and they could all go home? Arnold disagreed. 'People said that team spirit was poor and a few of the press blamed the presence of wives for part of the time for breaking up the camaraderie that you build up on tour. Not true. Team spirit was fine. Some of us weren't too keen on Denness as a captain but that was on the field. Off it, we got along fine and although results were not going our way, we did our best to enjoy it.'

He then went on to make a valid and significant point. 'Look,' he said, warming to his theme, 'people are *still* talking about that series. Often, I'm stopped and asked about that tour and what it was like playing against Lillee and Thomson. It was a famous series and we felt privileged to have been a part of it. Of course it was uncomfortable at times but what an experience!'

At the end of the series, after England had won the sixth and final Test at Melbourne (both Lillee and Thomson were injured, by the way), the Australian crowd unfurled a banner over the boundary railings, 'MCG fans thank Colin – 6 tours'.

Ever mindful of his manners and grateful for the gesture, Colin made a point of going over there to chat and to sign autographs, for an age it seemed. Nothing was ever too much trouble for him. Willis laughed at the memory and added a subtext to the happy scene. 'As Colin walked past, raising his bat on his way back to the dressing room for the last time, some young wag shouted out, "Hey, Cowdrey, you're a podgy fucker!" When Colin went over there to sign autographs, he signed himself PF!'

5

Ever the Bridesmaid

Test Cricketer 1955–67

'It would have saved me a great deal of pain.'

Colin Cowdrey's remark on being
recalled – again – to the England captaincy
and being sacked – again.

I T must have occurred to Colin as he set foot on the tarmac back in England on his return from Australia after the 1954/55 tour, if it had not occurred to him before, that everything had changed. He was still, officially anyway, an undergraduate of Oxford University, having been given leave of absence by Brasenose College to go on tour. He had not taken his finals.

His tutors were expecting him back. The college had a fine sporting tradition and it was hoped that he would lead the Dark Blues to victory against Cambridge that summer – at last. But he was now an established England cricketer. So what was it to be, Lord's in the Varsity match or Lord's in a Test match?

A.C. Smith gave a characteristic guffaw when I brought up this conundrum. He was also a Brasenose man and though he and Colin did not overlap at Oxford – four years separated the two – the precedent of the older student's experience impacted significantly on the younger.

'Colin had been given time off by BNC to go to Australia,' A.C. recounted, 'on the understanding that he came back to finish his studies and take his degree.' Again that Smith laugh filled the room. 'By that of course they meant to play cricket. But it was impossible. There was no way he could go back! The situation had changed. So when he left, they were not best pleased. I know that for a fact because when I asked for leave of absence to go on tour, they refused, worried that I would do a runner, like Colin.'

Brasenose's displeasure was not long-lasting. Colin later made his peace with the college and became president of the BNC Society and was instrumental in bringing A.C. back into the fold to succeed him in that position.

If Colin was quietly relieved that he would never again have to enter an examination hall, an examination of another kind was now at the forefront of his mind. He may have been able to extricate himself from further academic study but the RAF and National Service were not to be denied. To those of us from a different generation, the very idea of spending two years in the armed services when a military career holds no interest or appeal seems unimaginable but for Colin's generation it was a fact of life. He made his calculations; if he signed up immediately, he would be free to resume his cricket career in the summer of 1957, just in time for the West Indians. With hindsight, he would therefore have missed 11 Tests, one century and 626 runs.

The old injury, however, was to spare him the square bashing, though the resulting controversy left him in no doubt that being excused National Service on medical grounds was something of a mixed blessing. As instructed, he presented himself for a physical examination by the RAF doctors. Following the winter in Australia, he had, in his own words, 'a suntan like a Red Indian' and he cannot have appeared to be anything other than in the rudest of health. But somewhere in his notes, there was the reference to the trouble with his feet and the operation he had undergone while at Tonbridge. Perplexed, the medics referred him to a consultant in London, who took one look at his toes and had him discharged from service with immediate effect.

So far, so good. No doubt relieved to be excused from military duty, he discarded a blue uniform and donned a white one, at the same time running into a rich vein of form. Successive scores of 44, 101, 5,

139, 48, 44, 115* and 103* would have been welcome at any other time but he had not reckoned on the fierce censure of the British public. No matter that he had been a linchpin of Hutton's Ashes-winning team Down Under, he was now dodging the draft, pulling a fast one, taking the authorities for a ride, hoodwinking Matron for an off-games chit, in short, exploiting his connections in high places to evade his duty. How could anyone who scores 600 runs in a fortnight possibly be considered 'unfit'?

He went from hero to zero almost overnight. Once the press got hold of the story, the criticism was relentless and merciless. Worse, the poison pen letters started to pour in, some of them deeply upsetting. We shouldn't forget that Colin was still only 21 and though he had been through the fire of an Ashes series, he was yet an *ingénue* in worldly affairs. He was no seasoned politician, accustomed to public scrutiny and media derision. He was a sensitive soul, wary of criticism and uncomfortable with friction and discord.

Willie Hamilton, the Labour MP for West Fife, in a speech made this cutting observation, 'If he is fit to undertake a tour of Australia, surely he is fit to peel spuds in the RAF.' And then Colin's name was brought up in the House of Commons by Gerald Nabarro, Conservative MP for Kidderminster, he of the handlebar moustache and Terry-Thomas accent, in a question about the privileged few who were able to pull a few strings and 'dodge the column' when every other fit male of a certain age had to do National Service.

Up until now, Colin had done his best, as you would expect, to keep a low profile, taking the trouble to reply to all those letters – the ones that were not anonymous, that is – explaining the situation. But this attack angered him and he wrote a polite rebuke to Nabarro at Westminster, laying out the facts. 'By return of post,' he wrote, 'I was invited to meet him in his room in the House.'

The two had a fruitful discussion and it was not long before the young cricketer, naturally charming and emollient, had the crusty old parliamentarian eating out of his hand. Nabarro apologised profusely, his being ignorant of the facts of Colin's particular case, and they both agreed on the wording of a public communiqué, absolving Colin of any charge of exerting undue influence in high places.

In Colin's papers lies the original letter, on House of Commons notepaper, written in Nabarro's ornate, slightly rococo, hand:

'A meeting took place in the House of Commons on Wednesday evening 6th May 1955 between Mr Colin Cowdrey and Mr Gerald Nabarro to discuss the questions in the House during the last few weeks concerning National Service liabilities.

'Mr Nabarro wishes to state unequivocally that he recognises no attempt was made by Mr Cowdrey either prior to, or during, his service in the Royal Air Force to secure exemption or even deferment of National Service. Mr Nabarro expressed his regret to Mr Cowdrey for any construction to the contrary arising from Mr Nabarro's comments in the House.........

'Mr Cowdrey and Mr Nabarro have agreed that the matter is now amicably settled.

'Signed: Gerald Nabarro

'Countersigned: Colin Cowdrey'

Colin said he and the MP had parted on excellent terms. Thereafter, Gerald Nabarro concentrated on his endorsement of the Severn Valley Railway project, restoration of steam trains and dismantled lines being a particular hobby of his, and Colin returned to first-class cricket, perfectly executed cover drives being a particular hobby of his. The furore died down and the offensive letters dwindled, though never entirely. But the episode had scarred him. Thereafter, he remained wary of politicians, the popular press and public posturing.

There were in fact precious few cover drives in evidence when Colin was recalled to the Test side for the third match of the series against South Africa that season. Having been rapped on the knuckles for the umpteenth time by the Springbok pair of fast bowlers, Neil Adcock and Peter Heine, he might have thought wistfully that a bit of spud peeling in the RAF was not such a bad idea after all.

He made one in the first innings and therefore had plenty of time to watch one of Denis Compton's virtuoso displays with the bat. Not Compton's bat, you understand. He had left his own bat at home (all these stories about his forgetfulness, carelessness and lack of punctuality were true, it seems) so he had borrowed one of Fred Titmus's ancient blades and with England's score perilously placed at 75/4, he played like only he could to finish the day unbeaten on 155. Oh that such fluency had been at Colin's beck and call in the second innings; he scored 50, painfully accumulated over four hours. There was no way his bruised hands would allow him play in the fourth

Test but he was hopeful of declaring himself fit for the fifth and final match but another blow on the hand, this time from Trevor Bailey, put paid to that.

There was no overseas tour that winter and Colin was faced with an uncomfortable headache, one that had been afflicting him on and off ever since the RAF fiasco. He was an amateur and amateurs did not get paid. His father was now dead, his mother was back home but not in the best of health, he had no job and money was tight.

At which point in his life, enter, stage left, another individual who was to have a huge impact on his life. Stuart Chiesman, a member of the family that owned a large drapery store in Lewisham, as well as a chain of smaller stores around the south-east of England, was a Kent committee member and a great supporter and benefactor of the club. He served for 18 years on the committee before becoming chairman in 1959, a post he held until his death ten years later. His beneficence did not start and end with Kent cricket, generous though that might have been. He had been wounded twice in the First World War and as a result of his experiences, had set up and largely funded a charity for servicemen who had been blinded in the conflict.

According to Derek Ufton, a team-mate of Colin's in his early days at the club, Chiesman 'was a very nice man, much more approachable than committee men usually were in those days and he was in the habit of offering young players without winter employment a job in his store to tide them over'. Colin was no exception. Having been offered the job, he accepted with alacrity.

The eyes do widen a little at this point. We have Colin Cowdrey entering the lift of a department store owned by Grace Brothers, making small talk with Mrs Slocombe and Miss Brahms as he is whisked up to the floor for gentlemen's clothing, there to be instructed in the retail trade by Captain Peacock and Mr Rumbold. Colin professed that he found the experience 'fascinating' but I bet he wasn't being entirely truthful. Still, he was grateful and did his best not to confound his colleagues too much.

After a while, he began to forge a niche for himself. The intricacies of managing a department store may well have left him scratching his head but quickly he realised that his name 'began to have a certain commercial value'. This knack of chatting to people and making them feel at ease was to stand him in even greater stead in later appointments on boards and governing bodies. For the time being, he was content to potter, occasionally with time on his hands. Frustratingly, that never seemed to happen on a Saturday, when he was anxious, but would never dare, to slip away to watch Charlton Athletic at The Valley. Coincidentally, the aforesaid Derek Ufton, who gained a cap for England 'at football, let me tell you, though I would much rather it had been for cricket', would come along to see Colin in the store.

'Colin would be at a bit of a loose end,' he said. 'I was playing for Charlton at the time, so I had a winter job and had no need to take up the offer of work that Chiesman gave to the other young players. Anyway, I would get this call from Colin to go and have a coffee with him after training. I would present myself at the store and instead of being shown up to the boardroom or somewhere swanky like that, we would end up in the telephonist's office, a small pokey room right at the top of the building. To this day I remember the telephonist pulling out the wires and plugging them back in as they used to do on those old switchboards. And there we'd have our coffee and chat. Lovely, lovely man Colin. He had so much time for everybody, even the telephone girl.'

Cheekily, Ufton asked his Kent team-mate why he wasn't yet on the board at Chiesmans. Oh but he was, Colin answered, in fact there was a board meeting going on at that very moment. 'But I don't usually attend,' he added, with that wry Cowdrey smile.

Colin's financial well-being was now secure and he was free to pursue his career in cricket without those money worries that had forced the premature retirement from the game of innumerable amateurs down the years. Two of his contemporaries, Peter May and Ted Dexter, left the game before they might have done for that very reason. Dexter made no bones about it. 'Somebody's got to pay the bills,' he said.

But there was a bit more to Chiesman's generosity than merely securing employment for one of Kent's most promising. It was clear to anyone with half a brain that Colin was being groomed for the Kent captaincy. He had all the necessary attributes – Tonbridge School, Oxford University and now an established England player. And, above all, he was an amateur. Professional captains had broken into the officer corps but they were few and far between. Chiesman would have known this and as a mover and shaker at the club, he would have taken it upon himself to ensure Colin's smooth transition to the post.

He had taken care of the young man's financial future; now, what about his love life? Men in high places like to take on the role of puppet master, even if their motives are honourable and kindly meant. He had two daughters, one of whom regularly attended home matches with him and was very keen on the game.

Penny Chiesman was, by all accounts, a force of nature. 'I knew her well,' said Ufton. 'She would often chat to the players after the match and she was a delightful girl.' David Kemp had known her even longer, when she was a young girl. 'We used to play a lot of tennis. She was bright, attractive and, dare I say it, a bit naughty. She was expelled from school, as I remember, but I don't know what for, so it can't have been all that serious. I liked her enormously.' John Woodcock remembered her as a 'lively, striking woman with an energy bordering on the indefatigable'.

How much her father manipulated the situation is unclear but she was ever present at social functions at the club and it was not long before people noticed that she and Colin 'would pair off', as Kemp put it. 'She adored Colin,' he went on to explain, 'as indeed did all women, for he had such excellent manners and he was, let's face it, a good catch.' *At first slip now, it seemed.* 'You know what I mean,' he gently chided me.

Colin married Penny the following summer, in 1956. Peter May was his best man and Rev. David Sheppard officiated at the ceremony. It was a match made, if not in heaven, then on the playing fields of Kent, which supporters of that county would have you believe is one and the same thing.

Stuart Chiesman may well have privately harboured even warmer feelings than having the future Kent, and, who knows, England, captain for a son-in-law. Four years previously, he had lost his son in the most tragic and dramatic circumstances. The boy had been attending the Farnborough Air Show together with his governess. A De Havilland 110 had just broken the sound barrier but then broke up in a manoeuvre owing to a fault in the wing design and had plummeted to earth. Thirty-one people, including the pilot, were killed in the ensuing inferno. Among the dead were Chiesman's son and the governess.

Is it too capricious to imagine that Colin would become the son he had lost? And would it be stretching conjecture too far to suppose that Chiesman would become, in turn, another father figure to Colin? Certainly Colin's regard for his father-in-law never wavered and he was deeply upset when he died.

Like all cricketers who get impatient with an enforced winter break, Colin's pulse must have quickened as the 1956 season approached, and, what's more, the Australians were in town. His form was good leading into the Tests but his mood was possibly less so. The selectors again had asked Kent to open with him with a view to his opening the batting for his country on a full-time basis. Who was he to rebuff the request but he was ambivalent about the assignment. The selectors' ploy met with only moderate success. His partner throughout the series was Peter Richardson, who was by nature and upbringing an opener, and together they put on stands of 53 and 151, 22 and 35, 2, 174, 1 and 17 over the five Tests but Colin was unhappy with his contributions and felt, as did everybody else, that a series average of 30.50 was underwhelming.

Notwithstanding his own travails, he was right there in the middle of two memorable and extraordinary events in Ashes history. The first was over in a blink of an eye; the second took longer to evolve. At Lord's in the second Test, which Australia won, Colin was playing well in the first innings, on 23 at the time, when he received a half-volley outside off from Ken Mackay. He laid into it. Though the ball swung fractionally at the last moment, which meant that he hit it squarer than he had intended, he had timed the shot so well that he fully expected it to race to the boundary. Richie Benaud at gully intercepted it and with astonishing reflexes managed to hold on to it, the force of the shot knocking him backwards.

The moment was caught on camera and the press very soon dubbed it 'The Catch of the Century'. The photo shows Benaud with the ball in one hand, leading to the popular perception that he had caught it one-handed. He had not. As he was knocked off balance, one hand had shot out involuntarily to break his fall. When dismissed by such a flash of brilliance, there is nothing for it other than to give a resigned shrug of the shoulders and depart, which Colin did.

The second unforgettable episode took five days, more or less, if we take into account breaks for rain. Already, England's off-spinner,

Jim Laker, had undermined Australia's confidence by taking 11-113 in the third Test at Headingley, helping the home side to victory by an innings and 42 runs. In the fourth Test at Old Trafford, he crushed them, taking 19-90, in what was to go down in history as 'Laker's Match'. Merely writing down those figures, 19 wickets, has a surreal feeling to it.

To take every wicket bar one in a two-innings match is nigh on impossible but the eyes do not deceive, the evidence is there in the scorecard. It is a feat that has never been equalled and it seems scarcely credible that it ever will. Colin had the best view of unfolding events at his customary station at first slip.

The question perennially asked is how Laker took 19 wickets and Lock, an equally destructive bowler on these pitches, took only one. Like everybody else, Colin had no answer to this; that is just the way the cookie crumbles sometimes. He did offer an opinion, one that *might* have contributed to the disproportionate bowling analyses. He felt that Lock bowled a fraction too fast, so desperate was he to join in the turkey shoot, whereas Laker bowled with control and accuracy, eschewing variation of speed and turn, relying on the pitch to do its worst. It was 'ruthlessly efficient', he wrote.

In actual fact, he had caught Burke, Australia's opener, in the first innings to give Lock his one and only wicket. One wonders whether he might have spilled it had it been the last wicket to fall, in order to give Laker the chance of taking all 20. He did have a point about Lock's bowling. Laker, commenting many years later on what happened, wrote, 'I reckon I knew more about Locky's bowling than anyone and in fact he wasn't bowling well; he was pushing them through a bit too quick and tending to be a bit short. On his day, of course, he could be very nearly unplayable – but not this match.'

England won by an innings and 170 runs and a draw in the fifth Test secured the Ashes once again. And subsequent Australian whinges about the wicket? Richie Benaud had this to say, 'It was a terrible pitch but a terrible pitch on which England had made 459.'

Colin must have been relieved that, instead of attempting to master the intricacies of the cash register in Gentlemen's Clothing under the critical eye of Captain Peacock, he was on the MCC tour to South Africa the following winter. Traditionally, tours to the union (it was not until 1961 that the country became a republic) were considered to be the most hospitable off the field and the most hostile on it. This one was no different.

South Africa were doughty opponents, recovering from losing the first two Tests to square the series. Their bowling attack of Adcock, Heine, Goddard and Tayfield was the equal of any country in the world, Colin reckoned. The opening pair of Adcock and Heine was as fast as any and greatly underestimated by the cricketing public, if not by the English batsmen. As for the off-spinner, Hugh Tayfield, it was observed that he, for long periods, reduced Colin to something approaching strokelessness. *Wisden* wrote, 'Cowdrey on some days looked the highest class; on other occasions he found himself tied down completely by slow bowling, especially Tayfield.'

Mind you, he wasn't the only one. The whole series was characterised by slow scoring. The same *Wisden* correspondent gave this heartfelt lament, 'I hope never again to watch a series in which so many batsmen were frightened to make scoring strokes and mere occupation of the crease was the prime consideration of nearly everyone.'

The exception was Peter May. Throughout the tour, he stood head and shoulders in class and strokeplay above anybody else from either side and he alone seemed willing and able to take the initiative at the crease. It was a source of bafflement to all that he was unable to take this exceptional form into the Tests, where it seemed he couldn't buy a run. A charming man and a fine leader but not possessed of robust health, it was conjectured that the cares of captaincy were getting to him. Colin, by now considered a senior member of the team and possible future captain, took note of his friend's travails and wondered.

He said he felt very sorry for him and believed that one or two of his decisions, though proved wrong in retrospect, were understandable given that 'after five days under pressure in a match of ups and downs, you were often, as it were, punch drunk. That is the life of a Test captain.' Indeed. Colin would find out for himself soon enough. As for his own form, he confessed to feelings of disappointment. A series average of 33.10 would seem to bear this out.

Had he been accepted into the ranks of the RAF, Colin's two years of service would have encompassed the first appearance of the Vulcan bomber, action stations in the Suez Crisis and the dropping of

Britain's first hydrogen bomb on Christmas Island in the south-west Pacific. It is doubtful that he would actually have been in the cockpit of any of those aircraft; more likely he would have been playing for the Combined Services in the company of future international colleagues, such as Peter Richardson, John Murray, David Allen, John Edrich, Phil Sharpe and Raman Subba Row. Peeling spuds!

Some of those fellows said that National Service was great for their cricket. In 1957, the time when he would have been demobbed, one wonders whether Colin would necessarily have been an automatic selection for the first Test that summer against the West Indies, no matter how heavily he had been scoring for the RAF and Combined Services. If he had not been, the English public would have been deprived of witnessing the greatest stand in which Colin was involved, in a series when perhaps it could be safely claimed he came of age as a Test match batsman.

Way back in 1950, the West Indies had secured a very popular and highly unlikely 3-1 series win against England, thanks largely to their two spinners, Sonny Ramadhin and Alf Valentine. Between them, in the four Tests, they took 59 wickets and totally dominated the England batsmen. Their feats were immortalised in the calypso song 'Those Two Pals of Mine, Ramadhin and Valentine'.

In the first Test of the 1957 series at Edgbaston, it seemed that Ramadhin's dominance was undimmed; on the first day, on a flawless pitch, he teased and tormented his opponents, taking 7-49, as England were bowled out for 186. Colin did not face him for long – he was one of his victims, for only four – but he had plenty of time to study him from behind the bowler's arm in the dressing room. He watched and he analysed and he cleared the decks for his retribution. Since his troubles with Tayfield during the winter, he had been pondering how best to counter spin. Now he was ready to put his strategy into effect.

Ramadhin. Now, was he an off-spinner who bowled a well-disguised leg break or was he a leg break and googly bowler? These 'mystery' slow bowlers have bamboozled batsmen and fascinated spectators down the ages, from Bernard Bosanquet, who invented the googly (known as a 'bosie' in Australia), to Clarrie Grimmett, to Jack Iverson, to John Gleeson, to Bhagwat Chandrasekhar, to Saqlain Mushtaq, to Muttiah Muralitharan. They have all woven their magic for a time.

Sonny Ramadhin's wiles were never easy to unravel but by 1957, the England batsmen believed they had got his measure. After that first-innings rout, their doubts resurfaced. West Indies put the pitch into perspective by rattling up a large total (474) and the most England could aspire to would be a hard-fought draw. Reduced to 120/3, even that seemed a forlorn hope as Colin joined his captain in another one of those deep holes to which he had become accustomed to find himself.

By his own admission, neither of them at first could tell what Ramadhin was doing, which way it was going to turn. For the time being, Colin decided to play him as a leggie, playing down the line of the ball but with the hands ready to fall away if it turned, so he could let it go past the off stump. The trouble was he could not spot the googly, or the off-spinner, or whatever it was, the one that went the other way. Peter May came down the wicket to chide him whenever Colin was deceived, telling him to stop looking crestfallen. 'Keep a poker face,' he said. 'Don't let them know you're rattled.'

Good advice, Colin agreed, but not so easy to put into operation when bowler, wicketkeeper and close fielders are all hopping around excitedly as another one goes past the bat. Over the years, he learned to remain expressionless. 'Bowlers don't bowl so well when they get angry,' he observed in these unpublished notes of his.

He was finding it difficult to pierce the field. He would execute the correct stroke but the pitch was slow and Ramadhin's field well set. May, at the other end, seemed to be afflicted by no such problems. 'What he would do was to wait for the right ball,' noted Colin, 'plonk his foot down the line of leg stump, thereby giving himself room, to unleash a pick-up drive over mid-off or cover. By not getting his front foot close to the line of the ball, he was able to bring his whole body through with all his power.'

Colin went on to lament that this felt 'odd and alien to me' and he never felt confident enough to try the shot in the middle. There it is again, that word 'confident'. How extraordinary that one so gifted should ever confess to lack of it.

By contrast, May, whom many, Colin included, deemed to be England's finest post-war batsman, always seemed to be in control, no matter how treacherous the pitch, how intimidating the bowling and how tense the situation. Colin watched in admiration as May showed him how it should be done. 'He was completely deceived in the air by one ball. He was committed to the stroke far too early but nipped into top gear and hit the ball clean out of the ground.'

There was another shot that took Colin's breath, and nearly his head, away. May was on about 40 not out at the time, Colin recalled, and felt it was about time that he extricated himself from the tentacles that the medium-fast bowler, Dennis Atkinson, had wrapped around them. 'Suddenly, the windmill was in action, a fierce drive just missed me at the other end and sent the umpire ducking. The ball kept on climbing and disappeared over the broadcasting box and landed on the far side of the tennis court, surprising the two players.'

Colin's appraisal of the style and technique of his friend and captain is compelling reading, 'Peter May and I batted more together for England than any other pair in English cricket but we had contrasting styles. He was enormously strong, big hands, powerful forearms. I have seen him strike the ball off the back foot over the bowler's head into the pavilion at The Oval on several occasions. I wouldn't have reached halfway.'

This reminded me of a comment from John Woodcock about Colin's golf, 'He had great touch around the greens but he was no long driver of the ball. Go on, I would say when we were playing together, give it a rip. Just smash it and see how far it will go. "Wooders, I can't," he'd reply. "I just can't." And he was right. He just couldn't. It felt foreign to him. He needed pace on the ball. That was why sometimes, if the wicket was slow or his timing was a bit awry, he could be a bit pawky.'

It was a captivating contrast in styles as both batsmen started the day's long grind for safety. May was more fluent, occasionally executing a fierce drive, whereas Cowdrey eschewed any risk whatsoever. They counted the runs and the time off in tens and both passed steadily. 'Peter could stoke it when he wanted but he was more comfortable putting a strong punch through every ball he played... Whereas my game was based entirely on soft hands, bringing the bat in late and using the pace of the ball to find gaps in the field. Perfection of timing and accuracy of stroke – they provided for me the fun of batting.'

Their styles may have differed but their steely determination to see this through was identical. They both agreed that the flick on the leg side, a favourite shot of May's, was too risky, as they were not always sure which way Ramadhin was spinning it. 'For God's sake,' May instructed his partner, 'stop me from playing that shot.' They decided, as Colin put it, 'to show our Maker's name'. I assume that it was not the Almighty he was calling upon to bless their partnership but a slip of the pen, or rather a 'typo', as most of his notes are typewritten, for the capital letter. The maker he was referring to was the Slazenger logo on the face of his bat.

This self-denying ordinance made for slow going but it was highly strung, riveting Test match cricket. A mistake from either player would have meant curtains for their side. At the close of play, England had reached 378, both batsmen unbeaten, May on 193 and Cowdrey on 78. The lead was a mere 90 runs and when they resumed their partnership the next morning neither was kidding himself that they were yet out of the woods. The going was easier, Colin acknowledged, but not until he had reached his hundred did he feel able to relax and up the tempo.

At 5.24pm, perhaps the greatest, certainly the most famous, of England's stands finally came to a close. Colin was caught at long-on, trying to hit a six, by a substitute fielder. Which of the footsore West Indians had forsaken the field of play for the sanctuary of the dressing room is not recorded. What is recorded is that the partnership, of which Colin had contributed 154, had realised 411 runs in eight hours 20 minutes. It is still England's highest-ever stand for any wicket and remains a monument to both batsmen's concentration and stamina.

Godfrey Evans came in and tonked a breezy 29 before the declaration came, 583/4, May 285 not out, the highest score by an England captain, a record that stood until Graham Gooch hit 333 against India in 1992.

What of the disconsolate West Indian bowlers? A discreet veil shall be drawn across their figures but one statistic stood out like a sore thumb (or should I say sore finger, because Ramadhin's fingers were red raw). He had bowled 98 overs, poor fellow. I repeat, *98 overs!* He had sent down more balls in a single innings, first-class or Test, than anybody had ever done before, or has ever done since. Thereafter, he was all washed up and finished as a Test match bowler. His mystery had been revealed, his aura punctured, his effectiveness blunted and he was never the same force again. The match was drawn but West

Indian spirits had been broken. England won the rubber comfortably 3-0.

There was a humorous little postscript to Colin's recollections of the series, one that betrays his humanity and humility. In the final Test, in England's only innings, he failed to pick Ramadhin's leg break and was bowled for two. 'I was aiming to hit it through midwicket when it knocked back the off stump. On the way back to the pavilion, I passed the bowler and remarked, "He who laughs last, laughs loudest."'

There was no MCC tour that winter, which was a pity because Colin was in prime form and it meant a return to the Lewisham store and a renewal of his association with Captain Peacock. Not that he would have complained. He was fully aware of his obligations to his father-in-law and was no doubt a dutiful employee.

The phone calls to his friend, Derek Ufton, for a congenial coffee, showed no signs of abating, according to Charlton's captain and centre-half. For both of them, the beginning of the cricket season could not come soon enough, Cowdrey because the lure of the retail trade did not match that of leather on willow and Ufton because he was getting fed up with being injured and believed the grass at Canterbury might be softer on his dislocated shoulders than the hard ground at The Valley.

Regrettably for the English cricketing public, it was only the New Zealanders touring. I say *only* New Zealand, fully aware of the patronising tone of the comment but it is true that a weak and inexperienced team were outclassed in the Tests. Colin felt sorry for them, recognising that they really only had one player in their ranks, the captain, John Reid, worthy of international status. So one-sided had the contest become that there was popular clamour for the selectors to rest one or two of the established England players to try out some new blood.

Colin was asked to step down for the fourth Test and acceded to the request with characteristic good grace. He publicly stated that 'the selectors' decision was sensible and justified'; in private, I bet he slammed shut the lid of his cricket case with rather more force than usual.

The decks were being cleared, in any event, for the MCC tour of Australia that winter of 1958/59. By the decks, I refer of course to those of SS *Iberia*, the finest of P&O's fleet, entrusted with the precious cargo of experienced English cricketers. She was not a lucky ship. Unfortunate mishaps, collisions with other ships, frequent mechanical breakdowns and constant fuel leaks meant she was taken out of service and broken up long before her expected service had elapsed. The same could be said of the England side. They were comprehensively beaten 4-0 by the Aussies and the team was dismantled.

The strange thing was that nobody saw it coming. The party on board was considered by pundits and public alike to be one of the strongest ever to leave these shores. The 1950s had been a decade of almost uninterrupted success for England and there seemed no reason to believe that it would end anytime soon. 'Don't forget, we had won the Ashes three times on the trot,' Tom Graveney reminded me, 'and the Aussies were a pretty good side then.' So, what went wrong?

Colin confessed to one or two concerns before they left England but in no way could they be considered to be more than that, little niggles, hardly intimations of catastrophe. May was captain and there would have been not a single voice raised in opposition to that; his role as leader was firmly established and not open to question. Colin, however, was made vice-captain, a sure sign of the train of thought in the selectors' minds as to who was going to succeed May when the time came. In the same way that Colin had been openly groomed for the captaincy at Kent from a very early stage, it was plain to all that he was seen as May's natural successor. But the man himself wasn't so sure; he felt the deputy's job had come a little too early. There were more experienced and independently minded players in the team, Trevor Bailey being the most noticeable, who might have had other ideas.

On Hutton's tour of 1954/55, Colin had first got to know Bailey. It took a while, for Bailey was by then an experienced campaigner and Colin was the youngest of the side. Their relationship, which was to flourish and endure up to the time of Colin's death, started in the slips. In fact, Colin attributes his burgeoning reputation as a reliable slipper to Bailey. 'On that tour,' he wrote, 'fielding next to him, I took an early lesson in concentration.'

At first, not a word was spoken between the pair, Colin very much aware of his junior status. 'Once or twice, I glanced across at him to find his face in a frown, hand on chin, eyes disappearing behind the wrinkled eyebrows. Constantly he was muttering to himself. Once or twice an over, he'd double up in pain.' Alarmed, thinking he might be ill, he asked Bailey if all was well. A groan would emanate from the senior man and a stream of colourful epithets would drop from his lips, berating the inaccurate bowling or the inexplicable field placing. 'Whereas I was quite happy to enjoy the view, concentrating on the catch if it came my way,' Colin wrote in his notes, 'for him, every ball had its own life story.'

The point was that Bailey was not content to wait for the ball to come to him, he *willed* it, so that he could shape the course of the match in his image. He could not tolerate defeat. His commitment to England's cause had already been sealed in the public's consciousness during the Ashes series of 1953. In the second Test at Lord's, he and Willie Watson had shared probably the most famous of rearguard actions in a fifth-wicket stand of four hours for 71 runs, thus enabling England to escape with a draw and fight another day. And again, during the fourth Test. To stave off an Australian breakthrough, Bailey batted for 262 minutes, scoring 38, earning himself the sobriquet of 'Barnacle Bailey'.

Still he wasn't finished. In the same match, with Australia apparently cruising to victory, he seized the ball, operated off his longest run and bowled consistently wide down the leg side. His tactics hijacked a draw but irritated the hell out of the Australians. He rather enjoyed that. Although not cut from the same ruthless cloth, Colin admired his dogged determination to do whatever it took to gain the upper hand. 'Concentrate, concentrate, concentrate on every ball, whether you're batting, bowling or fielding – that was how he made his mark,' he wrote. 'His tenacity and great involvement in the game as much as his ability made him, in my view a most underrated all-round England Test player.'

Of course, his team-mates found this tightly wound coil of intensity rather amusing at times. 'We would watch him and smile at his antics,' said Colin, 'the way his face would be an open book. Occasionally, one or two would wind him up, commenting on the glorious strokeplay of this or that batsman. Trevor would explode in indignation, blaming the bowler, wondering how on earth this chap had managed to fox the selectors. Then that bowler would get a wicket and Trevor would say, grudgingly, that's more like it, that's why you were picked.' For all his quirks and mannerisms, Bailey was greatly admired for his commitment to the cause and had been a mainstay of the England team for a decade.

But could he be relied upon for significant contributions with the bat, now he was in the twilight of his career? Furthermore, looking down at the list of batsmen, Colin privately wondered where the runs were going to come from, should he and May ever come up short. In this, he was proved to be remarkably prophetic. But he did not dwell on these negative thoughts. He firmly believed, as did everybody else, that no team could live with England's bowling attack. And when you look at the depth of talent available, you would have been hard-pressed to disagree. Tyson, Loader, Trueman, Statham and Bailey were the quick bowlers, Laker, Lock and the untested Mortimore the spinners. The names alone should have sent a shiver down Australian spines.

However, Australian spines are not prone to shiver, especially when the Ashes are at stake. There were many reasons advanced for the unforeseen debacle but the obvious one was that Australia played the better cricket and were, despite predictions to the contrary, the more resourceful side. Yet the abject capitulation by the Englishmen rankled and the rasping note back home was the sound of knives being sharpened.

What did the players think? Peter Richardson made this observation to me, 'We were not a team. We'd been together for too long and frankly we'd all got fed up with each other's company.' Tom Graveney put it even more darkly, 'It wasn't a happy team. I can truthfully say it was the most disappointing and depressing tour I've ever been on.' Arthur Milton, whose first tour this was, and his last, said this of his experience, 'I don't think the management seemed a real part of the team.'

The vice-captain is part of the management team. Was Colin apart from the team in any way? Graveney blamed neither the captain nor his deputy. His criticism was levelled at Freddie Brown, their manager. Brown was hugely popular in Australia. He had led an MCC side severely weakened by war and its aftermath to that country in 1951/52 and had gained many friends for his cheerful and never-say-die attitude in the face of insuperable odds. 'Cabbages – large as Freddie Brown's heart,' shouted vendors at markets. But now, six years later, it wasn't Brown's heart that worried Graveney and others but his liver.

It was clear to everybody that he had a drink problem. 'He was worse for wear most of the time,' Graveney said, 'Halfway through the tour, he had to be sent off somewhere for a fortnight to dry out.'

Colin was naturally reticent about what went on off the field but he knew that things would have to change the next time MCC went on tour. In the same way that an elected leader of a political party, or a chairman of a company or a headmaster of a school is invariably the polar opposite of his predecessor, the next manager of an overseas tour was going to be a totally different kettle of fish. In this regard, Colin was not wrong. We have to read between the lines to guess whether the appointment met with his wholehearted approval.

He was quick to defend, both publicly and privately, his great friend and captain when he came under what he thought was undue criticism. Some of May's decisions, both in selection and team tactics, aroused fierce censure because it was felt that his largely unimaginative and defensive approach compared unfavourably with that of his Australian counterpart, Richie Benaud. Colin saw it differently. 'Peter was carrying a larger burden of criticism than usual by this time,' he wrote, 'and I felt it was unfair. There was little different that I would, or could, have done if I had been in charge.'

For an independent viewpoint, who better to quiz than the doyen of cricket reporters, John Woodcock? 'Peter May was no natural leader, like Benaud was,' he explained. 'His team greatly respected him for the very fine player he was and his position as leader was unassailable. But he was not a communicator. He was a very private man. What a shame he finished so soon, too soon. He would have made 100 hundreds if he hadn't retired early. I think he got fed up with the limelight and the press intrusion.'

And Colin would have been seen, not least by himself, as his natural successor? 'I think so, yes. That is why it was such a crushing disappointment for him to be continually overlooked.' *There was that famous photo of May with his wife beside the pool, as if that was a damning symbol of the whole tour.* He sighed. 'There were press men around, sniffing about for a story, looking for scapegoats. "Wives On Tour" I think was the unfavourable headline.' He didn't say as much but I was left with the distinct impression that Woodcock disapproved of sensationalised reporting. 'There were a few high jinks,' was as much as he would divulge, 'but what tour doesn't have its lively characters?

No, we lost because complacency had set in and we didn't perform as well as we should.'

Colin was incensed by the treatment his friend was getting. 'The photo implied that Peter was aloof from his team. In fact, no captain took more care over his team than Peter and he was justifiably hurt.' Clearly, captain and vice-captain, despite their firm friendship, were quite different personalities, one quiet, withdrawn, wary, uncommunicative and the other affable, sympathetic, forthcoming and full of bonhomie, but in the manner in which they put themselves at the service of their team, they were remarkably similar. It's just that May hid his insecurities better than Colin.

Today, the ill-fated tour is more remembered for the throwing controversy than May's sunbathing companion. By throwing I mean not the throwing *of* matches, a current blight on the game, but the throwing *in* matches.

'There was undoubtedly a lot of it around,' Woodcock agreed, 'so much so that it was threatening to get out of hand.' *Who were the worst offenders?* His faced creased into a grin, as if, even now, he could scarcely believe it. 'I remember Colin getting bowled by Jim Burke, the off-spinner. There is a photo somewhere of it, the look of surprise on Colin's face as he's bowled by someone who has the pose as if he's just scored a double top at darts!'

Burke was the least of the tourists' problems. He was a part-time spinner. Of much more menace were the quick 'chuckers', as they were known – Ken Slater, Gordon Rorke and Ian Meckiff. To give you a taste of what it was like to face a quick bowler with a jerky action, let me repeat Tom Graveney's description of facing Rorke, 'He ran in and from 18 yards, because of his exaggerated drag, he'd suddenly stand upright, all six foot four of him, and throw it at you.'

Meckiff was even more alarming. He was left-arm over and thus more difficult to pick up because of the angle of approach and the fact that his left arm was hidden from view until the last moment. Things had come to a head by the time of the second Test in Melbourne. The tourists had come across Meckiff in one of the state warm-up games and though his action had raised eyebrows, he had been far too wild and erratic for anybody to lose sleep over him. In fact, they didn't expect him to be considered for the Test team. 'Hmmm,' Woodcock chuckled. 'He was obviously keeping his powder dry because come the first Test, he was a different bowler. Or thrower, should I say.'

By the time of the second Test, England were 1-0 down and rumblings about Meckiff had become louder and more insistent. 'Chuckiff', he was now known as in the England camp. Their worst fears were soon realised. In the second innings, they were bowled out for 87, Meckiff taking 6-38.

Colin's analysis of Meckiff's action is, as you would expect, measured and downplayed. 'Whether he threw or not is not for me to say but there was something about the jerk with which his hand came over that made it difficult to see the ball until late. With most bowlers you know roughly where it is coming from and to some extent anticipate where the ball will go. There was a snatch about Meckiff's delivery that made you so much later in deciding which shot had to be played. This meant you were virtually playing someone twice as quick.'

Twice as quick! Never mind Colin's diplomatic use of the term 'snatch'. It seemed clear that Meckiff *threw* his thunderbolts. 'The sad thing about it all,' continued Woodcock, 'was that Ian Meckiff was such a nice man, a really delightful fellow. But I suppose we mustn't feel too sorry for him. He had been getting away with it for years. Throwing was rife in Australia. There were a couple of bowlers in the South Australian side... their names were Hitchcock and Trethewey. We called them Pitchcock and Trethrowy!'

But there were others dotted around the globe? We went through a quick list of suspected throwers at the time: Geoff Griffin, Roy Gilchrist, Charlie Griffith, Harold Rhodes. 'And Peter Loader, don't forget, who was on our side. Let me tell you a story. It happened during this tour.'

The uproar over throwing had reached such a pitch that both cricket boards in Australia and England had been drawn into it. Don Bradman, as a selector and soon to be appointed chairman, had his own views and he was not slow to express them. 'The problem is the most complex I have known in cricket because it is not a matter of fact but of opinion,' he publicly stated. To this end and in an attempt to quell the growing stridency of the debate, especially in the English press, he invited the team along to his house in Bowral in New South Wales.

'He had set up a small movie theatre,' continued Woodcock, 'and he showed a film to the boys, incorporating clips of film and newsreel of bowlers with suspect actions. Tony Lock included. To be fair to Lock, he was horrified when he saw his action in slow motion and he went back home determined to sort it out and re-model it. But it was a salutary lesson to us all. It wasn't just an Australian problem. Anyway, next year, Bradman came to England and with Gubby Allen, they started moves to get bowlers with illegal actions banned.'

That is until the appearance of Muralitharan 30 years later. My informant either did not hear, or affected not to hear, my comment. Perhaps the last word on the throwing controversy of this tour ought to be left to a former team-mate of Bradman's and by then a trenchant observer of the game in a newspaper column, Jack Fingleton. He brought out a book about the tour, titled *Four Chuckas To Australia*.

No tour is entirely devoid of its happier moments, even if the loss of the Ashes is a heavy burden to bear. Colin was quite right to think that he and May would have to shoulder the batting; the two of them were the only ones to average over 40 in the Tests. There were two stands when Colin believed they were both batting at their very best.

The second Test, at a packed MCG, started in dramatic fashion. Davidson removed Richardson, Watson and Graveney in a single over and England were 7/3. You might say that, by now, Colin Cowdrey was well used to walking out to bat in a crisis but this was different, as he described. 'On no other ground in the world can disaster strike more frighteningly than at Melbourne, where the dressing rooms are deep in the giant stands, the crowd larger than anywhere else and the din more deafening. When the first wicket fell that morning, the shuddering and clattering seemed to announce the end of the world. By the time the third wicket fell, it was like nothing I had ever heard before.'

When the fourth wicket fell, Colin made his way to the middle amid the cacophony of sound, there to be met by May. They had difficulty in hearing each other speak. No matter. There was no need for words. The match had barely started but was already in the balance. The series, the Ashes, the whole tour was on a knife-edge, the captain was under attack, his selections criticised and his captaincy doubted. The pressure was enormous.

But May batted as if he were facing no more than an average county attack on his home turf at The Oval. Cowdrey played almost as well and there can be no higher praise than that. Colin found the whole experience strangely exhilarating, as a batsman does when he is in form and dominating the bowling. They were parted the next day, having put on 118 runs. Colin was out for 44 and May completed a memorable century, one of his very best. 'Somehow,' Colin wrote, 'I felt that Peter and I had reached a peak that day.' All to no avail, however. From 210/4, England collapsed to 259 all out and in the second innings, they were bowled out by Meckiff for 87, to lose the match by eight wickets and effectively the Ashes.

There was another highlight for Colin in the third drawn Test, when he scored 'his customary hundred in Australia' as Woodcock wryly put it. He was the leading partner this time in another long stand with his captain, this time for 182, before the declaration came immediately he had reached three figures. The match was drawn, there was no way back and the least said about the comprehensive defeats in Test matches four and five the better.

One further point I wanted to clear up before this unhappy tour is consigned to history was the standard of umpiring, which had come in for a fair bit of stick from some of the England players. John Woodcock laughed hollowly when I brought this up. 'In 1954/55, when we won, the umpiring was considered to be the best in the world. In 1958/59, when we lost, everybody said it was the worst they'd ever seen. And do you know what? They were the same umpires!' No need to check his facts. But I did. And of course he was right. Messrs McInnes, Hoy and Wright were ever present.

Only two quick points need to be made about the summer of 1959. India were outclassed and had the unfortunate distinction of becoming the first Test nation to lose a series 5-0. And Colin Cowdrey had his first taste of international captaincy. Peter May had not retired, he had fallen ill and Colin deputised for the last two matches. The salient word here is 'deputised'; it was no permanent appointment. Not yet.

Some time during the season, May sidled up to Colin with the news, not wholly unexpected, that the manager for the forthcoming winter tour to the West Indies was going to be Walter Robins. The post-mortem at Lord's into the disastrous Ashes campaign had come to the conclusion that the *laissez-faire* tone and character of England's approach to their cricket was entirely inappropriate in this day and age. What was required was a more professional and disciplined regime.

To this end, MCC appointed the noted authoritarian Robins to take control of the side. Robins was a 'considerable figure in the game', Woodcock pointed out to me. 'He played football for Nottingham Forest, played for Middlesex and captained them to the county championship in 1947. He captained England before the war. He was a powerful and forceful personality. Some of the players were a bit frightened of him.'

I doubt that Peter and Colin were among that number but both had their reservations about the man. Or not so much the man – they recognised his dynamism and aura – but the way he was bound to try and run things. 'It was Walter's way or the highway,' noted Woodcock, 'he would brook no opposition.' The trouble was that May had been used to doing it his way and from the outset had his work cut out to maintain that authority. Colin, as his vice-captain (he had been restored to that position), did not operate at his most effective in the teeth of discord.

Of Robins, I will only say this. In the course of protracted conversations with George Chesterton, during the writing of his biography, he told me about an MCC tour to Canada in 1954 he had been on, captained by Robins. George was a mild-mannered man, not given to slinging mud, but he was deeply disparaging about Robins's man-management skills. 'We went on strike, you know,' he told me. 'We were a bunch of cricketing-schoolmasters, unpaid, who had given up our holidays to go on a goodwill tour for the MCC to one of its cricketing outposts and he treated us like squaddies. Naughty boy nets and curfews and physical training! Can you believe it? More like a boot camp than a cricket tour. He had to eventually, how shall I put it, moderate his approach. But he wasn't happy about it.'

The thing was that George and his fellow tourists were amateurs and therefore not beholden to their captain. May and Cowdrey were amateurs too but their situation was different. These were Test matches and the West Indies was no cricketing outpost. Colin smelt trouble.

Troubles come not in single spies but in battalions, as we know. How much May's illness, which had been troubling him for some time but now struck with a vengeance, was brought on, or exacerbated, by the cares of captaincy, not helped by an overbearing manager, we shall never know. His form was patchy and when Colin discovered the nature of his indisposition, all fell into place.

Yet, for some time, the truth had been hidden. The first Test, a high-scoring game, had been drawn. Against the odds, England had won the second Test, thanks largely to their now well-established opening pair of fast bowlers, Trueman and Statham, who had reduced the home side to 112 all out in their first innings. It was when the West Indies were 98/8 that the bottles began to fly. It was not long before a full-scale riot among the 30,000 crowd broke out and play had to be abandoned for the day. The mood was considerably more subdued as England went on to secure their victory by the huge margin of 256 runs.

But what was wrong with May? The official explanation was vague and the press were uncharacteristically discreet about the ailment and I, and all other England supporters back home, were told, with heroic delicacy, that it was 'an internal wound that refused to heal'. Other than that, we were left pretty much in the dark.

'Haemorrhoids!' Woodcock told me much, much later. 'The most extraordinary thing was that May kept it quiet from both his vice-captain and his manager.' *Do you mean to say that even Colin, his best friend on tour, was unaware of the problem?* 'Every evening, after play, Peter would go to the local hospital to have the wound dressed and he told no one.' Eventually, the problem became so acute that May was forced to return home. For the last two Tests, Colin was in charge. Again. But only holding the fort temporarily, until his stricken general could return to active service.

His relationship with his manager, though cordial on the surface – with Colin, it could hardly have been anything else – was uneasy. He did not have the authority, nor the iron will, of the departed captain and felt beleaguered and exposed. Furthermore, he had been asked – and it was a brave man to say no to Robins – to open, again, and he had reluctantly agreed. For the good of the side, again.

He tried to put aside these two perennial banes of his international career, opening and captaincy, and concentrate on finishing what May had started. They had seized the upper hand from their fancied opponents and he was damned if he was going to relinquish it. This required steadfastness in the face of a West Indian side stung by their humbling who fought back in the only way they know how, with a barrage of short-pitched bowling. Hall and Watson, later joined by Griffith, were at their most fearsome and Colin, as captain and opening the batting, was their target. Literally. He said that he had never been so bruised and battered in his career. His bravery was never in doubt.

His innings of 114 and 97 in the third Test, 65 and 27 in the fourth and 119 in the fifth were of the highest class and led the way for his team to eke out the three draws required to win the series. 'There you are, I said you were an opener,' Robins told him. Perhaps. But that wasn't really the point. Surely England's best batsman, now that May was gone, ought to bat where he feels most comfortable.

Colin's written account of the aftermath of the tour says it all really, 'Significantly, and on the strength of our victory in the West Indies, Robins was soon to become chairman of England selectors. Although I led England to victory in the series against South Africa the following summer, Dexter was the next England captain to tour Australia.'

Colin did indeed captain England for the five Tests against South Africa in 1960 but he was not, and did not consider himself to be, England's captain. Peter May was still indisposed and Colin was keeping his seat warm. He had no problem with that; it was what vice-captains do.

The series is best remembered these days for a highly dramatic, controversial and, looking back on it, very sad incident in the second Test at Lord's. Given the brouhaha over throwing on the recent MCC tour of Australia, what happened was an accident waiting to happen and could, and probably should, have been avoided. Geoff Griffin had been no-balled for throwing during the previous domestic season in South Africa but in spite of this, and in the face of the growing international disquiet, he had been picked for the tour of England.

Gubby Allen, chairman of MCC's cricket committee, had been to the forefront in the battle by the authorities to rid the game of this scourge; how much Don Bradman, by now the chairman of Australia's Board of Control, was behind him at this time remains a moot point. The two did meet, not long afterwards, and both agreed on a common policy on how best to tackle, and outlaw, this menace. What is certain is that England took the lead here and umpires were instructed that season to enforce the law on illegal actions. Which they did, with a vengeance.

Griffin was no-balled on several occasions in the warm-up county games but was picked for the first Test, during which he apparently passed muster because he was not no-balled in either innings, despite the deep misgivings of the England batsmen, Colin included.

That was to change in the second Test at Lord's. It just had to be Lord's, didn't it, cricket's headquarters and the spiritual home of the game. Frank Lee and Syd Bullar, both respected senior umpires, no-balled Griffin, five times in the first innings and six times in the second. Even from this distance, we can sympathise with the poor fellow; he must have felt that his world was crumbling around him.

Then an extraordinary thing happened. Returning for his third spell, he removed M.J.K. Smith, Peter Walker and Fred Trueman in successive deliveries, thus becoming the first South African to take a hat-trick in a Test match. Nonetheless, there was no disguising the fact that the match was a disaster, for him and his team – they lost by an innings and 73 runs.

But that was not the end of it. Because the match had been completed within three days and the Queen was due to arrive at tea-time to be presented to the players, both teams were instructed to go out there and play an exhibition match. I know of no professional player, either current or past, who does not have the utmost contempt for exhibition matches. Colin was no exception. If there is nothing to play for, if the result is immaterial, if there is no contest involved, what is the point? However, go through the motions is what they had to do and go through the motions is what they did.

Except the umpires. They took it seriously, very seriously. Griffin was no-balled repeatedly, such that he was forced to bowl underarm in order to complete the over. To add insult to injury, he was then no-balled again, for not informing the umpire of his change of action. That was cruel and totally unnecessary. Far better for him to have been allowed to complete the match (in point of fact, the match had already been completed) and to disappear into the sanctuary of the pavilion, there to have his future decided behind closed doors, not in the full glare of public scrutiny.

Although he was allowed to stay on the tour and play solely as a batsman, his international career was finished. Colin's reaction was one of sympathy but he felt powerless to intervene. Griffin wasn't in his team and he wasn't responsible for what he did on the field of play. His concern, as you would expect from a compassionate man, was 'that it was an embarrassment that he had been picked at all'.

As for the cricket, Colin was satisfied with his team's 3-0 success and pleased that his form returned in the last two Tests, including a masterful 155 at The Oval. The fact that The Oval was half-empty at the time worried him, not so much that the England supporters were missing a gem but that this series had failed to ignite the public's interest. Weak opposition and a rubber long since decided might have had something to do with it but the debate in the press and in the corridors of power was more about the moribund state of Test match cricket. Slow play, in other words, slow over rates and slow scoring, seemed to be strangling the game and there were those who seriously worried for its future. Among the strident apostles of 'brighter cricket' was England's chairman of selectors, Walter Robins. He turned a sceptical eye on the stand-in England captain and wondered.

There was no tour that winter so, once again, it was back to Lewisham and Chiesmans Ltd. Captain Peacock had now been spared the irksome duty of trying to instruct his tepid recruit, Colin having been, as it were, kicked upstairs, where he was introduced to the wider concept of selling, in other words, how to grow a business and make a profit. He said that becoming aware of the changing nature of large, family-run retail stores, such as this one, made a deep impression on him. My guess is that what he learnt, and what he stored away for future reference, was that running a business was not a lot different from captaining a team.

'The key to success,' he later wrote, 'is wrapped up in the ability or inability to solve essential human problems.' That, I believe, was at the core of his leadership style. Say what you like about his disinclination at times to make a decision or his essentially cautious tactical approach, nobody can gainsay the solicitude for the welfare of the teams he captained.

But come what May. Everybody expected the incumbent England captain to return for the Ashes series of 1961. May himself wasn't so sure. Privately (he only admitted this to Colin many years later) he wanted no more of it but publicly he bowed to pressure from Lord's and had made himself available. Not quite yet, however. He did not play in the first Test but felt unready to resume the captaincy when he did return to the side for the second Test at Lord's. Colin, having led the side for the first Test, was surprised to be asked to do it again for the second.

He was disconcerted at being informed so late in the day, not having done his usual homework as captain for a Test match but at least he was relieved that he was no longer being expected to open, England having settled upon the solid partnership of Geoff Pullar and Raman Subba Row. England had drawn the first Test, despite being well behind on the first innings. They were saved any embarrassment by a magnificent 180 from Ted Dexter, ably supported by a century from Subba Row.

At this point, it is as well for us to pause and take stock of Dexter the player, if for no other good reason that Colin, in his notes, does the very same thing. Several paragraphs are devoted to the man who was to become his rival but always his good friend.

'Ted Dexter was without doubt the most talented all-round games player I have ever met,' he wrote. He remembered when he was at Oxford practising on the rackets courts at nearby Radley College and playing with the young Dexter and immediately coming to the conclusion that he must be one of the best schoolboy players in the country. The professional at the school agreed. So good was Dexter at all games, he said, that it was the devil's own job to get him on court. 'Ted was superbly built,' Colin went on. 'Six foot tall, immensely strong and quick over the ground. He was a good 100- or 200-yard sprinter, fine centre at rugby and good at football. At tennis, rackets, squash, golf and of course cricket, he had the ability to strike the ball better than anyone else on earth.'

Dexter's prowess at golf is well known; there are some who believe he could have made a name for himself in that game had he not chosen cricket. Colin gives an interesting insight into this theory. While on tour in Australia, somehow or other, Dexter had arranged a foursome in Adelaide with Jack Nicklaus, Gary Player and Norman Von Nida, on the day before the Australian Open. Colin pulled Dexter's trolley that day, accompanied by several of their attentive team-mates. 'On the way round, I whispered to Norman, "Come on then, how good is Ted *really?*" He answered that he was the best striker of the ball to come out of England since Henry Cotton.' As it happened, Colin believed that Dexter did not play as well as he could in that round, notwithstanding the fact that 'he pulled off a number of dramatic iron shots'.

Afterwards, the three golf professionals encouraged Dexter to lay aside his cricket career to try his hand on the American circuit. 'Of course he didn't,' Colin tells us, the relief in his voice almost tangible, 'but it must have been an attractive financial proposition.' Dexter was an amateur, we must not forget. Did he ever regret his decision? Colin remained none the wiser. 'Ted was such a philosophical fellow that we never knew his true feelings. He was not one to look back and be bowed down by might-have-beens. He was always able to pull a veil over the things of yesterday and prepare to make the best of tomorrow.' Len Hutton always said of Wally Hammond, 'Invent a new game today and he will have mastered it tomorrow.' Colin had the same opinion of Dexter. 'If only I had one quarter of his talent,' is his final observation. Lament, you might call it.

Colin had been out of luck in the first Test, scoring 13 and 14, but he felt he was in good nick and came into the Lord's match on the back of a couple of hundreds for Kent. May was now fit and ready to return. But not as captain. The thinking was that it would be better for him to ease his way back into Test cricket without being burdened with the cares and responsibilities of the captaincy. So Kipper, be a good sport and hold the fort for a bit longer, will you, there's a good chap. What else could he say?

On later reflection, he believed his acquiescence, always immediate, always unconditional, did him no favours on this occasion. 'This was the Test in which I should have clinched the captaincy for years to come,' he wrote. 'Had the Lord's Test taken a different pattern, I think I might have begun a long reign of leadership and so avoided the many rumpuses and embarrassments of the next few years.'

Not a few of which disappointments were his own. But the match was a disaster; England lost a game they were expected to win. Everything that could go wrong, did go wrong. He misread the pitch, not the first captain ever to have done that, but it meant that England played two spinners and Australia none, on a surface better suited to their battery of four seamers. England batsmen played and nicked, Australian batmen played and missed. England's batting collapses in both innings were inexplicable. Colin scored 16 and 7 when he felt that he could, and should, have scored a hundred. And there were times when it seemed every decision he made, in the field or back in the dressing room, backfired. It was a calamitous performance. England had lost by five wickets. 'That Saturday was the blackest day of my life.'

Had they won, or even drawn creditably, he remained convinced to his dying day that Peter May would, there and then, gladly have handed over the reins and the Cowdrey reign would have commenced.

Instead, the knives were out. Colin was sacked as captain and May reinstated. He was not led into the headmaster's study and summarily expelled but let down 'gently' as he called it. But let down he was. Thereafter ensued a decade of 'captaincy merry-go-round', as the press labelled it. I prefer to call it more of a beauty pageant, with all its attendant embarrassments, as one by one the contenders were led out to face public scrutiny. All were worthy aspirants, all had their strengths and all had their supporters, either in the press or behind closed committee room doors.

Always Colin was in the wings and sometimes he was in the spotlight, hating the frenzy and the hoopla but privately believing the crown should be his. At one time or another, his rivals were Ted Dexter, David Sheppard, Mike Smith, Brian Close and Ray Illingworth, all of whom were team-mates and all of whom he had the greatest regard for personally (with the possible exception of the last named). In the meantime, there were runs to be scored and Tests to be played.

This Ashes series was lost, in one disastrous session, if folklore is to be believed. This was at Old Trafford, when Dexter was leading the charge for victory, batting imperiously as only he could, before Richie Benaud, the Australian captain, gambled by bowling his leg-spinners around the wicket and into the rough. Dexter was dismissed for 76, May was bowled around his legs for a duck, England collapsed to 201 all out, losing the match and the Ashes, with Benaud taking 5-12 in 25 deliveries. In such a manner are legends born. Benaud was a genius, May a general lacking inspiration.

It left a deep scar on the England psyche. For May, it was the end. He retired from Test cricket following the final Test at The Oval and a great batsman and a very fine captain was lost to the game. Incidentally, Colin was ill and did not play in this momentous encounter. He returned at The Oval but scored 0 and 3, to round off a thoroughly disappointing season. One for which he had had the highest hopes.

The demeaning beauty pageant continued during the following season, with the captaincy for the series against Pakistan passing from Dexter to Cowdrey and back to Dexter. Furthermore, appearing like an Old Testament prophet out of the desert, strode the imposing figure of the Rev. David Sheppard. What a twist of the tale this provided for the newshounds.

Sheppard had been persuaded temporarily to lay aside his ministry – in which great things were expected of him – in order to resurrect his cricket career, with a view to leading the MCC side to Australia that winter. Thus the three of them were thrust on to the stage and the judges eyed them critically. Ironically, Colin was in magnificent form against the Pakistanis, scoring 159 in the first Test and 182 in the fifth.

Even more ironically, he had again been asked to open, the dependable Subba Row, like May, having retired from the game early. A further irony was provided by the fact that in the fifth Test at The Oval, he opened the batting with Sheppard. They put on a stand of 117. Say what you like about the vexed problem of Colin's disinclination to open; he was the most technically correct batsman in England and a good fit for the role, he always gave of his best and he played some splendid innings there.

Colin believed he was third favourite for the Australia job. The press had their money on Sheppard. Colin believed that Dexter was a shoo-in. After some unnecessary diversionary tactics from the chairman of selectors, Walter Robins, the announcement was made. Colin was right. Dexter was named as captain, Cowdrey as his vice-captain and Sheppard as an opener. The confidence Colin had in his instincts was born out of a shrewd awareness of Robins's agenda. In a nutshell, it was encapsulated in the catchphrase 'brighter cricket'.

Robins had a point here. Following the upsurge in public interest in the game after the Second World War, enthusiasm seemed to be waning. Test cricket had become stale and defensively minded. Most Tests were drawn and the game seemed to be stagnating. The riveting series between Australia and the West Indies in the previous winter (which included the famous tied Test) had shown the way and Robins was eager that English cricket should follow suit. To that end, he favoured the fearless, swashbuckling, cavalier

Ted Dexter rather than the more orthodox, dare one say cautious, Colin Cowdrey.

What Colin thought of the appointment is difficult to tell; rarely did he confide his inner feelings with anybody. Usually, he trod the diplomatic path. Were there any clues in his notes? Interestingly, he writes about Dexter more than any other cricketer, with the exception of Ranjitsinhji, both Sussex men, incidentally. Ranji had long since been dead; Dexter was very much alive (still is, of course). Colin's assessment of Dexter's personality is fair, balanced and affectionate. 'So gifted is Ted in so many things,' he writes, 'he found it hard to give much time to people.'

There was an innate shyness about the man, he believed, that made it difficult to get to know him. He had this habit, when asked a question, as he frequently was by pressmen and commentators, of pondering his answer at length before giving a reply. 'While doing this, he'd look upwards or away, scratching his nose as he sniffed, giving every impression of aloofness. It was totally unintended but unfortunate. This apparently leisurely and arrogant air gave rise to the nickname "Lord Ted", which stuck.'

For all that, he was a deep thinker, not only about the game – and Colin later gives Dexter full credit for his quick understanding and effective execution of tactics of the new, limited-overs game – but about life too. Every sport he commented on was subjected to intense scrutiny of technique and strategy. Colin asks the hypothetical question, was Dexter too much of a theorist? He gives no definitive answer, possibly fearful that the same question could be asked of him. Nonetheless, Dexter the theorist was 'always in pursuit of the best' and would display scant regard for anyone with inferior knowledge who had not made sufficient attempt to gain it.

'I have not met anyone else in my life who has been able to shut his mind so single-mindedly to outside distraction. If only I could do the same,' Colin finishes wistfully. You do wonder whether he was too hard on himself sometimes. Sadly, and frustratingly, at that point he breaks off, promising to come back to his audit of Dexter's captaincy, but he never did. Death intervened.

Having gone with the maverick to lead the side on the field, who would the selectors choose as manager? 'There's no doubt that Dexter can handle a bat,' Colin reported one of the selectors as saying, 'but who's going to handle Dexter?' The answer to this Colin *does* give detailed appraisal, for reasons that shall, in due course, become obvious.

The appointment, when it was announced, astonished the cricketing world. Bernard Marmaduke Fitzalan-Howard, the 16th Duke of Norfolk and England's Earl Marshall and senior duke of the realm, was no stranger to official posts but he was a novice, went up the cry, as a manager of a cricket team. Not quite so, as it happened. He had taken his own team on a tour of the West Indies, he had instigated the traditional pipe opener of the season for the tourists to play his team, the Duke of Norfolk's XI, at his own ground in the family seat at Arundel Castle, he had been president of MCC and he loved his cricket.

Furthermore, he was president of Sussex and had been instrumental in appointing Dexter as club captain. In fact, the choice was an inspired one. After initial scepticism among the players (he caused considerable amusement at their first official function when he told them, 'Gentlemen, I want this to be an entirely informal tour. You will merely address me as "Sir".'), he won them over with his natural charm and courtesy and his evident love of the game and his desire to do his best for them. The Australians took to him; in the end, he had them eating out of his hand. 'He was a lovely chap,' Tom Graveney told me. 'Utterly charming.' And then he laughed, making a reference to the 'Sussex Mafia' on that tour and the fact that the duke, Dexter and Sheppard were all Sussex men. Even Fred Trueman was eventually won over and the two became good friends.

Colin, with his background, natural politeness and ease of manner, got on with him like a house on fire. 'I admired the Duke of Norfolk most of all for the way he always sought to play second string to the captain yet was willing to take any of the load off his shoulders whenever it would help.' Quite when and how the close relationship between the duke and player took hold is unclear but take hold it did.

In an effort to glean a little insight into their friendship, I asked Alan (A.C.) Smith, who was on that tour as the reserve, initially anyway, wicketkeeper-batsman, what his memories of the duke were. 'First of all, you must appreciate that there were four amateurs in the party, Dexter, Sheppard, Cowdrey and me.' *I thought the distinction between amateurs and professionals had been abolished – that very summer, wasn't it?* 'Actually the distinction was abolished during the tour, to take effect at the beginning of the next season, 1963. In fact, the barriers had been breaking down for some time before that. When on tour for England, there hadn't really been any distinction at all. But socially, vestiges of the old class system still prevailed. For instance, the duke's three daughters joined him later in the tour.

'One day when we were in Melbourne, the duke announced he had theatre tickets for that evening's performance and needed two more escorts to accompany his daughters. Of course, it was expected that Colin and I should be the two escorts. We went out for dinner afterwards. It was a very pleasant evening.' And then he started laughing. 'Those girls – they were known as the Norfolk Broads!'

Another aspect of Colin's temperament that Smith was eager to convey was his propensity for networking. Now, that word 'networking' often has unfavourable connotations, hinting at manufactured intimacy and self-serving social climbing. Of all the people I have spoken to about Colin's extensive circle of friends in high places, none has ever intimated that he used their influence for his own purposes. What he enjoyed was putting people in touch with each other for their mutual benefit, not his. He loved matchmaking. Sometimes, personal advantage accrued but that was not the primary purpose.

Smith gave an involuntary whistle as he marvelled at the number of people Colin knew in Australia. 'Mind you,' he added wryly, 'he did tour there six times.' Everywhere they went, it seemed, Colin had friends and contacts. 'He even organised cars for the boys. I got one and I was a junior member of the party. Yep, Kipper looked after me on that trip.'

He told me another story about the 1974/75 tour, on which he was an assistant manager. 'Just before the Perth Test – Colin had only been in the country for two days – he said to me, "Come out this evening with me. We're guests at Government House with the state governor." He had a car ready and off we went to meet him. All I can remember was that the governor's language was *awful!* Typical Aussie, really.'

Of course, MCC tours were not all about receptions and theatre visits. The serious business was the cricket and in this regard, the team's mission statement, clearly articulated in press conferences before they set out, was two-fold – to win back the Ashes and to play 'brighter cricket'. They failed on both counts. Dexter was magnificent with a bat in his hand, especially early on in the tour, but his reputation, together with that of his opposite number, Richie Benaud, as enterprising captains intent on playing attractive cricket, did not last the series. All this talk of positive intent was forgotten in the Tests, according to *Wisden*, 'where victory, or rather the avoidance of defeat, became the all-important factor'.

The narrow margins between the sides could have provided an interesting tussle, one that should have gone down to the wire, but sadly, when all was set for a thrilling climax in the final Test at Sydney, with both sides locked at 1-1, 'the game turned out to be the dullest and by far the worst of the five'. Which is saying something, for *Wisden* in conclusion gave this damning verdict, 'Overall, much of the cricket was grim, especially the Tests.' So much for brighter cricket.

And how was it for Colin, 'the most stylish of the batsmen', as *Wisden* described him? Not at all bad, as it transpired. He averaged 43.77 in the Tests, the highlight coming at Melbourne, his favourite ground, where he scored 113 and 58 not out, to help England to their solitary victory, by seven wickets. Another milestone was his 307 against New South Wales, which remained forever his highest score in first-class cricket (MCC 307 became his personal number plate on his Jaguar thereafter). 'I would never have managed it without my old friend, Tom Graveney,' he always said. 'He was batting with me for most of the time and he kept on encouraging me towards the triple century, telling me that now was no time to lose concentration.'

One game that certainly was not grim was held at Canberra towards the end of the tour. Sir Robert Menzies, the Australian prime minister, was a cricket nut. Accordingly, he would assemble a Prime Minister's XI to play the tourists and a swift glance at his team (including Cowper, Harvey, Benaud, Mackay, Grout and Loxton) indicated that MCC would not have taken them lightly. Nor did they, especially once the guest player was announced. Sir Don Bradman was enticed out of retirement, much against his better judgement, to lace on his boots and buckle on his pads once more.

A.C. Smith takes up the story. 'There was huge public interest. The Don back at the crease! He came in at number five. Tom Graveney was bowling his leggies at the time. He hit Tom for a four past mid-on. The next over there was a single and Don was now facing Statham. I was keeping and I remember what happened very clearly. Obviously Statham was not going to let rip so I was standing, what, five yards back. Statham trundled in and delivered the ball at military medium, Don played back, the ball came off the face of the bat, on to his boot and rolled slowly on to the stumps and the bails fell off. It was agonising really.'

Tom Graveney chuckled as he recalled the incident. 'I am the man off whom Sir Don Bradman scored his last runs!' he announced proudly. Both men made the point that Colin and The Don knew each other well. Of course they did. I have ploughed through reams of letters from Bradman to Colin, mainly from their time as administrators of the game in their respective countries. Whatever their differences of opinions, the tone remained staunchly cordial, warm even.

'Before we leave this tour,' cried A.C. during our conversation, 'what about the world record stand with Colin in New Zealand?' I confessed my ignorance. He put me right. 'It was the second Test at the Basin Reserve in Wellington. Colin had damaged his hand in the field so he came in down the order at number eight. I was batting at number ten. God knows why. F.S. Trueman went in before me at number nine!'

Having seen you bat, Alan, I should have thought that ten was about right. 'I always knew I should never have sent my son to your school. Anyway, Colin was batting like a dream, despite his injured hand. And, though I say it myself, I wasn't batting too badly either. We shared an unbroken ninth-wicket partnership of 163, a world record.' It was indeed. And so remained until bettered by Asif Iqbal and Intikhab Alam at The Oval in 1967. Colin scored 128 and Smith 69 on that memorable day. All three Tests were comfortably won by England. New Zealand's development as a Test nation had a while to go yet.

'After that tour, I never played for England again,' A.C. rather wistfully said. 'As team-mates, Colin and I got on very well but I got to know him much better after we had retired.' Retired from playing that is. As did Colin, A.C. Smith later became a significant figure in the administration of the game.

What better antidote to a drab series between the two Anglo-Saxon nations than the arrival on these shores in that spring of 1963 of those calypso cricketers from the Caribbean, with their compelling brand of enterprising cricket and their loud, colourful, exuberant supporters? Once more, hitherto half-filled grounds were packed to the rafters. England lost the first Test by ten wickets and it was imperative for the sake of the series that they fought back in the second at Lord's. This they did, in a match that has gone down in the annals of the game as one of the most gripping, spellbinding ever played. Colin's role in the final act is unforgettable.

West Indies were bowled out for 301 (Trueman 6-100), no mean feat by the home side, given the strength of their opponents' batting. On the second day, with two early wickets in the bag, and with Hall and Griffith in full cry, they scented blood and circled their prey. In an innings which Colin described as one of the greatest seen at Lord's, Dexter pushed them back, then contemptuously dismissed them. 'Not only did his innings reflect completely his volatile nature and almost arrogant confidence, it also thrust England right back in the game,' he wrote.

Dexter's counter-attack caught the public imagination. Why, a whole book was even written about it (Alan Ross's *West Indies at Lord's*). I read it, hidden inside the covers of a large, dull tome on the British Constitution, in the school library during a history lesson. It made a huge impression on me too. Sadly, and this may have contributed to its enduring appeal, Dexter's onslaught came to an end all too soon. Hall and Griffith were replaced and he was LBW to Sobers for 70. England's total was a mere four runs in arrears.

On the Saturday, the queues were snaking around St John's Wood long before the gates opened. Colin, captaining the side in the field in the absence of Dexter who had a sore knee, describes the scene, 'I have played before crowds three times as huge in Melbourne but nowhere on earth do my stomach muscles tighten up a full hour before play as they do in this special place.' Had it not been for a masterful 133 from Basil Butcher, England would have been home and dry. As it was, their target for victory was 234. Nip and tuck.

At this point in his notes, Colin breaks away to raise once more the contentious issue of throwing. The England players, while accepting that most of Griffith's deliveries were legitimate, were certain that, when he strained for extra pace, 'his action altered perceptibly and he could produce the most brutal, lethal delivery, fast yorkers or short-pitched bouncers'. The atmosphere in the home dressing room when he came on to bowl was always tense, sometimes acrimonious. They'd seen enough of it all on that tour of Australia in 1958/59 and the problem hadn't gone away.

It wasn't a chuck that did for Colin but 'the ridge'. Officially, the ridge at Lord's did not exist. Groundsmen, pitch inspectors, turf experts, geologists, surveyors, all came out strongly against the theory that there was a ridge that ran across the square, saying that it was a myth. No, it wasn't. Ask any cricketer who played there. I hit it once, by accident. I bowled a rank long-hop and even at my gentle medium pace, the ball flew over the wicketkeeper's head (he was standing up). Andy Roberts, who was at mid-off, doubled up with laughter.

When the ball flies off the ridge, delivered by the world's fastest bowler at the time, Wes Hall, it is no laughing matter, as Colin found out to his cost. 'He let loose two very nasty ones and then, by chance, pitched one only just short of a length. It reared straight up and would have struck me under the chin at full speed had I not flung up my left arm in an instinctive parry.' The sound of the forearm breaking was sickening. As Colin had it set and plastered in hospital, he knew that his match and his season were over.

Or was it? Like the best of dramas, there was an unexpected twist to the plot. England's advance on the winning total underwent so many alarms and excursions that even experienced onlookers in the pressroom were chewing their fingernails. This time, there were no fireworks from Dexter. The responsibilities lay heavy on the shoulders of Close and Barrington, as well as their arms, torso, knuckles and other parts of the body, as they were subjected to a barrage of short-pitched bowling from Hall and Griffith – in poor light, too.

Close, in particular, was hit frequently, never flinching, always ready for the next ball. Then he lost control of his senses, or so it seemed to the onrushing Hall. Close was walking down the wicket towards him, bat raised, face grimaced. So disconcerted was Hall that he aborted his run-up. But Close persisted with the tactic, giving Hall the charge, and if he wasn't able to get his bat on the ball, he was quite content for it to thud painfully, but harmlessly, into his chest.

There was method in his madness, according to Colin. Far from losing his mind, Close was adopting a deliberate ploy in an attempt to disrupt Hall's rhythm and induce him to lose length and direction. 'It wasn't a maniacal innings of blind courage,' he asserted, 'but a carefully premeditated assault.' It may not have been the product of blind courage but it took courage all right. It so nearly succeeded too. The following day, the newspapers printed a picture of Close stripped to the waist; his torso was a patchwork of bruises, lesions, contusions and swellings. You could even see the outline of the ball's seam on one purple mark. 'It was, surely, Close's finest hour,' Colin said.

The match was always going to be a balance between runs to be scored and wickets to be taken. Now, on account of a delayed start to the final day because of rain, time entered the equation. Eventually Close's incredible innings came to a close, caught Murray bowled Griffith for 70, and the maths were simple. England needed 15 to win, West Indies needed two wickets and there were 19 minutes left to play.

Back in the dressing room, Colin was padding up, with some help from team-mates. Dexter was adamant that his stricken batsman should not bat unless it was absolutely necessary to do so. As the minutes ticked by and England's score advanced in singles, it became increasingly clear that he probably would. He started to practise batting one-handed in front of the mirror, with a left-handed stance. That was the only way he could keep his broken left arm out of the way.

The 6pm news on the BBC was put on hold as the nation sat round their television sets, transfixed by the live broadcast from Lord's. Final over, to be bowled by Hall, eight to win, eight wickets down. Dot ball. Second ball, Shackleton dropped the ball at his feet and set off on a run. It became a race between bowler and non-striker, Allen, to reach the far end first. Allen won. Seven to win. Third ball. A yorker. Allen squeezed it to square leg for a single. Six to win, three balls left. Fourth ball. Shackleton swung and missed and already Allen was down at his end. Murray, the wicketkeeper, threw the ball to Worrell at short mid-on and, rather than risk a shy at the stumps, he took on Shackleton, both 38 by the way, for a race to the stumps. Worrell won, whipped off the bails and Shackleton was run out. Two balls left, nine wickets down, six runs to win. Lord's held its breath and all eyes were turned to the pavilion. Surely that was it. England's last batsman was *hors de combat* and they had lost.

Then that familiar, slightly stooped and portly figure slowly made its way down the pavilion steps, through the gate and on to the outfield. The ovation Colin received going out was every bit as thunderous as any coming in after another of his magical hundreds. He was 19 not out, by the way. There is that famous photo of him at this very moment, giving the photographer a shy little smile as he passed. Did he quietly mouth, 'Gosh, this is fun, isn't it?'

He recounted later that it was bedlam by the time he reached the pitch. The West Indians were shouting to each other and Frank Worrell was trying to make himself heard above the tumult of the crowd as he beseeched his fast bowler not to bowl a no-ball. And the calmest man in St John's Wood was David Allen, Colin recalled.

Nothing was said between them. Nothing needed to be said. Colin, thankfully, was at the non-striker's end and would only have to face one ball at the very most. Allen was intent he should be spared that. Calmly, he blocked the last two deliveries and a game of almost unbearable tension had ended. The match was drawn, the series re-ignited, popular interest in Test cricket reborn and the myth-making began. Colin had this to say by way of a final comment on one of the great Test matches, 'My injury apart, it was perhaps the best cricket match I have played in, for tension and excitement and constant changes of fortune.'

For all that, it was a long period of inactivity, which lasted well into the winter, as the bone healed, no doubt interspersed with bouts of introspection and self-doubt. He joked that 'it was a good place to get hit', the significance of which would not be lost on any batsman cognisant of the eternal verities of an orthodox technique; in other words, he was in the correct place, left elbow up, leading with the top hand, when the ball struck. All right, it was unlucky that it had bounced more than he had expected, but at least he had not abandoned ship, turned away and taken his eye off the ball. One happy consequence of his injury was that he was able to spend a rare Christmas at home.

It was in that fallow period following the holiday season and the excesses of New Year that the phone rang in the Cowdrey household. MCC secretary Billy Griffith was on the line. Conversation soon turned to the current travails of the MCC party in India, not so much poor form or loss of matches but the catastrophic injury and illness list. It seemed that one by one the team were being picked off as if at a turkey shoot and reserves were being urgently sought.

Colin had been lined up to captain the side but his arm had not healed in time and in his absence, M.J.K. Smith had taken hold of the reins. It was not odd, therefore, that Griffith should seek the advice and opinion of the leader left behind. And then an uncontrollable urge took hold; Colin volunteered himself. He had been deeply disappointed to miss out on the privilege of leading an MCC side to the land of his birth. His arm was fine. After all, it had stood up the strenuous task of carving the turkey. What possible fears could the Indian bowlers present in comparison? Almost as soon as he blurted out his wish to help out, he was having second thoughts. Too late. Twenty-four hours later, he was on a plane to the subcontinent.

The parallels between that telephone call and one made by Mike Denness ten years later are extraordinary, the only difference being that on this occasion, Colin volunteered himself whereas the *cri de coeur* from Australia had come from the team. The bottom line was no different, however. He was abandoning the comfy hearth of home in the middle of winter to play in a Test match in possibly the harshest environment in which to adapt. His team-mates had been in the country for longer and they were dropping like ninepins. Furthermore, he hadn't picked up a bat for seven months.

Batting one-handed was all very well for a desperate two balls but more would be expected from him than just bravery. Ah, but this is *India*, he told himself, my birthplace, where the people, the food, the culture are familiar. Had things turned out a little differently, I could have been playing for the home side. How much the teeming, bustling metropolises of Delhi, Calcutta and Bombay were going to remind him of the green rolling slopes of the Nilgiri Hills remained to be seen. Not at all, as he unsurprisingly discovered.

When he arrived, the situation was even worse than he had imagined. In the first two Tests, for the visitors it was simply a case of if you're upright, you're playing. A brief glance at the scorecards underlines how short the selection meetings must have been. In the first match, Micky Stewart, an opener, is batting at number ten. In the second, he is batting at 11 and the only entry alongside his name is 'absent ill'. Furthermore, both wicketkeepers have been pressed into action, Jimmy Binks with the gloves and Jim Parks as a batsman. England had to borrow a 12th man from India when they fielded.

So with just a couple of nets as preparation, Colin was playing in the third Test. Under the circumstances, his innings of 107 out of a total of 267 was a creditable effort, though hard going. His 151 in the fourth was less easily excused. 'It killed English hopes,' *Wisden* reported, so slow and sluggish was the run rate. 'Cowdrey appears unaware of his vast potential...he stood suspiciously aloof in Delhi, leaving others to attempt the scoring rate needed.' It was on this tour that his great friend, John Woodcock, was moved to criticise his batting in print, calling it 'pawky' and 'stodgy' and wondering aloud what on earth it was that persuaded Colin to go into his shell like that. Even Colin admitted that neither innings was 'a work of art'.

In all fairness, the tedious rate of play was not all Colin's fault, nor was he solely guilty. The pitches were uniformly slow and low, which meant that all five Tests were doomed to stalemate from the outset. So lifeless were the playing surfaces that 'even a competent craftsman could bat successfully with a broom handle', thundered our Woodcock, 'and the nature of the play inflicted sore wounds on the game of cricket.' Even I, a loyal fan with all the enthusiasm of a 14-year-old, was bored reading about it in the papers.

The Ashes contest back home in 1964 wasn't much better either. Three out of the five Tests were spoiled by rain, Australia won a dull series 1-0 and international cricket seemed unable to sail out of the doldrums.

Colin was similarly deflated, struggling to find wind to fill his sails. For the first time in his Test career, he was dropped. Recalled for the fifth Test at The Oval after some scintillating innings for Kent, he found his touch, at this level at any rate, just as elusive as before but slowly confidence surged, the strokes began to flow and during his second innings of 93 not out, he passed 5,000 Test runs.

However, it is not his batting in this match, or indeed during the series, for which he is best remembered but a catch, not a difficult or spectacular one – in fact, it could be described as 'regulation' – but a historic one nonetheless. The photo of him pouching the ball at first slip, at a comfortable height just to his right, following a snick by Neil Hawke, is as famous as they come.

Like Colin, Fred Trueman had been dropped from the side, frustratingly three wickets short of the magical number of 300, never before achieved in Test cricket. Together with Colin, he was recalled for The Oval. Everybody knew, including him, he was coming to the end of his illustrious, 14-year career as a fast bowler. This final Test of the summer could conceivably be his last. Predictably, nerves set in (as they would some years later, when Colin approached his own personal milestone of 100 first-class hundreds), he could not find his rhythm and he bowled like a drain. In the end, Dexter had to take him off, wicketless.

John Woodcock clearly recollected the dejected walk, from short leg at one end to short leg at the other, a once proud and fearsome fast bowler dispirited, down on his luck and inwardly cursing the cricketing gods. There would probably be no last burst, there would be no second innings (rain had seen to that) and in all likelihood, there would be no more Tests. For his team-mates, his misery was hard to witness.

As fate would have it, a stand developed and Dexter was in a bit of a fix. In an instant, Trueman was at his shoulder. 'Give me t'ball,' he demanded and without waiting for a reply, he snatched it from Dexter's grasp and marched to the end of his run. There were only three overs left in the morning session, so Dexter laughingly gave in.

Trueman's first three balls were high, wide and handsome. He regained his line sufficiently in the remaining balls to gain one more over, the last before lunch. Suddenly, he ripped out Redpath's middle stump and the next ball he had McKenzie caught by Cowdrey at slip. With a characteristic predilection for the dramatic, in front of a full house on the Saturday of an Oval Test, Trueman was on a hat-trick, on 299 wickets, on the verge of immortality – and it was lunch.

Even the corporate diners forwent their pudding, intent on not missing that first ball after the break. There was no hat-trick but Trueman was bowling like a man inspired. He would not be denied. Not long after, he found the edge of Hawke's bat, the ball flew to first slip and to a tremendous roar from the crowd, Colin clung on to it. Gratefully, Trueman sank into Colin's arms. Asked later how he felt at breaching the hitherto unthinkable record of 300 Test wickets, his reply was true Trueman, 'Bluidy knackered.'

So it was that neither of the two cameos of Colin that had imprinted themselves in the public consciousness of the mid-1960s had anything to do with his batting; one had been walking out to bat at Lord's with a broken arm and the other catching Fred Trueman's 300th wicket.

Colin was at the mid-point of his career and at something of a crossroads. Of course, he was not to know he was halfway through his cricket career. As with all sports, he was but one serious injury or catastrophic loss of form from the *coup de grace*. He was fortunate; his playing career lasted longer than many.

I remember during my one and only conversation with him at Tunbridge Wells back in 1973, for some reason or other – probably because I had recently had a knee operation – we briefly discussed knees, the most troublesome and badly designed of all the joints. 'I've been lucky,' he said with feeling, 'I haven't had problems with my knees. Brain, yes, but not knees.'

By and large, he was lucky with injury, though when it did strike, it always seemed to be at the most inopportune moment. He had been playing at the top level for ten years but now he had been dropped from the Test side and the suspicion was taking hold that he was not, for the time being at any rate, an automatic selection, the first name on the team sheet, one of the 'untouchables', as Jose Mourinho put it.

His form had been erratic. Did he privately harbour negative thoughts? Was he going through another crisis of confidence? Was the belief in his ability starting to erode? He is no longer here so we cannot know. Ah, but wait a minute. Browsing through his notes, I noticed a whole chapter entitled 'Flaws In My Game'. A whole chapter! This from one of the most technically gifted batsmen of his generation. I looked for a chapter entitled 'Bowling Attacks I Have Put To The Sword' but in vain. Blowing his own trumpet was just not his style. He really did not think he was as good as everybody said he was. Some of the critical detail contained therein – it is a very long chapter, incidentally – is interesting and illuminating.

'The particular criticism levelled at my batting,' he begins, 'is that all too often I would allow ordinary bowlers to dominate me when really I ought to be lifting myself above them and destroying them.'

He does not ascribe this to any weaknesses in his game but rather to the different venues where he performed, or more specifically, the different types of pitches on which he played. He accepts that the best batsmen should be able to play on all surfaces and agrees that he, to some extent, learnt over time how to cope with varying conditions. But he certainly felt more comfortable and more confident about going for his shots on certain wickets than others. He pinpoints slow pitches as his bugbear. 'Slow, low, spongy surfaces, with accurate bowlers operating to defensively set fields, would find me like Samson without hair,' he confesses.

Basically, he felt that he could never hit through the line of the ball. In other words, he simply could not open his shoulders and give the ball a crack. As he relied so much on timing, with soft hands, bringing the bat in late and using the pace of the ball to ease it on its way, he found it difficult to free up his arms and basically smash it in the opposite direction. On quicker wickets, he came into his own. It is no surprise, therefore, that he flourished on the harder, faster pitches of Australia and the West Indies.

Undoubtedly, this is why he was so good at rackets. The hard ball, no bigger than a golf ball, whizzes around the concrete walls and skids off the concrete floor of a court the size of a hangar and somehow you have to get your racket on it. The best players merely lean on it, hitting through the line and easing it on its rapid course. No strength is required, merely timing and a good eye. That is more or less how Colin batted. May, Dexter, Sheppard, Smith, even Barrington when he was in the mood, could smash the ball out of sight. Colin could not. He caressed it.

The nearest of his contemporaries in impeccable timing and elegant strokeplay was, I guess, Tom Graveney. Both were brought up in the days before one-day cricket and both were still playing when it was introduced, dipping their toes in the water, so to speak. I asked Tom how he would have adapted to the crash, bang, wallop of the modern limited-overs game. He gave me an old-fashioned look. 'I think I might have scored a few.'

The same with Colin. He made the point in these notes that the fundamentals of batting do not change. He would have trusted his technique and looked for the gaps in the field, as he always did. Where his jaw dropped in admiration is when he analyses the fancy new shots that contemporary batsmen have fashioned and perfected. He makes mention of the reverse sweep, 'I keep my mouth firmly closed here for I was no good at all in this department. I marvel just how good at it a number of players have become.' But caution still informs his opinion. 'These shots are a big risk and each batsman has to work out his own way of extemporising.'

I wonder. Had Colin, and indeed Tom, been brought up in a later generation, would he have thrown caution to the wind in limited-overs cricket and unfurled, without inhibition, his vast range of strokes? I am reminded of the example of the New Zealander, Glenn Turner, who attributed the influence of the one-day game in transforming him from a plodding journeyman into a thrilling shotmaker. Where Colin would have struggled, and did, even in the early days of the Gillette Cup and the John Player League, was in the field.

Recognising his batting sometimes seemed as burdensome to him as turning a heavy millstone to make grain, Colin candidly admitted that, if he had his time again, he would have practised harder at developing more aggressive strategies to combat slow pitches and defensive fields. 'I should have spent more time in the nets improving my batting on slower wickets.' When forced to adapt his technique and give the ball a 'biff' as he called it, he really didn't know what he was doing. 'It was not a matter of looking odd, I felt odd and tended to cling to the style that had served me so well. This was a MISTAKE.' The capitals are his. 'I should have applied myself with determination to add new methods to my game.'

He remembers batting with Peter May in a one-day exhibition match in Canberra, in other words, not a terribly serious contest. The wicket was slow and low and a couple of goodish off-spinners were operating. Colin was playing orthodox shots against the off break, that is, turning the wrists and closing the face of the bat when the ball was wicket to wicket, thus hitting with the spin on the leg side. If the ball was pitched outside the line of off stump, he would look to hit it through the off side. But he was having trouble piercing the shrewdly set field.

May, by contrast, was having no such problems. He simply placed his front foot straight down the wicket and hit the ball in the air, over the infield, in an arc between mid-off and cover point, 'inside out', as cricketers call it. It was the same when a slow left-armer came on. Colin was hitting the ball with the spin, in other words into the off-side field, which was heavily populated. May merely plonked his foot down the wicket and 'fetched' the ball over to the leg side, which wasn't heavily populated. Mike Smith had played in the same way, to Colin's great admiration, when he got his double hundred in the Varsity match of 1954.

The crucial point of May's technique, Colin observed, was 'getting hurry on the bat through the ball – what golfers call speed of the club head through the ball.' This being an exhibition match, Colin was minded to try and follow suit. It felt alien to him. 'I tried it in the nets or when the pressure was off, like here, but I rarely had the confidence to do it in the middle, during a Test match. My method was a light bat, a calm frame of mind and stillness at the crease, moving only when the ball was released. I found it difficult to make up my mind where and how to hit it before the ball was bowled.'

He finishes his searing self-examination with regret, 'I should have copied Mike Smith, by fetching the ball pitched outside the off stump on to the leg side, and done the same as Peter, and practised hitting over the top.' Try as he might, he could not do it regularly as a means of getting out of trouble or breaking a deadlock; he could only manage it when well set.

The other bane of his cricketing life, the scourge of the England captaincy and his ambition to lead a side abroad, continued to bedevil him throughout this period. Press speculation resurfaced when the incumbent, Ted Dexter, in his mercurial way, had made himself unavailable for the tour to South Africa in 1964/65 because he was contesting the seat of Cardiff South East as a Conservative candidate in the general election. His opponent was Jim Callaghan and he lost but by then the selectors had already appointed his successor – not Colin, but Mike Smith. Colin had originally made himself unavailable but then changed his mind but it was too late. His inclusion would have unbalanced a side already decided upon.

Smith did a fine job in South Africa, winning the series 1-0, on the strength of which he was retained as captain for the home series in 1965 against New Zealand and South Africa. In the meantime, Dexter had been the victim of an unfortunate accident, breaking his leg when his Jaguar pinned him against a warehouse door as he was pushing it to the nearby garage to fill an empty tank. It signalled, more or less, the end of his Test career. The way was clear for Smith to make the job of captain his for the foreseeable future.

The thing is that Colin had no problem, either on a personal or a professional level, with Smith's appointment. No qualms, no misgivings, no resentment, no apprehensions. In fact, he went so far as to say, 'Mike Smith was one of the best captains I have played with.'

They had known each other since their Oxford days, they had been team-mates, they respected each other as cricketers and both knew that they had the interests of the England team at heart. Colin found him calm and unflappable, even in the most dramatic of situations.

'Mike's answer to a problem was usually to doze off or do the *Daily Telegraph* crossword. And then he would give his decision, clearly and definitively.'

Colin's high opinion of Smith as a captain was shared by most of the players in the teams he led. They appreciated his undemonstrative style, his absent-minded, professorial approach, his cheerful confidence, in himself and his players, and his sensible, thoughtful decision-making. Above all, he allowed the individuals in his side to be themselves, believing that if they were good enough to be picked for England, they would be good enough to make up their own minds how they should play.

Above all, he had no ego; everything was subordinate to the needs of the team. The tours to South Africa and Australia were deemed to be among the happiest undertaken by MCC since the war. 'Look, I skippered most of the sides I played in,' he told me, 'so I was pretty experienced in the job. I enjoyed it. I trusted the boys and we had very little trouble off the field. And we had a good side, which helps!'

One hopes that Colin put all thoughts of the captaincy to one side and concentrated on his own game, mid-career wobble or not. His form that summer was greatly improved. Against the New Zealanders, his 119 at Lord's helped to clinch a victory by seven wickets and in the third Test at Headingley, where England completed a clean sweep of the series, he witnessed the most improbable triple century of all time.

It seems absurd to report that John Edrich's 310 not out was lucky – but it was. The wicket was greenish in colour and each ball left a mark as it seamed about, sometimes extravagantly so. It was not easy to bat on, as Colin found out for himself. His innings of 13 was painfully accumulated, with much playing and missing, before he was bowled. Meanwhile, at the other end, Edrich was swatting the bowling seemingly without a care in the world. He would play and miss on average twice an over, Colin reckoned, but then he would hit a four. Then another four. Sometimes a six. His tally contained 57 boundaries, the highest number in any Test innings. Colin was in awe. He wrote, 'I am convinced I shall never see another innings like it.'

He was particularly impressed with Edrich's total concentration, how he put aside at once the ball that he had just missed and set his mind to playing the next. 'It is a gift that all great champions have, whatever the sport.'

The South Africans later that summer were made of sterner stuff, determined to avenge their defeat at the hands of Smith's team that winter. This they did, with a solitary victory in the second Test at Trent Bridge. The Nottingham crowd, together with Colin at closer quarters, had their first sighting of the new *wunderkind* from the Cape, Graeme Pollock, whose majestic 125 (out of 269) in the first innings paved the way for a 94-run victory. The only other player to reach three figures on either side was Colin (105 out of 240).

Apart from GP, as Graeme Pollock was known, the other player from the visitors who captivated English supporters was Colin Bland. For his fielding, not his batting, though he was a formidable batsman in his own right. It is difficult to explain to a modern audience what an impact he made wherever the South Africans were playing. There is no really outstanding fielder around today and that may be because the overall standard of fielding has greatly improved over the years, an undoubted by-product of the proliferation of one-day cricket. They're all good fielders now.

The South Africans were always acclaimed for their athletic fielding and this side were no different. But Bland stood out, even among these naturally gifted sportsmen. One's mind wanders down the list of magnificent outfielders over the years – Alan Ealham, Derek Randall, Paul Sheahan, Viv Richards, Clive Lloyd (before these two West Indians took to the slips), Jonty Rhodes – but none of them could hold a candle to Bland. He was phenomenal.

Colin was not alone in his wide-eyed astonishment of Bland's two run-outs in one afternoon in the Lord's Test. His victims were Ken Barrington and Jim Parks. Jim told me that when he knew he was in trouble and was sprinting for the other end, making sure that he had put his body between Bland and the stumps, Bland actually threw the ball *under* his legs to send the middle stump cartwheeling out of the ground. It was breathtaking.

I remember attending the Oval Test that summer and I couldn't take my eyes off Bland all day as he prowled about in the covers. He had an extraordinary throw, not really overarm, more of a mid-shoulder flick, and the ball would arrow to bail height, with no discernible arc in its trajectory. More often than not, the wicketkeeper would have to lean slightly over the top of the stumps to prevent Bland's throw from wrecking them. It is from that afternoon that I can date my abiding love affair with fielding. It was not only players from other countries who feared Bland with a ball in his hand.

His own countrymen were petrified of him. Barry Richards told me a story of a Currie Cup match. Whenever the ball went on the side of the wicket where Bland was lurking, a great shout from the dressing room, let alone the two batsmen, went up. 'NO!' Bland drifted deeper and deeper, practically patrolling the boundary. Still no one dared take the proffered single. Bland would lope in, pick up the ball and lob it back, underarm, to the bowler. How many runs were shunned is not recorded. It was only after the match had finished that Bland admitted he had thrown his arm out.

We are indebted to Colin for a snippet of the most riveting piece of sporting television from that era. So impressed was he by Bland's fielding that he asked him whether he was prepared to put on a little exhibition when the South Africans visited Canterbury. The ever modest Bland agreed, surprised but delighted. A large crowd gathered to watch the spectacle. A set of stumps was put up, a box of balls was produced and one of the Kent team rolled each ball along the ground some 25 yards in the direction of the fielder, to his left and right.

I will let Colin describe what happened, 'With Bland's first throw, he knocked the stumps sideways, with the next two he missed narrowly, with his fourth he lifted two stumps out of the ground and with his fifth he laid the remaining one flat.'

There was no sixth. The spontaneous applause was long and appreciative. Colin bemoaned the fact that no video footage was taken of the exhibition but in this he is wrong. It was broadcast on television later. I know. I saw it. Sadly, he ends his reminiscences of the summer with the observation that this was the last the English public were to see of a South African side poised on the cusp of greatness. The political storm clouds were gathering and, as we know, Colin was about to be caught in its eye.

Though he did not wish it, speculation among one or two reporters that Colin was seriously being considered for the captaincy of the forthcoming tour to Australia resurfaced in the weeks before the party was announced. In the event, he was content that the selectors kept faith with Smith in spite of losing the three-match series against South Africa and more than happy to support his friend as vice-captain on his fourth tour of that country, his third as second-in-command.

This time, he was not press-ganged into opening. There were three openers in the party, Boycott, Barber and Edrich, and they all played in all five Tests, Edrich going in at number three.

'You know, I never understood his problem with opening,' Mike Smith confided in me. 'Technically, he was well suited. It was a reflection of everybody's regard for his ability that he was asked to do it. I know he never really fancied it but he was so good he could have made it his own.'

Making room for another middle-order batsman was the unspoken supplement, of which England had a few – Dexter, Barrington, Smith, Graveney, with Parfitt, Close and others in the wings. Smith believes that Colin ought to have been given full rein as captain in the West Indies in 1959/60, when May was ill, shouldn't have gone and was forced to come home early. 'It would have settled things a bit,' Smith said. But this was 1965/66 now and Smith had his own way of doing things.

There was a marvellous piece filed by Ian Wooldridge for the *Daily Mail* about a press conference early on in the tour. He describes the England captain thus, 'He strolled in with an open-necked shirt, a white linen jacket which appeared to have been slept in for a week and a carrycot containing a slumbering junior member of the Smith dynasty. Apparently, Mrs Smith had gone shopping and MJK was left holding the baby.' This calmness, Colin knew, was part of his philosophy, which some people mistakenly took for softness.

The avowed intent of MCC was no different to the aims of the previous tour to Australia under Dexter, to win back the Ashes by playing attractive cricket. Oddly, the narrative of events followed more or less a similar pattern. England played well, took a 1-0 lead but their impetus faltered, Australia fought back immediately, the series was tied at 1-1 and stalemate came to pass. Thus Australia retained the urn and what had promised much for the Englishmen ended in disappointment. Colin had a good tour. He missed the first Test through illness but scored his usual hundred at Melbourne, his favourite ground overseas, and ended up with an average of 53.40.

How was Colin as a tourist and vice-captain? Smith's reply was unhesitating. 'He was a good tourist, very helpful, as you would expect. He wasn't a drinker and didn't prop up the bar after play but the thing is, he knew so many people everywhere he went that he was always asked out for dinner somewhere. No surprise really. He was such a nice bloke. I always got on well with him.'

And as a player? 'I loved watching him bat. The purity of his batsmanship was a joy. His temperament was not to bash the ball but ease it away with perfect timing. He would provide the anchor of the innings. Everybody who played with him said he was one of the best. And don't forget his slip catching, *par excellence.* Not the most mobile and not given to flinging himself around. But great hands. All the bowlers wanted him in the slips.'

In his book, Colin refers to the 1960s as the era of the West Indies. He was not to know at the time of writing that the era was to extend through the 1970s and 1980s to the 1990s, before it came to an end. The 1966 vintage were lying in wait that summer and England were duly ambushed. The first Test was lost embarrassingly easily, by an innings and 40 runs, and heads were going to roll. Why that should always have to be a natural consequence of defeat I am never quite sure but the experts and pundits seem to think as much, so it must be so.

The head most likely to roll – it always is – was the head himself, the captain. Colin, for one, thought this was unfair. Smith had done well in Australia and had the team's confidence. Jim Parks believed the result of the game rested on the toss, which Smith lost. I have my own theory. It was because the West Indies had more initials before their names, an advantage we would normally associate with the amateur, public school tradition of the English. Only M.J.K. Smith could be put in the same bracket as the splendidly initialled A.D.A. St J. McMorriss, G. St A. Sobers and his cousin, D.A.J. Holford. The selectors however blamed the captain and Smith was sacked.

And that was it? 'Er, not quite. I was recalled for the 1972 series against Australia. But it was the end of the England captaincy for me, you're right.' *Any qualms?* 'None whatsoever. I wasn't getting enough runs. That was the long and the short of it. No, I had no problems with being dropped.' *I'm intrigued, Mike, what was Colin like as a runner between the wickets?* He laughed. 'For someone who got rejected by the RAF because of his feet, he wasn't too bad. You wouldn't be pressing for two very often, mind you. But he was a good judge of a run.' *You kept in touch?* 'Indeed we did. We'd meet up at Lord's from time to time and we were on the same MCC cricket committee for a time. Nice chap.

Couldn't help but be fond of him. He was the obvious choice to take over once I'd been dropped.'

It was with a resigned shrug that Colin took the expected call from the chairman of selectors. Yes, of course he would be delighted to step once more into the breach. It is always an honour to captain one's country. No, I'm sure the boys will readily fall in behind me. It's a pity I have no time to plan, to prepare, to put my mark on the team but we all know what to do and we're all professionals. Well, of course, I'm not a professional myself, but you know what I mean. Yes, I understand it's not a permanent appointment. So how long will...? Ah, three Tests. I see. But there are four left. Never mind. I shall do my best.

He could have written the script himself. He had been there before, on more than one occasion. At least the next match was at Lord's. He never lost the sense of anticipation and awe whenever he stepped on to the playing surface at HQ. And it *was* an honour to captain his country at the home of cricket.

To rejig the batting, in came Boycott, Graveney, after an inexplicable three years in the wilderness and D'Oliveira, who will be looming large in our story shortly. Nobody who saw, and heard, the thunderous welcome the MCC members gave to Graveney as he walked out to bat on his return to the Test side will ever forget it, only exceeded perhaps by the reception as he came back, four agonising runs short of a triumphant century. The England team seemed energised.

When West Indies subsided to 95/5 in their second innings (effectively 9/5), a home victory seemed all but assured. One man stood in their way, however, and when that man was Sobers, you always feared the worst. Together with his cousin David Holford, they moved the score up to 369 before Sobers declared. They were both undefeated, Sobers on 163 and Holford on 105.

Colin came in for some predictable but slightly unfair criticism for his lack of imagination in attempting to dismiss Sobers. But he would not have been the first, nor was he to be the last, to be thwarted by the brilliance and the genius of the greatest cricketer the world has ever seen. Sobers was at it again in the third and fourth Tests, scoring 94 at Trent Bridge and 174 at Headingley. England had drawn at Lord's but there was no hiding place in the other two Tests, which they lost heavily.

No prizes for guessing the gist of the phone call Colin received at the completion of his temporary three-match stint in charge, 'Really sorry, old boy, such a shame...but we feel the time has come for a change, new blood and all that...you do understand, I'm sure... but thank you for your efforts, much appreciated...oh, by the way, we feel it best that you take a rest at The Oval...go away and recharge your batteries at Kent.'

That is precisely what he did. He was grateful for the enveloping blanket of support and sympathy from his home county because the hurt was considerable. His last chance of nailing down the captaincy of his country had come and gone and he felt sore. In retrospect, he believed it was a mistake by the selectors to call on him again; they would have been better served if they had made a complete break from the past and appointed someone new. His last words on the matter sound so sorrowful, 'It would certainly have saved me a great deal of personal pain.'

6

Man of Kent

Kent CCC 1950–76

'Cricket without fun...well, it's just no fun at all.'

Colin Cowdrey

'KIPPER – he's a god here among the hop-pickers.' I gave a wry, sidelong glance at my driver as he negotiated the high-hedged lanes of Kent. I was amused by the fact that he had combined the image of a fish, a deity and a seasonal industry, all in one short sentence. Mike Taylor, my friend and team-mate at Hampshire, had a rich lexicon of expressive idioms, including a whole glossary of Cockney rhyming slang. He also had an encyclopaedic knowledge of his fellow pros.

He was right about Colin Cowdrey. I noted that when he came in to bat – it was at Tunbridge Wells – the members stood to applaud him to the wicket. When he went out to bat, mark you, not when he came back; it was as if he was making his farewell appearance. He was not. There was plenty of life in the old dog yet but clearly he enjoyed an exalted position in the affections of the Kent faithful.

Kent is a bit of an odd county, I have always thought, and this is from one who lived there for a time. For the most part, people drive through it, on their way to the continent, rather than stop off in it, as a destination. Despite the fact that road and rail links with London are second to none, the place always felt a little cut off. I am reminded of a bizarre exchange we had with our opponents in a Second XI Championship game between Kent and Hampshire at the Crabble Ground in Dover, a quite beautiful and spectacular arena carved out of the side of the hill. The cause of the dispute between the two teams escapes me, so it cannot have been very important, probably something to do with a breakdown in communications between the captains about a declaration. The conversation went something like this:

'Typical. How can you trust a county that plays at nine different venues?'

'To paraphrase Winston Churchill.'

'Eh?'

'He was being rude about the French. He said, how can you trust a nation that has 300 different types of cheeses.'

'That was de Gaulle, not Churchill.'

'Whatever. Didn't know the Frogs played cricket.'

'What's cheese got to do with it anyway?'

The point was – I think – that Kent had no home. Well, they did, it was Canterbury, but they played so many of their home games at other places that they seemed to lack a base, a focal point, a fortress. Most home games to their own players must have felt like away matches. Not that the Kent members worried much about that. What was indisputable was that the support for their team around the county was as passionate and as vociferous as anywhere.

And at the apex of their veneration was Colin Cowdrey. County members always hold a special place in their hearts for one of their own, a loyal and dependable member of the team who is born and bred in their midst. Colin was not born in Kent but he was locally grown. Moreover, he was an England player, captain no less, revered around the world, and he was *theirs*. I'm sure Colin was aware of the eminence of his stature at Kent – he certainly gave a little, shy smile as he was applauded to the wicket that day – but I expect he found it a strain too.

'Some are born great, some achieve greatness and some have greatness thrust upon 'em.'

How did Colin Cowdrey attain such an exalted position in the affection of Kent supporters? In which of the three categories of greatness, enunciated by Malvolio in Shakespeare's *Twelfth Night*, did he fit? Colin's prowess as a batsman, you could argue, he was born with. So far as his leadership qualities can be traced, undoubtedly his background and education prepared him for positions of authority, greatness by any other name. As for Malvolio's final dictum, Colin may have had the captaincy of Kent 'thrust' upon him rather more quickly than he had anticipated but I doubt he demurred.

Few were in any doubt at the time that Colin was destined, sooner or later, to assume the captaincy of his home county. 'Kipper was probably inked in as a future skipper when he was at Tonbridge,' A.C. Smith told me. 'Think about it – captain at Tonbridge, captain at Oxford, established England player and, crucially, an amateur.'

It was while he was on tour in South Africa in 1956/57 that he got the call – actually, of course, it was a cable – from the Kent cricket committee, one of whose members was his father-in-law, Stuart Chiesman, asking him to take over the captaincy the following summer. Colin was now 25, not exactly a youngster, but there were plenty of older, more experienced players in that Kent team, not least of whom was his England team-mate, Godfrey Evans. How would they take to being led by a relative rookie? The clue lies in that one word of Alan Smith's – 'amateur'.

You see, the 1950s were quite different to the 1960s and 1970s, in cricket as in so many things. Colin's career spanned two generations, from Lindwall and Miller, ocean voyages, short back and sides, jackets and ties, big bands and Gentlemen and Players to Lillee and Thomson, jet travel, shoulder-length hair, flares, big collars and definitely *no* ties, stadium rock and stroppy egalitarianism.

This being 1957, in an altogether more deferential age, it is unlikely that any of the senior players of that Kent team would have considered his appointment out of order, and if they did, they would have kept their mouths shut. Godfrey Evans gave his immediate, unequivocal support, 'Give it a go, Master. We'll be behind you.' Colin was already known as 'Master' in the Kent dressing room.

There were two reasons Evans was so confident that Colin would have the full support of his Kent team-mates. First, they knew that the committee would revert to the practice of having an amateur captain, following the less than successful tenure of the professional, Doug Wright. Wright had been a fine servant of both Kent and England but as Colin diplomatically put it, he was finding the job of captaincy 'burdensome'.

So, if it is going to be an amateur, most of the team would have reasoned that at least we will have an amateur who is worth his place in the team. After all, some counties had amateur captains foisted upon them who were simply not good enough players. Not only will we have a good player as a captain, they would have argued, but also we will have one of England's finest. The other reason was that Kent were struggling, and had been for a number of years. The halcyon period of the pre-war years, with Frank Woolley, Tich Freeman, Les Ames and Doug Wright strutting their stuff, was long ago. Perhaps this young man will usher in a new era.

If that was to be so, it wasn't going to happen overnight. As was his wont, Colin sat down and pondered the task ahead, its magnitude and how best to set about it. A plan was what he needed and he loved planning. First and foremost – and in this regard he was very much to the fore of current thinking – he recognised that he needed help to run things, to wit, a manager. The role, to the best of his knowledge, had never been initiated at county level. But it made sense the more he thought about it.

He assumed that he was now an England fixture and would be for some time so it was likely he would miss a fair number of county games each season. He would therefore need someone to run things in his absence, someone he could trust and someone the rest of the team would follow. Not on the field of play – he could leave that to his vice-captain – but as a permanent presence around the place, to organise, to support, to control, to censure, in short to ensure that always things were done the Kent way.

It needed a special person with special qualities and in truth there was only one such man. Les Ames had been an outstanding wicketkeeper-batsman for Kent and England before the war and was, to put it mildly, a legend in these parts. Retired now, he needed persuading to return to the fold, albeit in a non-playing capacity, but Colin was confident by now of his ability to twist arms. Sure enough Ames agreed. The partnership endured and flourished until 1972 and their friendship until Ames's death in 1990.

But Rome wasn't built in a day. For a start, there were only 15 players on the staff. Yes, a team comprises 11 players so, in theory, four reserves in case of injury does not sound so bad. Several factors have to be taken into consideration,1 however. Regular calls were made on Kent players for Test match duty, more and more as they became increasingly successful. Fifteen contracted professionals suddenly seem slim pickings.

Furthermore, where was the next generation going to come from if there were not enough players to compete properly in the Second XI Championship? Up until this point, Kent had been relying on a cohort of amateur club players to make up the numbers, most of whom were no more than that, stocking fillers. Compared to other counties, Kent were woefully understaffed. The players they had were past their peak. The war had deprived the county stalwarts, Fagg, Todd, Valentine, Wright et al, of their best years and this was reflected in the two decades afterwards when results were generally disappointing. This was true of all counties of course but Kent seemed less equipped than most to make up the shortfall.

The grounds were rackety, dilapidated and barely fit for purpose. Colin remembers the team having to change in shifts in some dressing rooms because they were so small and the continual hazard of splinters from wooden floors raked by studded boots was a nuisance they could have all done without. Facilities across the board were in urgent need of upgrading. But where was the money coming from? The year before, 1956, the club had made a loss of £12,000, an almost catastrophic figure in those days. One ray of sunshine in all this gloom was that Kent seemed to be maintaining its plentiful and loyal support around its outposts.

Colin's job was threefold, he believed. First, he needed to improve standards and draft in younger, better players. To this end, he set in motion a system of recruitment that left no changing room or club bar in the county unvisited in Kent's pursuit of new talent. He was going to build a team for the future. Secondly, he had to turn a deficit into a profit. This was not his prime responsibility – that was the committee's job – but he saw it very much as his duty as captain to beat the drum around the cricket clubs and centres of influence. To this end, by his own calculation, he attended 164 functions during the winter of 1957/58, there being no overseas tour that year, to spread the gospel. Fine practice, you might say, for his later calling as an accomplished after-dinner speaker but I bet Penny, his new wife, was not that impressed.

However, needs must, and his beloved Kent demanded fealty. And lastly, he had to convince his team that they *could* do it. Many were of the firm conviction that it was impossible to win the championship playing at so many out grounds. Conditions varied and it was like playing every home game away. Not so, averred their captain; we have to build a team that is multi-functional, capable of winning in all conditions, on all surfaces.

That took time. It is clear enough from the records that Kent were everybody's whipping boys once those fine players who had lost their best years to the war began to lose their edge and retire. Colin was still a young man and though he had made his debut way back in 1950, he was not really part of the scene until he returned from Australia in 1955.

What was it like during those fallow years, playing in a weak team, expecting to get beaten every time you took the field? I spoke to Derek Ufton, whom we have already met in these pages, about that depressing time. 'The big players who had served us so well and for so long were simply not being replaced,' he said. 'Furthermore, we had a succession of not very good captains. It's all right if you have a good team and everybody knows his job, then tactics become not so important and you can get by with a moderate leader. But we were a poor side from about 1950 onwards and for all that time we were without a proper captain.'

So what was the prevailing reaction to Colin's appointment? 'We were delighted. He was young, yes, but by no means inexperienced. The team had stability at last. Slowly, things started to improve.' *What about the influence of Les Ames?* 'Crucial. But Colin too must take a fair share of the credit for Kent's revival. Les may have uncovered the talent but Colin built a team around that. While I was there – I retired in 1963 – we became a steady, consistent side. Good Lord, I was batting at number eight! And I can safely say I was the best number eight in the country.'

I was keen to ask him of his views of Colin as a captain. 'Well, he was immature at the start. He needed to do a bit of growing up. Probably this had a lot to do with his being an only child, who didn't see his parents for seven or eight years. Occasionally, he'd have problems with one or two of the older players but Les was a huge help and support. Slowly, Colin grew into the job. What's more, he was getting a lot of hundreds for us. Such a wonderful player. Peter May was regarded as the best player in England after the war but there were times when Colin made him look like a selling plater.'

I beg your pardon? 'A selling plater. Never heard of it? It's a racing term, meaning a horse that's not very good.' I had to admit that my knowledge of horse racing jargon had never stretched that far but his judgement was clear enough. I had heard it said about Colin's batting more times than I care to mention. Sometimes, he made it seem he was batting with the gods.

'The point is, Colin was such a nice man. Every day of his life, he became a nicer man. He was no tactical genius, though he knew the game inside out. His strength as a leader was his personality. The rest, how we all played, what our jobs were...well, we knew what we had to do and we got on with it.'

There was one last word Ufton was keen to have. 'Colin was president of Kent in 2000. He died in office. The position of president was in the gift of the incumbent. Before he died, he invited me to succeed him, which I did, in 2001. It was the kindest act and the greatest privilege.

Colin's opinions on these stalwarts of his early years as captain are equally fulsome. In his notes, he refers to Ufton as 'a marvellous person to have in your side, an excellent wicketkeeper and doughty left-handed batsman'. He said that Ufton was patient and understanding in his role as Godfrey Evans's understudy, only coming into his own when Evans was injured (rarely) or on England duty (frequently). He also remembered being present at Wembley when Ufton made his first and only appearance in an England shirt against the Rest of the World in 1954. Colin knew his football so we can have faith in his judgement when he referred to Upton as a 'hugely competent centre-half'.

Another footballer/cricketer who played for Kent at the time was Stuart Leary. Colin called him 'one of the most gifted games players of all'. He was a regular fixture in the Charlton side, 'small but fast, he held the ball for that vital, extra second, able to distribute the precision pass that would send the opposition into a panic'. Leary came over from Cape Town when he was 16 and 'loved his cricket more than anything else'.

An exceptional close-to-the-wicket fielder, useful leg-spinner and fine batsman, he might well have become, according to Colin, an automatic Test cricketer had it not been for his football commitments. 'He was an automatic selection for Kent when I was playing,' said Colin, 'but his batting did not quite blossom as we expected, no doubt on account of playing both games under the spotlight, which took its toll.'

At this juncture in the story of Colin's county career, we might as well confront a controversy that started to swirl around him, namely the vexed question of 'walking'. This refers to the unwritten law that pertained in the domestic game that you should walk if you know you are out without waiting for the umpire to be forced to make a decision.

Obviously, this did not include LBWs; no batsman is *ever* out LBW, as we know, and if he is given out LBW, that is only because of the incompetence of the umpire. No, it referred to whether or not the batsman had hit it, usually a snick to the wicketkeeper. The logic of this tacit understanding among the players was that the batsman invariably knew he had hit it and if he remained at the crease, feigning innocence, he was in effect 'cheating'. One or two players on the circuit got a name for themselves as being a 'cheat' and unfortunately but incontrovertibly Colin was one of them.

I put the epithet in inverted commas to declare my misgivings about the whole business. First, it has to be pointed out that it only applied to county cricket. Test matches were exempt, for the very good reason that other countries simply did not abide by the custom; Australians, for one, were self-confessed non-walkers. They preferred to wait for, and abide by, the umpire's decision.

Famously, Richie Benaud, captain of the visiting Australian touring team in 1961, when asked in a press conference about his views on walking, replied that he would leave it to each individual in his team whether to walk or not. Fair enough. Everybody knew where he stood. As long as there was no argument with the umpire once the decision has been made, right or wrong. But English county players, a tight-knit, relatively small band of brothers, felt that honesty should prevail and that the tradition of walking should be upheld. And if anyone fell short of the ideal, this being a small world in which word of mouth spread rapidly, he would be labelled a 'cheat'.

All I can say is which of us can put hand on heart and state categorically that we have always walked? Even when it was the thinnest of edges? What happens if no one else hears the snick and doesn't appeal? Do you walk off anyway? What if you have been the unfortunate victim of a succession of umpiring blunders? Are you not entitled to level things up a bit? What happens if it is the last ball of the match and yours is the last wicket? The temptation to stay would be nigh on overwhelming. What if this was your final chance to make a score before being dropped – yet again – and more than likely shown the door, the end to your career? Say you hated the bowler. He had been peppering you all day with bouncers, accompanied by muttered threats and evil glares, and your animosity had been fermenting for years? Are you really going to give your wicket to your worst enemy?

As you can see, the problem is hedged in with ambiguity and equivocation. For clarification, I sought the opinion of John Woodcock. 'Les Ames used to say that everybody walked in the 1930s. Rubbish! It's human nature not to walk on occasions. I know of no single player who walked every time. The Rev. David Sheppard – now, if you would expect anyone to be completely honest and walk every time, it would be him – he didn't always walk.' After a moment's consideration, he added this, 'With the possible exception of Ted Dexter. I do believe he walked, every time.'

So what about Colin? 'Look, Colin never set himself up as a disciple of walking. The trouble was, I suppose, that he made a show of walking off immediately when he had obviously hit it, you know, bat under the arm and stripping off his gloves, as he quit the crease. But there were times when he didn't, just like everybody else, and perhaps, *perhaps,* one or two umpires were swayed by that.'

Another person who knew Colin well and played against him was Hubert Doggart, captain of Sussex in 1954, headmaster of King's School, Bruton in Somerset, treasurer and president of the MCC, a fellow administrator and lover of the game. *What about Colin and the question of walking, Hubert?* 'We got to know each other well on a tour to the West Indies, organised by Jim Swanton, to heal the wounds of an acrimonious England tour there the year before. He was hit on the hand and he came up to me at the other end when the over was finished and made the extraordinary observation that batting is so difficult! Now Hammond would never have said that.'

Yes, but what about walking? 'One minute. Don't be impatient. I shall get there in the end. As Colin eased the ball to the boundary, I stood there in amazed admiration. What timing!' *And walking?*

'Walking! What nonsense. We were never encouraged to walk. It was never an issue in our era. I think it only became one later, long after I had finished playing. My sense is that this controversy about walking and Colin was all a bit manufactured. He never held himself up as an advocate of walking.'

So, there we are, as clear as mud. Was Colin a walker? Yes, most of the time. Was he a cheat? Not in my opinion and in the mind of others. Did some regard him as a cheat? Quite possibly, but as we have seen, the morality of the whole thing is cloudy at best. Let me leave the final word to Woodcock. 'Colin played in a good era, where standards of sportsmanship were upheld. I don't think he would have liked playing today. Even when he was alive, he was dismayed by the gradual erosion of manners and etiquette. He was the complete good man. Was he a saint...?' He paused for effect. 'I know of no saintly cricketer, do you? Not even the Rev. David Sheppard.'

By now, if not yet canonised, Colin was a hugely experienced county captain, to say nothing of his success in that role with the England team, so this seems as good a place as any to examine his style, his way of doing things. To my great good fortune, there is practically a whole chapter in his notes laying bare his thoughts on this very topic. There is nothing particularly revolutionary in the breakdown of his principles – he does not advocate new ideas like 'leg theory' (Jardine) or slow over rates (Hutton) or four-pronged pace attack (Lloyd) or 'mental disintegration' (Waugh) – but it does reveal the man under the cloak of office. In short, he captained as he lived his life, cautiously, considerately, conservatively but knowledgeably, thoughtfully and diligently.

Only a great captain – and he does not include himself among that small number – can get all of his team to perform at their maximum all the time, 'So the skill and fun of leadership is to see how much he can get from his men.' He is greatly exercised by temperament. 'We are all temperamental and need careful handling,' he writes. 'As far as humanly possible, a captain must treat each individual as a special case.' For example, to get the best out of Boycott and Snow, as he did on the tour of West Indies in 1967/68, both of whom were vastly different characters, he had to employ different strategies. As another example, he makes mention of his two England compatriots from Surrey, Jim Laker and Tony Lock. 'Lock needed the stick and Laker the carrot.'

As you would expect, common decency informs all his actions. 'The best captains in my experience never let slip a word of criticism against any of his players in public,' and he goes on, 'Look for the best and expect the best but be ready to make allowances, rather than carping at weaknesses.'

Easier said than done. Any cricketer who has captained a side knows what it is to have a sore tongue from biting it as he helplessly watches a dolly dropped or a careless fumble in the field. 'Some captains stride around making a lot of noise,' Colin observes, 'but I have seen many good captains who have extended their authority and influence in a much quieter way.'

We can hazard a guess which style he espoused. Ah yes, here it is a little further down the page, 'Personally, I prefer the quieter way. It suits my temperament.' That is not to say that a captain should be a soft touch. I am reminded of Tom Graveney's remark about his captain on that West Indies tour, 'Colin was usually such a gentle and nice man... but on this tour he cracked the whip.'

There is an interesting and illuminating paragraph in these notes underlining his *modus operandi*. He believes that trial and error (e.g. experience) are needed to bring out the best of each member of his team. For example, when he first started out as a captain, the custom was for the captain (an amateur) to set and alter fields, even if it meant overruling the bowler (a professional). Colin tended to follow suit but then changed his mind. 'I became very reluctant to do this. The bowlers were picked on merit to bowl sides out. I cannot do it for them. They must do it for themselves. I don't expect them to tell me how to bat.'

Perhaps not. But there, he was one of the best batsmen in England. There might have been one or two amateur captains around, purportedly batsmen, who probably came in for a bit of *sotto voce* stick from their professional team-mates, but not the Kent captain. But listen to this, a telling affirmation of his captaincy style, 'I regard the captain in the field as the chairman of the board, carving out an overall policy and leaving it to his departmental heads to get on with their jobs.'

His father-in-law, Stuart Chiesman, had he been still alive, would have nodded his head in agreement. Others might not. I am put in mind of more dictatorial captains, such as Jardine, Close, Illingworth, Greig, who employed different methods. That is not to say one way is right and the other way wrong. The two Mikes, Smith and Brearley, notably operated in a more collegiate manner.

As a captain, Colin felt that you had to enjoy the game and, crucially, convey your enjoyment to the rest of your team. 'Cricket is a game of fun,' he insists. 'By fun, I do not mean hilarious social entertainment. The fun is in the heat of competition.' That much is true, certainly from his perspective. Elsewhere, he admitted that he did not always bat as well as he might when there was nothing on the game, in a benefit, charity or dead match. He was at his best when something was riding on the result. When you are the captain, something is always riding on the result. Should your lack of enthusiasm for the contest manifest itself in any way, your players will soon pick this up and they too will find their energy draining away.

This concept of having 'fun' while still engaged in the combat of a Test match was very important to him. 'I feel very strongly about this and felt ever more strongly about it as the years went by,' he writes. He accepts that others might not agree with him, that all Test captains 'would not put at the top of their lists of attributes for being a good captain fun or enjoyment or good cheer'.

One cannot imagine Raymond Illingworth, for example, encouraging his team to have fun out there in the middle of an Ashes Test. But Colin saw no paradox in playing to win while enjoying the contest. You can play just as tigerishly with a smile upon your face as a scowl. 'In my time, I have seen the game become harder, tougher, sharper, more competitive, more commercial, more difficult. All the more reason,' he contends, 'for captains to foster this sense of fun.' And he ends this homily with a passionate exhortation, 'CRICKET WITHOUT FUN – WELL, IT'S JUST NO FUN AT ALL.' The capitals are his.

That may be so, and there is little doubt that this principle remained the lodestar of his playing career and beyond, but one aspect of captaincy, which he did not particularly relish, was team selection. 'Who'd be a selector?' he ruefully asks at the beginning of one sub-section. But he was; it went with the territory. His first painful lesson was at Tonbridge. He was no longer the tiny 13-year-old but now the captain. His closest friend had been having a hard time of it recently and was about to be dropped from the XI. Colin persuaded everyone that he should be given one last chance.

It was the wrong decision. He lay himself open to criticism – 'captain's pet' and all that – and the poor boy under the spotlight had clearly lost form and confidence and deserved to be dropped. Sure enough, he failed the next week and then the axe really did fall. 'I had learnt a lesson,' Colin admits, 'perhaps the hardest and one most relevant to life. One must be strong when making decisions which concern other people's destiny.'

Colin's detractors would say that he did not always follow his own advice, that he was not always strong as a captain. I cannot comment on that but at least I can say that he *had* guiding principles. And who of us can say we have always abided by our guiding principles?

If unpopular decisions have to be made, he contends, then it is always a comfort to have allies around you. This might sound like a truism but it is particularly important at county level where a team spends six months in each other's pockets and tempers can flare. 'During a season, I had to make numerous tough decisions at Kent.'

One problem grew out of their increasing success and recruitment of better players, some of whom would be on regular international duty. Should an England player be automatically restored to the team on his return, even if his replacement in the Kent side had just played a blinder? Colin's answer to this conundrum was to try to build a squad system, so that certain players were 'rested' from time to time. All very well and good in theory, he discovered, but the reality was that no player wanted to be rested; he always felt that he had been dropped. This is where his manager, Les Ames, and the club coach, Colin Page, played such a crucial role, in helping to smooth ruffled feathers and foster a genuine team ethic, all for one and one for all.

The ideal situation, Colin argued, was for one captain to run his own ship, with help from his lieutenants, of course. In his notes, he cites the example of Stuart Surridge, the legendary Surrey skipper during their years of hegemony of the county championship in the 1950s. First, it is important to point out that a captain does not have to be the best player in the team, though he has to be worth his place. Surridge was no great batsman nor was he more than an occasional bowler, a partnership-breaker. But he made himself an inspirational fielder, close to the wicket, always in the thick of the action. 'As a striking fielder, he was seen to be a dynamic leader,' is Colin's observation, adding admiringly, 'which was very clever.'

The point is that Surridge had no selection committee; he picked the team, and that was that. It is true that such a wonderfully gifted team that had all bases fully covered practically picked itself but, Colin argues, 'This really is the ideal situation and the greatest fun for everyone when the team clearly understands that the captain is fully in charge and responsible for his own ship.' The unspoken validation here is that the reason for the success of HMS England in Caribbean waters in 1967/68 was that there was no argument about who was skipper. Captain Cowdrey was in sole command.

That was not always the case when he captained England. He gives an amusing account, almost a short one-act play, which underlines the problems of a committee picking a team. The scene is set in 1961, when Colin was deputising as captain for Peter May. The team for the first Ashes Test has to be decided:

Scene I
It is in Gubby Allen's flat, adjoining the grounds of Lord's Cricket Ground. Allen, chairman of the selection panel, is a lifelong bachelor and the details of even basic hospitality have long escaped him. He is dressed in his dressing gown.

Cowdrey: *Good morning, Chairman. Am I early?*

Allen: *Ah Cowdrey. Eight o'clock, I said, and what time is it?.....Oh, eight, on the dot. Come in.*

Cowdrey: *Are the others on their way?*

Allen: *Not 'til nine-thirty. Thought we'd get together first to agree on what side we want.*

Cowdrey: *What happens, Sir, if they don't agree?*

Allen: *Oh, don't let's worry about that, my boy. Now, what do you reckon – tea or coffee?*

Cowdrey: *Tea, please.*

Allen: *Damn! I've only done coffee. I shall have to go and make some.*

Cowdrey: *Oh no, please. Coffee will do fine.*

Allen: *Good. Should've known you were a tea man, shouldn't I? Born in Nagpur or somewhere, weren't you?*

Cowdrey: *Bangalore.*

Allen: *Exactly. Enough of the waffle. We've got to time these eggs properly. I'm a three and a half minutes man myself. What about you?*

Cowdrey: *Three and a half will be just fine, Chairman.*

Cowdrey, as best he can, tucks into burnt toast, hard-boiled eggs and lukewarm coffee as the nucleus of a team is pencilled in. The doorbell rings. Enter the other selectors, Les Ames from Canterbury, Wilf Wooller from Cardiff and Herbert Sutcliffe from Leeds. All are immaculately attired in blazers and ties. Allen is still in his dressing gown.

Allen: *Come in, chaps. Breakfast?*

All three in unison: *No thanks, Gubby. Had some on the train.*

Allen: *Good. You all know young Cowdrey? Excellent. Right, down to business. We've more or less agreed on the side. Here it is. What do you think?*

Ames: *Not sure about him, Gubby. I think ---- is a better bowler.*

Allen: *Les, I told you he would never be picked again.*

Ames: *Yes, Gubby, but that was two years ago.*

Wooller: *I see yet again there's no representative from the Principality. We've got some excellent players down in Glamorgan, the equal of anyone on this list.*

Sutcliffe: *What about -----? Have you considered him?*

Allen (aghast): *Whaaat? Are you being serious, Herbert?*

Wooller: *He wouldn't even get in the Glamorgan Second XI.*

Ames: *That's because he can't speak Welsh.*

Allen: *No no, Herbert, that's a ridiculous suggestion. And you know it.*

Sutcliffe: *Oh, all right, if you say so, Gubby. Anything to keep the peace.*

Allen: *Now, for God's sake, can we possibly agree on these 12 names?*

Argument rages. Eventually....

Sutcliffe: *I'll have to leave it to you chaps to agree.*

Allen: *Why?*

Sutcliffe: *Got to go. It's one-thirty. My train's at two.*

Allen: *But you can't go now. We haven't agreed on the 12. We're still two short.*

Sutcliffe: *Sorry, Skipper. This meeting has gone on an awfully long time, you know. And I do have a train to catch.*

Allen is speechless with anger. Sutcliffe gets to his feet.

Sutcliffe: *Anyway, you know my feelings on the last two places.*

The doorbell goes. It is Sutcliffe's taxi. He departs. Allen is rather gloomy.

* * * * *

Scene 2

Leeds Railway Station. Sutcliffe has missed his two o'clock train. It is now early evening and the England team for the First Test has already been announced on the 6 o'clock news. The platform is thronged with newspaper reporters.

Reporter 1: *Herbert, Herbert! Yorkshire Post here....*

Reporter 2: *Mr Sutcliffe, The Times wonders whether you---*

Reporter 3: *Herbert! The Telegraph....can we quote you on----*

Reporter 4: *Any comment on the team, Herbert?*

Sutcliffe: *The team selected, gentlemen, was the unanimous choice of the committee.*

Reporter 1: *Why did you leave out Close, Herbert?*

Sutcliffe: *Oh, my God, did we?*

The whole point of this pastiche is not to denigrate the characters involved. These men, Colin is keen to emphasise, were not buffoons; they knew their cricket. But committees are unwieldy beasts and he felt happier at Kent, and with the England set-up for a time, when a small, hand-picked and loyal cadre was solely responsible for team affairs and selection. The issue of who is responsible for picking teams has always been a bone of contention at county level, he believed. 'In successful times,' he writes, 'most county committees are content to leave team affairs to the captain and manager. In lean times, the call goes out for a selection committee, which would be totally responsible for picking the XI. We at Kent wanted to change all that.' And he did. By the time he finished playing, Kent was one of the powerhouses in the domestic game.

The change, slow in coming, at last began to manifest itself in the early 1960s. A gradual improvement in Kent's position in the county championship reassured the committee that Colin was right; good times were just around the corner. In 1964, they came seventh. In 1965, they came fifth, and fifth again the following year. In 1967, they finished as runners-up to the mighty Yorkshire, the team of the decade, much as Surrey had been in the 1950s.

This was satisfying enough but the real breakthrough came at the very end of the season when Kent won the Gillette Cup, the first piece of silverware in their history. The competition at that stage was only five years old. Philosophy and tactics for limited-overs cricket were still in their infancy; a quick glance at the scorecard will show that this was a world away from the big-hitting run fests of the current game. Nevertheless, Kent won. To compare eras is fun but ultimately fruitless. By winning the cup, Kent had proved they had beaten the best around at the time and the hop-picking county celebrated as only they can.

Lord's was packed as it always was for the last showpiece of the summer. Kent were up against Somerset. Colin won the toss and elected to bat. Denness and Luckhurst, opening, made a half-century apiece, Shepherd at number three scored 30, and that was about it. From smelling the roses when they were 138/1, they tumbled into the mire, all out for 193. Colin made one.

Kent's total – and we're talking here of a time when it was 60 overs a side, not 50 – would have been undefendable in today's game. But this was 1967, not 2017. Par for the course, depending on the wicket of course, was usually regarded to be between 220 and 230. So, in these terms, Kent were by no means out of it. In fact, they secured victory with comparative ease, dismissing Somerset for 161. Look at these extraordinary bowling figures. Norman Graham bowled his 12 overs for 26 runs and John Shepherd his 12 for only one more. You will be unsurprised to hear that Underwood was the main destroyer, taking 3-44.

The list of previous winners throws up an interesting fact. For the first two years, Sussex, captained by Ted Dexter, were victorious. The following year it was Yorkshire, captained by Brian Close. The previous year, Warwickshire were winners, captained by M.J.K. Smith. So, Colin had been preceded by three England captains, all of whom had been regarded as successful in the role, tactically astute and flexible in their thinking. Who would have thought that Colin would have been among the first to crack the code of this new game and adapt to its peculiar demands? But he was. What were his strategies? What plans did he draw up? How did he put them into action? Yet again, he opens up in the typewritten pages of his notes.

Typically, he did not consider himself physically or technically suited to this particular form of the game. Whether or not he was mentally willing and able to embrace the new format, he remained ambivalent. He recognised its commercial value and enjoyed playing in front of large crowds and a big TV audience but was unsure if he ever really got it out of his mind that it was a bit of a 'hit-and-giggle' rather than a serious and technically demanding variation.

He describes in detail a recurring nightmare. It is a Sunday League match of 40 overs in front of a packed Canterbury crowd. The day is swelteringly hot and the game is being televised. Batting at number five, he had scored a hastily and not very elegantly cobbled together 25, composed mostly of scrambled singles, some of which would have resulted in a run-out had the throw hit the stumps. On one occasion, he had to dive for his life, thus covering himself in dirt, and on another, he was hit on the back of the leg by a wild throw as he scrambled for safety.

During the tea interval, he had chewed at a few sandwiches with his leg wrapped in a towel filled with ice.

Now it is time to take to the field. Absent-mindedly – he has just noticed that his sleeves are bloodstained where he had grazed his elbows – he makes his way to his usual position at first slip before a curt word from his captain reminds him that it is a Sunday and of course, there are no slips on a Sunday. He trots off to point, that being the safest place, it had been decided, for the most immobile fielder in the side.

The off-spinner is opening the bowling. He looks mournfully to his left. No third man. There does seem to be an awful lot of unoccupied outfield down there. Sure enough, the batsman plays that extraordinary shot, well, it's not really a shot at all...what's it called... oh yes, the 'reverse sweep' and damn, it's running down to third man. With a helpless look around – there's nobody else within 20 yards – he sets off in hot pursuit. He hopes, he prays, that the ball will beat him to the boundary but drat, it's slowing up. With a desperate dive, he stops it before it crosses the rope but his impetus carries him into the advertising board, which collapses with a loud clatter. Ouch, that hurt.

He picks himself up – 'Sorry, madam' – and retrieves the ball, making sure that both feet are within the boundary. He looks up to locate the wicketkeeper, who has one arm aloft, more in hope than expectation. He hurls the ball in as hard as he can, wrenching his shoulder in the process. 'Yes,' shouts the batsman running to that end. He makes it easily as the ball finally reaches the wicketkeeper on the third bounce. They have run five.

And then he wakes up. It is the middle of winter, the log fire is crackling, he sips at his gin and tonic and he wistfully thinks of all those happy years he spent fielding at first slip for England and Kent. In many ways, he comes to the conclusion as he looks back on his career, he would rather have played between the wars. The wickets were, by and large, firm and true, overs were bowled at 20 an hour and runs came quickly. Bowlers targeted the off stump, 'always looking to attack and bowl people out, with fields set for the catch on the off side'.

The leg side was full of gaps. The best players would have exploited these gaps. 'Hobbs and Bradman,' he judged, 'would never have scored at 60 or 70 an hour without plundering these gaps on the leg side.' After the war, when he learned to play, more grass was left on the wickets and as a result the quick seamers and the medium-pacers thrived: Trueman, Statham, Tyson, Loader, Bedser, Bailey, Jackson, Gladwin, Shackleton and their own Ridgeway at Kent. There were no easy runs in that era.

The 1960s changed all that. First came the Gillette Cup in 1963, followed by the Sunday League in 1969, and first-class cricketers had to learn how to play a new type of game, as well as maintaining enthusiasm for, and competence in, the traditional longer form. Colin, in keeping with a few others, found the shift challenging. But when did England's most experienced player ever shirk a challenge? He set himself the task of understanding the nature of the new beast and then taming it. That he succeeded in the first but failed in the second is not ignominious. He had plenty of goodwill in the bank; it was not a huge stain on his reputation. We can be thankful that he applied his instinct for forensic analysis, allied to his vast experience, to give us a personal insight into one-day cricket.

The advantages, as he saw them, were many, some obvious, some less so. Cricket was in the doldrums at the time and needed an injection of something new, something exciting, something fashionable, 'trendy' in the parlance of the time. Limited-overs matches, completed in one day, with a winner and loser, was just the ticket for a new generation growing up in a world that was rapidly changing.

If the 1950s were in black and white, the 1960s were in garish technicolour, and limited-overs cricket seemed to embody all that as much as miniskirts, bell bottoms, long hair and the Beatles. Although it is hard to conjure up a mental image of Colin wearing beads, a tie-dyed tee shirt and jeans, he was not so reactionary as not to recognise the new game's potential. As a financial boost, it was unquestionable and long overdue. It brought in the crowds, 'and who does not thrill when performing in front of a full house?'

There were new skills to be learnt and perfected. Fielding improved in leaps and bounds, rather too literally for his less than svelte frame but he marvelled at the athleticism of the modern player. He had one caveat though. He cringed when he saw opening bowlers flinging themselves around in the field and risking injury. 'I would ban my three strike bowlers from ever diving in the outfield. Saving a run and hurting a shoulder for the rest of the season?' The cake was not worth the candle.

The revolution in batsmanship was startling, he observed. 'From the batsman's point of view, he had to learn three things and this has broadened and improved the art. One: Be alert to playing the ball for a quick single. Two: Improvise to keep the scoreboard ticking over. Three: Learn some "slog shots" so as not to get bogged down.'

He is quite honest in these pages about his inability to adapt to these demands. He occasionally played a cameo innings, which would 'catch the eye'.

But he knew that was not enough. 'As I look back, I am rather disappointed with myself for not being quicker to adapt.' He does not say it but I will for him. That was the way he was brought up, to keep the ball on the ground at all times unless there was a clear opportunity to clear the ropes. 'I am amazed at how much the ball is in the air nowadays,' he does remark. He adds a disconsolate admission, 'If I had played more one-day cricket as a young man, I am sure I would have been a better player.'

He relied on touch and timing, not strong forearms and bigger bats. When his touch deserted him, as it did from time to time, he would have 'benefitted from being able to give it a bash'. He felt too constricted by his upbringing, 'I was stuck with a sound technique and a rigid game plan.'

If he was slow to adapt, he was in no doubt that the great players of yesteryear would have coped, indeed flourished, in the one-day game. 'They would have *revelled* in it. Grace, Ranji, Hobbs, Compton, Bradman, Worrell, Weekes, Walcott, Headley, Trumper...I could give you 50 more. But equally, I could give you a couple of hundred who would have been totally submerged.' Where he puts himself in the pantheon is unclear. Modest or simply realistic?

Perhaps this image gives us a clue. He imagines a scenario in a Gillette Cup Final. He comes in at number six with five overs to go. Underwood is bowling. How come? They are both on the same side, aren't they? Well, this is a nightmare after all. He is bowling over the wicket from wide of the crease with a 6-3 on-side field, pitching the ball at a fair old pace just outside leg and going down. 'In my first 12 years as an England player, I would have had no idea how to unravel that equation.' By this time he had already scored 18 of his 22 Test hundreds. That is quite a confession from one of the most gifted, technically speaking, of his era.

What about the bowling? On this, he is unequivocal. The whole point of one facet of the contest has been turned on its head. Bowlers used to try to get batsmen out. Now their only objective is to stop the batsman scoring. In short, their purpose has shifted from attack to defence. Furthermore, an integral part of the game, the draw, has been removed. This meant, in effect, that the art of trying to get someone out, thinking about how to dismiss a batsman, even if the plan might involve sacrificing a few runs, will 'wither on the vine'.

However, if the stated aim of bowling becomes purely the drying up of run-scoring opportunities, he cites one or two bowlers of his generation, Bedser and Statham to the fore, who would have been a nightmare to chase a total against, bowling at will straight into the blockhole. 'In these two, you have two bowlers who could do it with their eyes shut all day long.'

In short, what Colin is saying, I guess, is that the great players – bowlers and batsmen – from any era would have had the skill to adapt and prosper. The ordinary players, among whom he seems to include himself, would have had to learn how to play limited-overs cricket effectively, preferably having grown up with it from an early age. That would not have incorporated hours and hours practising hitting the ball correctly on the off side, the leg side being out of bounds and guarded by a barbed-wire fence enclosing a tennis court. There is one last comment, a daydream really, on the subject of one-day cricket. 'How I would have loved to do what Barry Richards did once to Derek Underwood, stepping outside leg stump and hitting it through the vacant gaps on the off side. The bowler I have in mind is

Bob Appleyard, just to see the expression on his face and to render him speechless for the first time in his life!'

Back to more familiar territory, the three-day game. Following their near miss in the 1967 season, finishing second to Yorkshire, Kent repeated the feat in 1968, yet again runners-up to the white rose county. I say feat but to Colin and his team-mates, it felt like a crushing disappointment. In fact, they had won one more game than Yorkshire that season but had finished below them on account of the bonus points system, odd though that might sound. This failure to garner sufficient bonus points was something that the team made note of and committed to memory.

High hopes therefore were not unrealistically held for the next season. 'Huh, dashed hopes and good intentions,' said George in *Who's Afraid of Virginia Woolf?* about his career prospects. Colin might well have said the same of the 1969 campaign. He snapped his Achilles tendon and Kent plummeted to tenth place. The two might not necessarily have been directly linked but the loss of their captain and main run-getter cannot have helped. He was undeterred. For him, the pursuit of the county championship had become something of a crusade.

To this end, he worked hard to get himself fit for the new season and in addition, something else stirred his sense of destiny. Kent's centenary year was 1970. What happier alignment of the constellation of stars could there be than to win the championship pennant on the hundredth birthday of the modern Kent CCC?

Somebody else thought so too. Edward Heath was born in Broadstairs, his constituency as an MP was Bexley and he was a Kent man through and through. He also enjoyed his cricket and was thus invited to speak at the centenary dinner held in Maidstone in January. He did well to make it. At the time he was heavily involved, as leader of the Conservative Party, in skirmishes with the prime minister, Harold Wilson, in preparation for a general election that summer.

And not doing too well, it would seem. The polls were looking bad for the Conservatives; informed opinion had Labour well in the lead. Undaunted, Heath rose to his feet and made this extraordinary, prophetic declaration, 'If I win the general election, you will win the county championship.' He elicited a roar of approbation though few took him seriously.

But Colin did. For some time he had been building a team for that very purpose and now he believed all the building blocks were in place. The stars, the game changers, the match winners were there in abundance. Denness and Luckhurst were as fine an opening pair as there was in the land. Asif Iqbal (Pakistan) and John Shepherd (West Indies) were all-rounders of the highest class. In Underwood, he had at his disposal the most destructive spin bowler of the day and in Alan Knott, he had the greatest wicketkeeper-batsman of the age, some might argue of all time.

The trouble was that the Englishmen among them would more than likely be called up for England duty, so would the cupboard look a bit bare in their absence?

Not a bit of it. Colin, and the other members of the ruling triumvirate, Ames and Page, had already identified this potential problem and made sure that they had in place a number of talented reserves, ready to step in and do the business when required. This was sensible planning. It came to pass that five, Cowdrey, Luckhurst, Denness, Underwood and Knott, made 18 Test appearances between them that summer. Some hole to fill.

Colin was not worried. He had singled out three youngsters in particular who were full of promise and who would, he believed, step into their boots and not let the side down. The three he had put his faith in became Kent legends: Graham Johnson, Alan Ealham and Bob Woolmer. The championship, if it was to be won, would not be won by 11 or 12 regulars. It would have to be won with a large, coherent and united squad. Colin was good at making people feel that they were wanted, that they were special, that they belonged, that they had a role to play.

To find out more, I sought out Graham Johnson, whom I knew from our playing days, not well but well enough from 22 yards. He was kind enough to share his memories of that eventful season and the part played by his captain. 'I remember bowling to Kipper in the nets when I was a trialist, a kid really, sometime in the mid-1960s. He hit one back at me and I attempted to stop it. "Don't do that," he said. "You might hurt yourself." Anyway I was taken on the staff. The trouble was, I wanted to go to university. So I approached Colin and explained my dilemma. "I'm building a team here," he said, "and I want you in it." Very flattering.'

But knowing you, I guess you were undaunted. You went to LSE, didn't you? 'I did, with his blessing. But he told me that any spare minute I had, the deal was that I would play for Kent.' *And there weren't many of those, considering all the demonstrations you had to go on.* He had the decency to laugh. 'I was on half a salary, which was fair enough. By 1970, I had graduated. It was my first full season.' *How did you find Colin as a captain?* 'I knew none better. He was great with individuals. He made young players like me feel very important.'

It wasn't only young English players who basked in the glow of Colin's affable personality. One West Indian and one Pakistani were to become household names in Kent on account of his powers of persuasion. On 25 February 1965, a young all-rounder made his first-class debut for Barbados at the Kensington Oval in Bridgetown against the International Cavaliers. He took 1-54 and 1-57, scoring 22 and 33, a reasonably satisfying performance but hardly one to set alarm bells ringing in opposition dressing rooms.

However, the captain of the Cavaliers took note; something in the young man's enthusiastic demeanour had caught his eye. After the match, he sidled up to him and engaged him in friendly conversation. The upshot of their chat was that John Shepherd would travel to England that summer and join Kent. Colin had secured his man.

In 1967, Pakistan were touring here and one of their warm-up games was at Canterbury. A young Asif Iqbal opened the bowling, without much success, it has to be said, but batted well in a partnership with his captain, Majid Khan, scoring 44 at number seven. Colin again watched with an appreciative, critical eye. He had been informed by Les Ames that Asif, whom Ames had seen play in a schoolboy side over here in 1963, was a useful prospect.

For the moment, Colin reserved judgement. He was to get a further look at Asif later that summer. In the third Test at The Oval, Asif, still opening the bowling by the way, and reasonably successfully on this occasion, scored a majestic 146, this time batting at nine! The measure of his achievement was that the next highest score in the Pakistan innings was 17. Single-handedly, Asif had saved his country from humiliation, if not defeat.

Colin's mind was made up. He was not alone in beating a speedy path to the Pakistan dressing room door. Several other counties were also sniffing around.

I was fortunate enough to be able to ask Asif about Colin's influence on his Kent career. He was as obliging as I had been led to believe. 'I first visited Kent in 1963 with a Pakistani Eaglets side. I managed to get a few runs and take a few wickets. I remember talking to Majid Khan, who was also on the tour, and telling him it would be nice to play county cricket in England, especially for a county like Kent. When an England under-25 side, captained by Mike Brearley and managed by Les Ames, came to Pakistan, at the end of the tour, Les casually mentioned to me that he would like to see me playing for Kent.'

And then Colin spoke to you after the Test? 'We had a chat and it didn't take long for me to be persuaded to play for Kent.' *And how was it when you arrived?* 'Well, it was a long way from home and the thing most difficult to come to terms with was the weather. The games played in April were not much fun and many a time I found myself wishing to be in front of a log fire rather than on a cricket field.' A not unfamiliar tale. I don't think I have ever met an overseas player who has not had similar first impressions of an English spring. However, Kent warmed up, both metaphorically and literally. 'Everybody at Kent bent over backwards trying to make me feel at home.' And nobody can say that Asif did not repay this generosity of spirit – in bucketfuls.

The trick of captaining a county side, or at least, one of them, I always felt, was to galvanise overseas stars in early season conditions, such as Asif describes. Nothing can dampen the spirits and undermine collective enthusiasm more than an unwilling overseas player, or worse, two of them, hanging back as everybody else takes the field, desperate to remain in the warm fug of the dressing room for a few more precious moments. It is hard not to sympathise with them, their having just jetted in from warmer climes, but come on chaps, this is the start of the new season, when it's all going to change and this time we're really going to make our mark.

The best, the most emotionally sensitive of the overseas players, recognised this and got stuck in straightaway. Shepherd and Asif were of this ilk. The triumvirate of captain, manager and coach had recognised this; you expect your principal players to lead from the front and that is what they did. What of Colin as the team prepared for the centenary season? Was he greatly in evidence during pre-season practice? Derek Underwood chuckled when I brought this up. 'Dear old Colin. His preparation was laughable, really. He was not one to hit the gym, that I can tell you.' *But pre-season training wasn't like that in the Middle Ages, was it?* 'That's true. But he wasn't a regular netter. Nor was he one for cross-country runs or anything like that.'

Many a time in the writing of this book have I tried to imagine Colin in one situation or other. Here's one more. The captain flogging himself up and down the hills of the High Weald at the head of his troops? No, neither can I. Graham Johnson rushed to his leader's defence. 'He was there at nets all right.' But then he laughed. 'Mind you, that's only because they were doing a TV piece about Kent's prospects and the cameras were present.'

Lest anybody runs away with the idea that Colin was a bit of a dilettante, above the tedious exertion of training and practice, I should point out that this was far from the case; it was just that he did things differently, something that as an amateur, he was perfectly entitled to do. Christopher says that he was no great netter, like, say, Tom Graveney, but he would go in there and work on a particular element of technique that he felt needed fine-tuning. Once he was satisfied, out he came. For one thing, he preferred to remain fresh and keen. Too much practice dulls the brain, he believed. And another thing, he did not want to become too 'grooved' in his strokeplay. The thing was to remain still and alert at the crease, ready to play what's in front of you rather than the shot you have been rehearsing for half an hour.

It was the same with his fielding. Derek Underwood mentioned that he was a surprisingly agile fellow for one who did not look terribly athletic. 'He was a big man but a fantastic catcher,' he whistled in admiration.

But even the most fantastic catchers drop the odd one from time to time. David Kemp made an interesting observation on this point during the course of our conversations. 'If he'd dropped a couple – which didn't happen very often – he would stop off at my house on his way home. "Come and throw some balls at me," he would say. Which I did, for an hour. First the right hand, then the left. When he was satisfied, he would call it a day.'

This chimes with James Graham-Brown's story about Colin hauling him out of his house to bowl at him – well, to throw at him, from 18 yards – in the nets, privately and alone and away from the madding crowd, after Andy Roberts had broken his jaw at Basingstoke.

In short, Colin had worked out what was best for him and he stuck to it. Cricket has never been a game of one size fits all.

Talking of size, I tackled Christopher about his father's weight. *Nowadays, they have bleep tests and calipers to calculate body fat percentages. If you don't measure up, you're out. So was your father ever concerned about his weight?* 'You know, once or twice he went on a diet. But it never seemed to work. When he started to lose a bit of weight, he said he felt uncomfortable and unbalanced, as if his strength had ebbed away. I think that was just the way he was built.'

I've seen pictures of Colin after he had been ill and not long before he died. He had lost weight and he looked drawn and emaciated, not himself at all. I believe that a sportsman, specifically a games player rather than an athlete, has his natural weight and body shape. Colin was a bit pear-shaped but my goodness, could he caress a cover drive.

On 16 June, Edward Heath was handed the keys to 10 Downing Street, much to many people's surprise. Colin, by contrast, far from having one hand on the championship trophy, found himself with his other hand holding a wooden spoon. As June slipped into July, Kent were at the bottom of the table. Had they been a football team, by now there would have been panic in the boardroom, the manager would have been sacked and a real fear of relegation would be gripping the team.

I wondered what the mood was like in the Kent dressing room at the mid-point of a season that seemed to be going catastrophically wrong. I sought the opinion of Graham Johnson. 'Look, this may seem a bit odd to say but we didn't think we were playing that badly. We'd been a bit unlucky and not quite done the business but we weren't a bad side. In actual fact, although we were bottom, there was not that much of a points difference between top and bottom. All we needed was a couple of wins to kick-start our season.'

Nonetheless, you <u>were</u> bottom. It cannot have been comfortable propping up the rest of the table. So what happened? He said the turning point came after their dismissal from the Gillette Cup by Sussex on 8 July. It wasn't so much that they had lost but the manner of their defeat – a lame capitulation, by all accounts – that dismayed and rankled. 'We had a couple of days off and a meeting was called for all the staff, to clear the air.' *Whose initiative was that?* 'I can't remember whether it was Colin's or Les's. It doesn't really matter. The point is that we all knew that something had to be done.'

Les Ames led the discussion. 'Well, I wouldn't exactly call it a discussion, not at first anyway. Les really laid into us. Voices were raised and it got a bit heated,' said Graham. I understood. I have been in dressing rooms when tempers have flared; the only surprise was that it didn't happen more often. 'But once people had got one or two things off their chest, things settled down and we began to analyse more calmly.'

The outcome of that meeting was to change the course of the season. 'There was no magic wand waved,' Johnson maintained, 'but we felt we needed to believe in ourselves. We're better than this, we told ourselves. Let's be more positive and get ourselves up the table.' Apart from a renewed sense of purpose, one or two concrete strategies were agreed. 'We felt we'd been too passive. We needed to be more aggressive, especially in our hunting down of bonus points. That was something that made all the difference by the end of the season.'

Another resolution was that there should be a greater emphasis on team ethic rather than individualism, always a thin dividing line in such a game as cricket. 'Well, there is *no* game like cricket, is there?' he grinned. 'Anyway, someone made the point that our B team had been more successful than our A team. Should the Test players simply walk back into the side when they came back from international duty when the reserves were playing so well?' *And the upshot of that dilemma?* 'We all agreed that the strongest side should be picked for each game, no matter whose nose was put out of joint. That collective spirit was crucial and saw us through to the end.'

The transformation was remarkable. It was as if Lord Nelson had paid them a morale-boosting visit and re-issued his famous instruction before the battle of Trafalgar, 'No captain can do very wrong if he places his ship alongside that of the enemy.' And blow it to pieces was the unspoken command. That is precisely what Captain Cowdrey and his troops proceeded to do. First to feel the brunt of a Kent broadside were Derbyshire. The match was drawn but ten bonus points were accrued, mainly through explosive batting. The die was cast. There was no going back. Hampshire and Sussex were beaten and the slow but inexorable climb up the table had begun. As so often happens in these situations, confidence was now flooding through the team.

The epithet 'flooding' I used advisedly. Pay heed to this tale of a professional cricketer's lot at the time. At the conclusion of one match at 6pm – at Lord's against Middlesex, on this occasion – the Kent team clambered into their cars, negotiated the Friday rush hour traffic through north and west London and headed off to the West Country to play Somerset the following day. With minimum hold-ups and a following wind, that journey is a long one. With torrential storms, flooded roads and several detours, their destination became Weston-super-Nightmare. They arrived at their hotel at 3am. Later that morning – no delayed start to accommodate their late arrival, or anything like that – they lost the toss. It always happens like that. No matter. This team was now equal to anything. They dispatched Somerset by ten wickets.

Graham, I see you were batting at number seven in this game. Yet three weeks earlier, you were opening the batting – and scoring a hundred. 'Positions in the batting order were not really fixed,' Johnson replied. 'We were a team of all-rounders so we were pretty flexible.'

Weston-super-Mare to Cheltenham is an altogether easier journey but not for Colin – he had to make the return journey to London, to face the Rest of the World at The Oval. Where he batted rather well, as it happened, top-scoring in the first innings with 73.

Here I shall allow myself a little diversion from Kent's pursuit of the title. Originally, these matches against the Rest of the World – hastily organised following the cancellation of the South African tour – had been granted Test match status. Then, quite arbitrarily it seemed to most cricket lovers, the authorities saw fit to remove that status. To this day, these matches inhabit a strange twilight category, first-class yes but not Test class. That means that these games are not added to Colin's 114 Tests and neither is this 73 added to his 7,624 runs.

Before we feel too sorry for him, spare a thought for poor Alan Jones of Glamorgan, picked for the first 'Test' of that summer and then dropped, having scored 5 and 0, never to be picked again. So he joined the exclusive band of the 'one-cap-wonders'. Ah, but no, he didn't. Having been presented with his England cap, he had it taken away from him. The decision defied logic then and it defies logic today. You play in a five-day match for your country against the finest players in the world, including *inter alia*, Barry Richards, Eddie Barlow, Rohan

Kanhai, the Pollock brothers, Garry Sobers, Mike Procter and Clive Lloyd, and it is not deemed a Test match? Ludicrous.

Colin had other things on his mind than debating the status of the match he was engaged in and the quality of the players he was playing against. In common with the rest of the England team, he deemed these true Test matches, whatever the TCCB decreed – retrospectively. He was worried how his beloved Kent were doing in his absence, down at Cheltenham. He had every reason to be concerned. The pitch was a shocker and the visitors were having the worse of it. All seemed lost. Time for Deadly to rescue his team. Not with the ball, as you would expect – though he did take five crucial wickets in Gloucestershire's second innings, in addition to his six in the first – but with the bat. Underwood's 16 not out, in the company of John Dye, last man in, saved the follow-on, which, had it been enforced, would have been curtains for Kent. As it was, they had been set a total of 340 to win.

Underwood may have relished bowling on this minefield but Gloucestershire had to hand Mortimore and Allen, two of the finest exponents of the art of spin bowling, backed up by Bissex, no mean bowler in his own right. Nobody gave Kent a hope. Except Colin. I take up the story of what happened from Asif Iqbal. 'This was the match on which our chances of winning the championship rested. Make or break. It was a raging turner and I managed to get a few runs. Colin was constantly on the phone telling me he knew Kent would win.' I just love Asif's description of his innings as 'a few runs'. In fact, he scored 109 to steer his side to victory – by one wicket – in a display of supreme confidence and technical brilliance that had even his team-mates lost for words.

I asked Asif about his captain's qualities as a leader. 'I think a large part of my development as a cricketer had to do with the faith that Colin put in me. Much of cricket at the highest level is about confidence and nothing gives a player more confidence than to know that his captain believes in him.' *Can you give me more of a clue about his style of leadership?* 'Colin was one of the most outstanding cricketing personalities it has been my privilege to have known during my career in the game. Quite apart from being perhaps the most stylish batsman of his era, he was a terrific human being and a true captain – on and off the field. He cared for everyone and always wanted the best for all his players. Like a true leader, he could absorb pressure like a sponge, never allowing it to go down to his players.

'He never lost his temper, even when unacceptable mistakes were made on the field and I never remember him shouting at anybody, not even those who came back into the dressing room looking very sheepish after playing a shot that looked, for all money, an imitation of Charlie Chaplin playing cricket.'

Not much that I can add, or needs to be added, to that assessment, other than Asif never played a shot like that.

Although Colin had an intuition that Kent's centenary year would be the one, he freely admitted there were times during the season when he suspected his optimism might have been misplaced. One who had an almost mystical belief that nothing could prevent Kent from walking away with the championship was Asif. Colin told a good story about Asif and his unshakeable faith in their destiny. Following the narrow win against Gloucestershire, they were taking on Surrey at Blackheath and it was during a fruitful and unbeaten partnership between the two, in which Asif scored another hundred, that this conversation ensued. Colin bemoaned the fact that the season did not go on for a few weeks more, so that they could profit from their recent good form. Perhaps the charge up the table had come too late. 'No no, skipper,' Asif countered. 'We shall win it in our last match at The Oval.'

His conviction was infectious. Before beating Surrey at The Oval in the final match of the season, they had to dispose of them here, at Blackheath. Graham Johnson, together with everybody present, vividly remembers the last ball of the match. It had been another nail-biter of a game.

Set a total of 263 to win, Surrey were always going to chase it down as they too were in with a chance of being champions. With the last ball of the 21st over in the final hour, with time for maybe one more, 12 runs to win, last pair at the wicket, Pat Pocock launched a huge slog off Johnson over wide mid-on. 'He really connected with it and I thought, hello, that's going for six. Asif set off from wide mid-on, sprinted all of 45 yards and caught it one-handed above his head. It was one of the most remarkable catches I've ever seen.' *Incidentally, Graham, I see that you took 12 wickets in the match.* 'Told you we were a team of all-rounders.'

Now, if the Kent boys believed, after the win against Gloucester-shire, that they *could* win the championship, this astonishing victory convinced many of them that they *would* win.

But not without further tension and excitement, and a bit of luck, it has to be said. The following week at Folkestone, Garry Sobers hit them from pillar to post and into the English Channel. He eventually took pity on the Kent bowlers by declaring when he was 123 not out, Nottinghamshire on 376/4. Once Kent, in reply, had subsided to 27/5, the game, to say nothing of the championship, was up, according to the folk circling the boundary.

But in this most extraordinary of seasons, there always seemed to be someone who stepped up and took control. On this occasion it was Brian Luckhurst, with an unbeaten 156, who steered the innings to calmer waters, enabling the captain to declare 50-odd runs behind. Now it was Sobers's time to throw down the gauntlet, something, as we know, he was never afraid to do. He set Kent a total of 282 in two hours plus the mandatory 20 overs in the last hour – more challenging than his gamble in Port of Spain but a fair one, thought Colin. The home side made it, just, by three wickets with a couple of overs to spare.

Beat Leicestershire with a reasonable haul of bonus points in the bag as well and Colin could throw away that spoon and put one tentative hand on the trophy. This they did, by an innings and 40 runs, crucially picking up a king's ransom of 23 points. The mathematicians in the side did their calculations and assured the skipper that they did not even have to win their final game against Surrey at The Oval to clinch the championship: five bonus points was all they needed.

Graham, I see you scored another hundred in this match, your third of the season. Johnson was keener to talk about the first, earlier on, in June, against Sussex. He'd scored 92 three weeks before and this time as he approached the landmark, his maiden first-class ton, he was naturally anxious. Colin was batting with him as he negotiated the nervous 90s. 'He couldn't have been more helpful and encouraging. He kept on coming up to me between overs, suggesting where runs could be got, asking me which bowler I would prefer to face so that he would take the other one, constantly chivvying me and making me concentrate. It was a marvellous moment for me when I made it, with my captain at the other end coming up to shake my hand.'

So to The Oval, scene of many a dramatic denouement to the season in Colin's career. This was special, however. This was Kent. In a season that had brought acute personal disappointment – the loss of the captaincy to Illingworth for the tour to Australia – he had found returning to his roots, in a dressing room full of friends, a considerable balm to his hurt. Now his team were on the cusp of being crowned champions.

But hold on, was the weather going to provide one final, nasty twist? The rain did eventually relent and play commenced at 2.50pm. To secure the requisite bowling points, Kent had to bowl out Surrey cheaply, and rapidly. Rain was all about and the forecast was not promising. They nearly did, Surrey declaring on 151 with nine wickets down, thus depriving Kent of that vital fifth bonus point, the beastly fellows. In point of fact, that action was quite encouraging, a reassurance that Kent were not going to be handed the title on a plate and that the integrity of the competition remained intact.

The stage was set for Captain Cowdrey to seize his destiny. By his own admission, the pitch, rain-affected, was a pig to bat on but he always relished a challenge and seemed to save his best innings for the times when conditions were at their least favourable. I shall leave it to Graham Johnson to describe it all. 'It was one of the best hundreds I've ever seen him play. We all felt that it was a fitting tribute that he should be at the crease, batting as only he can, when we got the bonus points we needed, putting the destination of the championship beyond reasonable doubt. The Master giving a masterful exhibition of batting. It couldn't have been more appropriate.'

Did you paint the town red that night, not that it would have been Colin's style, but did you celebrate? 'Not truly. You see, we hadn't actually *won* anything. Mathematically, it was still possible, but highly unlikely, that Lancashire could overhaul us as they had one more match to play. But they didn't. So we had our party later, at Number 10.'

At Number 10? 'Yes, Ted Heath, now the prime minister, invited us all for a celebration at Number 10.' *Did you misbehave in the garden, like the 2005 Ashes-winning team?* Johnson gave me one of those looks that he used to give batsmen who had just played a streaky shot off his bowling, as if to say, of course not, we were all better behaved in those days.

Before our meeting drew to a close, he was anxious to share with me his assessment of Colin as a man, away from the public eye and his fame as a cricketer. 'There were layers to him. Gradually, over time, you would peel them away and come to a place where you really felt you had got to know him. These were the times I treasured, chatting to him after he had retired.

'I started my career under Colin and finished it with his son, Chris, as captain. He was around a fair bit, watching Chris, and Graham, his third son, playing for Kent, so we had plenty of opportunities to catch up. He helped me with my career at Barclays after I stopped playing. I found he was prepared to open up more. For example, when he became president of Kent – it was after his heart attack – he wasn't at all well and found the official functions something of a strain. He would sidle up and say, "If I need to slip away, you will make sure everybody is having a good time." It was as if he was letting you into his closed, private personality.'

I got the impression that the normally granite-jawed, imperturbable Graham was getting a little emotional here. 'One more thing,' he insisted. 'That 1970 team was *his*. At his memorial service in Westminster Abbey, we were all sitting together. Asif came in, dressed in his Kent blazer. Instead of sitting with the high and mighty, as he was expected to do, as a former Pakistan captain, he came and sat with us. "We're Colin's team," he said. And he was right, we were.'

The loyalty shown towards Colin, both at the time of his death and earlier, when the heat was on, out there in the middle, was genuine and deep. In a way, they were merely repaying the loyalty he had shown them. Colin said, 'The year of triumph became possible only with the development of a host of good players together.'

The bit-part performers are sometimes overlooked, with the majority of the attention bestowed upon the stars; Colin made sure this did not happen. The foundation of a successful side had been laid down, the young players matured together and, for a while, Kent enjoyed an unparalleled period of success. Under a different captain, of course, but Colin was happy with that. Mind you, he did have this to say about his overseas stars, 'We could not have done it without John Shepherd and Asif Iqbal.'

One could be forgiven for believing that Colin's Kent career gently slipped into the twilight thereafter. The following season, he contracted pneumonia halfway through the summer and did not play again until 1972, by which time he had handed the captaincy over to Mike Denness. There was of course that unexpected final tour of Australia in 1974/75 but after that, he decided enough was enough and announced his retirement at the conclusion of the 1975 season.

However, one last milestone still beckoned him. The prospect of scoring 100 first-class centuries hove tantalising into view and though personal targets, as far as run-making was concerned, never really rowed his boat, joining that small, elite band was an opportunity not to be spurned. To date, only 25 batsmen have achieved that target. Jack Hobbs was the first – incredibly, he fell only three short of making it 200 – and Mark Ramprakash the latest, and probably the last, for few believe that anybody will achieve it in the future, the number of games in the season having been severely reduced.

The feat has only ever been feasible for batsmen playing county cricket, there being no such professional set-up anywhere else in the world. The fact that Don Bradman is the only cricketer to have joined the club who has not played county cricket serves to underline his pre-eminence.

As would be expected, nerves set in as the landmark approached. Not just with Colin but his team-mates, Kent supporters and, so it seemed, the whole of England. 'Everybody knew the significance of the moment,' James Graham-Brown told me. 'But no one dared to mention it in the dressing room for fear of tempting fate.'

Maidstone Festival week in late June and early July 1973, Somerset were the opponents and Colin scored 123, his 99th century. Excitement built. He was in good form. Would he do it in the next match, in the second game of the festival, against Surrey? Asif was batting with him at the time. They had many fruitful partnerships together. The respect and admiration they felt for each other was obvious, both great batsmen, though cut from different cloth. 'They were very close,' said Graham-Brown, 'and loved batting together. We called one Master and the other Maestro.' *Which was which?* He laughed. 'I'll leave you to work that one out.'

Asif's account of what transpired is rather touching. 'One of the moments that I will always remember of my association with Colin was batting with him when he got his 100th hundred.' The last few runs came agonisingly slowly. Finally, he was on 99. Asif went up to him. 'Wherever you hit it, I will make it,' he said at the time, later telling me, 'I was much quicker than Colin.' That is putting it mildly. Mind you, Asif was quicker than just about anybody in the game. 'Colin looked at me quizzically and replied, "That's all very well but what about me?"' *But you made it?* 'We made it.'

It was an emotional moment. Immediately, Denness declared with Colin on 100 exactly and Asif on 119. Graham-Brown described the scene as Colin reached the dressing room. 'He sat down quietly, not saying a word. Naturally, we all went up to him to congratulate him but then left him alone. He seemed... serene. He knew the significance of what he had just achieved but there was no wild celebration. He looked – he was – physically and emotionally drained. It was as if Anthony Sher had just played King Lear and he had returned to his dressing room and was coming down from playing one of the most intensely taxing parts in the Shakespeare canon. The humility of the man in the immediate aftermath of such a great achievement in the game was what struck me.'

Graham-Brown would not let me go until he had unburdened himself of his own insight into the enigma that was Colin Cowdrey. 'He got a bit of stick for being an Establishment figure, friends with the great and the good, and all of that sort of stuff. But he never lost the common touch. He would chat to me, an ordinary, run-of-the-mill county pro just the same as if I was a prime minister or the Duke of Edinburgh. I think the people who didn't like him were the ones who didn't know him.'

Professional jealousy perhaps? 'Maybe not so much that as inverted snobbery. People think he was born with a silver spoon in his mouth. But he wasn't actually. He was no snob! It is absolute b******s that he would look over your shoulder while talking to you to see if anyone more important had entered the room. He made you feel *you* were the most important person in the room and that it was a privilege for him to be speaking to you.'

Another less obvious character trait of Colin's he was keen to highlight was his sense of humour. He gave a couple of examples. 'It is true – though he was keen to deny it – that occasionally he would toss up on the phone.' *What on earth do you mean?* 'Colin Page told us that once Colin was in a phone booth just outside the Blackwall Tunnel.

He had been delayed for some reason and got hold of Ian Buxton, the Derbyshire captain, so they could toss up on the phone.' On another occasion, Graham-Brown forgets which game, Kent needed 99 to win in their second innings. 'Colin stood there in the dressing room. "If we all get nine," he said, "we'll win!" We lost a couple of wickets and John Shepherd had to go out with a further two runs needed. "Get out there, Shep," he said, "and get me a quick two!"'

Asif added his two-pennyworth on the same theme. 'Colin had a great sense of humour. In those days, we used to share the driving and he was deeply impressed with my sense of direction and my knowledge of Kent roads. On one occasion, while I was ploughing our way through traffic, following my directions, he mumbled, "Never thought in my life I would be shown the way to Kent grounds by a Pakistani taxi driver." I told him it was a sign of changing times. He gave me another of his quizzical looks.'

Colin was to score another seven hundreds before he called it a day. The final one probably gave him as much satisfaction as his first. It is given to few top-ranked sportsmen the opportunity to sign off with your loyal public on a triumphant note. What better occasion for your last hurrah than Kent v Australia at his cricketing home of Canterbury? The match was towards the end of June during that sweltering hot summer of 1975. On the final day, Kent had been set an improbable target of 355 to win, having been rolled over in the first innings for 202. So confident of an easy win was the Australian captain, Ian Chappell, that he ordered the team coach to be ready outside the gates at 3pm, in the hope and expectation that they would get away early and avoid the Bank Holiday traffic on their journey along the south coast to Southampton.

'But I was given a last memory to savour,' Colin wrote in his notes. 'In the last 20 overs, we eased home to a famous victory by four wickets.' His memory uncharacteristically lets him down here; he is full of praise for Bob Woolmer's unbeaten hundred. In fact, well though he played, Woolmer scored 71 not out. The victory owed everything to a wonderful innings of 151 not out by Colin. He remembered that all right. 'It was one of the best innings I have ever played. The Australians were generous in their unexpected defeat. Ian Chappell found it within himself to clap me on the shoulder and say, well done.'

Far from avoiding the traffic, the Australians did not reach their hotel in Southampton until past midnight. They didn't look too bad on it though the next morning when they took the field against Hampshire. They did for me all right; I was bowled by Ashley Mallett for 12.

And that was it, pretty well. Colin finished his career with a first-class average of 42.89, rather lower than you might expect. A quick glance at the records of the other 24 with 100 hundreds to their name underlines this surprising statistic. Only Tom Haywood, of Surrey, has a lower average, of 41.79, and he played in a different century, second to the milestone after the great W.G. Grace in the pre-First World War era.

So why has Colin, comparatively speaking, got such a low average? If nothing else, his presence in this august company is a tribute to his stamina and longevity but surely he was a better player than this. One clue, I believe, lies in the fact that he rarely went on to make big scores, what Graham Gooch used to term 'daddy hundreds'. If we leave aside the famous 307 he made against South Australia on the 1962/63 tour of Australia, there are no double hundreds and few in excess of 150. He scored 107 centuries and 231 fifties which is not a very impressive conversion rate.

How come? He was aware of this conundrum as much as anybody and gives it some thought in his autobiography, 'Most of my best innings have been fused with some problem or adversity.' The unspoken assumption is that if there was not a great deal resting on his innings, he often found it hard to motivate himself. Scoring runs merely to boost his batting average gave him no pleasure whatsoever. What satisfaction was there in scoring a double hundred against weak opposition? He cites the fact that he never scored a hundred against Leicestershire or Glamorgan who had, at the time, moderate attacks at best.

He admits that he got out too often once he had scored 50. 'I used to relax and try to experiment or to practise a particular shot and get out.' Alan (A.C.) Smith told me a good story about Colin on this very topic. 'Warwickshire were playing Kent at Edgbaston. Colin was 105 not out at tea. After tea, I expected him to open out and play a few shots. In fact, he seemed to go into his shell and was barely able to hit it off the square. I sidled up to him. "What's up, Colin?" He looked surprised. "Nothing. It's just that I'm experimenting with a new grip." Extraordinary!'

The point, I think, is that he was not greedy for runs. He reminds me very much of Barry Richards, who should, by his own admission, have scored many more than his 80 first-class hundreds. 'Jeez,' he said. 'The number of times I got out in the 70s or 80s because I got bored and hit it up in the air.' Vintcent van der Bijl told me that he would put his life on Barry scoring 50 but his money on Graeme Pollock scoring a hundred once he had passed 50. 'GP was run-hungry in a way Barry never was. He would *never* give his wicket away.'

It was the same with Colin. Sometimes, he did give his wicket away, through carelessness or lack of concentration. He needed the stimulus of competition, the thunder and smoke of battle, the man-to-man confrontation of bowler and batsman. A good bowler, that is. 'I was never a run-gatherer,' he says, 'like Bradman, Barrington, Sheppard, May, and Boycott of the current generation.' A.C. Smith puts it in a nutshell. 'Colin a great batsman? Not quite. In my view. Peter May was the best. Now there was a tough nut. Ted Dexter was the best against the best, if you see what I mean. Colin was... enigmatic, almost as if he could not quite believe how good he was.'

By now, questions of how good a player he was, whether he had been the best he could be, were academic. He belonged to the ages. 'I look back on that sunlit day at Canterbury,' he wrote, 'with fond recollection. It was now time to bow out.'

7

Those Two Imposters: Triumph and Disaster

The England Captaincy 1967–71

'No other captain could have led the side so well and performed the numerous duties of captaincy so flawlessly in the exacting circumstances of this tour.'

Wisden on Cowdrey leading MCC in the
West Indies, 1967/68

I KNEW Brian Close. Not well but well enough to form a firm impression of him. I first came across him in South Africa during the winter of 1973/74 when he captained a Derrick Robins team touring the country. For a sports-mad nation starved of Test cricket, the tourists, who were as close to a fully fledged international side as you could get, attracted great interest and huge crowds wherever they played.

I was not playing for Eastern Province but as I knew a number of players from the two sides, I spent a lot of time in both dressing rooms and with them afterwards in the bar. There was no doubt whose show this was. Close led from the front, both out on the field of play and afterwards in the pavilion at St George's Park. The extraordinary things that man could do with a full glass of beer could have put Paul Daniels out of a job. To say that he was the life and soul of the party is a bit like suggesting that Ian Botham enlivened the odd Test match.

Talking of Ian Botham, by the time he had made his debut at Somerset, Brian Close was the club captain and it was in matches against the Wurzils, as they were known, that I saw Close at close quarters, if you will forgive the pun. He was surrounded by a group of fun-loving, but talented, youngsters and they were very fond of pulling the old man's leg, sometimes mercilessly. But it was clear that they held him in the highest regard and listened to him when he spoke. He had the gift of authority and he turned a bunch of under-achievers into a trophy-winning side. He was also, let us not forget, a mighty fine cricketer in his own right.

You may be wondering why I am beginning a chapter with a thumbnail sketch of Brian Close. Because it is with Close that this particular narrative starts. The man chosen to succeed Colin as captain of England for the final Test at The Oval against the already victorious West Indians in the summer of 1966 was Brian Close.

With popes, football managers, presidents, headmasters, whatever sort of chief executive you choose to mention, a change always seems to come with a violent swing of the pendulum. So it appeared with the new captain. Close was a northerner, a native of Yorkshire, the self-proclaimed 'God's Own Country'; Cowdrey was a southerner, Kent was his county, known as the 'Garden of England'. Close was blunt and outspoken: Cowdrey was agreeable, conciliatory and modest. Close was a punchy, occasionally reckless, leftie: Cowdrey batted right-handed in a more classically moulded and orthodox style. Close was a professional: Cowdrey was an amateur. And that perhaps says it all.

However, on closer inspection, certain similarities emerge. Both were youthful prodigies, taken on a punt to Australia with MCC, Close in 1950/51 and Cowdrey in 1954/55, arguably before they were ready. Both had chequered international careers, though Cowdrey's was the more enduring; he played 114 Tests and Close only 22. And their bravery in the face of fast bowlers was equally admirable.

What Colin thought about being replaced by Close is not recorded. Probably not a lot. By that I mean he most likely did not give it much thought, preferring to lick his wounds back at Kent.

There is no reason to believe, by the way, that he and Close, though not bosom buddies, did not get on perfectly amicably whenever their paths crossed or whenever they shared an England dressing room. As luck, and a certain amount of bold leadership, would have it, England defeated the West Indies at The Oval. Close took a lot of the credit, justifiably, and that seemed to be that as far as the England captaincy was concerned. Colin was now right out of the picture.

There was no tour that winter and Colin was not selected for the three-Test series against India, which England won 3-0, at the beginning of the 1967 season. Nor was he picked for the first Test against Pakistan in the latter stage of the summer. However, weight of runs in the county championship made demands for his recall difficult to ignore and he was restored to the England side for the second and third Tests, both of which England won. Close's grip on his team seemed firm and incontestable. Colin did not set the world alight with his form; he scored 14, 2*, 16 and 9.

When asked what was most likely to blow the government off course, Harold Macmillan, prime minister at the time, famously replied, 'Events, dear boy, events.' Just before the third Test at The Oval, an event had taken place, one that was to have extensive consequences, not only for the two protagonists involved but the game of cricket too. In a match between Warwickshire and Yorkshire in mid-August at Edgbaston, the two sides captained by Mike Smith and Brian Close, there had been an unseemly scene at the conclusion of the final overs. Warwickshire had been set a target of 142 runs in 100 minutes. They had fallen nine runs short and the game was drawn.

However, Yorkshire had only bowled 24 overs in that one hour and 40 minutes, unconscionably slow, at a snail's pace, you might say. As the Yorkshire team left the field, Close took exception to one of the Warwickshire supporter who barracked him and, it was alleged, he manhandled him. The story broke the next day. Yorkshire were accused of blatant time-wasting and Close of assault. Close denied the assault but made no apology for his tactics. Lord's stepped in, a disciplinary hearing was convened and Close ordered to attend.

All this happened in the days leading up to the Test match. Colin was very much aware of the press interest in the affair because speculation was rife and he was, once again, slap bang in the middle of it. Was Close going to be sacked? And was Cowdrey going to be asked to lead MCC on the forthcoming tour to the West Indies? He was horrified. He knew as little as anybody else of the goings-on behind the scenes at Lord's and hated the press intrusion. Everywhere he went, through the Hobbs Gates at The Oval, at the doors of the pavilion, to and from the nets, he was hounded and pressed for comment, of which he had none and made none. He must have felt like fleeing, as he did from Lord's as a schoolboy. He was no schoolboy now; he was England's senior player and he was in the eye of the storm.

In the event, Close was stripped of the captaincy and told that he would not be leading the side in the West Indies but in order to spare him embarrassment, as the team for this Test had already been picked, news of his sacking was withheld until after the match had finished. The game proceeded but newspaper speculation did not abate. Close led his team to an impressive eight-wicket victory to seal the series 2-0, an amazing feat of single-minded application, considering the furore swirling about him.

Colin was none the wiser about the selectors' deliberations until the Saturday of the game, when the chairman took him aside and confided in him that they wanted him to captain the side that winter. Yet again, he felt he was caught between a rock and a hard place. His sympathy was with Close and the situation he had found himself in. 'But I was back in the nightmare of the previous summer,' he later wrote. 'The publicity then had left its mark and I could not bear a repeat.'

But a repeat was precisely what he was getting. He had to accept. As his friend and mentor, Les Ames, said to him, 'You do not alter any decision that may be made over Brian Close by moving out of the picture.' Colin knew he was right. If your country comes calling, you must go. On the Monday, once England's victory had been secured, the touring side was announced, with Cowdrey as captain. The Fleet Street presses were red hot that evening. And the story had a sting in the tail. When pressed by a persistent reporter whether Close would have been first choice as captain had the Edgbaston incident not taken place, Doug Insole, the chairman of selectors, was forced to admit yes. Thank you, Doug, second choice again and now everybody knows it. It was just as well that the two of them were firm friends. That they remained so says much about Colin's magnanimous nature.

Incidentally, as a direct consequence of Close's time-wasting, the laws of cricket were amended to stipulate that a minimum of 20 overs must be bowled in the last hour of a match. Though that hour seems to last much more than 60 minutes, given the funereal rate that those 20 overs are bowled in the modern game.

That four months elapsed between the announcement of the team and setting off for the Caribbean worked to Colin's advantage. The controversy slowly died down, if not disappearing altogether, and he was able to put it out of his mind and concentrate on his plans to take on the unofficial world champions in their own back yard. On previous occasions when he had been asked to step into the breach, there had been no such period of preparation; he had, more or less, walked through the door of the dressing room to take charge of someone else's team.

This time it felt different. Yes, the majority of the players had flourished under Close and were upset at his dethronement but these were professional cricketers and they were used to these upheavals, unwelcome though they may be. Cowdrey was now in charge and they all had to get on with the job. Captains come and go, selectors come and go, team-mates come and go – that is the way of the world of sport. Nothing for it but to band together and make the most of it. Because if they didn't, it was going to be a mighty long tour. West Indies had thumped England in 1963 and 1966 and with Sobers, Kanhai, Butcher, Griffith, Hall and Gibbs on board, there did not appear to be any cracks in their supremacy.

Colin thought otherwise. He alone believed that the fearsome fast bowling pair of Hall and Griffith, if not a spent force, had reached their peak and were on the slow descent down the other side. In Snow, Brown and Jones, he was sure he had the equal, if not the superior, pace attack and as everybody knew, the key to success in the Caribbean was fast bowling. So, like any general worth his salt, he sat down and drew up his strategy for the forthcoming campaign. The Five Year Plan, he called it. If that sounded a bit like one of Stalin's brainwaves for 1930s Communist Russia, we can forgive him for that. Up until now, forward planning at MCC had stretched no further than the next membership sub-committee meeting. In this, Colin was ahead of his time. Besides, he always felt more comfortable when he had time to organise and prepare.

Not wishing to tempt fate and no doubt touching every piece of wood within reaching distance, he studied the future international programme. He was 37, going on 38, and he reckoned, with a favourable wind and barring injury, he had perhaps another five years left of playing at the top level. He was in fine fettle, batting as well as ever and felt ready, champing at the bit, you might say, to take charge of the England team. This was his time and he was determined not to waste it. For the task ahead was formidable. They were about to take on the West Indies in the Caribbean.

Following that tour, back home in 1968, the Ashes would be at stake, not won since 1956. Then there was a winter tour to South Africa, to face a team that were rapidly emerging as one of immense talent and potential, followed by a return series against the same opponents at home. And then – whisper it quietly – there was the Holy Grail for any captain of England, the opportunity to lead MCC on an Ashes tour of Australia in the winter of 1970/71. It had been his lifetime's ambition to take a team Down Under in search of the Ashes. Dare he dream? Yes, he did. That would be a fitting way to sign off a long career. Whatever transpired, he reasoned, there would be no doubt in anybody's mind at the conclusion of this five-year cycle which country could consider themselves world champions. For England, he wrote, it would be 'five campaigns of the highest and most demanding order'.

Looking at the team they had selected, he had every confidence. In Boycott and Edrich, he had a redoubtable pair of openers; in the middle order, he had the vastly experienced Barrington and Graveney; spin was provided by Titmus and Pocock; the wicketkeeping duties, as well as useful runs, would be determined by one of Knott or Parks and the fast-bowling trio of Snow, Jones and Brown would not lack for variety of attack nor rawness of pace. Furthermore, England's recent record, with one or two notable aberrations, had not been half bad. No, this was a team in which he could place his trust. The question was whether they would trust him.

To this end, he produced another rabbit out of the hat. He organised a pre-tour, two-day get-together. A boot camp it most certainly wasn't but indoor nets at Crystal Palace were appropriated and sessions set aside for discussion and planning. He gave a speech, more of a rallying call to the troops, outlining his vision and how he wanted to implement it. He was getting rather good at this sort of thing, an accomplishment which would stand him in good stead as part of his duties as captain of an MCC touring team and one for which he was to become acclaimed in later life.

In brief, he explained that he had accepted the captaincy in circumstances unfortunate and beyond his control. But, for better or worse, he was now the captain and this was his thinking. Continuity, both of selection and ethos, was critical, he believed, and therefore he saw in front of him a squad of players which would form the nucleus of England's assault on world domination in the next five years. Some would fall by the wayside – they always do – and others would come in to fill their shoes but he was convinced that together they had the talent, the experience and the resolve to take on all-comers. He ended with these words, 'I hope we shall unite as one in this period to achieve solidarity, both on and off the field.'

Whether this Churchillian address aroused his listeners to a fever pitch of passion is not recorded. Cricket pros are sardonic and hard-nosed by nature but even the most cynical would probably have been nodding their heads in agreement. What he had said made sense and besides, dear old Colin was dear old Colin; he had his heart in the right place and nobody doubted his commitment to the cause.

What the troops thought of the indoor nets would be much easier to figure out. Waste of time, they would have quietly said. How can a gloomy net inside a dimly lit cavern with a restricted run-up and a low ceiling possibly replicate the conditions in the Caribbean? Of course they couldn't. That was not the point. It was a show put on for the cameras and the press, to drive home that this team meant business.

In this, Colin was ahead of his time. Nowadays, teams go off to the jungle or to the desert or to the swamps or to the forest to bond; then the whole idea was a novelty. Furthermore, the concept of an England squad, enshrined in central contracts, is nowadays accepted as custom and practice; back then, England teams were plucked from the counties on an ad hoc basis. Getting the press on board was a stroke of genius. Colin was only happy that the lads seemed to have got behind him and that he had prepared everybody, himself included, as well as he could possibly have done. Now, the proof of the pudding was in the eating.

Perhaps it would be more accurate to recount that the pudding had already been eaten, seeing as they set off on Boxing Day. Time was taken to acclimatise. They needed it for the early showings from MCC were far from encouraging. Colin was not unduly alarmed; it was nothing that he had not expected and was something he had accommodated in his plans. He had always believed it took roughly three weeks for a touring side to adjust to a new country and different playing conditions. In this he was proved right.

It doesn't need a brain of Einstein proportions to get this but it still surprises me that cricket boards around the world persist in parachuting touring teams into immediate action and expect them to hit the ground running. Colin believed that his side would be ready for the first Test, and they were. He would have been happier if his main strike bowler, John Snow, had not fallen foul of a nasty virus and was clearly not fit to play but there you are, the best-laid plans of mice and men.

And here's another thing. The gentle and mild-mannered Colin Cowdrey, considered by more than a few to be too nice to be a captain of England, was revealing a more ruthless streak. Tom Graveney outlined to me the significant change he had noticed in his friend's demeanour, 'I'd always believed he was too much of a good-natured sort of bloke to be a wholly convincing England captain. But on this tour he cracked the whip.'

Indeed. Jim Parks imparted this piece of information about a selection decision that Colin made before the Tests had even started, 'He came up to me after one of the warm-up games and told me that Knotty was having a shocker and that they just couldn't pick him for the first Test. I was going to play instead of him.' The juxtaposition of 'Knott' and 'shocker' seems astonishing, even impossible, for the generation brought up on the unshakeable assumption that Alan Knott was the greatest wicketkeeper ever to have donned gloves. But there you have it, from the horse's mouth.

Jim may well have been his rival for the keeping berth in the England side but he has ever been a fair and honest man. He knew the potential of the young Kent wicketkeeper and recognised that the future belonged to him. But he privately agreed that Knott had not had an auspicious game. So he quietly prepared himself for duty while the news was broken to a dismayed Knott. The point here is that Knott was *in situ* – he'd made his England debut earlier that summer against Pakistan – and did one poor game justify the chop? Furthermore, Knott was a team-mate of Colin's at Kent. Would future car journeys for the two of them around the country develop into frosty, silent tracts of time?

Whatever Knotty thought of the news – it is doubtful he was best pleased – the decision had been made and Parks played. 'I broke my finger in the third Test,' said Parks. 'Knotty came back into the side, and the rest is history.' History records that the incomparable Alan Knott remained England's first-choice wicketkeeper from that day until his final Test, against Australia at The Oval, in 1981.

On his previous tour here in 1959/60, Colin had noted with some surprise the lack of adequate practice facilities, nets particularly, at the main venues. It was the same for both sides but he reckoned this shortcoming affected the home side more than the visitors. The West Indies team was drawn from a loose confederation of islands spread over the Caribbean, many of whom would have jetted in to Port of Spain, Trinidad, where the first Test took place, short of practice and in need of a net. The tourists, by contrast, had been involved in their warm-up matches – first-class, it should not be forgotten – and were more battle-hardened.

This was an ascendency that would steadily dissipate, Colin predicted, as the series wore on and the West Indies found their stride but he expected, correctly as it turned out, that they would be undercooked in the first and probably the second match of the series. It was important to take full advantage of this while it lasted.

Colin won the toss, a good start. Boycott hit Hall for four fours in his first two overs, an even better start. Yes, we all know that Boycott could bat stodgily at times but he had all the shots and sometimes, when the moon was in the right quarter, he was willing to unfurl them in all their technical perfection. He and Colin played beautifully, though neither went on to score centuries. However, Graveney and Barrington did; Barrington's was his fourth in successive Tests and Graveney's was no less than 'a glorious exhibition of cultured batting', according to *Wisden*. England's total of 568 was their second highest in the West Indies. The best of starts.

Tom Graveney laughed when he recalled this innings. 'I had just heard that I had been awarded the OBE in the New Year's Honours

List. To stick two fingers up to my team-mates who kept on telling me that OBE stands for Other Buggers' Efforts, I went out there to make sure that this time it was my own effort. And then, I never got another run all tour!' Not quite true, as the scorecards tell, but he did fail to rediscover the fluency of that first innings. He was currently experiencing something of an Indian summer in his Test career. Although he was unwilling to ascribe this late flowering of form wholly to the appointment of his friend to the captaincy, he always felt that he flourished as an England batsman when he believed his captain had confidence in him. 'Colin batted me three or four, where your best batsmen should be. That was the vote of confidence I needed.'

Although the young Clive Lloyd announced himself with a maiden Test hundred on his debut, West Indies fell five runs short of saving the follow-on. In their second innings, David Brown, 'bowling with great fire, shot out Butcher, Murray and Griffith in one over, to reduce them to 180/8 at tea' in the words of *Wisden*.

I sought out David on his farm in north Worcestershire for memories of this tour. He remembered this spell of bowling all right. 'Aaargh!' he cried, the anguish still evident in his voice, 'I had Wes Hall within a gnat's whisker of bowling him the last ball before tea. It nipped back, cut him in half and how it missed the leg stump I shall never know.' *After tea, you never looked like taking another wicket.* 'I wouldn't quite say that. Boycs dropped a sharp chance at short leg off Hall, but he didn't usually field there, did he? Anyway, I'd shot my bolt by then.'

Hall and Sobers put on an undefeated ninth-wicket partnership of 63 and West Indies escaped with a scarcely deserved draw. England departed Trinidad greatly buoyed by their performance despite the disappointment of not being able to force the win. 'If only I'd had Snow to call upon,' Colin lamented.

How much he was missed was illustrated, to devastating effect, in the second Test in Jamaica. England's first innings was held together by a magnificent, fighting 101 by their captain on a surface already beginning to crack. Altogether, he batted for six hours and 96 overs to steer his side to a total of 376. This innings was put into context by John Snow, who exploited the untrustworthy pitch as only he could, to skittle the West Indies for a paltry 143, taking 7-49, including Sobers for a first-ball duck for the second time in succession.

The one before no doubt remains firmly embedded in the reader's memory. It was at The Oval when Close had stuck himself suicidally close to Sobers at short leg and instructed his fast bowler to bowl a bouncer. This he duly did, Sobers hooked, got a bottom edge which ricocheted off his thigh pad to nestle gently in the hands of an unblinking Close, who had not moved a muscle. It was without doubt the greatest short leg catch I have ever seen. There was no need for Close to loiter nearby this time (though he was in the press box, reporting for one of the dailies); Snow had his man LBW.

West Indies, for the second time, were forced to follow on. With half the side gone and the score on 204/5, 'we were unquestionably sailing home to victory when a bottle, swirling high up in the sunlight, not only changed the course of the match but transformed it into one of the most remarkable Tests ever played', wrote our hero, with a rare poetical flourish that he surely did not feel at the time. One bottle followed another, and another, the mood turned ugly and soon the local police had a full-scale riot on their hands.

Before we examine the possible reasons for the disturbance, the measures taken to quell it and the immediate aftermath, let us recall the exact circumstances of the spark, which set the whole thing ablaze in the first place. I am indebted to Jim Parks's sharp recall of what happened. 'Basil was batting and Basil was bowling – er, Basil Butcher batting, that is, and Basil D'Oliveira bowling,' he added with a grin. 'Anyway, I was standing up at the time. In previous matches, I had noticed that Butcher tended to flick the ball away off his legs if the ball strayed down the leg side but often in the air. So I went up to Bas and suggested I stay back, he would slide one down the leg side and let's see if we could strangle Butcher that way.'

Note that Parks did not refer to D'Oliveira as Dolly. Nobody did. That was a coinage of the world's press. To his friends, team-mates and opponents – and it would be difficult to differentiate between any of these categories – he was simply known as Bas. He did exactly as Parks had suggested. Butcher suitably obliged and Parks took the tumbling catch. 'The trouble was,' said Parks, 'he didn't walk.' That may have been so but in fairness to Butcher, it must be said that it is not always clear to the batsman, who is perforce for a second or two unsighted, whether the catch has been taken. So he stood his ground before, reluctantly it seemed, the umpire gave him out. But

Butcher's hesitation had given the crowd, now pretty well rum-fuelled and soured by their team's capitulation, an opportunity to vent their displeasure, convinced that their man had been the victim of English cheating. So the bottles started to fly.

John Snow, down at third man, was right in the front line. He turned and made gestures appealing for calm. It must have surprised even the most ardent disciples of this fiery, enigmatic man that he, of all people, was trying to play the peacemaker. In this he was doomed to failure.

Tom Graveney remembered the riot on his first tour of the Caribbean, way back in 1953/54. On that occasion, there had been a run-out decision against the home side, which the local population had disagreed with. A hail of bottles rained down on the England players and things threatened to get out of hand. 'Then Johnny Wardle, one of the team jokers, picked up a bottle, pretended to drink from it and proceeded to give one of the best impressions of a rubbery-legged drunk I've ever seen,' he said. 'Immediately everybody started to laugh, the mood lightened and a full-scale riot was averted. But this was different. This was ugly.'

David Brown takes up what happened next, 'Colin wanted to go with Garry Sobers, who was batting at the time, over to the area where the trouble was worst, to plead with everybody to return to their seats so that the game could continue. Garry was not too keen but he went. It was futile. A bottle came whistling over, narrowly missing Jeff Jones's head, and that was it. We scarpered.'

The riot police in their white helmets and wielding their truncheons waded in, which only seemed to inflame passions and increase the level of violence. They commenced firing tear gas canisters. 'Wrong decision!' Jim Parks guffawed at the memory. 'They took no account of the wind direction. The cloud of gas, instead of drifting towards the trouble makers, came in the opposite direction towards us in the dressing rooms.'

It was said that the air conditioning units inside the pavilion sucked in the tear gas, where the Governor General, Sir Clifford Campbell, and senior members of the Jamaican government were being entertained. By this time, the chief of police had ordered a complete evacuation of the playing area and a disconsolate Colin Cowdrey led his team off the field. Those who were left on it.

Back in the dressing rooms, the players watched with some alarm as a pale grey cloud of gas, 20 feet high and 60 feet wide, slowly blew towards them. As best they could, they wrapped their heads in wet towels, finding the whole experience thoroughly unnerving. 'Most unpleasant,' reported the *Daily Telegraph* correspondent, with rare Swantonian pithiness.

Later, Colin cogitated on the reason, if not the cause – palpably Butcher's dismissal – for the ugly scenes. Perhaps it was a local political demonstration that had little to do with the cricket. Or perhaps it was a communist-inspired insurrection. Or perhaps it was simply a case of too much rum, a hot day and West Indies disappearing down the pan.

He had not much time then and there for sociopolitical analysis; he was soon in deep discussion with the Jamaican Cricket Association about what to do next. The hosts, as well as the club members and the genuine cricket supporters, were horrified by what had happened and deeply ashamed at the damage that had been done to the reputation of West Indian cricket. Colin, who always had a soft spot for people from these parts, was affected by their genuine expressions of apology and sympathetic to their plight and was mindful to agree to whatever the Jamaican Cricket Association decided.

In the event, play was not abandoned for the day and on reflection this was a mistake, he felt. They should not have been made to go out to play again that day. It somehow didn't feel right. Grateful for the England management's supportive stance, the association's chairman made this immediate, unusual, quixotic gesture to the visitors. Clearly England had been disadvantaged by any delay in proceedings; therefore he proposed that extra time, equal to the amount of playing time lost, be added on to the scheduled hours of play, even if it meant continuing on the sixth day. In the event, a period of 75 minutes was agreed. Not that England would need it. They were going to win easily.

Creekit – it's a foony old game, as Geoff Boycott never tires of saying. He may well have said it on this occasion too, if anybody could hear him among the coughing, spluttering and wheezing of his England team-mates, their heads covered in wet towels. No game is over when the greatest cricketer the world has ever seen is still at the crease, even if the odds are stacked against him.

When the cloud of tear gas had dispersed, the ground for the most part emptied of rioters and the playing area cleared of bottles and debris, Colin led his side back on to the pitch. There were still a few demonstrators about and sporadic outbursts of stone throwing and immediate police response did little to settle their nerves. The match took on a surreal atmosphere; clearly unsettled and thinking they shouldn't be out there at all, England took a while to get back into their stride. Sobers sensed this and before anybody knew what was happening, he was off and away, playing as irrepressibly as only he could, evoking unpleasant memories, for England supporters anyway, of a similar impossible rescue mission at Lord's in 1966. Colin remembered it well and wondered from his station at slip, with shots scorching the grass at Sabina Park, whether the West Indies captain was going to do for him again. Very nearly, he did.

Sobers was able to declare his innings closed at 391/9, carrying his bat for a peerless 113. 'The whole episode had knocked the stuffing out of us,' Colin wrote. They had seen a position of near invincibility melt away from them and now they were in a situation where they could not possibly win yet could conceivably lose. An awkward last session to bat out time and a pitch cracking up – anything could happen.

What happened next was as predictable as rain at Old Trafford. Sobers, as inspired with the new ball as he was with the bat, immediately bowled Boycott, had Colin LBW, both for ducks and England shortly found themselves at 19/4. The creeping alarm in the away dressing room was as palpable as that low, grey cloud approaching earlier that afternoon. Stumps were pulled at 5.30, as per the ground rules, but as expected, Sobers popped his head around the door and said, 'Well, we'll just have to claim the extra time tomorrow, Colin.'

Of course he did. Nobody expected otherwise. Colin would have done the same, had the roles been reversed. Incidentally, Colin had been given out incorrectly. He had hit it. But he made no fuss and quietly departed, shaking his head at yet another strange decision by the home umpires.

The next morning was expectedly torrid. England had 75 minutes to hold out, with West Indies needing six wickets. The crowd was in a fever pitch of excitement, though there was no hint of the previous day's trouble, and the West Indians circled for the kill. Spin was now being employed at both ends, Gibbs with his fizzing off breaks and Sobers with his slow left-arm variety. The score progressed from 38/5 to 51/6 then 61/7. Only Test match cricket produces such nail-biting tension. Has that clock stopped, was all Colin could think, as David Brown strolled out to stem the tide.

'Garry was bowling his left-arm spinners into the cracks,' he told me. 'I couldn't lay a bat on them. One ball at me, he let go a bouncer. It whistled past my ear! Obviously, he had made a sign to Deryck Murray, the keeper, because he had gone back a few paces. And then he bowled me.' Back in the dressing room, John Snow, no doubt with a wry comment, stood up, picked up his bat and made his way to the door.

'Hang on,' somebody cried. 'It's all over!' Amid all the excitement and the drama, one man alone had kept a cool head and was perfectly aware of the unusual playing conditions agreed the previous day. The 75 minutes had elapsed. The draw had been secured. So Basil D'Oliveira, even though the over had not been completed, tucked his bat under his arm and followed Brown off the pitch. He was right. There had been no stipulation in the agreement about the number of overs to be bowled, merely time, and the 75 minutes had been played.

The umpires dithered, scratched their heads and eventually pulled up the stumps. The West Indians, obviously disappointed, realised the game was up and trooped off. England, perilously placed at 68/8, had escaped with a draw in a match they could easily have lost. But in departing Kingston later that day, their mood was far from buoyant, as you would expect of a team that has just dodged a bullet. They were downcast and not a little cross at having dominated the home side for two Tests and come away empty-handed.

Drama, like Banquo's ghost, seemed to stalk this England team as they made their way around the Caribbean. Their next port of call was Barbados, where they repaired to their hotel on the west coast, the renowned Sandy Bay Resort, to lick their wounds, or to be more specific, bathe their tear-gassed eyes, with a bit of rest, recuperation, sunbathing and swimming. It was here, several miles from the cricket ground, that the second of three major incidents of the tour took place.

The Titmus Boating Accident was certainly no laughing matter, even if the major protagonist later attempted to laugh it off. Taking a dip in the seductively aquamarine waters of the Caribbean Sea, Fred Titmus swam over to a motorboat idling nearby. He hung on to the side as he engaged the occupants in cheerful conversation before attempting to haul himself over the side and on board. By the greatest of misfortunes and unbeknown to anybody in the party, this boat was of a most unusual design. The propellors were under the hull and to the sides instead of to the rear and, as Titmus grabbed the edge, his legs floated up and under the hull.

'Suddenly there was a loud bang,' reported an eyewitness and Titmus, unaware for a second or two what had happened, lifted up his foot and was horrified to see it coursing blood. Colin and team-mate Robin Hobbs helped him ashore where they wrapped the foot in a beach towel and carried him to a car. The dreadful injury was obvious to all bystanders. John Woodcock was one. He later wrote, 'As I watched him carried from the sea, I saw little chance of him playing again.' Two of Titmus's toes were missing and the another two were hanging on by a thread of skin. St Joseph's Roman Catholic Hospital is nearby and it was there that Titmus was driven with all speed.

Fred Titmus was not a Catholic but the Holy Ghost was by his side that day. As chance would have it, the surgeon on duty at the hospital was a Dr Homer Rogers, a visiting Canadian orthopaedic surgeon who specialised in ice hockey injuries. He took one look at the damaged foot and observed laconically, 'Oh, we'll soon have that sorted out.' Titmus, whenever asked about the accident, always heaped praise upon Dr Rogers for saving his foot. He firmly believed that had he been left in the hands of less experienced practitioners, all of the toes, if not the whole foot, would have been amputated, and that surely would have been the end of his career.

As it was, Rogers told him that he had seen far worse injuries in ice hockey players and all had resumed their playing careers. He amputated the four little toes but left the big toe, vital for balance, intact. And Titmus did play again, the following summer. As Woodcock commented, 'That he did is a remarkable story of good doctoring, good luck and irrepressible spirit.' Fred Titmus continued to play a significant part in Middlesex cricket for years to come and, marvellous to relate, he made a return to Test cricket, at the same age as Colin, 41, on the MCC tour to Australia in 1974/75.

Of course, Titmus being Titmus, there were a few amusing stories accompanying the accident. Tom Graveney was deputed to ring the then Mrs Titmus back in England to reassure her of her husband's well-being and no, it was not necessary for her to fly out to be at his bedside. Titmus's social arrangements meant that such a mission of mercy could well have had unfortunate consequences.

Jim Parks, who had been sunning himself on another part of the beach and had been unaware of the unfolding drama, came back to the hotel and when apprised of what had happened, jumped into a car and drove straight to the hospital. 'And there was Fred,' he said, 'sitting up in bed with a large grin splitting his face and a cigar in one hand and a brandy in the other!' *And where was Matron?* 'Probably poured him the brandy. You know our Fred.' Asked by one of the visiting journalists how he was, Titmus quipped, 'Fine. Only I feel a bit lighter.'

As Colin surveyed the bloody and damaged foot, he would have known in an instant that he had lost the services of his senior spinner and vice-captain for the rest of the tour. And it would not have taken him more than another moment's reflection to fear for the professional career of his team-mate. As he admitted, he was 'as close to personal panic as I have ever been in my life'.

His angst was heightened by the knowledge that it was his wife, Penny, who was at the controls of the motorboat at the time of the accident. Although absolutely no blame could possibly have been attached to her – and never was – he would not have been human if he had not felt pangs of guilt mixed with foreboding as he awaited the outcome of Dr Rogers's expertise in the operating theatre. The news, when it came through, was a relief. The report was as sobering as it was welcome. Titmus had been very lucky, Rogers explained. Had the propeller struck half an inch higher on the foot, he would have had to amputate at the ankle.

Some years later, nine to be precise, I fell into conversation with Fred about the accident. At the time, he was coaching the Surrey team and I was waiting to go in to bat. For some reason I found myself in the Surrey dressing room – the viewing of the playing area was more advantageous at Guildford from that spot, being right behind the bowler's arm – and I was trying to size up the bowling attack that I was soon to face. The trouble was that the window was quite high up which necessitated standing on a bench on tip-toe. *Can't be too comfortable for you, Fred, being short of a toe or two.* He laughed. 'Do you know how much compensation I got for that accident?' he demanded. I confessed I did not. 'Ninety fackin' quid! Didn't even pay me bar bill.'

As if the gods had decreed that was enough excitement for the time being, the ensuing Test match in Bridgetown was a dull affair, a bore draw as it is known in the business. The wicket was slow and lifeless and batsmen on both sides cashed in. When the batting side is so much in the ascendency, nothing much happens apart from the steady accumulation of runs and interest slowly wanes.

'Edrich and Boycott for us and Lloyd for them batted superbly,' Colin wrote, 'and Snow, on an unhelpful surface, showed what a fine bowler he was turning into by taking 5-86 off 35 overs.' Other than that, there was very little to say except that Colin's misgivings appeared to be materialising; West Indies were indeed improving and the balance of power had shifted.

Tom Graveney did provide me with one observation about this forgettable encounter. It concerned Clive Lloyd, who had now completed his second century in his first three Tests. 'Mighty fine player, Clive. And, my God, didn't he hit the ball hard.' Then he started to chuckle. 'We reckoned he gave away a dozen runs every innings.' *What, by not running singles?* 'No, when he was fielding, he could never resist shying at the stumps and he was so quick nobody had time to back up and the ball would fly away for four overthrows.'

When West Indies eventually declared their first innings of the fourth Test in Trinidad at 526/7, those misgivings of Colin's had become real fears. It was crucial in order to save the match and keep the series alive that England should reach something approaching parity when they batted. Thankfully, the captain was in one of those moods when he made batting look so effortless and every stroke is a joy. Jim Parks, watching on as a spectator, couldn't see how anybody would get him out. Nobody did.

Well, none of the West Indian players anyway. It was one of the umpires who did for him, giving him out caught behind for 148. It was, according to *Wisden*, 'a highly dubious decision'. Colin, as usual and significantly, I believe, in view of the muted controversy of 'walking' that forever seemed to swirl around his playing career, makes no mention of being the victim yet again of an umpiring mistake. He took the rough with the smooth, always uncomplainingly. Ironically, this injustice was to change the course of the match, and the series, though that was not apparent at the time.

Although Colin, together with Knott (69*), had ensured that England saved the follow-on and therefore presumably putting themselves out of danger of defeat, the possibility of victory seemed non-existent. Already, Colin was mentally preparing himself for the scenario of going into the final Test with the series locked at 0-0. This was dispiriting. England, he felt, had played the better cricket but now they were tiring and West Indies were getting stronger. All that was to be done was to hold on, keep their nerve and hope that the fates were kind to them in Guyana, in a match that was increasingly likely to be a winner-takes-all occasion. Then Sobers took a gamble.

To this day, arguments rage about Sobers's declaration. It was the third dramatic incident that occurred off-field on this tour, the others being the riot and the boating accident. I can just about get away with calling a declaration 'off-field' because the decision is usually taken in the dressing room, as it was on this occasion. West Indies were pootling along in their second innings on the final day of the match. They were 92/2 and the game was meandering towards a draw. Suddenly, Sobers appeared on the players' balcony and signalled to the two not-out batsmen, Kanhai and Carew, to come in. He was declaring. The decision astonished everybody.

Colin was anxious as they walked off the field; what was Sobers up to? The experienced pros, as well as the pressmen, were swiftly doing their sums. Ken Barrington, none more experienced than he, immediately came up with the correct bit of mental arithmetic; 215 to win in 165 minutes. 'That's 78 an hour, Skip,' he informed his captain.

What *was* Sobers up to? What surprise had he hidden up his sleeve? Why declare now? Why declare at all? All these thoughts were swirling around Colin's mind as batsmen padded up and discussion about how to respond seethed all around. Declarations are a notice of intent. Presumably Sobers thought he could win. But so could England. The game, dying on its feet, had suddenly been thrown wide open.

Barrington was convinced that Sobers had got his sums wrong and that this target was eminently achievable. Colin, naturally more cautious, was not so sure. The pitch was taking spin. To underline this, he only had to point to the first innings figures of Butcher's (5-34) – and he was only a part-time leg-spinner. Also in their ranks, they had three genuine spin bowlers, Gibbs, Rodriguez and Sobers himself, in his slow style. 'He was convinced we would put up the shutters from the start,' Colin wrote of his adversary's decision, 'and he would torment us with four spinners wheeling away at 20 overs an hour.'

Well, there was nothing for it but to see how things went. If quick wickets were lost, they could shut up shop and play out time. If they got off to a good start, then they should go for the runs. Simple as that. And that is precisely what they did.

Later, after victory had been secured, Colin pondered the reason for Sobers's gamble. Several theories came to mind. First, Garry Sobers always was – still is – an inveterate gambler and this throwing down of the gauntlet, to break the stalemate, appealed to his risk-taking temperament. Secondly, he firmly believed that his two leg-spinners, Rodriguez and Butcher, would prey upon England's 'historic insecurities against this type of bowling'. Thirdly, he was fed up with England's slow over rate, turgid scoring and perceived negative tactics. Fourthly, he could not stomach another draw.

He later explained his reason thus, 'I made that declaration for cricket. If I had not done so, the game would have died. This way, the West Indies could have won. England had never scored at 40 an hour during the tour and I did not expect them to do so then.'

Fine words. Fine sentiments. But he had fatally miscalculated. And for this he was slated. Port of Spain for him became known as Port of Pain and he never lived it down. Colin was kinder. He said this of his opposite number, 'In the face of fierce criticism, it was typical of him, true sportsman that he was, that he remained so generous in defeat.'

It was fitting that Colin, whose stature as an England captain was growing by the match, should lead his team home to victory. He said that it was important they did not lose early wickets. They did not. Edrich and Boycott put together an opening stand of 55 and the chase was on. Colin joined Boycott and by the time he was out for a masterful 71, the game was practically theirs. It still required some judicious batting from Boycott to reach the required 38 runs, with three minutes to spare.

Man of the match? Captain Cowdrey with a total of 219 runs. Not that they had such awards in those days. The cynical Trinidadian crowd might have awarded it to the home captain for declaring. Discourteously, Colin was booed as he came off the pitch. 'His offence was to have played two superb innings and to have led England much more skilfully than Sobers led the West Indies,' noted *Wisden*, tartly.

Two points need to be made about this extraordinary game before we move on to the denouement in Guyana. First, why was Colin's controversial dismissal in the first innings so crucial for eventual victory? Quite simply, had he batted and batted, as he gave every indication of so doing, England would have reached, if not passed, the West Indies total, there would have been no time for West Indies to make a score and Sobers would not have been in any position to declare and set a target. Secondly, to modern readers a target of 215 in 53 overs (which was what it worked out) seems straightforward, easy even. All I can say is that it was different then. Limited-overs cricket, and attendant run chases, was in its infancy. Nobody should underestimate the tension of the climactic stages of a dramatic Test match in the Caribbean.

Strictly speaking, Guyana is not in the Caribbean, being part of the South American mainland, but it does of course share many cultural and historical connections with the region. One distinction its cricket ground does not share with the rest of the Caribbean, nor indeed with any other major cricket ground in the world, is that Bourda is below sea level. No surprise therefore that the pitch is usually low and slow and frequently flooded. And no surprise either, that Colin and his selection panel decided to dispense with their usual three-pronged pace attack in favour of playing two spinners.

I was reminded of this fact by David Brown during our conversation. *Which of the three pacemen did Colin leave out?* That was a disingenuous and slightly naughty question. I already knew the answer. 'Me,' he answered ruefully. *How did you feel about that?* He gave me an old-fashioned look. 'What do you think? Not terribly impressed. And I told him so.' *Did that affect in any way your relationship with him?* He relaxed into the more familiar Brown amiability. 'Not at all. He was the captain. He had to make these decisions. He explained why and I respected him for it. Even if I disagreed. It's what you do, isn't it, when you're part of a team.'

Perhaps so. But I have known players who have not been so sanguine when dropped by their captain. One such was Ken Higgs, the Lancashire seamer. It was Chris Cowdrey who told me the story. After retiring from county cricket, Higgs was persuaded to renew his career with Leicestershire. Whenever Kent played Leicestershire and Chris went out to face Higgs, he was immediately greeted by a vicious bouncer. 'That's because your old man dropped me,' would be the snarled accompaniment. 'It happened *every* time,' said Chris, 'so much so that I had no option but to laugh. He never forgave Dad for dropping him.' So, not all fast bowlers are as forgiving as Brown.

With Titmus having gone home and Robin Hobbs, the other spinner in the party, deemed too inexperienced for Test match duty, the veteran Tony Lock, at the time playing for Western Australia, had been summoned to join the side. He, with Pat Pocock, would form England's spin attack. Lock had made his England debut in 1952 and he and Colin went back a long way. Indeed, the older members of the side would recall that it was Colin who caught Lock's solitary wicket at Old Trafford while Laker did for the other 19 Australians. Because of his fierce competitive streak and his mean bowling, Colin greatly admired Lock and that is the reason he believed that Lock was the right man for this particular task. Little did he anticipate that at the end of this taut, tense thriller of a Test match, it would be Lock's batting, not his bowling, for which he would be eternally grateful. A gratitude that deepened with Lock's help and encouragement when Colin was called out to Perth on that 1974/75 tour of Australia.

West Indies' first innings was all about Sobers and Kanhai; they made 152 and 150 respectively. It was just as well the rest of their side were not in a greedy mood for the total might have been colossal rather than the manageable 414. Snow bowled magnificently on an unhelpful track to take 4-82 and Lock, though taking only a couple of wickets, was as miserly as ever. Yet again, England relied on Boycott (116) and Cowdrey (59) in their response before a collapse threatened to derail them. 259-8 is a perilous position. Had they been forced to follow on, the game would surely have been up, especially as the match was scheduled – unusually – to be played over six days. Two guardian angels, Lock and Pocock, the most unlikely saviours of a longish tail (Snow was batting at number eight!), put on 109, Tony Lock smiting the ball with uncommon belligerence to notch up 89, his highest first-class, let alone Test, score. 'The cost of his air fare from Perth was beginning to look like a steal,' Tom Graveney drolly observed.

Snow versus Sobers... again. Or that is how it seemed. John Snow was emerging as England's foremost fast bowler and his battles with Sobers, unarguably the greatest cricketer ever to have laced on boots, were becoming the stuff of legend. Snow did not get him out but he did snaffle six other West Indians. His match figures of 10-142 underlined his growing stature and his value to this team. Sobers was simply magnificent. He batted chancelessly and it was only lack of partners that prevented him scoring his second hundred of the match. 'Sobers's 95* out of a total of 264 was a great innings,' *Wisden* reported simply.

'I always loved it when Garry got a big score,' Graveney told me. *Why, Tom? Were you in awe of his strokeplay?* 'Not 'arf. But that's not the reason. If he batted a long time, he didn't want to do much bowling.' *But it worked the other way too. If he didn't bat for long, he would want to do a lot of bowling.* 'Ah, but you see, Andy, I was a batsman.' He chuckled long and hard over that one.

England started the last day, the sixth, needing 330 to win. Whether that was a realistic target, whether they approached the final innings minded to seek the victory or to see out the draw, and thus claim the rubber, soon became no more than an academic question. Their score of 41/5 was calamitous.

All the hard work, all the good cricket played, all the best-laid plans lay crumpled in the dust. Lance Gibbs was spinning a deadly web, West Indian fielders were swarming around the bat and the West Indian umpires' fingers were twitching. Colin alone stood firm, a captain intent on remaining on the bridge even as the waters came lapping around his feet. His fellow Kentish man, Alan Knott, remained faithfully at his side and together they blocked and blocked. After tea, improbably, they were still there. Eventually, the captain's long vigil came to an end, LBW to Gibbs for 82. There were still 70 minutes for Knott and the tail to hang on. Those 70 minutes, as Colin pointed out in his notes, were 'the longest and most excruciating of my life'.

Brown, a spectator in the dressing room but biting his nails as much as anyone, chortled at the memory. 'Let no one say that Colin was a soft touch. Off the field, he was an utter gent; on the field, he was no pushover, I can tell you. He employed all the tricks of the trade to waste time. I can't remember how many times he sent out the 12th man to change Knotty's gloves.' In his own, inimitable style, Knott remained obdurate while wickets steadily fell at the other end. As *Wisden* reported, 'Knott was well nigh as assured as Cowdrey and no less courageous.'

It was a race between the clock and the West Indian bowlers. I say a race. In the England dressing room, it felt more like a slow march.

Indignation knew no bounds as Pocock was given out caught, clearly off a bump ball. Jeff Jones (first-class batting average of 3.97), last man in, slowly trudged to the wicket. Last over of the day, of the match, of the series. Six balls to survive for England glory. Or six balls for West Indies to snatch victory and tie up the rubber. 'A capacity crowd,' wrote Colin, 'will never forget the last over bowled by Lance Gibbs to Jeff Jones with every West Indian fielder sitting on his bat.' How would Colin have known that? According to Brown, Colin spent that last over hiding in the toilet.

As he returned home, together with his victorious team, Colin must have reflected that life doesn't get much better than this. He had only to read the *Wisden* report of the tour, penned by E.M. Wellings, to appreciate how high, both as player and captain, his reputation now stood. 'I am quite certain,' went the end-of-term report, 'that no other captain could have led the side so well and performed the numerous duties of captaincy so flawlessly in the exacting circumstances of this tour... Now, for the first time, he had his own command and he assumed it with authority, growing rapidly in stature as a leader and becoming more and more assertive as a cricketer.'

The 'exacting circumstances' to which Wellings refers is a hint not so much at the unruly crowds and of course the riot but more at the standard of umpiring, which was poor, sometimes downright biased. In fact, he went so far as to hazard a guess that Cowdrey's team had to be '30 per cent better to come out on top'. Substandard umpiring was always a bugbear of England teams abroad. It wasn't surprising really when you take into account that only in England was the game professional, so you would expect the officiating to be proportionately better supervised. Of course it is different now, with a fully trained and well-paid cadre of neutral umpires circling the globe. Back then, 'home umpires' or 'whingeing Poms', depending on which side of the fence you sat, was the familiar soundtrack to MCC tours.

It was undoubtedly a happy team, both Graveney and Brown were keen to emphasise, despite the unpleasant incidents and considerable provocations. They played good cricket, often in the most testing of circumstances and above all, they kept their nerve at crucial junctures. Wellings believed they were 'well-controlled'; in other words, there was never any doubt who was in charge. Graveney was convinced this was because, 'Colin, at long last, was captain of his own ship.' The team was thus cast in his own image: urbane, courteous, well mannered but patient, tenacious and tough as teak when battle commenced.

Mind you, as he pointed out in his notes, he was blessed with some pretty good players. 'Snow, Brown and Jones were as potent a fast-bowling attack as any in the world, considerably faster and more hostile than the West Indies.' That says something. More potent than Hall, Griffith and Sobers? Yes, it seemed he had been right all along. Hall and Griffith had seen their better days. 'Snow was our match-winner,' he continued. 'He took 27 wickets in only four Tests and was a handful for even their best batsmen.' Furthermore, he reckoned that Boycott and Edrich were developing into England's finest opening pair of batsmen since the war. 'Boycott in particular emerged as a superb player.'

No doubt, Geoffrey would agree with that sentiment. 'Above all,' Colin concluded, 'I needed a number of players to play above themselves, especially when the chips are down, and that happened on my tour. Alan Knott, the find of the party, was an excellent case in point.' Note the use of the possessive pronoun *my*. Colin really did feel this was his team. The Five Year Plan had got off to a good start.

Perhaps the last word on England's triumphant adventure in the Caribbean ought to be left to *The Times*'s cricket correspondent, John Woodcock. 'Yes, it was a happy tour, the unfortunate accident to Titmus notwithstanding. But there, I find that the happiness or unhappiness of a touring party is usually in direct proportion to whether they are winning or not.'

Back home, as a signal of Colin's authority over England cricket at this time, he was appointed captain for the whole of the forthcoming Ashes series that summer before a ball had been bowled. As it happened, cricket lovers had to wait a long time for that first ball to be bowled; the weather was miserable, the traditional pipe opener at Worcester was completely washed out and rain severely curtailed the other matches of the tourists' preparation. The weather did not improve; it was a wet summer and none of the Tests escaped delay and interruption. In all, it was calculated that the Australians lost over 100 hours of cricket during their tour. It was the soggiest and most disappointing Ashes series that many, including me, could remember. The Five Year Plan, you might say, got a soaking.

There's no such thing as a weak Australian side. Who first mooted that is unrecorded but countless England captains, down the ages, have repeated the mantra. That said, Bill Lawry's team that visited these shores in 1968 neither sent shivers down the spine nor stirred the blood. England had the stronger side, they were playing at home and they had just triumphed in the West Indies.

They should have reclaimed the Ashes but did not. They were ambushed in the first Test and thereafter Lawry and his men played a stubborn brand of cricket, intent on avoiding defeat, and England, partly to do with bad luck with the weather, but more to do with their failing to capitalise on opportunities when they arose, seemed powerless to do much about it. There was that thrilling finale to the series at The Oval, which England won, but that only papered over the cracks of a disappointing campaign. A decade is a long time without the urn.

After the frustrations of the second Test at Lord's, which England would surely have won had it not been for the rain, a hugely satisfying and emotional milestone beckoned Colin in the third at Edgbaston. Nobody had ever played 100 Tests. Colin was about to reach that landmark. He had already passed the record of 91, set by his Kent team-mate, Godfrey Evans, and to say he was anxious was an understatement.

Never mind the record, this was a game England had to win and once again, rain decided to play the spoilsport. Day one was washed out. On day two, having won the toss and coming in when the score was 80, Colin produced another of those innings when he seemed to be on a different playing field to everyone else. On 58, he pulled up lame, clutching his hamstring. Wild horses would not have dragged him off, however. Geoff Boycott, the dismissed batsman, had to re-don his pads and act as a runner, one of the very few occasions that team-mates and opponents could ever remember him running somebody else's runs. When he reached 60, Colin passed Wally Hammond's record of 7,000 Test runs. Could he mark his 100th Test with a century?

Despite his handicap, he was timing the ball as sweetly as ever. There seemed no earthly reason why his supporters should not hope. Alas, stumps were pulled with Colin on 95 not out. Resuming in considerable discomfort the next morning, he managed to eke out the remaining five runs to record his 21st Test hundred, one of his very best. It came at a price though. He took no further part in the match, Tom Graveney deputised as captain and steady rain from 12.30pm on the final day put an end to any hopes England had had of forcing the win. There was no chance that Colin would recover in time for the fourth Test, another disappointing draw, which ensured that Australia kept hold of the Ashes.

'Nothing happened in Acts One, Two, Three and Four. Then suddenly in Act Five, the stage was littered with corpses.' So commented a pupil of mine after a trip to the Royal Shakespeare Theatre in Stratford. You might be forgiven for believing that is a fair summation of the English cricket season of 1968. All the drama, excitement and bloodletting were saved up for the fifth Test and its immediate aftermath. And when the curtain finally dropped, reputations, if not bodies, were lying, broken, all over the place.

It all started with a phone call. Graveney gave me the inside story. Basil D'Oliveira, apart from being able to count to 75, had not exactly covered himself in glory in the West Indies and had been dropped from the team following England's defeat in the first Test. This was strange as he had top-scored with 87 not out in England's second innings but there you are...it was a summer of strange selection decisions.

Following the draw – and the loss of the Ashes – in the fourth Test (remember, Colin had been unfit and Graveney had led the side in his absence), Graveney received a call from his captain. 'Roger Prideaux is ill,' Colin told him, 'and we need a replacement. How is Basil playing?' Graveney and D'Oliveira were team-mates at Worcestershire. 'Back to his best,' Graveney replied unhesitatingly. He admitted to me that this was not strictly true; D'Oliveira had been struggling for runs but there had been signs very recently that he was rediscovering a semblance of his old form. Besides, Graveney believed in his friend's ability and mental toughness and never doubted his calibre as a Test match player. 'Fine,' said Colin. 'We'll stick him in.' It was a fateful decision, one that was to reverberate around the cricketing world.

I cannot imagine that Colin's choice of replacement for Prideaux did not send a frisson of alarm through the committee rooms at Lord's. Basil D'Oliveira was a Cape Coloured and being barred by the apartheid laws of South Africa from playing first-class cricket in his own country, he had forsaken his homeland to try his luck in England. That he had made it to the England Test team was a story in itself, a triumph of talent and tenacity over prejudice and bigotry. Now, Colin Cowdrey was no political *ingénue*.

His later career gives the lie to any suggestion that he was naïvely unaware of the possible ramifications of his decision to pick D'Oliveira. He knew as well as anyone that the scheduled MCC tour that winter was to South Africa and as a man of colour, D'Oliveira would not be welcome in his home country. This needs to be kept in mind as the 'D'Oliveira Affair', as it was called, unfolded and Colin's role in subsequent events came under the closest scrutiny.

Back to the game. On purely cricketing terms, there was an unarguable case for recalling D'Oliveira and so it was proved when he played one of the great Test innings of modern times. Consider the context as he strolled – Basil always strolled – out to the middle on the first day of The Oval Test. The Ashes may have been lost but England could still square the series; they were playing for pride and besides, their opponents were *Australia*.

England were in trouble, having lost Milburn, Dexter and Cowdrey cheaply. Edrich and Graveney stemmed the tide but when Graveney went, there was still much work to be done. D'Oliveira had just come back into the side and was playing for his place. Furthermore, there was a tour of South Africa in the offing and it had been his dream to return to the country of his birth, one that had branded him a second-class citizen and denied him any opportunity of representing them, now wearing the cap of his adopted country. What a beacon of hope he could provide in that bitterly divided land. And Alan Connolly, a vastly under-rated bowler, especially in English conditions, was bowling seriously well.

Spread over two days, an hour on that first evening and the following morning, he scored 158. Together with Edrich, who made 164, he held the middle of the innings together. The total of 494 had given them a fighting chance. 'D'Oliveira,' *Wisden* reported, 'hooked the short ball superbly and next day drove magnificently.' Graveney was equally fulsome. 'It was an absolutely magnificent innings,' he told me. 'He had such powerful forearms and he struck the ball so cleanly that it would rocket to the boundary. He hooked and drove so commandingly.'

Colin wrote, with some insight, that he 'batted as if this was a mission utterly divorced from a Test match'. Charlie Elliott, the umpire, put it another way. When D'Oliveira had scored his hundred, he muttered to him out of the corner of his mouth as play resumed, 'You've put the cat among the pigeons.' When he was out and had returned to the sanctuary of the dressing room, D'Oliveira sat quietly for a while, without removing his pads, seemingly oblivious to the congratulations of his team-mates, and gave that characteristic little blow out from the cheeks. He must have thought his place on the tour was secure.

Australia averted the follow-on, owing solely to a typically obdurate 135 from their captain, Bill Lawry. In search of quick runs, in order to set a total and give themselves time to bowl Australia out, England threw bat at ball, mustering 181. Australia had to score 352 to win, highly improbable given that the Ashes were already secured and all Australia needed to do was bat out time for the draw. For England, the prize was victory and the task was to take ten wickets.

'Easy-peasy,' Graveney grinned at me. 'We had 'em on the ropes at 85/5 when we went in for lunch.' At which point, a sudden and violent thunderstorm struck south London. In no time at all, the playing area was flooded and once again, in this sodden summer, it seemed that the weather was going to thwart England. When the deluge had ceased, Colin donned his blazer and, alone, went out to inspect the wicket. 'Inspect the wicket!' Graveney chuckled at the memory, 'You couldn't *see* the wicket. The square was under water. All the Aussies were laughing and joking in their dressing room. They were convinced that was it for the day. And quite frankly, so did we.'

But not Colin. Restlessly, he paced about, urging the willing groundstaff to ever more endeavour in their mopping-up efforts. In this, they were joined by a volunteer force of spectators. Graveney was convulsed with laughter at the memory. 'Surrey members were walking around spearing the ground with the tip of their umbrellas to drain the water away. Wouldn't be allowed today.'

At 4.45pm, the umpires deemed the conditions fit to play. In a nutshell, that meant England had 75 minutes (that number again) to take five wickets and save the series. What the Australians thought of this surprising turn of events can be scarcely imagined.

Or could it? By sheer coincidence, I was put in touch with one of the not-out batsmen who had to buckle on his pads and renew battle with the Englishmen. John Inverarity had stood firm throughout the morning while wickets fell around him. He was determined to carry his bat and see it through to the end and felt confident he could. He had given every indication of relaxed permanence and England knew that to have any chance of squeezing home, they had to get rid of him. He played in only six Tests – and this was his finest hour, incidentally – but he had a long and distinguished career playing for Western Australia. Later, he was chairman of selectors for Cricket Australia. His profession was teaching and for a time he took up a post at Tonbridge School, hence his connection with Colin Cowdrey.

What did your lads think of the crowd helping to mop up the water? 'Mop it up! They were down on their hands and knees drinking it.' *Was it fit to play when you started?* He was surprisingly sanguine about this. 'Well, we played. And nobody died. So it must have been fit. Anyway, when the umps say time to go, boys, out there you go, don't you?' He did say that he swapped his usual batting boots for his fielding boots with longer spikes because he felt he was less likely to slip when batting. 'I won't say it was wet but the water did come over our boots walking out there.'

In other words, it was a moot point whether play should have recommenced. Here, I disagree with myself, if you see what I mean. When I was playing, I was always of the opinion that conditions should be, if not perfect, then adequate enough to perform at your best. Now that I no longer play, I believe that players are too precious about it all. They are paid to entertain and this they cannot do sitting in the pavilion. So I guess Inverarity had come to the same conclusion. It was not in the Australians' best interests to restart; they had nothing to gain and all to lose. But the umpires took a different view, so out they went.

England of course couldn't wait to get cracking. They knew the batsmen would not fancy facing Underwood on a wet pitch, even if they only had 75 minutes to survive. The problem was that, for a while, the pitch was *too* wet. 'It was a fifth-day pitch,' Inverarity reminded me, 'and in actual fact it was more difficult facing Deadly in the morning before the storm, when the pitch was dry and dusty. So, although it was turning, it turned slowly.'

For a while, not a lot happened. Colin fretted and changed his bowling around, searching for a breakthrough. It was provided by

D'Oliveira, a noted partnership breaker. 'Basil nipped one back to Jarman,' said Inverarity, 'and it just clipped the bail as it went through.' Immediately, Colin whipped off D'Oliveira and replaced him at the Pavilion End with Underwood. The pitch had now started to dry out and he was at last able to gain some real purchase as he fired the ball in. The Australians collapsed spectacularly and he took four wickets in 27 balls for only six runs. There is that famous photograph of the last ball of the match with poor old Inverarity, who had defied England for so long, padding up to Underwood and the whole of the England side in shot, gathered around the bat, appealing in unison for LBW. The umpire's finger is pointing to the sky.

Was it out? Inverarity laughed. 'Ask Charlie Elliott.' *But he's dead.* 'Look in the scorebook, then.' Taking pity on me, he finally admitted, yes, it was out.

How do you think Colin captained that day? Well, not just that day, but whenever you played against him? 'He was a vastly experienced player and he knew the game, and the participants, backwards. So he usually arrived at the right decisions. And Colin was Colin. You know, a thoroughly agreeable bloke and people followed him because they were fond of him. Occasionally, I felt he dithered a bit and wanted everybody's opinion before making up his mind. He wasn't an inspirational leader, an up and at 'em sort of captain, but he knew his way around the block and nobody would want to rock the boat and take him on. He was like that. He got people to do things for him because he was so damn *nice!*'

Rather than dwell on Australia's defeat, Inverarity was keen to take me back a few years, to the 1954/55 series. 'I was ten at the time,' he said. 'My dad, who played for Western Australia, was invited, together with my mum, to a reception to meet the MCC players. When he came back home, he told me that he had been speaking to a delightful young chap by the name of Colin Cowdrey.'

He then fast-forwarded to the current tour, 1968 in England. 'It was my first tour. One Sunday, I was invited down to his house in Limpsfield where we played tennis and pool and chatted a lot. Both Paul Sheahan and I were schoolmasters and if there's one thing that Colin was interested in, other than cricket, it was schools and education. I met him again when he was on the 1970/71 tour and when I was over with the 1972 team, we met up again. He knew I was interested in a teaching post, so he arranged a meeting for me with David Kemp, who was, as you know, an influential figure at Colin's old school, Tonbridge. As a result, I was offered, and accepted, a temporary post there to teach maths. That was 1976/77. That was what he did. He knew so many people and he liked to put individuals in touch with each other. He was a fixer.'

Classic networking, you could call it. 'Yes, but not for him but for others around him.' On account of this typical piece of Cowdrey contact-making, John Inverarity and his family became close, personal friends. 'When we arrived in England, he met us at the airport and drove us down to our temporary home. He loaned us a car and had us round for Christmas. Jeremy, his son, used to babysit for us!' *That was very brave of you and your wife.* He laughed. 'Ah, I see you know Jeremy. Well, the whole family were very kind to me, Jane and the girls and we never forgot it. We remained close and saw each other whenever I was in England or he was in Australia. I was so sad when he died.'

He still would not let me go without another illustrative story about Colin. 'It was on that same tour of 1968. We were playing Kent at Canterbury. Colin was playing; he was captain. And here was this great batsman, on an easy pitch, which didn't seem to be giving anybody else any trouble at all, scratching around at the crease as if he was an absolute novice. Strange that. There were days when he could look a world-beater and there were other days when it looked as if he didn't know which end of a bat to hold.' Ah yes, the puzzle that was Colin Cowdrey. I was becoming quite familiar with the enigma.

No more so was that enigma in evidence than in the days and weeks that followed England's win at The Oval. The touring party for South Africa had to be picked, and quickly; public announcement of the team was to be made on the following day. Colin had already been named as captain, so that very evening he jumped into his Jaguar and crossed the Thames to meet the other selectors at Lord's. The selection panel, in addition to Colin, comprised: Peter May; Don Kenyon; Alec Bedser; with Doug Insole in the chair. Also present were senior figures at MCC: Arthur Gilligan (president); Gubby Allen (treasurer); Billy Griffith (secretary); and Donald Carr (assistant secretary). Also in attendance was the nominated tour manager, Les Ames. I make no comment on the composition of the committee but I do note the number – ten. A lot of opinions, you might say.

According to Colin, discussions went on well into the night. It would not have needed a fly on the wall to tell us what took them so long. When the touring party was announced the next day, D'Oliveira's name was not on the list of 16. Unsurprisingly, all hell broke loose. Or, as Colin was fond of exclaiming in his diaries, the balloon went up. Nobody, pressmen, pundits, fans, politicians, columnists, correspondents, soapbox orators, even the man on the Clapham omnibus, could believe that D'Oliveira's omission had not been politically motivated.

MCC, so it was claimed, had been advised by their counterparts in the South African Cricket Association that their government would not welcome D'Oliveira back into their country as an official member of England's Test team. So D'Oliveira had been sacrificed in order to maintain cricketing contacts between the two countries.

The selectors, including the captain, were not unprepared for this and had their defence to hand. Categorically no, it was asserted, they had not, at any stage, been subjected to political pressure; the team had been picked on cricketing grounds only. Then why had D'Oliveira, who had, incidentally, just scored 158 in a Test match, not been included among the top seven or eight batsmen in England? That can be explained by the fact that the balance of the side demanded a bowling all-rounder, such as Tom Cartwright, who had been picked, rather than a batting all-rounder, as D'Oliveira was, who had *not* been picked. It was a shame but there we are. Selection is a tricky business and sometimes, unpopular decisions have to be made.

'I think we have got rather better than him in the side,' said Doug Insole, rather insensitively. 'Anyone who would swallow that,' thundered *The Guardian*'s editorial, 'would believe that the moon was a currant bun.' Rather ominously, the Rev. David Sheppard weighed in with the comment, 'The MCC have made a dreadful mistake.' Tom Graveney, D'Oliveira's great friend and team-mate, was incandescent with rage and his anger had scarcely abated as he talked about it many years later when I was writing his biography. 'To get 158 and then get *dropped?* Nonsense. It was political.'

To this day argument over the affair rages. First, let us consider whether it is at all possible to construct a feasible scenario where

D'Oliveira could have been left out on purely cricketing grounds. Yes, it is true that Cartwright was in a class of his own as a medium-pacer. D'Oliveira was no more than an occasional bowler, a partnership-breaker. His strong suit was obviously his batting. The batsmen chosen ahead of him were Cowdrey, Graveney, Boycott, Edrich, Barrington, Prideaux and Fletcher. No Dexter; he had declined to tour. All of those players had distinguished Test careers, with the exception of Prideaux. Fletcher was inexperienced but it was not unusual to blood a youngster on tour. After all, Colin had been taken to Australia before he had even scored a hundred for Kent. Prideaux only played two more Tests after his debut that summer against Australia, but he had not been dropped. He had been ill, so it would not have been unreasonable to restore him. However, the fact that D'Oliveira had just scored 158 was inescapable and in cricket, as in all team games, it is always a case of possession is nine-tenths of the law. He was the man *in situ* and the logic for his inclusion was surely watertight.

There was however a hidden subtext here, and one that had nothing to do with politics. D'Oliveira's talent was undeniable. His story, his background, his tenacity in the face of seemingly insurmountable obstacles was the stuff of folklore and he was rightly lauded for it. Furthermore he was a thoroughly decent and honourable man, greatly loved by friend and foe alike. But he had a weakness, one that had manifested itself on Colin's tour of the West Indies earlier that year. 'You see, he was a man of colour, playing for the Mother Country,' Jim Parks said to me, 'and as such, he was feted wherever he went. Everybody would buy him a drink, and Bas being Bas, he couldn't say no. That was his trouble really.'

Graveney went even further, half sad, half amused by his friend's antics. 'Kanhai got him on the rum and coke. And once he started... You know, before Bas came to England, he never drank. He had this weakness. He couldn't handle it. And of course it got the better of him.' Indeed it did. Basil, with a few drinks inside him, was impossible to handle. Colin was perfectly aware of this, though he was too discreet to make known his private reservations. It is possible that the selectors felt that this was a risk not worth taking. South African hospitality was – still is – legendary.

The political argument, that pressure to omit D'Oliveira was exerted from above, is more difficult to refute. The British government,

MCC, cricket boards around the world, informed observers, were all aware that a train crash was in the offing. If this controversy wasn't going to highlight the growing moral repugnance of sporting contacts with apartheid South Africa, then something would. It was as plain as a pikestaff. Cricketers, and their administrators, were generally a conservative bunch; most, if pressed, would have deplored the mixing of cricket and politics and would have preferred to maintain playing links between the two countries, even if the South African regime and its policies left a nasty taste in the mouth.

Let us continue to play them, thus keeping open channels of communication, so that influence can be brought to bear and change effected. We can't possibly deny the cricketing public the opportunity of seeing our chaps take on a young, emerging, exciting Springbok side including Peter and Graeme Pollock, Eddie Barlow, Mike Procter, Barry Richards, Lee Irvine and others, can we? That would have been the thinking, I guess, of MCC and I'm sure Colin, by nature a fixer and conciliator, would have been sympathetic to that view.

The selection panel could be criticised for wearing blinkers – after all, apartheid had been sustained for years by passivity from governments worldwide – and the imputation of moral cowardice is difficult to ignore. But put yourselves in their position. Knowingly to cut ties irrevocably with one of the Test-playing powerhouses is a heavy burden to bear.

Without exception, the selectors denied that they had been subjected to pressure, of any kind, from any quarter. I'm sure they were being honest in this. However, saying that no pressure was exerted is not the same thing as saying that no pressure existed. Pressure was all around. It is perfectly feasible that they were subconsciously affected by the ramifications of their decision-making. Alas, all those who were in that committee room at Lord's are now dead, with the exception of Doug Insole. He has never wavered from the official line, that they omitted D'Oliveira on purely cricketing grounds, and it seems futile to pursue him further. He's in his 90s now and must be sick of being asked to defend himself.

There have been dark mutterings about the minutes of the meeting having mysteriously disappeared but even if Sherlock agreed to look for them, I would remain sceptical of the point of the exercise. I have taken minutes at many a meeting and the written account I subsequently produced often bore little resemblance to what actually took place; either I could not exactly remember or I had unconsciously (all right, sometimes quite consciously) slanted it the way I wanted it to read. The point is, nobody read them and nobody cared.

MCC was not a government department, it did not have Hansard stenographers noting down every word, every interjection, every cough in every meeting. It was a private club and I bet a pound to a penny that the minutes, if they exist, would reveal nothing startling. I think we just have to accept Colin's version of what occurred. For better or worse, that is what they decided. Whether it was the right call is another matter altogether.

Just when the storm was at its height and MCC felt that things could not get any worse, they did. About a fortnight later, Tom Cartwright, about whose fitness there had been some doubt, withdrew from the party; a stubborn shoulder injury had not healed enough for him to risk undertaking a long and arduous tour. To Colin, the response was straightforward. D'Oliveira, the unnamed first reserve, should take his place. 'Fine,' you can imagine him saying to his fellow selectors, as he said to Graveney, 'We'll stick him in.'

It may have appeared straightforward to him but to many observers, it was anything but. If the selectors had ignored D'Oliveira in the first instance because he was not regarded as a front-line bowler, why had they replaced a front-line bowler with a front-line batsman who only bowled occasionally? It didn't make sense. But there was no other medium-pacer of Cartwright's stature, Colin countered. Be that as it may, and few were convinced, the whole affair then took on a discord that expanded way beyond the confines of the game of cricket.

If anybody had any doubts about how widely it spread, then a speech given by the South African prime minister, B.J. Vorster, in Bloemfontein in the Orange Free State, the very heartland of Afrikanerdom, provided a nasty reality check. In it, he railed against what he saw as the cricket authorities in England capitulating to anti-apartheid agitation and D'Oliveira's belated selection had given force to his words, 'We are not prepared to receive a team thrust upon us by people whose interests are not the game but to gain political objectives which they do not attempt to hide.' Hmm, black pots and kettles come to mind.

He did not, there and then, call off the tour, being mindful of South Africa's delicate relations with other world bodies of sport, most notably rugby, but he had left MCC precious little wriggle room. In short, he was stating what everybody had known for a long time; D'Oliveira would not be welcome in South Africa as part of an England cricket team.

A week later, MCC bowed to the inevitable and called off the tour. Criticism of them and the selection panel that put them in this undesirable position hardly abated however. David Sheppard, possibly the most vociferous disparager, was unhappy and accused MCC, and by implication his old friend and team-mate, Colin Cowdrey, of 'a lack of foresight and weakness'.

From their time at Oxbridge, Colin had never been able to share Sheppard's utter moral certainty and self-conviction in life. It was no wonder they found themselves at opposite ends of the spectrum in this affair. It seems clear to me that Colin, though publicly abhorring apartheid, was keen to act as peacemaker and go-between, keeping all avenues open for reasoned and sensible discussion, but got lost in the moral maze as he went along.

He felt enormously sorry for Basil and was greatly relieved and hugely obliged that he did not blame him for his dream being snatched away from him. Over a mournful but companionable dinner, Basil told him, 'I'm terribly sorry that I should be the cause of you and the lads missing the tour.'

Rev. Mike Vockins was appointed secretary at Worcestershire shortly after this affair, a post he held for 30 years, and he got to know D'Oliveira well. Over coffee and chocolate biscuits in his study near where I live, he gave me his take on D'Oliveira's view, 'Basil always told me that he never blamed Colin Cowdrey for what happened. He said that Colin had, privately, assured him during this Test match that he would be "on the plane" but he always believed that he had been put under intolerable political pressure and been outvoted at the selection meeting. The two of them remained the greatest of friends until Colin's death.'

I was interested in John Woodcock's take on the whole sorry saga. 'Ah yes, the D'Oliveira Affair,' he reflected sadly. 'It was not the MCC's finest hour. Nobody came out of it well, I'm afraid to say. Except Basil.' Undeniably so. Basil D'Oliveira had cemented his affection in the minds of the British public by his restraint and dignity throughout.

Although there were much larger issues at play here than just missing a cricket tour, Colin was bitterly disappointed that he would not now lead MCC in a tour of South Africa, something for which he had been planning for months. The Five Year Plan, though not destroyed, now had a whole chapter ripped out.

Being of a buoyant and idealistic disposition, he still harboured hopes that relations between the two cricket governing bodies had not fractured permanently. After all, South Africa were scheduled to play five Tests in England the following summer. Prime minister Vorster would not want to scupper that as well. Colin wrote, 'I feel that eventual good will come out of it all.' Chapter four of the plan was still on, surely. However, Peter Hain and the Stop The Tour campaign put paid to that.

With their choice of Pakistan as an alternative touring destination that winter, MCC swapped what might be deemed a domestic civil war for the real McCoy. Verbal conflict, press opprobrium and public anger were usurped by firebombs, firearms and machetes. The country was in chaos after a bitterly disputed general election, which would result in the total breakdown of law and order. One million died in unrestrained blood-letting, which prompted a war with India, military humiliation and the loss of East Pakistan, later to reinvent itself as Bangladesh. And into this socio political cauldron, MCC sent 15 unsuspecting cricketers.

Colin was still captain. His grip on the job was as secure as ever; there was no obvious rival and it was generally accepted he was doing a good job under circumstances that were far from easy. This tour was about to test his powers of blandishment and conciliation to the utmost. It is one thing to plead with a bottle-throwing mob, drunk on rum; it is quite another to confront gun-toting agitators, drunk on murder.

The party smelt trouble as soon as they set foot on Pakistani soil. The country was seething with unrest. All was confusion and turmoil. The itinerary was constantly changed, travel arrangements fluid and hotel accommodation hit-and-miss. The Pakistan Cricket Board was anxious for the tour to take place, despite the mayhem and violence that was being unleashed all around. Playing games of cricket would give the impression that all was calm and normal; at the very least it might provide a source of distraction from the rioting. The players felt isolated and not a little frightened. The impression that they were being used as pawns in a bloody game of chess was difficult to shake off.

That they were expected to play a Test match amid this lawlessness and violence seems surreal but play cricket they did. Beyond the stands, Lahore was burning; within the ground, the crowd was restless, with students in strident voice, their demonstrations teetering on the brink of open revolt. Disturbances were frequent and the game occasionally disrupted as police waded in to restore an uneasy semblance of order.

Commentators and onlookers often referred to Colin's batting throughout his career, when he was playing at his best, as seemingly occupying a different plane to everybody else. On this first day, so at ease with the bowling was he that he could have been at Canterbury, with the famous lime tree just inside the boundary, or at Tunbridge Wells, with the rhododendrons in flower just outside the boundary, rather than in riot-torn Lahore, with fires lighting up the stands and rabble-rousers stirring their followers to a pitch of insurrection. He scored exactly 100 out of a total of 306. It was his final Test century and in many ways his most extraordinary.

Wisden recorded, 'Among the hubbub of student unrest, his innings was a magnificent performance in which he kept his cool despite the many distractions.' Beauty in the face of chaos; calmness and serenity as hell is let loose. How often has a Cowdrey innings been thus described, except in this case it was not a country's fast bowling attack he was facing but a country's population on the brink of civil war. His powers of concentration were never better in evidence than during his four hours at the crease that day.

The match, shortened to four days on account of the unrest, was a largely forgettable draw. Drama was saved for the off-field machinations that were a daily feature of this ill-fated tour. At the last minute, a Test in Dacca, in East Pakistan, was inserted into the schedule. When the players found out, they were horrified. Tom Graveney remembered a meeting, which he in his capacity as vice-captain attended, of the tour committee with the representatives of the Pakistani government. The politicians were desperate for the tour to continue and the detour to Dacca to go ahead if only to appease an angry populace.

Messages coming back from Lord's were ambivalent. Of course, the players' safety was paramount but if the tour could proceed, despite current difficulties, it would greatly assist relations between MCC and the Pakistan Board of Control. The advice given by British diplomats, both in Pakistan and back home, was at best vacillating and at times downright misleading. Graveney was adamant that they should not go to East Pakistan. News from there was that law and order had totally broken down. In his strongly expressed opposition, he believed he had the voice of the team, especially the younger and less experienced tourists. 'Huh,' he grunted. 'The only reason we went was that the students in Dacca, who had control of the city, threatened to burn down the British consulate if we didn't.'

His words fell on deaf ears. Nobody at that meeting is still alive but it is not hard to imagine its tone and content. Graveney, never one to mince his words, spoke up challengingly. Les Ames, the manager, was courteously attempting to lead his party as best he could through a political minefield. And that was no figure of speech; the acrid smell of burning buildings was in their nostrils. And Colin, no doubt with head in hands, was mournfully brooding on what had befallen his beloved game of cricket. The decision was taken to soldier on, ironic really, considering there was not a soldier to be seen when the team landed in Dacca. The army, and the police, had completely withdrawn from the city, leaving it in the hands of firebrand agitators and left-wing students.

'We were escorted everywhere we went by these students,' said Graveney. 'They said they were in charge and we would be safe.' *Did you feel safe?* 'Hmm. I did ask one of them why he wasn't at university attending lectures. He just gave me a wink and pointed to his rifle.'

Much like the social fabric of the country, the pitch for the Test did not take long to unravel. It was basically 22 yards of rolled mud and it soon broke up. England were saved from defeat only by a superb unbeaten century from D'Oliveira. So, it was back to West Pakistan for the final Test of this unhappy campaign. The tension and violence in Karachi if anything had worsened and now the players were seriously concerned for their safety. Several of them openly expressed their desire to go home.

Graveney remembered a fractious team meeting in the hotel. He told me that he, as vice-captain, gave utterance to their fears and strongly recommended that the tour be abandoned. Cowdrey and Ames, having taken advice from the British Embassy, were still of the opinion that they should carry on. For the sake of cricket, and future relations between the two countries, argued Ames, they should not cut and run because of domestic adversity.

I have only Graveney's testament of those difficult last days of the tour and now he is no longer with us for me to probe deeper. I did ask him about Colin's leadership during this crisis. His affection and respect for his friend had not wavered but he did feel that Colin, and Les Ames, had been put under intolerable pressure by MCC to see things through, come what may. 'Colin seemed...distracted. As if he really wasn't sure what to do.' Graveney wasn't the only one to find fault with his captaincy.

Wisden gave him a bit of a roasting, 'Cowdrey found the making of decisions more and more difficult in the bewildering circumstances.' One assumes that the correspondent was referring to decisions *off* the field, for little of note was happening on it. My only response is that bewilderment would have been totally understandable given these exceptional circumstances, none of them to do with cricket. Colin Cowdrey was the captain of a touring team, not the president of a war-torn country, nor an army general ordered to restore control. His instinct was, always, to accommodate and to meet halfway. His loyalty to MCC and the game of cricket was unimpeachable and total. Let us do our best and get on with the game, would have been his mantra. It was so in the West Indies and it was so here. It wasn't his fault they were caught in the middle of a civil war. And it probably wasn't his decision to abandon ship anyway. That was more likely the manager's and Ames's inclination was to carry on too.

So the match started. That it was never finished came as no surprise to anybody who was there. While violence and disorder, total anarchy in effect, raged all around, England, by the third day, had amassed a total of 502/7. One wonders how much the Pakistani bowlers were intent upon their task; they must have been as frightened as the Englishmen. At last, the powder keg exploded, as it had been threatening to do for days. 'When we saw the marquees on the far side of the ground set alight, we knew we were in trouble,' said Graveney. 'The army advanced on the mob, rifles ready to fire. This wasn't just a riot, this was war!'

David Brown has the moment etched on his memory. 'Knotty and I were at the crease. Knotty was on 96 not out. He'd never scored a Test hundred before. Suddenly, the whole Pakistani team started to leg it off the field. I ran too, but I had to pass Knotty, who was oblivious and taking guard for the next delivery. I practically had to drag him off. He wanted to stay to score his hundred.'

Back in the pavilion, the only sensible decision open to them was quickly taken. The team piled on to their bus and lay down on the floor on the glass from the smashed windows as the driver – 'a brave man' said Graveney – drove hell for leather back to the hotel. A flight out of Karachi was secured that very night. As an interesting footnote in cricket history, the Karachi Test remains the only game that finished before the first innings had been completed. Not that anybody cared. 'After we had taken off,' Graveney recalled, 'the captain of the flight came on the intercom to inform us that we had just cleared Pakistani air space. And a great cheer went up.'

Colin was not with the party making their escape. Personal tragedy heaped on professional disappointment. He had been informed earlier on in the match that his father-in-law, Stuart Chiesman, had died. 'I flew home immediately,' he wrote. 'In many ways, he had been a second father to me and our friendship was close.'

Wisden may have been critical of Colin's captaincy in Pakistan but the England selectors clearly had no such qualms. There was never any suggestion of a change at the top for the forthcoming Tests that summer against West Indies and New Zealand. Now in his late 30s, Colin was enjoying his cricket, playing as well as ever and saw no reason, injury aside, why he should not realise his life's ambition to lead England in Australia in 18 months' time. In early May, it happened that Kent were playing Glamorgan in a Sunday League fixture. Nothing untoward seemed in the offing. Colin was batting with his usual composure and had reached 39 when he set off for a quick run. The Achilles tendon in his left foot snapped and he collapsed in a heap on the ground.

When such an injury occurs, the sound – not unlike the report from a pistol – is unmistakeable. To take that simile one step further, it was as if a marksman had lined up the Five Year Plan in the sights of his high-velocity rifle, squeezed the trigger and blown the document to kingdom come. Up until this time, Colin had remained remarkably free from injury, given his heavy schedule and heavy frame. 'Oh, that I am fortune's fool!' He might well have echoed Romeo's cry as he was carried off the field but in truth he uttered no such words.

Clearly in shock, he refused to believe he was seriously hurt. 'He wanted to go out there and carry on,' Chris told me. 'He kept on trying to stand up and wouldn't listen.' In the end, pain got the better of him and he sank back on the chair. It cannot have been long before he came to the conclusion that his season was ended. Surgery was performed the following day and with his leg encased in plaster he had plenty of time to contemplate the final ruination of his plan for the immediate future of England cricket.

As he wrote dejectedly in his biography, it had been something of a sentimental yearning 'to captain an England team that I had built, nurtured and encouraged' to win back the Ashes in Australia and he had allowed himself to dream. 'I was to learn of course that such romantic conceptions are not only born in the minds of fiction writers, but die there as well.'

The selectors moved quickly to appoint Raymond Illingworth in Colin's place. To some, this came as a surprise. Illingworth's Test career had progressed in fits and starts, he was now 37 years of age, he had left his native Yorkshire to take over the reins of captaincy at Leicestershire but had only been in the job for a month. His maturity as a cricketer was never in doubt; his lack of experience as a captain, especially in the Test arena, certainly was. Those who doubted his suitability, however, simply did not know their man.

Colin was in no doubt as to his competence, judging that his 'calm, shrewd, steadying lead' would bear fruit. He was right. West Indies were beaten 2-0 and New Zealand by the same scoreline. Any reservations about his value to the team as a player were dispelled at Lord's in the second Test against the West Indians. England had collapsed to 61/5 before Illingworth, batting at number eight, rescued them with an innings of 113. The captain had cemented his place. Colin could only grit his teeth, watching on from afar, and persevere with his rehabilitation.

He returned for the start of the 1970 season, fully recovered, fitter than he had been for a long time, with appetite renewed and confidence unimpaired. However, it is not always as easy as that. He needed time in the middle and for a while, that just did not happen. A string of low scores for Kent meant that he was not considered for the first Test, against the Rest of the World. Peter Hain and his Stop the Tour campaign against the South Africans visiting these shores had been successful, so a Rest of the World team had been hastily assembled to play five Test matches against England in their stead. This had not been in the original Five Year Plan but nobody, least of all Colin, had a copy of that anymore.

However, centuries against Sussex and Essex prompted the selectors to recall him for the second Test. Not as captain, of course, because Illingworth was now firmly seated in the saddle and had given no sign that he was prepared to dismount. Why should he? The team was now his and they were doing well enough. That did not stop the press from resurrecting the unwelcome captaincy debate. Illingworth or Cowdrey to lead MCC to Australia that winter? The brusque northerner or the approachable southerner? The hard-as-nails professional or the courteous amateur?

The clichés were old and hackneyed but the press played them for all they were worth. Colin, frankly, could have done without it all and simply wanted to concentrate on establishing his place in the side again and Illingworth too was put out, believing it was an unwelcome distraction from the job in hand. The Rest of the World – Sobers, Lloyd, Kanhai, Gibbs, Intikhab, Barlow, Richards, Procter, the Pollocks et al – were seriously formidable opponents.

In order to close off further public discussion on the matter, it was decided that the issue would be resolved after the third Test, earlier than usual but you could see the selectors' point. Colin was batting when they met in the committee room in the pavilion at Edgbaston. If they had glanced out of the window, as I am sure they did from time to time, they would have witnessed a classical Cowdrey innings, all effortless timing and precise placement of shot. He was out, caught Murray bowled Peter Pollock, for 71, and no sooner had he unbuckled his pads than he was approached by A.C. Smith, one of the selectors, who told him that the chairman, Alec Bedser, wanted to see him in the secretary's office.

Heaven knows what his thoughts were as he made his way along the corridor. Expecting the worst but hoping for the best, I imagine. The news was what he had feared. Gently, Bedser explained that they had decided to go with Illingworth. He was perfectly aware that this would be a great disappointment to Colin, knowing how much he had set his heart on the job, and he was very sorry for that. But the choice had been made. What else could Colin do but accept the inevitable? It was indeed a crushing disappointment but it could hardly have been unexpected. He mumbled something innocuous and turned to go before Bedser delivered a quicker ball. 'We'd like you to go as vice-captain,' he said.

Now this, the vexed subject of the vice-captaincy rather than the captaincy itself, was what caused him sleepless nights, much soul-searching and deep regret for the rest of his life. A vista of potential problems immediately opened up in front of him so he asked for time to think it over. Colin always liked to ponder and consider his options but in this case, delay only exacerbated the situation. Why would he hesitate? Did this signify equivocation on his part over the selectors' choice of leader? Could it be construed that by reserving judgement he was indicating a reluctance to give the appointed captain his full support? No, none of this guided his thinking but the delay set tongues wagging and did him no favours.

This was going to be his fifth tour Down Under. He had been vice-captain on three of them, under May, Dexter, Smith, and now he was to be vice-captain again, under Illingworth. Ever the bridesmaid would have been his private misgiving. He had wanted to run his own show but that was now no longer possible. Fair enough, but should he have his arm twisted to act as the loyal lieutenant – again? If they did not want him as captain, then presumably he was not in their plans for the future. In which case, would it not be more sensible and more forward-looking to appoint a younger man, one whom they had their eye on as a possible future leader? All this makes perfect logic and he could hardly have been blamed had he expressed it.

But things never were entirely straightforward with Colin. As usual, he was anxious to do what was best for everybody, the team, the management, MCC, England cricket and its good name abroad. He needed time to think. As it happened, the announcement of the tour manager had thrown a considerable spanner into his works. David Clark went to school at Rugby and served in the Parachute Regiment during the war, being wounded, taken prisoner and remaining a POW until 1945. He made a belated first appearance for Kent at the age of 27 and became captain in 1949. He it was who gave a first-class debut to a promising 17-year-old schoolboy by the name of Colin Cowdrey.

Later, after retirement, he became successively chairman and president of Kent. He managed the successful MCC tour to India with Mike Smith as captain in 1963/64. So, in more ways than one, he would have been the perfect fit as manager now, with Colin as captain. Whether he had been appointed in the expectation, or even hope, that Colin would be made captain is unrecorded. The two naturally got on well and Colin had great regard for his administrative and diplomatic capabilities. The partnership with Illingworth was not such a natural fit. Perhaps Colin envisaged, if not trouble, then at least friction between manager and captain. If he did, then he was remarkably prescient. In any event, he felt that he owed his friend and mentor all the help and support he could give.

So, reluctantly, Colin agreed to be Raymond Illingworth's second-in-command. It was a disastrous decision, which led to personal unhappiness, professional disappointment and a dismal finale, or so he believed, to his international career. 'Oh dear, the vice-captaincy,' said John Woodcock, running a crestfallen hand through his impressive full mane of hair. 'He should never have taken it. It backfired on him in so many ways.'

The least said about the tour the better, certainly from Colin's perspective, who found it a miserable experience. He devotes a mere two short paragraphs to the campaign in his autobiography and mentions it not at all in his notes. The irony is that Illingworth's tour to Australia in 1970/71 was hailed as a famous success. England won the series 2-0, regained the Ashes and so demoralised the Australian team that they sacked their captain, Bill Lawry, before the final Test.

Illingworth gained few friends in the country for his aggressive and uncompromising approach but he gained the respect of his team, led them well, brought the best out of his two mavericks, Snow and Boycott, and performed well with bat and ball when the situation required. That he had trodden on a few Australian toes in the process was neither here nor there to supporters of England's cause.

Then what ailed the vice-captain? The problem was twofold, as I understand it from reading between the lines of reports and observations from those who were there. First, he felt out of place and out of harmony with Illingworth's regime. Then his form deserted him, the runs dried up, his confidence evaporated and the catches started to go to ground, hitherto unheard of. Eventually, he was dropped from the side, a humiliation which had to be borne alone. Whether the one led to the other is impossible to say. Sometimes a player can put aside personal problems when he is out in the middle and still perform effectively. On this occasion, Colin could not.

A hint of his state of mind is given in his autobiography when he contemplated the tour ahead. 'Would cricket – the whole game – be richer for our visit?' he asked. What on earth did he mean by that? He did not answer his own question, so we have to draw our own conclusions. My understanding is that he was worried that the hard-edged, combative, quarrelsome, even venomous, climate creeping into the modern game – something that was totally alien to him – would spoil the cordial relations that historically obtained between the two sides. If there was going to be a fight, he wanted no part of it.

His fears were not groundless. In the face of some provocation, it has to be said, Illingworth instilled in his side a sort of siege mentality, where they tended to close ranks and treat umpires, press and public as potential enemies. This would have horrified Colin. But it was a state of affairs that was to become more and more prevalent in Test cricket as the 1970s moved on. Either consciously or unconsciously, he became more and more detached from the team. His isolation did not go unnoticed. *Wisden* commented, 'His cricket might not have been such a disappointment if he had allowed himself to become absorbed into the body of the team.'

A friend of mine, who happened to be staying in the same hotel as the England party – I forget at which venue – told me that he encountered Colin ploughing a lonely, if gentle, furrow up and down the hotel pool. When asked why he was not with his team-mates at the cricket ground, he gave a resigned shrug and said, 'I'm not needed.' Bob Willis was on this tour as a young, untested fast bowler. He told me, 'Colin was not part of the inner circle of decision-makers. By this time, Illy had become totally disenchanted with the manager and had decided to rely on help and support from his senior pros, Boycott and Edrich. And Clark, being a fellow Kentish man as Colin...well, you could see that the management team was not a good mix. Colin seemed...disconnected. Bit sad really.'

Chris Cowdrey put his finger on the nub of the problem. 'The trouble was that Illingworth hated Australians. And Dad loved them.' I doubt he meant that Illingworth hated *all* Australians but it was undeniably true that on the field of play they were bitter enemies. Is this right or wrong? Should sport replicate the enmity of the battlefield? Illingworth would say yes. You do what you have to do to win. Colin would probably have demurred. What is not in any doubt is that Illingworth returned home with his victorious team a hero and Colin came back, saddened, dispirited and no doubt fearful for his international future.

Was Illingworth the correct choice, the right man for the job? 'Of course he was!' cried Alan Smith, one of the selectors. 'Illy did a superb job. Much as I was fond of Colin, there is no doubt in my mind that we made the right choice. Nobody else could have got the best out of Snow and Boycs and the way he handled his team in the face of considerable provocation was outstanding. The cock-up was not the choice of captain but the appointment of the manager.' *Which wasn't in your remit as a selector?* 'No. The manager was appointed by the MCC. The team was selected by us.'

The sad irony of the breach between captain and vice-captain is that it arose not from personal but cultural differences. There was no gulf in ages between the two; they did not come from different eras. But they came from different backgrounds, different environments, different traditions. Nothing wrong with that. Cricket is a broad church – always has been – and dressing rooms down the ages have accommodated all types. But Colin wanted to lead his side in his way, embracing his values and his methods, and Illingworth had a different vision.

There is a photo somewhere that I have seen that says it all. The team are gathered together, in their MCC blazers, before they left London. They are recording their tour song. As far as I can recollect, the recording did not make much of an impression on the charts, hardly surprising when you see that it is Brian Johnson who is conducting, not Gareth Malone. Everybody seems in jovial spirits. We know we can't sing, seems to be the expression on most faces, but let's give it a go and have a bit of fun. In the background can be spotted Colin Cowdrey. Now, a raucous sing-song may not have been his cup of tea so it would not be unimaginable if he felt a wee bit uncomfortable. But he looks *haunted,* as if he has taken a sideways glance along the seated row to the captain in the middle and thought to himself I could – should – have been there. And now I never will.

He never openly admitted to a rift with Illingworth, though some might say his silence spoke more plainly than words. But to dispel the common perception, or perhaps in an attempt to heal old wounds, he is nothing but complimentary about Illingworth in his notes for the unpublished book. The occasion, the circumstance, was the appointment of Illingworth as the England team manager in 1994 and Colin was analysing the problems facing English cricket at the time and how well suited to the job he felt Illingworth was. Another twist is provided by the fact that Illingworth's tenure as supremo of English cricket proved to be less successful than his captaincy.

Colin's appraisal of Illingworth's fitness for the task makes interesting reading, and makes you wish they had more of a fruitful partnership when they were playing. 'He demanded high standards as a captain,' wrote Colin, 'while instilling an air of confidence and encouragement in his team.' So acquainted was he of Illingworth's strengths as an all-rounder that he was keen for him to join Kent when it seemed he might leave Yorkshire because of a contractual dispute. In the event, he went to Leicestershire but Colin wanted him in his side. Whenever he had captained Illingworth in the England side, he had found him 'quiet, straightforward, and well-organised with his bowling and field-placing'.

He looked back with regret to the first Test against Australia at Edgbaston in 1961, at the time when he was holding the fort for Peter May, who was still recovering from illness. In retrospect, he believed that was the time when he could – should – have secured the England captaincy for the next decade. He did not do himself justice and neither did Illingworth. 'Many a time I have looked back on that day and wished he had taken 7-110, not 2-110. That would have established him more quickly as a natural successor.' Successor to Colin, obviously, but a future England captain nonetheless.

He then made mention – quite touching really – of Illingworth's magnanimity towards his son, Christopher, when he was playing for Kent. By this time, Illingworth had gone back to Yorkshire as their coach/manager. Owing to crises of various kinds – there always seemed to be a crisis at Yorkshire – he had resumed the captaincy and so, by a quirk of fate, the two of them were in direct opposition as captains of their respective counties. It was now 1982 and Kent, on the last afternoon, having had the worse of the game, were grimly hanging on. Chris, with 51 not out, had held Yorkshire at bay and denied them their victory, just, with nine wickets down. Illingworth shook Chris's hand as they departed the field of play. 'Tha were bluidy lucky with weather, lad,' he said, 'but well played.'

Colin appreciated that. It was just how the game should be played, tough, with no quarter given and none asked, but in the end you shake hands and accept success or failure with generosity of spirit. He was equally generous in these final words on his successor, and some may say rival, as England captain, 'Raymond has known every type of weather, with great championship-winning sides at Yorkshire, success with Leicestershire and the thrill of captaining an Ashes-winning series in Australia. I congratulate him!'

Twenty years too late? He didn't think so. 'It was the press which had built up a Cowdrey/Illingworth feud over the decades, not us,' he wrote. 'He is a good man.'

All this was some time in the future. Colin's immediate priority, once back in England with the new season of 1971 soon underway, was to regain his touch and reclaim his England place, if it wasn't too late. Not quite. Not yet. Form made a welcome return, runs came a-plenty and he was recalled for the first Test against Pakistan at Edgbaston.

He spent the first two days watching from first slip as Pakistan amassed 608/7 declared. That was the game that Zaheer Abbas scored 274, his country's first double hundred. For good measure there were centuries from Mushtaq Mohammad and his Kent colleague Asif Iqbal. Forced to follow on in their reply, England did manage to avoid defeat but Colin's contributions of 16 and 32 were not significant and not enough to save him from being dropped for the second Test.

Later that month, he contracted pneumonia. Chris has a theory that it was brought on by his father's habit of coming to cricket grounds already changed and going home still dressed in his kit, often damp from the day's exertions. Whatever the cause of the inflammation of his lungs, it put paid to any further cricket that summer. And put paid to his Test career according to most informed observers, including him. That pretty well seemed to be that.

Until he picked up the phone at Christmas three years later.

8

The Long Goodbye

After cricket 1976–2000

'Keep cricket a happy game.'

Colin Cowdrey's message from his hospital
bed to MCC and their guests at the bicentenary
celebrations at Lord's in 1987.

IT happens to all professional sportsmen. The time might be of
their choosing, it might come unexpectedly, too early, or it might
have come, on reflection, a little too late. But it is never welcome.
For cricketers, the end comes with a wrench of particular savagery. I
have long pondered the reason for this. After all, a cricketer retires at
an age not a great deal older or younger than any other sportsman. So
why have so many cricketers confessed to difficulties in adjusting to
'civvy street', with a distressingly large number, in statistical terms,
who have subsequently taken their own lives? What is so different
about cricket as a career?

The answer lies, I think, in the nature of the game. It takes up so
much time, in fact, all of your time. Not only that but when he was at
home, he wasn't really, because he was playing cricket every day, often
away. So it would not be unreasonable to assert that cricketers spend
more time with their team-mates than they do with their family. In
fact, the team becomes a sort of surrogate family and the dressing

room more comfortable and embracing than anywhere else, a cocoon protected from the rest of the world. Then, suddenly, that protective cloak is stripped away and 'who will then stand upright when the harsh winds blow?' as Thomas More said.

For Colin, the time was of his choosing – Thomas More enjoyed no say in the timing of his – and you would expect no less, given his record and length of service. However, the question of what to do with the rest of his life was no different than for any other of his colleagues coming to the end of their careers. It was not as if he had not been pondering it for some time. When a cricketer reaches his late 30s and early 40s, as he was, thoughts of retirement intrude willy-nilly. His initial leaning, just as it was at the end of his school career, was towards teaching, well, schoolmastering, if I can make the distinction.

It is not clear from his notes what subject he would teach. He just thought he would slip easily into common room life at a school much like his own Tonbridge, running the cricket in the summer term and coaching rugby and rackets during the winter. What school could possibly turn him down? But then he got distracted. 'With the captaincy of Kent, playing for England (sometimes as captain), I became rather blinkered as to what I was going to do next.' Before he hung up his boots, he was made many offers from companies and businesses to come on board 'but a couple of Kent victories, a satisfying hundred, selection for another England tour, and I forgot about them'. It was not until he had achieved the milestone of his 100th hundred that 'the shutters of my mind were opened and the prospect of working in the City became more attractive'.

There was one further distraction, the unexpected call-up to Australia on the 1974/75 tour, before he really sat down and took stock. It was an old school friend who opened the door to the City, enabling him to explore the workings of merchant banking, insurance, Lloyd's, and other financial institutions. The trouble was, he discovered, he knew next to nothing about the City and how money worked. His contemporaries who had followed this career from school were now well up the ladder of success. He would have to put his foot on the first rung. He claimed to be fascinated by the inner workings of stock broking and the like but I am not sure how genuine the appeal was. He said the same about the retail trade when working for his father-in-law but everybody knew where his heart truly lay.

Staying at Kent, in some administrative capacity or other, was not an option. The year following his retirement, his eldest son, Christopher, joined the staff and it was clear he was set, at the very least, for a successful county career. Colin decided it were best to keep his distance and let Chris develop at his own pace and in his own style. Having the surname Cowdrey was burden enough without having his father queering his pitch. Colin judged that discretion was the better part of valour and vowed to keep his distance.

Soon after returning from his sixth and final tour of Australia, he was invited on to the board at Whitbread, the brewing company. 'Following the Packer Revolution in the late 1970s,' he wrote, 'it was obvious we needed an influx of good young players to replace the ones who had been, or might be, snatched by World Series Cricket.' He and the chairman of the company had a little chat over morning coffee – the way you do – and the upshot of their conversation was the formation of the Whitbread Scholarship Scheme, designed with the specific purpose of sending three or four talented youngsters overseas in the winter, to learn their trade and mature as future professional cricketers. 'I am pleased to say that among the first beneficiaries were Ian Botham, David Gower and Mike Gatting,' he announced proudly.

Before Colin's career as the City's answer to Gordon Gekko had taken off, he found himself on the front pages, not of the *Financial Times* but of all the tabloids. For one who fled a posse of reporters outside the Lord's pavilion at the age of 13 and who harboured a lifetime's distrust of what his son, Chris, called gutter journalism, as opposed to the true cricket reporters, with whom Colin had a warm relationship, the experience must have been excruciating.

However, it was not a good day to bury bad news nor was it the sort of story that could be hidden in a short paragraph on one of the inside pages. In 1978, it was announced that Colin Cowdrey was leaving his wife after 22 years of marriage to live with Lady Herries, the eldest daughter of the Duke of Norfolk. His family, his friends, his former team-mates, the folk of Kent and indeed the whole cricket fraternity, were shocked. David Brown, who had bowled his heart out for Colin on that successful tour of the West Indies in 1967/68, probably spoke for everyone when he told me, 'Kipper? He was probably the *last* one we expected to get divorced!'

In many ways, this chapter of Colin's life was the one I least looked forward to chronicling, the one I would rather not have had to write. Not because it inevitably casts a shadow on his reputation but because it cast, and continues to cast, a shadow over other people whose story this is not. The fact of the matter is that Colin divorced his wife and remarried. It happens. The reasons for the separation were no doubt as complex and as impenetrable as in any relationship and little is to be gained, in my view, in digging around in the dirt to find evidence to blame one party or the other. I would have preferred to make mention of it and move swiftly on. But it became known, it was in the public domain and it provided food for thought, among his friends as well as the intrusive press, about the enigmatic and private personality of one of England's most recognisable sporting figures. It was, like it or not, newsworthy.

The effect on the family can only be imagined. All four children, Christopher, Jeremy, Graham and Carol, dealt with the emotional upheaval privately, and in their own way. Their wish to be spared the harsh glare of publicity is understandable and should be respected. Penny was devastated; that much was obvious to everybody. 'She adored Colin,' David Kemp told me, 'and the whole family was knocked by the divorce. It was a very, very difficult time for everyone.' As the wife of the club captain, she had been very much in evidence at Kent while Colin was still playing. Then two of her sons joined the staff and being the extrovert personality she was, it was always unlikely she would quietly fade into the background.

Nevertheless, Colin must have had his reasons. Kemp, a fair and even-handed man if ever there was one, tried to make sense of the conundrum. 'Much as he loved her – and I believe he truly did – he found her difficult to control sometimes. She was, how can I put it, quite highly strung and what he wanted above all was *peace*. His life was stressful enough, an England player always in the public eye, and he hated all the attendant fuss and brouhaha. For example, when Illingworth was chosen ahead of Colin to take the MCC team to Australia, she was incensed. "Illy's got it!" she cried and rushed to Colin's defence. She felt he needed her support. The thing is that he didn't need it and didn't want it. He just wanted the whole sorry business to disappear. They were two completely different personalities. Perhaps his new wife, Lady Herries, and the world she inhabited, gave him the tranquillity he craved. Who knows.'

I plucked up courage and asked Christopher whether he felt that his father, towards the end of his life, had found peace. He paused and gave it some thought, 'I think so. I hope so.' Obviously a lot of water had flowed under the bridge and time seemed to have healed most of the old wounds, as it had with all of Colin's children. They were in close touch with him right until the end and I got the sense that, if they believed he had let them down and betrayed their mother, later exposure to life and all its vicissitudes had softened their judgement and calmed their spirits. After all, the four of them have met with personal unhappiness themselves and that tends to put a different perspective on things.

'Don't forget,' Chris reminded me, 'that Dad had a heart attack in his late 40s, followed by a triple bypass.' Indeed that was so. 'He'd gone to see a specialist,' continued Kemp, 'who had told him he had a dicky heart and he needed to ease off and take things more gently. But Colin could never say no, so I am not sure there was too much easing off there.' Kemp went on to tell me that Colin got a lot of stick for his actions in the press, especially when it later emerged that he was going to marry the Duke of Norfolk's daughter. He must have sensed my puzzlement. 'Why? Because he was the premier earl of England and a Catholic to boot. The most important family in the realm, aside from the Royals, was committed to a religion that forbade divorce.'

If the relationship between man and wife is private business, the role of parenting is perhaps fairer game for analysis, if only because nobody knows a father better than his children and we have, in the course of this book, been trying to unravel the paradox at the heart of Colin Cowdrey. 'Penny was a wonderful mother,' said Kemp, 'but Colin adored his children. He was a good father but found the marriage...*difficult*.'

The reason for this, he maintained – and on this, just about everybody I spoke to agreed – was undoubtedly his upbringing. For seven years of his childhood, at the most formative stage of his life, he had no parents. Thus he had no model on which to base, for better or worse, his own experience when the time came. 'He didn't really know about parenting,' said Chris. 'He was never there. Not his fault but that was the way it was. He was a bit naïve like that. He thought if you played sport then everything would be fine. He never asked how my work was going at school, for example.'

Chris then told me an amusing story, one that he had recounted at his dad's memorial service. Mother and father had just received the dreaded call from son's headmaster of his prep school, Wellesley House, requesting their presence at a meeting to discuss Chris's less than impressive academic results. 'I was playing a footie match,' Chris remembered, 'just as they turned up. It so happened we had won 5-0 and I had scored all the goals. After the game, Mum and Dad came over and I was told to get in the car, obviously for the parental bollocking. There was silence. Then Mum said, "Go on, Colin, say what you were going to say." Dad turned to me. "I particularly enjoyed the second goal, the near-post header. I loved the way you caught it just right." Mum was furious with him. But that was it, you see. Sport solved all problems.'

Paradoxically, the divorce and Colin's marriage to Lady Herries brought Carol closer to her father. 'Lady H wasn't one bit interested in cricket,' she told me. 'In fact she was totally unsociable. All that interested her was her horses. So, for all these cricket functions that Dad attended, I was his date.' No doubt deputed to keep an eye on him – his health was not good by now – she relished the role. 'I was what, 18 or so, and I had a whale of a time, meeting all these interesting and famous people.' She too had an amusing story about her father. 'Chaddy! He was the duke's chauffeur and he *adored* Dad. When we had to go to Lord's or wherever, Chaddy would arrive in the car to pick me up. Except he would be sitting in the passenger seat.' *So your father would drive?* 'Oh yes, every time. He was very old by now, Chaddy.'

I was about to ask her more of her memories of her father but she got there first. 'I want to stress this. Dad taught me, an impressionable young girl, how to behave. I don't just mean how to hold a knife and fork but how to treat people. For example, when he was at Barclays and we'd walk into the building, not only would he recognise Fred and remember his name, he would stop to have a little chat. "Now, how's your wife?" he would ask. "Last time I spoke to you, she hadn't been well."

'It was little gestures like that. People would always come up to him and say, I remember when you scored that hundred at such-and-such a place and Dad would answer, "Ah, yes, the wicket was wet, wasn't it? And we'd just followed on." And so on. Nothing was too much trouble. That was the lesson of life I learnt from my father – how to take time and trouble with people.'

I had a long conversation with Jonathan Smith, the English master at Tonbridge School when all three Cowdrey boys came under his wing. Apart from his successful career subsequently as a writer and playwright, he has a great love and knowledge of the game of cricket. His son, Ed, played for Kent and Middlesex and for England in three Test matches against South Africa; following his retirement from the game, Ed is now an author and commentator on *Test Match Special*.

Initially, I wanted to talk to Jonathan about the effects of Colin's divorce on the boys. He was Chris's tutor for the five years he was at the school and he also taught Jeremy and Graham English. 'For the period of roughly 1970–80, I saw a fair bit of the family. Yes the divorce was awkward and we all had to scramble around, hiding the newspapers that had awful things said about their father. Graham was the worst hit, I think. He'd just come to the school and was at a vulnerable age when you really don't need to be dealing with this sort of thing.'

However, Smith was eager to move on. Clearly he found talking about someone else's domestic problems as uncomfortable as I did. It soon became evident that he knew and understood Colin well but in a completely different context from cricket. 'I saw him a lot around the school and at cricket matches on the Head. He was a great chatter. He would pass no one without a hello and a word or two. He was utterly without arrogance or self-importance. "Hi, I'm Colin Cowdrey," he said to me when I first met him, as if I didn't know. "I hear you're taking on my son. Good luck!"' *How was he as a parent?* 'He worried about the boys, as any parent does. Frequently, he would ring up and we'd discuss their progress, though I sensed he was more concerned about what scores they were getting on the cricket pitch than in the examination room.'

As a dramatist himself, Smith was drawn to the comparison as a performer between an actor and a cricketer. Both are entertainers in the broadest sense and are expected, on a daily basis, to go out there in front of their audience and strut their stuff. 'Cricket can unman you,' he said. 'You are in the spotlight and all your frailties, your weaknesses are exposed to the public gaze. And often you fail.'

Although Colin was an essentially shy man, who did not enjoy the pitiless scrutiny of the national press, he was, regardless, a public figure, recognised wherever he went. 'That was why Tonbridge was so important to him,' Smith insisted. 'It was a steadying influence in his life, even after he left. There was nothing he enjoyed more than walking into a hall of 200 boys and talking to them about cricket. He was a great raconteur. He had them in the palm of his hand. The way he would play the crowd, as it were, as he walked around the school or the boundary...he had a special touch, leavened by a lovely, self-deprecating sense of humour.'

Smith also compared Colin's charisma with the great actors he had known. 'Out there, on stage or in the middle, nobody can touch you. You feel safe and in control, doing what you do best. Like all great performers, there was a certain aura that surrounded him. So, although he was shy off the pitch, he must have enjoyed the limelight, playing those marvellous innings in front of those large crowds. He was no wilting wall flower, was he?'

And what of Lady Herries? She was a racehorse trainer, her relatively small but successful operation based in Angmering Park, near Arundel. The two were married in 1985 and of course she became Baroness Cowdrey when Colin was ennobled in 1997, but she chose not to use the title, being a peer already in her own right. By all accounts, the union was a happy one. Colin was pleased to support her business and her passion, though he knew little of horses himself. Former England team-mate David Brown found himself rekindling his friendship with his captain and his new wife through their shared occupations, he as a breeder and she as a trainer of racehorses. 'I saw a lot of Kipper at race meetings. We got on well and would natter on for hours once the races had finished. Presumably he knew what he was letting himself in for when he went to live with her. I think he enjoyed playing second fiddle to her in an environment away from cricket, where he was always the central figure.' Lady Herries had no interest in the game and, either by design or choice, kept well away from Colin's world.

Ah, but what was Colin's world now? I have waded through armfuls of letters in his files, replies mostly from friends, friends of friends and friends of them too, politely exploring possibilities of gainful employment, obviously set in train by Colin after his retirement. Which correspondence bore fruit?

One morning, I was walking back from the shop in our village, having just bought a paper, when a car pulled away from our neighbour's driveway. I noticed out of the corner of my eye the driver and immediately did a double take. Was that Geoff Arnold, the same Geoff Arnold who had given me a little insight into the Illingworth tour of Australia in 1974/75? Indeed it was. Apparently he is a good friend of one of my neighbours in the village, Ray Jepp. It transpired that Ray, now retired, had been Arnold's bank manager. I paid him a visit. 'Colin Cowdrey!' he exclaimed when I told him about this book. 'Knew him well. We both worked for Barclays.' Hastily I fetched my notebook and settled down to mine this rich and wholly unexpected source of Colin's later life.

'It was Sir AFT!' he cried, once I had located a pen. *I beg your pardon?* 'Sir Anthony Favill Tuke, chairman of Barclays. He loved his cricket, you know. President of the MCC, wasn't he?' Sir Anthony Tuke was president of MCC 1982/83, succeeding Hubert Doggart. He was also chairman, successively, of Barclays Bank 1973–81, of RTZ (the acronym refers to the merged companies of Rio Tinto and Zinc Corporation) 1981–85 and of the Savoy group of hotels 1984–94.

He was no great sportsman himself but was an enthusiastic sponsor and enjoyed nothing more, Jepp told me, than watching a Test match from the Barclays box at Lord's or The Oval. 'I met Sir Anthony by chance,' wrote Colin in his notes. I bet it was not quite as serendipitous as that. However engineered, the association became a happy and profitable one for both parties. 'Basically,' Colin continued, 'I became a travelling representative for the bank around the cricket-playing globe.' No doubt doors opened for him wherever he went.

'Colin knew everybody,' said Jepp. 'And everybody knew Colin. Look, he would ring up the governor of the Bank of England... now, what was his name? Oh yes, Leigh-Pemberton, Robin Leigh-Pemberton. He'd ring him up – and of course, he was put straight through – to ask whether he was free to come to Lord's for this or that function. And it would go straight in the diary. Colin was a sort of PR man, excellent at bringing people together for their mutual benefit.'

What was your connection with him? 'I was a branch manager at Barclays in Kennington.' *Next door to The Oval?* 'Yes indeed. I knew Micky Stewart through amateur football. He introduced me to the lads at The Oval and eventually I found myself looking after the personal accounts of 23 out of their 24 players.'

Apparently, it was part of Colin's duty to look after the branch managers and assist them when they were entertaining clients at sporting venues, particularly cricket matches. 'I'd be with Micky Stewart at The Oval for lunch at a Test match and head office would say, we'd better get Colin down so you can talk about cricket. I had a job to convince them that all cricketers were not thick and that Micky, being a very intelligent bloke, could talk about any number of things, including stocks and shares.'

Thank you, Ray, for defending the IQ of cricketers. 'You're welcome. I met Colin loads of times and I found him an absolute gent, a very nice man. He would be walking around Lord's, accompanied by the high and mighty, and he'd spot you in a crowd and *always* make a point of coming up to greet you. He made you feel you were the most important person he'd met that day.'

What was that story you were telling me about Len Hutton? 'As you know, Colin was very fond of Len. He said he had looked after him in Australia when his dad had died. Anyway, as I lived nearby, Colin asked me to pick up Len to give him a lift to Lord's. You just stop me, was my reply. Len Hutton was a great hero of mine. Anyway, after that, I became his regular chauffeur.'

So, once more, Colin's knack of bringing people together had got a result. 'I should say so. For the bicentenary dinner at Lord's, Colin came up to me to say that Len was the guest of honour but he couldn't come unless I picked him up. Could I do it for him? I said I'd do it for myself! Colin made sure there was an invitation for me too.'

I guess he didn't have a desk or anything. 'Oh yes he did. He had a desk in head office. And a secretary. He was there, really, for who he knew. He was an excellent front man. He was a good face for Barclays. He had great clout for someone who never had a job in his life.' At which, Ray Jepp roared with laughter. 'Well, not a *real* job,' he added, 'not like the rest of us, nine to five, Monday to Friday.'

I asked Ray whether he had met Penny. Or Lady Herries. He shook his head. And then told me a story, which was clearly his wont.

This was one that was printable. 'Look, you know as well as me that cricketers are usually doing one of two things in the dressing room, either reading *The Sun* or ringing up a bird to fix that evening's entertainment. But Colin wasn't like that. He was no womaniser. We were at a lunch in head office on one occasion. We gave him a lift back to Sloane Square afterwards. When we had dropped him off, my friend looked at me and said, "I can't believe that bloke has had two wives. He just doesn't seem to be the type." Colin was such a nice and personable fellow. So modest. No side to him at all.'

Barclays had strong connections with South Africa (controversially), Zimbabwe and Kenya and was beginning to open up close contacts in Australia and New Zealand. In all these countries, Colin was probably the best-known face in the whole company. He records in his notes his particular pleasure in liaising with MCC over sponsorship by Barclays for cricket tours of East Africa. 'I like to think my influence helped a little to enable these visits to take place.' He saw his role thus, 'I played two parts. My first was a walk-on part, listening and absorbing the details of how a large bank like Barclays worked. My second was at the forefront of the stage as an international cricketer and an ex-England captain.'

He was often called upon as a guest speaker at special dinners or occasions and at this, according to just about anybody who knew him, he was a past master. I use the term deliberately. It originally referred to one who has held the office of worshipful master of a guild, club or society. As we shall see shortly, Colin was elected Master of the Skinners Company, which of course founded his alma mater, Tonbridge School. He was as well a master of the spoken word.

Here are the assessments of three of many who should know.

'Colin was adept at all the social graces,' said A.C. Smith. 'He was a brilliant off-the-cuff speaker. He never spoke too long, he always pitched it just right and invariably hit the nail on the head.' Alan Dowding knew him well and listened to him often. 'He spoke fluently, without notes. He was brilliant at remembering people in the room and making the necessary references to them.' Hubert Doggart was a headmaster and they usually know a thing or two about public speaking. 'Colin was warm, relevant, easy on the ear and aspirational for all potential, as well as existing, cricket lovers.' I could go on but I think the point has been made. Colin knew how to turn a phrase.

In his notes for the unpublished book, I came across a chapter entitled 'On Your Feet'. Eagerly, I seized upon it, intrigued as to whether he was going to expound on batting or fielding at slip. But no, it was wholly devoted to speech-making. Immediately, he makes this astonishing admission, 'I've always been terrified at the prospect of having to rise to my feet and say a few words.'

This from a practised exponent of the art. He says that it was a skill he learnt; it was not something that came naturally. He ascribes his diffidence to his upbringing. As a child, ferried from pillar to post with nowhere he could call home and in environments where he was expected to be seen and not heard, he thought it best to keep his mouth shut.

Likewise, when he first entered adult dressing rooms. They were not places of peace and quiet. By and large, they were populated by characters whose wit and speed of repartee he could only admire. He makes mention of John Warr and Doug Insole as having the gift of oratory combined with humour, and of course Fred Trueman, who was famous as a great story-teller with a photographic memory. His best turn, Colin insists, was a set piece in cod Chaucerian English, which he could deliver at the drop of a hat, word perfect, with not a gesture or intonation out of place. Colin believed he could never compete with that. Who could? Trueman was a natural comedian. But with practice and one or two tricks, Colin reckoned that most people could turn themselves into a reasonable performer.

He goes back to his first, disastrous attempt to say a few words in front of an audience. As head boy at Tonbridge, he was invited to the annual OTs dinner, at which he was expected to make a speech. 'After one or two initial strokes, I simply couldn't lift the bat. I froze. My mind went blank. The chairman recognised my plight and asked aloud, "What sort of year has the school had in sport?" I got my confidence back and spoke for a few minutes without my notes and the audience seemed to come alive.' Everyone gave him a sympathetic round of applause as he sat down but he had learnt his first lesson, one he never forgot.

Thereafter, he claims, he never went in to bat, so to speak, without these three tricks up his sleeve:

'1. On the menu card, write out in capitals a couple of subject headings with the first sentence. Just in case.

'2. If you are next to anybody standing up to speak, have one or two relevant topics written down to help him out if needs be.

'3. Follow Winston Churchill's advice. Try to use words of one syllable if possible. Don't bore them with two words where one will suffice. He did his homework. Make sure you do yours.'

Colin was obviously a fan of Britain's wartime leader. 'His best impromptu speeches were carefully prepared. Nothing was too much trouble to Winston when it came to fashioning English composition.'

Of all the fine preachers he listened to in his life, Colin names two of the most inspirational. 'Lawrence Waddy, my headmaster at Tonbridge, was a superb preacher, after-dinner speaker and lecturer. Another was Billy Graham, the evangelist whom I heard preach at Oxford. He began with four of the funniest stories I've ever heard. Then, having warmed up his audience, he warmed to his task. He was an extraordinary orator.'

The most difficult speech to make, Colin tells us, is what he terms the 'five-minuter'. This was the one that he was called upon most to deliver, at cricket clubs, dinners and in his roving commissions for Whitbread and Barclays. 'I was often asked to "talk cricket" for five minutes or so and all this practice helped when I was appointed chairman of the International Cricket Council.'

Some critics unkindly hinted in their obituaries of Colin that his work for Barclays was largely inconsequential and incidental. He does not tackle head on this assumption, if ever he got wind of it, but he does claim in his notes, 'Ten years immersed in varied interests and concerns, meeting a wide range of people, led to three unexpected positions of responsibility. In 1985, I became the Master of the Skinners Company. In 1987, I was invited to become president of the MCC in its bicentennial year. And in 1989, I was elected chairman of the ICC, a post I held for four years.'

Far from frittering away his time in retirement, he was now embarking on what many regard as the most profitable and influential period of his life. Even his detractors admit that he rose to the occasion.

First, the Skinners. The company developed from a mediaeval trade guild of the furriers, who dressed and traded furs. In those times, furs were very much a luxury item and their use strictly controlled. It was a part-religious, part-trading organisation and was one of the first guilds to obtain a royal charter, from Edward III in 1327. Thus they go back a long way, further even than MCC. As their wealth and influence grew, it became possible for their members to set in train various philanthropic ventures. One of these was the founding of schools. Their first was Tonbridge School in 1553.

While I was teaching English at Malvern College, one day I encountered our headmaster in the common room. I noticed the unusual tie he was wearing. It seemed to be raining the numbers six and seven. *That's an interesting tie, Headmaster. A cricket club, perhaps?* He gave me a withering look. 'I am very surprised, Mr Murtagh, as a member of my English Department and as a noted wordsmith, that you are unacquainted with the phrase "to be at sixes and sevens".' Actually, I was acquainted with the phrase though not of its origin but I felt it politic not to argue. The use of my surname did not bode well. He might have been joking but you never know with headmasters. 'Well, let me tell you.' I felt a history lesson coming. I waited patiently. He was after all a history teacher. 'You've heard of the Lord Mayor's Show?'

Yes. After the Lord Mayor's Show. 'There had been a long-running dispute between the Skinners and the Merchant Taylors and it came to a head during the Lord Mayor's procession of barges down the Thames in 1484, when both guilds disputed the right to be number six during the procession and who should be relegated to number seven. Violence erupted but the Lord Mayor at the time came up with the inspired compromise that they should take it in turns each year. And to this day, we still do. Hence the term "to be at sixes and sevens".'

It was as if the scales had fallen from my eyes. I knew that Hugh Carson was an Old Tonbridgean. He never stopped reminding me of their prowess in the Cricketer Cup. Tonbridge was a Skinners school. Colin had always been a loyal servant of their old boys' cricket team, for whom he never failed to turn out, when county commitments did not intrude. He played for them for many years after retirement, 'But never as captain,' David Kemp told me. 'He preferred to be just one of the boys. He didn't want to hog the limelight or throw his weight around. His enthusiasm for the Cricketer Cup set the tone for the OTs' success.'

When you think about it, considering his enduring affection for Tonbridge, with its Skinners connections, the former head of school and England cricket captain was an obvious choice to become their Master. He accepted with humility and delight. Besides, he probably had more furry sweaters in his possession than all the furriers in the guild put together.

Now, Hugh, I wonder if you could outline for me the function and responsibilities of a Master of the Skinners Company. This was asked of my former boss many years after our retirements from teaching, with a glass of wine in my hand on this occasion. It was after he had served his year as Master in 2011 and was intended as a lead up to my exploration of Colin's year of office. 'It's a bit like being a headmaster,' he told me. 'You need to be able to handle people and try to get them playing to their strengths and not worry too much about their weaknesses.'

And Colin was good at that. 'Indeed. He had vast experience of handling people in his job as captain of a county team and his country. He had all that in spades. But more than that, he was a good man. By that I mean a true Christian. He wanted to do good. And you must realise that the Skinners is a charitable organisation. Its *raison d'etre* is to do good. That was why he was such a marvellous Master.' Colin's team-mates who referred to him as Master got there before the Skinners.

I am not sure that Ernest Cowdrey was an emotional man but I should imagine that even he, had he been alive, would have felt a frisson of pleasure as the news emerged that the son he had so presciently christened Michael Colin Cowdrey had been appointed president of MCC. The year was 1987, the 200th anniversary of the founding of that great club. It seemed so apt, so right, that Colin's presidency should coincide with the bicentenary; nobody could fulfil the role as honourably and as diligently as he. The price he paid, however, was grievous.

He regarded the honour as the pinnacle of his career and was determined to make a success of it. The appointment is routinely for one year and the question I was keen to discover was what influence can be brought to bear in such a short space of time when more permanent officers at the club – secretary, treasurer and other officials – were more familiar with the corridors of power and where they led.

For this, I sought the aid of Roger Knight, a former secretary and president. 'It's a strange hybrid really. The president is the top man but the day-to-day business is done by the permanent staff. As president, you can play it how you want really. You can get involved in the politics or you can play the role of figurehead.' Colin could have played it safe and confined himself to meeting and greeting the dignitaries from around the world at Test matches, celebratory dinners and the like. He would have been very good at it.

But he chose not to. He was at an age when he felt comfortable at throwing off the shackles of caution and self-doubt. There was business to be done and he knew it. For one who had been criticised as a captain for dithering, there was no sign of that immediately he took up office. He proved himself to be an able and dynamic leader at a time when cricket found itself at a major crossroads. Radical changes were required from a body not exactly known for innovation. Accompanying his noted charm and powers of persuasion was now added a steely resolve, which quite surprised those who had known him a long time. The cricket world was changing and if his beloved MCC were to survive as anything other than a charming relic of a bygone age, he needed to get a grip, and swiftly.

'There was turmoil at the club,' Alan (A.C.) Smith told me. He should know. In the spring before Colin took up office that autumn in 1986, he had been appointed secretary of the Test and County Cricket Board. 'There had been friction between the MCC and the TCCB for years ever since the control of the domestic game had been removed from the MCC and handed over to the new body, the TCCB, in 1968. It was felt that the governance of the game in England should not be in the hands of a private members' club.' Mike Vockins, who was the secretary at Worcestershire at the time and knew his way around the MCC, remembers the period as 'a tricky time'. He continued, 'You would have thought that the MCC and the TCCB, both splendid organisations which had the good of the game at their very heart, would have been hand in glove. But the relationship was not as close as it ought.'

He went on to tell me with an amused chuckle that one secretary would communicate with the other by mail, 'even though they were housed in the same building!' I then made mention of the resignation of the club's secretary, Jack Bailey, which caused a furore at the time and still manages to ruffle feathers today. Did he jump or was he pushed? The answer to that largely depends on whom you talk to. Vockins furrowed his brow. 'We're talking about events that happened 30 years ago. I don't really remember. What I do remember is that Colin walked into a difficult situation, saw that something had to be done and acted quickly and decisively.'

It seemed that Bailey understood that the two bodies had two different agendas and believed fervently he should protect the rights and privileges of the club he represented, therefore keeping the TCCB at arm's length. A considerable number of the club's members were in agreement with him. At the heart of the dispute was that the TCCB ran Test matches but the MCC owned Lord's. So who was in charge when Test matches were played at HQ? It was, quite simply, a power struggle.

Whether Colin had a direct hand in Bailey's resignation remains unclear. 'Things did settle down,' said Vockins, 'as they tend to do. The Colonel [Lt Col John Stephenson] took over and relations between the TCCB and the MCC became more harmonious.' Alan Smith agreed, saying this about Colin's influence on affairs, 'That is why I saw Kipper's appointment as a good thing. He was a conciliator and I felt sure he would help to smooth over any friction. The thing with Jack...well, I don't know. All I know is that Colin *dealt* with it.'

For a thoroughly impartial view, what better source to consult than *Wisden*? The bicentenary year was meant, and organised, to be a fitting celebration of the durability and prestige of the famous old club, one that Colin loved and was honoured to serve. There was much to look forward to.

'Sadly, the year was not always blessed,' went the editor's notes to the 1988 edition of *Wisden*, 'not even for the Marylebone Cricket Club in its bicentenary year. Concerned at what they felt was an encroachment by the Test and County Cricket Board on their rights at Lord's, the club's premises, a group of members voted at the Annual General Meeting in May not to accept the club's Report and Accounts. There were also calls for the resignation of the President, MC Cowdrey. The dissatisfaction of those members had been prompted by the resignation of the Treasurer, DG Clark, the previous December, and the early retirement in January of the Secretary, JA Bailey. At a Special General Meeting at the end of July, the Committee received by a large majority the support of the Club's members but they had been reminded of the importance of proper consultation and communication in today's world.' It was, the editor admitted, an 'unhappy episode'.

My guess, having got to know Colin well, I believe, in these pages, is that this 'unhappy episode', coming during his presidency and at a time which should have brought him pleasure and pride, must have hurt him deeply. It was not meant to be like this, with a fractious membership, ancient quarrels stirring, the premature departure of the secretary and the treasurer, a testy AGM, the annual report not being passed and journalists outside the Grace Gates sharpening their pencils. It was meant to be a festival of cricket, not a hotbed of politics and recrimination.

I sought the opinion of Colin's old friend Hubert Doggart, who took over the role of treasurer at the club at this epochal moment in its history. 'History. What a caper!' he cried. 'Soon there will be nobody left who remembers what happened during a difficult period at the club 30 years ago.' He then made this poignant observation about Colin's year in office, 'No president could, surely, have had a sadder presidency.' Without taking sides – indeed he was at pains to steer a middle path, something as an ex-headmaster he was uniquely qualified to do – he wanted only for me to understand the effect that such complications had on Colin, who could see no complications in cricket. Cricket was a game to be loved and cherished, not to bicker over.

It was clear from our conversations that Doggart had a huge affection for Colin. Their friendship went back a long way. Doggart saw the relationship as a partnership of sorts but one of equals. They both captained their respective universities, Doggart skippering Cambridge in 1950, Colin Oxford in 1954. Both incidentally had a future England captain playing under them; Doggart had Peter May in his team and Colin had Mike Smith. There was an extraordinary synchronism in that encounter in 1954 when they played against each other. Doggart was captain at Sussex and his team were playing Oxford at The Parks, captained by Colin. They both scored 140! They had been on that MCC missionary tour of the West Indies, managed by E.W. Swanton, 'binding the Commonwealth together' as it was termed.

They were drawn to each other, finding their temperaments, especially in their love of cricket, to be entirely compatible. Later they partnered each other at the amateur doubles in rackets at Queen's, in 1958 and 1959. They went in to bat together at a Special General

Meeting of MCC in 1983, to speak against the motion to send a touring side to South Africa during the apartheid years. Colin would not have wanted to speak, Doggart said, but his persona, reputation, knowledge and standing within the game were such that he was persuaded otherwise. The motion was defeated in the Hall, even before the postal votes were counted, Doggart told me with evident relish.

And now this. At the AGM in May 1987, when the annual report and accounts was not accepted by the membership, Colin looked shocked. He went for a decision review, long before the technology had been invented, and called for another vote. The motion to accept the report was defeated for the second time. Swiftly he brought the meeting to a close. He had no option. But the report had to be passed at some stage otherwise the club would descend into anarchy.

A Special General Meeting was called, this time at the Central Methodist Hall, Westminster, more of a suitable venue than the crowded Long Room at Lord's. On this occasion, wiser counsel prevailed, the more vociferous critics were outnumbered and the annual report was accepted, by a whopping 80 per cent majority. The president must have heaved a sigh of relief. He did, but he was not in the chair. He was in a hospital bed, recovering from a triple bypass operation, necessitated by the first of his heart attacks. The meeting was chaired this time by the club treasurer, none other than the aforesaid Hubert Doggart.

Privately, Hubert and I mused over the strain Colin must have been under during these difficult months and how much it might have contributed to his heart attack. The only conclusion we could possibly come to was that it cannot have helped. We agreed that it was a sad climax to Colin's career – not that he was no stranger to personal disappointment – but more importantly, it could have spoiled what was intended to be a festival celebrating a special birthday of a special club. In fact it did not, though Colin's absence from the two stellar, pre-eminent events, the dinner in the Guildhall and the match the following day, MCC v Rest of the World, was keenly felt. How he must have gnashed his teeth in frustration at missing all the fun.

Characteristically, he sent a message to the Guildhall diners from his hospital bed, 'Keep cricket a happy game.' They did. The celebrations and the match at the centrepiece of the whole thing were a resounding success and for this Colin gave full credit to Hubert, who stepped into his shoes and fulfilled the president's role with energy, competence and aplomb. The bicentenary year was a private disappointment but a public triumph.

After the Lord Mayor's Show... The ancillary to this celebrated saying is not so well known. After the Lord Mayor's Show comes the dustcart. One might have expected at the conclusion of his year's presidency that Colin would have retired quietly to Angmering Park, to watch the gallops and recover from his heart operation. Not a bit of it. His diplomatic skills were required at another place, which also needed an urgent makeover.

The Imperial Cricket Conference – the name says it all really – was set up in 1909 to govern world cricket and comprised only three members, England, Australia and South Africa. It was renamed the International Cricket Conference in 1965 to reflect its wider membership but, according to Colin, 'It had no teeth,' amply illustrated by its impotence in the face of the Packer Revolution and the introduction of World Series Cricket. 'So, for ten years it had stagnated,' wrote Colin in his notes, 'not strengthening its position. What it needed was a chairman who could travel the world, consult with the cricket-playing boards, and put in place a proper governing structure with adequate financial support.'

Traditionally, the chairman of the ICC was the extant president of MCC. Thus, in 1987, Colin had chaired meetings of both establishments. This was clearly not a good idea. For a start, that person would change every year and continuity became impossible. Furthermore the president/chairman had a foot, uneasily in Colin's case, in both camps. Thus, the leadership of world cricket lay in the hands of a man who had not been elected but had been nominated by his predecessor, in whose gift the appointment lay. Colin set about exploring means by which the two roles and therefore the two governing bodies could be detached from each other.

Times were a'changing and credit must go to Colin for recognising this and, what's more, doing something about it. 'Basically,' A.C. Smith told me, 'the ICC were expected to look after the minnows in the world game, the Hollands, the Canadas, the Argentinas, while the MCC were in charge of the Test-playing countries. The ICC needed to become independent, just like the TCCB, and run world cricket. Colin was just the man to supervise the passing over of power, to make the transition as smooth as possible.' *And did he succeed?* 'Yes he did. You see, everybody liked and trusted him. Why, he even got the Indians onside!'

In 1989, when he took up the chairmanship of the ICC (renamed the International Cricket Council, to reflect the changed nature of its governance), Colin was no longer president of MCC. The two roles had been separated.

He was not entering the lion's den blindfolded; he was aware of the huge task that lay before him. Whether it was a good idea for a man not in the rudest of health was a moot point, he was not about to shirk this challenge, whatever his doctors advised. And, like the planner he was, he sat down and drew up a synopsis of the problems confronting him. It is neatly laid out in his notes.

There were three areas of major concern, he judged. The first was: slow over rates; continual interruptions in play; short-pitched bowling; bad behaviour and confrontational attitudes; loss of respect for umpires; sledging; the demise of spin bowling; the need for an international panel of umpires and referees. Much of it sounds all rather familiar, doesn't it?

The second uncertainty was commercial. The ICC needed to act as a central body independent of its member boards. It depended on the charity of the richer members to function. It was crucial to develop its own source of income and sustainability. The ICC still had its offices at Lord's. The move to Dubai was yet a pipe dream. To that end, the search for sponsorship and advertising revenue needed greater emphasis. Colin saw the rights to the World Cup as crucial in this regard.

The third gridlock was political. When was it ever not? Colin was aware as anyone that South Africa's isolation, necessary as it was, 'cast a dreadful shadow over the health and prosperity of the world game'. Hand in hand with that thorny bramble went the proposed invitation to the top table of Test cricket for Zimbabwe (who were opposed to any contact with South Africa) and Sri Lanka (who were in the middle of a civil war). There was also the continued refusal of India and Pakistan to play each other and the enveloping financial crisis afflicting the West Indies. What perturbation! How he must have wished for the powerfully reassuring presence of Les Ames at his side.

Unsurprisingly, the commercial and political details of the job interested him less than the cricket, though he argued in his notes that all three were interdependent. More than anything else, he was becoming increasingly 'fed up' with the belligerence displayed by players under the bogus justification of professionalism and competitiveness.

Quite possibly, his distaste for unnecessarily aggressive behaviour on the field of play had come to a head during his last two tours Down Under. Certainly, he had no rapport with Illingworth's hard-nosed brand of captaincy in 1970/71 and what he thought of being called 'fatso' by Jeff Thomson on the 1974/75 tour can only be imagined. But this was not personal. He observed a trend and he abhorred it. The game was becoming professional; that he endorsed and applauded. Then why should the players not behave professionally? If they did not, why were there no means to ensure that they did?

Sledging was a new phenomenon, one that he had never before encountered. Personal abuse directed at a batsman? It just never happened. 'The ground rules of good manners and a proper spirit of sportsmanship seem to have been abandoned overnight.' He put the blame, and the responsibility, firmly in the court of the captains. He quoted the Laws of Cricket, which state perfectly clearly, 'It is the responsibility of the captain at all times to see that the game is played within the spirit of the game as well as within the laws of the game.' What part of that sentence could possibly be open to interpretation, he reasoned. 'Yet captains are abrogating their responsibility,' he thundered, in so far as it was possible for Colin to thunder.

In addition, what Colin referred to as 'the flow of the game' was exercising him greatly. He recognised that limited-overs cricket had caught on in a big way, in spite of his earlier misgivings, and was encouraged by that. 'A wider and sometimes quite new audience has been opened up,' he wrote with enthusiasm. However, he feared for the future of five-day Test matches and three- or four-day championship cricket. 'I travelled the world in my capacity as ICC chairman and met boards,' he wrote, 'and the possible scenario that the days of Test cricket were numbered came as a douche of cold water.'

This was at a time when West Indies, with their tactic of employing four fast bowlers delivering a relentless barrage of short-pitched bowling, operating at the funereal pace of 12 overs an hour, were sweeping all before them. People were being turned off by the tedium of the spectacle. Slow over rates, the preponderance of fast, short-pitched bowling and the paucity of spin bowling were 'unacceptable', in his opinion, and were 'shining an amber light on the future of Test cricket'.

There was another headache but this one he makes no mention of in his notes. I doubt that he would have publicly admitted it anyway because it was brought on by the ceaseless pestering of a man he knew well and had come to respect enormously. If I say that man was none other than the great Sir Don Bradman then you might appreciate the cleft stick in which Colin found himself.

Who in the world of cricket, with the possible exception of Sir Garry Sobers, was more celebrated and honoured than The Don? Notwithstanding his incomparable exploits on the field, he had carved out for himself an eminent niche in the administration of the game, particularly in his home country of Australia. In short, when Bradman spoke, folk tended to sit up and take notice. Including Colin. Bradman had been kind and well disposed to him whenever they had met and they had struck up a warm friendship that endured to their deaths, coincidentally within two months of each other.

But Bradman clearly had a bee in his bonnet. Once it became public knowledge that Colin had been appointed chairman of the newly constituted ICC, and was therefore now a major player on the world stage, Bradman, believing he had the chairman's ear, proceeded to bend it, remorselessly. When you have waded through dozens of Bradman's letters to Colin, as I have, all written in his small, neat hand, banging on about his pet subject, you would have demanded not one tablet but a packet of paracetamol.

What was the bone of contention that exercised the mind of the greatest batsman in the history of the game? The back foot law. Not wishing to teach grandmother how to suck eggs, I shall endeavour to explain briefly Bradman's concern. The no-ball law used to be determined by where the bowler's back foot landed in relation to the return crease, the line adjacent to the stumps. If the back foot landed behind the crease, the ball was legitimate. The problem was that some bowlers, usually of the fast variety, tended to drag their toe across and beyond the crease, in effect delivering the ball several feet nearer the batsman. Some of the photos from that ill-fated MCC tour of Australia in 1958/59 (the generation of the 'chuckers' and 'draggers') showed bowlers with their front foot way in front of the popping crease. An unfair advantage, cried horrified onlookers and irate batsmen.

The worst offender was Gordon Rorke; so exaggerated was his drag that he actually was delivering the ball from 18 yards. 'If I'd played forward,' observed Colin at the time, 'I would have been standing on his foot.'

In 1963, the law was changed. Henceforth, if a bowler's front foot landed beyond the popping crease, that constituted a no-ball. To me, and to anybody else who has been brought up knowing no other, that seems to be an eminently sensible and logical law. After all, it applies to most sports. If you serve at tennis with a foot on the line, it's a foot fault. If you hit the board in a long jump, it's a no jump. If you intrude beyond the white line of a football pitch for a throw-in, it's a foul throw (or should be). A javelin thrower must not overstep the line even if his momentum carries him over subsequently.

A certain leeway is allowed for a bowler in that he can cut the line but not overstep it but the principle is the same. However, Bradman strongly disagreed, partly for technical reasons but probably because the old law had stood for over a century well enough so why change something that didn't need fixing? He lined up his sights on Colin and bombarded him with letters.

Attentively solicitous and ever cordial, Bradman always begins with the customary civilities and polite enquiries after the health and well-being of Colin, family and friends. Having had news of Colin's heart attack, he writes, 'Had a letter from Gubby [Allen] telling me you're OK. Great news. Just take it quietly for a while.' Congratulations are extended on a recent England win, 'Well done on England's fine win in the Test match against West Indies. It was not only good for England, it was good for cricket. The breaking of West Indian domination will have favourable consequences at all levels of the game.'

It is not long before he gets down to business. Obviously, he sees the chairman as a guiding rather than disinterested presence in committee and urges Colin to make use of his influence, 'As chairman, you are charged with a neutral stance. I believe you also have a bounden duty to make your convictions known. Your prestige as a person and former distinguished player is such that it is right for you to influence matters.'

What Colin's convictions were we do not know, as I am in possession of only Bradman's letters, not Colin's replies. No doubt they are among Bradman's papers but it is not hard to imagine that Colin kept his convictions to himself, if indeed he had any on this less than pressing subject. His job, he saw, was to gain consensus from a widely divergent and notoriously quarrelsome committee of board members on matters of more immediate concern than the back foot law.

But Bradman was not so easily put off and renewed the campaign. 'I hold the view, rightly or wrongly, that by and large the cricket law makers are too complacent.' He nudges Colin in another letter, 'I've been thinking of this back foot no-ball law and hope you are making progress.' Not enough, clearly, because in a later letter, he says, 'Whilst naturally I am a little impatient and frustrated at the delay in full consideration being given to my back foot proposal, I do understand that no law of cricket should be hastily altered without full consideration.'

After a while, patience starts to run out. 'Right now you have people who do really have a deep seated feel and appreciation of the problem being in danger of getting outvoted by people whose knowledge is 1 out of 10.' After further stonewalling, as he sees it, the tone of his letters becomes more strident. 'I confess to be totally frustrated...Is there no progress at all?...This matter is crying out for revision...If such a wide and knowledgeable group of people such as Richie Benaud, Colin Egar and Ian Chappell are in agreement with me, why is my voice not being heard?'

If that were so, and I have no reason to believe it was not, it must have been the only occasion in their long and bitter relationship that Don Bradman and Ian Chappell were in agreement. What hurt Bradman more than anything else, I sense, was that he felt he was being sidelined, something that had rarely happened to him before. He complained at being cut dead by Peter May and being fobbed off by Donald Carr when the subject of the back foot law was brought up. 'It seems to me that so long as Peter May, Doug Insole, Donald Carr and others sit pat and refuse to listen to reason, the game of cricket will continue to be saddled with this monstrously stupid law.'

The law was never changed. There was no appetite to do so. As far as I know, it was not even discussed. I presume that Colin deflected the tricky deliveries from his old friend with a dead bat and judicious use of the pad, much as he had defied the wiles of Ramadhin at Old Trafford in 1957.

Bradman was without doubt a powerful and persuasive figure in the cricket world but he was notoriously thin-skinned, a complex and highly driven man, obsessed by detail and not a little consumed by his own self-importance. Not given to close friendship, he remained loyal to those who gained his trust, not least of whom was Colin. He was for example fulsome in his compliments to Colin on the news of his knighthood. And his civility never let him down, even after the dismay at not getting that law changed. 'I hope you're not finding the exertion of the job too taxing. Jessie was 82 on Monday and sends her love.'

Nor was his competitive instinct on the wane, it seemed. There was always news of his golf. 'Still on 11. Played this morning and did the last nine in 38. Not bad for an ageing 79.' And who cannot, if not warm to, then at least commend, someone who takes the trouble to write this? 'So glad you are on the mend but please don't overdo things too soon. Look after yourself. Warmest regards. Don.'

If the back foot law did not make it on to the list of ICC priorities, drawn up by Colin at the outset of his chairmanship, how fared the others that did? In short, was Colin a success in the job? The general feeling, I believe, is that he was the right man in the right place at the right time. First and foremost, he managed to secure the independence of the ICC from the MCC and any of the national boards of control. 'The appointment of Colin was a masterstroke,' Alan Smith believed. 'He was a key player in making this happen. No one could have done it better than he. And for this, he must take a lot of the credit.'

Regulation was put in place that a minimum of 15 overs an hour should be bowled, with appropriate fines doled out to teams failing to meet this requirement. 'For the most part,' Colin was pleased to report to the council in 1992, 'this has been achieved by everyone, with just two instances of fining to date.' The principle of match referees had been adopted and his opinion was, 'The presence of the match referee has acted as a deterrent, so providing protection of the umpire and helping to restore his authority and status.' Bad behaviour on the field, aggressive conduct and unacceptable sledging 'have been reduced but the umpires will continue to keep a rigorous eye on this'. The appointment of neutral referees had been agreed and thereafter, in Test matches one of the two umpires would be 'neutral'. I thought all umpires should be neutral but the word was taken to mean 'not from the home team's country', as used to be the case.

Of course, in Colin's view, this was no more than a stop-gap measure. He wanted to see in place an international panel of umpires, wholly independent and responsible for the officiating of international matches worldwide. The Elite Panel of ICC Umpires did not come into being until 2002 but a start had been made. In the meantime, he encouraged board members to give much thought to 'this complicated and controversial subject' and looked forward to the day 'when the financial climate improves and sponsorship is forthcoming'. He did not live to see that day but he had set in train the impetus to bring it about.

It has been my opinion, and that of others I have consulted, both within the game and interested onlookers, that behaviour on the field of play, both at international and first-class level, is, on the whole, acceptable and greatly improved since the bad old days when Colin's career was coming to a close. 'The problem is not in the professional game,' John Holder, the former Test umpire told me, 'which is, by and large, properly policed and effectively enforced, but in the recreational game, where behaviour is, frankly, appalling.' Colin would have been shocked at that. As was I. As would anyone who laboured under the naïve belief that cricket was a game to be enjoyed. MCC are currently much concerned about this and are taking sensible measures to deal with it. Colin's remit was not the recreational but the international game and the introduction of match referees, neutral umpires and a closer watch on player behaviour all came into force on his watch. As A.C. Smith observed, the credit was his.

The concerns over too much short-pitched bowling and the demise of the spinner slowly disappeared, or at least faded into the background. A lot of people, Colin included, had become disenchanted with the ugly spectacle of four very fast bowlers being used in rotation throughout the day, as employed by the West Indies throughout the 1970s and 1980s, with a half-volley as rare a sighting as Lord Lucan, and believed something should be done about it. Quite what, nobody was sure. The West Indies were not complaining. They were world champions and had no desire to have their wings clipped. And, to be honest, nor would any other country had they had the same armoury at their disposal.

But for many reasons, which do not concern us here, the deep well of terrifyingly fast bowlers from the Caribbean started to dry up. Reverse swing came to the fore, perfected by practitioners such as Imran Khan, Wasim Akram, Waqar Younis and copied by others, and relentless short-pitched bowling, aimed at the body, fell out of fashion. I abjure the use of the word 'intimidatory'. *All* fast bowling is intimidating. It is up to the umpires to step in if it gets out of hand and threatens life and limb. 'And don't forget helmets!' Alan Smith reminded me. Indeed not. The introduction of helmets has gone a long way to reducing the negative effect of short-pitched bowling. Thus the problem, much to Colin's relief, faded into the background.

Spin bowling, to everybody's chagrin, did indeed appear to be dying out. Then a genius appeared on the scene and single-handedly, it seemed, he saved the breed from extinction and reinvigorated the art. Shane Warne made his Test debut in 1992 and the rest is history. Colin could sleep easy at night. The heritage of spin bowling, stretching back through the ages, including in its family tree Abdul Qadir, Bhagwat Chandrasekhar, Derek Underwood, Bishan Bedi, Sonny Ramadhin, Jim Laker, Hedley Verity, Clarrie Grimmett even back to Bernard Bosanquet, the inventor of the googly, was safe in Warne's hands, or fingers.

Those who claim – and there are a few – that Colin enjoyed more than his fair share of good fortune in his life point to several serendipitous events and juicy half-volleys during his career, on and off the pitch. All I can say is this. What batsman has ever scored a hundred without a slice of luck somewhere along the line?

The same goes for what is probably regarded as Colin's crowning achievement during his stewardship of the ICC. I refer to the re-admission of South Africa to world cricket in 1991. It is undeniably true that political and social forces were already in motion, which would result in the release of Nelson Mandela from prison, negotiations with the national government, led by F.W. de Klerk, towards free and fair democratic elections and the eventual assumption by Mandela of the presidency. Over these momentous developments, Colin had no influence; of course he didn't. But he saw the opportunity and used his considerable authority and powers of persuasion to pave the path for South Africa's re-admittance.

Private negotiations had been going on for months, involving not only cricket boards but also governments. I do not know which airline Colin used as he travelled the world in his capacity of chairman but the air miles must have been totting up handsomely. One key player in all the comings and goings of the South Africa business was Ali Bacher.

He and Colin were old adversaries on the field of play. Bacher had made his Test debut at Lord's in 1965, in a three-match series, which South Africa won. Following the end of his playing career, he had become an administrator in the game, overseeing a controversial period when he organised a number of rebel tours of his country during the apartheid years and isolation. But, to his credit, he saw, quicker than most, which way the wind of politics was blowing and worked tirelessly to put in place the amalgamation of the two warring factions of domestic cricket in South Africa, the South African Cricket Union (white) and the South African Cricket Board (multi-racial). Once that significant step had been taken, the decks were cleared for total re-integration.

But not so fast. Colin, by nature a cautious man, knew that it was imperative to get the politicians, as well as the cricket administrators, of all the countries on board. India, in particular, remained sceptical. The more emboldened of the ICC delegates and supporters of South Africa's re-admittance had targeted the World Cup in March 1992, to be held jointly in Australia and New Zealand, but Colin thought that was probably premature. In July 1991, at a meeting of the ICC, he had made up his mind to disallow South Africa's participation in the World Cup, believing that insufficient groundwork had been done by the two boards of control still operating in that country; true democracy, in cricket as in politics, was still in its fledgling state.

However, events took a surprising turn. The newly released Nelson Mandela replaced the ailing Oliver Tambo as the president of the ANC and he was anxious to bring an end to the 'armed struggle', secure peace to the country and open negotiations to end apartheid rule in South Africa. He needed international backing.

One of his masterstrokes was to lobby the ICC for South Africa's inclusion in the World Cup. He used the same masterstroke, the country's abiding passion for sport, to even greater effect at the rugby

World Cup in 1995, when he presented the Webb Ellis Cup to the victorious South African captain, Francois Pienaar, dressed in a green Springbok jersey. He was a master of public relations. Accordingly, he set in motion a campaign to promote South Africa's cause, leaving no stone unturned, no government minister undisturbed, no prime minister or president at peace; even the chairman of the ICC had the full beam of his attention turned in his direction.

In Colin's papers there are a number of faxes between members of Mandela's team and the British government. Here is an excerpt from one, Thabo Mbeki, Mandela's deputy and later successor, to Douglas Hurd, the foreign secretary, 'I write to you, Sir, to inform you of our support for this application. As you are undoubtedly aware, the ANC has for many years been involved in the struggle to end apartheid in sport...In light of these developments, we request you use your good offices to encourage the admission of the United Board of South Africa into the ICC.'

Two things should be noted. The use of the word 'united' in the new name for the governing body of South African cricket was significant, crucial even. And Hurd's prime minister was John Major, cricket lover and clandestine friend and confidant of Colin.

Still Colin was minded to remain cautious. That is until he received a personal fax, with the ANC logo at the top, from Nelson Mandela himself, from which I quote, 'The ANC wishes to inform the International Cricket Council that the ANC fully supports the application of the United South African Cricket Board...The United South African Cricket Board is a non-racial, democratic body and it has cricket development programmes which it is implementing throughout South Africa. Further, their participation in that competition [the World Cup] will enhance the process of unity in sport as well as the spirit of reconciliation generally in my country.'

Those words, 'unity in sport', must have been music to Colin's ears.

The cricket lover at heart may have been rejoicing but in public he had to be more measured. This was now September 1991. The World Cup was in the following March. Time was short, very short. Colin moved swiftly. He wrote to Andrew Turnbull, the Parliamentary Private Secretary to prime minister John Major thus, 'The more I think about it, the more I realise this letter makes it game, set and match with the Test-playing countries. There is no way I could envisage telling the cricket world we had knocked back Nelson Mandela.'

Two days later, he wrote to Michael Melhuish, the MCC president, who had incidentally been in the Cambridge team in 1954 when Colin was captain of Oxford and M.J.K. Smith had scored that double hundred, 'There is now no logical reason why South Africa should not be admitted to the World Cup.'

A Special General Meeting of the ICC was immediately called – it took place on 23 October – in which Colin made a statement. The minutes were in his papers, 'The chairman stated that since his own decision was made in July to disallow South Africa from participating in the World Cup in 1992, several significant changes have taken place... Above all, Nelson Mandela had personally written to the chairman of the ICC to allow South Africa to play in the World Cup. That in itself was a major development.' General discussion ensued. 'After consultation with the delegates, the chairman announced that since there was no opposition to the proposed resolution and the delegates had achieved consensus, South Africa would be included as the ninth team to take part in the 1992 World Cup.'

It would not take a leap of imagination to picture Colin and John Major raising their glasses of G&T in celebration in the private flat above 10 Downing Street. More publicly, of the many letters and notes of congratulation that Colin received, two will suffice, 'Surely the most positive and productive ICC meeting ever. Well played indeed, Mr Chairman!' Signed, Peter West. Another came from an old friend and ex-England colleague, who had also played against Coin, twice, in the Varsity match, Raman Subba Row, 'Very well played, Chairman!'

The acclamation was not universal however; it never is. *The Times* took exception to ICC inertia in the face of rapidly changing socio-political circumstances, 'This should have been firmly and irrevocably decided three months ago.' Subba Row sprang to his friend's defence. Colin kept a copy of the letter that Subba Row sent to *The Times*. 'Politics – like cricket – is a game of timing. Too slow and you get too far behind the clock. Too quick and you may have no wickets left to win the match. But the right pace brings its rewards – in this case the happy and universally accepted return of South African cricket. Securing the endorsement of Mr Mandela, as well as the Commonwealth heads of government was a triumph for South African cricket administration and for Colin Cowdrey as chairman of ICC. Far from decrying a well-timed innings, we should be applauding the near perfect performance of the players in this match.'

Generally, it was accepted that Colin had played a blinder. He was able to report thus at the AGM of the ICC in July of the following year, after the World Cup, 'With the full blessing of the ANC, the ICC conference of 1991 saw the restoration of our formal links with that country and the new United Cricket Board of South Africa has been welcomed as a full member of the ICC. They made an historic visit to India and played in the World Cup in Australia and New Zealand. This was followed by a short tour of the West Indies with their first full Test match against the West Indies in Barbados. A full international programme lies ahead.' Indeed it did. South Africa were back.

Colin wrote to Ali Bacher after the tour to India. Of course he did. He single-handedly kept the Post Office solvent. 'Congratulations on your triumphant tour through India. I would think that you were quite overcome by the welcome you received...It is really marvellous that the ice has been broken and you will be going from strength to strength.' Prescient words. Twenty years later, South Africa were ranked number one in the world.

News of Colin's knighthood later that year – 'for services to cricket' – came as no surprise but with considerable delight and satisfaction to his many friends. Letters, faxes, telegrams of congratulations poured in from all over the world. One obviously amused him because he kept it and I came across it buried in his papers. It was from Buckingham Palace, addressed formally to Sir Colin Cowdrey, with the usual (I imagine) stuff about procedure and protocol. It concludes with this paragraph, 'In the past there have been occasions when a person to be knighted has been unable to kneel. To avoid any possible embarrassment, I should be grateful if you would answer the question below. Are you able to kneel? YES/NO' With evident glee and no doubt a smile playing about his lips, Colin crossed out NO and signed it.

One can imagine Colin swapping the medal on his lapel for a trainers' pass at any race meeting where his wife had a runner and this he frequently did, proving to be a loyal and enthusiastic supporter of her career, even though his knowledge of horses was minimal. Notwithstanding the calls of his new-found hobby, his diary was full with other commitments. Christopher, at his father's memorial service, referred to his 'enduring fault' of never being able to say no. Except when he was batting with Boycott, he privately added.

There would be a ribbon to be cut here, a plaque to be unveiled there and a new pavilion to be opened somewhere else. He was perpetually in demand at dinners, commemorative functions, charity auctions, benefactors' galas, benefit matches – you name it, if the occasion had cricket somewhere in its headline, Colin would be there. He was invited on to boards, councils, governing bodies, committees. I did a rough tally of the organisations he represented, those at any rate that I found evidence of in his papers. They included: chairman of, variously, MCC cricket committee, county pitches committee and Southern Sports Council; member of the Winston Churchill Fellowship Awards Committee; treasurer of the Percy Bilton Charity (for disadvantaged and disabled children); non-executive director of Bilton plc: member of the council for the British Heart Foundation; president of the Lord's Taverners and the Association of Cricket Umpires; trustee of MCC; Fellow of the University of Durham. The list is exhaustive.

Exhausting too. Why did a man with a dicky heart spread himself so lavishly instead of gently embracing the sixth of Shakespeare's Seven Ages of Man, 'the lean and slippered pantaloons/with spectacles on nose and pouch on side', with the occasional round of golf thrown in? In short, why could he not say no?

His life had been blessed; he would have been the first to admit that. He had been able to play cricket, at the highest level and for longer than anyone could dare to hope, and rarely did a day pass when he did not give thanks for this. As a result, he felt he owed a debt of gratitude to the game. He wanted to give back, to repay, to share and to enthuse. Cricket was more than a game to him, it was a way of life and his life now was to spread the gospel. This he did in spadefuls. The consequences, as we shall see, were heartbreaking. If cricket was his life, it cost him his life.

Before the umpire raised his finger, there was another honour for which Colin could respectfully raise his bat. His close friendship with John Major, known only to a small circle of trusted aides and one of which the wider world was largely ignorant, was to have an extraordinary outcome. In June 1997 it was announced that Colin was about to be made a peer of the realm. Immediately, unsympathetic commentators, cynical journalists and scribes with a bee in their bonnet leapt upon this as evidence of naked cronyism, the prime minister rewarding his old chum and cricket hero with a nice little sinecure in the House of Lords. The quip of Colin swapping one cushy seat at Lord's for another at Lords gained plenty of traction.

The truth was quite different and took a while to come out. For some time, Colin had been working quietly behind the scenes on a scheme to unearth and nurture sporting talent from a young generation becoming increasingly inert and lacking in ambition and, crucially, opportunity. He had suggested the idea to Major and the prime minister, being a sporting fanatic himself, picked it up and ran with it. He needed a voice and a platform. The voice was provided by one of the most public – and respected – sporting personalities in the country, Colin Cowdrey, and the platform, a political one that did not need a constituency and an election, was provided by the House of Lords.

Thus Colin was ennobled as Baron Cowdrey of Tonbridge. Note the geographical location contained in the title. His friends had suggested Canterbury but he had rejected the very idea – he would be stepping on a certain archbishop's toes, he reasoned. His old England team-mate Basil D'Oliveira, who always mischievously referred to Colin as Mr Choudary, now proposed he should be known as Lord Choudary of Bangalore. Instead, Colin settled upon The Lord Cowdrey of Tonbridge, thus indicating where his heart, and his abiding gratitude, lay. 'But what shall we call you now, Master?' cried another old team-mate, Brian Luckhurst. 'How about Lord and Master?' came back the droll reply.

The carping upset Colin's many supporters. Ian Wooldridge, the well-known *Daily Mail* sports columnist, rushed to his defence in print. 'Throughout his life, Colin Cowdrey has been a modest, almost self-deprecating, man and as such he will assuredly be aware today that there are those who will ridicule his preferment. There always are...Colin Cowdrey now has a public platform from which to press home his scheme. It is called the House of Lords and he intends to use it...I am delighted for him as I am for all other sportsmen so honoured today. These men have contributed hugely to British sport and the day some disgruntled old runt seeks to destroy the system, this country will be the poorer for it.'

And so say all of us was the message from hundreds of well-wishers. I select but a few from many in his personal files. 'It is a great honour for you and the game. You will wear it lightly and with distinction as you have carried many other honours,' Rev. David Sheppard, Archbishop of Liverpool. 'My dear Kipper, Will hope to speak to you on the blower soon but if I don't, may I be the last to congratulate you on your appearance up the order,' Doug Insole. 'Dear Kipper, I hope your ears have been burning just a little because I have told all and sundry that there never has been an award more deserved than this one to you, You are truly a marvel to have achieved so much for which all in cricket can be very grateful. Good on you, my Lord!' Ted Dexter.

And this writer needs no identifying. 'My dear Choudary, What a star! Absolutely wasted on this earth. I am sure there are higher things awaiting you. I am sure there were huge celebrations (tea parties) in Bangalore for one of their long lost sons...You are truly a lovely man.' What would have warmed Colin's heart was that all these letters, and many more, came from cricketers, ex-colleagues and opponents, his tribe, if you like. Lest anyone assume that it was only the fraternity who were happy for him, let HRH Prince Edward speak for the great and the good throughout the land. 'Very many congratulations on your elevation to a life peer. This is great news and I am delighted for you.'

Colin did not waste time. This was no undemanding half-volley he had been delivered. The demise of sport in schools was a national scandal, exercising the minds of people from many professions, not just politicians. Colin rose to make his maiden speech in the Upper House a mere six months after his investiture. Some peers wait for years before strapping on the pads. Some peers never get changed. Was he nervous?

'I rise with some trepidation and with many more butterflies in the tummy, I can assure noble Lords, than ever I endured at the other Lord's, almost as hallowed, but no less noble.'

Quickly, he warmed to his theme, sport in schools, 'It is a subject dear to my heart and to many across the land...I long for time, almost more than money, to be given to the school curriculum for sport...This time last year, I was set a task by the then prime minister, the Right Honourable John Major, as part of his initiative, Raising the Game. I was charged to form a small group comprising Sports Council, head teachers and PE teachers to see whether it would be practicable if we could persuade leading sportsmen and sportswomen to visit schools and demonstrate their skills...The task is daunting. There are too few of them [skilled PE teachers] to cope with the vast numbers, the limited playing fields, inadequate facilities and too little time given to each pupil.'

He then went on to evaluate the importance of his message, 'The great thing about sport is that one is never as successful for very long. When one starts to get above oneself, it is a terrific leveller because one loses very much more than one wins. This is a wonderful teacher for life.'

He concluded with this heartfelt rallying cry for those who would take up the initiative, 'I hope this debate today will send a signal to all head teachers, urging them to give a little more time to sport and, what is more important, when they do so they will be able to do so with government approval.'

Did the House rise to him, as they used to do at that other place (I refer to Lord's, not the Commons) as he resumed his seat? No, they did not. It is not custom and practice to do so. But the praise he received afterwards was unstinting.

Once again, a copious number of congratulatory letters dropped through his letterbox. Here are three that I have chosen from his files. 'Heartfelt congratulations on your speech today. After 51 years in the House, I count it as one of the great ones,' Earl of Longford. 'You made the most magnificent speech. Many congratulations... one of the best speeches in the House for many a long year,' Lord Moynihan. 'I thought I should drop you a line to thank you for initiating Wednesday's invaluable debate on sport,' Trevor Brooking in his role as chairman of Sport England.

Mischievously, I have occasionally wondered how their lordships behave during a debate in the Lords in which they are not participating and in which they might have little interest. Do they sit and listen quietly or do they heckle and behave rudely, as they seem to do in the other House? Or, to put it another way, when they are on the back benches, do the more playful of their number keep slumber at bay with furtive chatter like naughty schoolboys in the back row in class?

I asked a fellow peer and old friend of Colin's, Ian MacLaurin, whether they ever attended debates in the chamber together.

The former chairman of Tesco, Vodafone and the ECB, The Lord MacLaurin of Knebworth fixed me with those unwavering eyes, much as he did back in the days when I used to teach his son. Then he grinned, 'Colin and I got to know each other well, particularly when I started to run English cricket.'

MacLaurin, we must remember, like Colin, was something of a schoolboy prodigy as a cricketer and had pretensions of playing for his native county, Kent, before a career in the retail trade claimed him. With this in mind, he was keen to share one of his memories. 'Whenever we attended functions together and he was down to speak – which was often – Colin would turn to me and say to his audience that he was pleased and honoured to have his old friend, Ian MacLaurin present. "Though I could never understand," he would add, "why he turned down playing for Kent to become a *grocer!*" The way he said "grocer" never failed to bring the house down.'

Talking of houses, what happened when you attended debates together in the Lords? 'I would be pretending to listen to a speech on something or other and there would be a little nudge in my ribs, accompanied by a written note. "Why on earth are you contemplating splitting the championship into two divisions?" it would say. Or, "What's this Twenty20 thing you're proposing? What will that do to our great game?" I'd write back, "Because I think it's a good idea. After all, we've just lost the Benson and Hedges competition. We think it might catch on." And so on. It was wonderful banter, great fun. It was a huge honour and pleasure to have known him. It was a very, very special time for me.'

Colin did not rest on his laurels. He knew as well as anyone that you are only as good as your last innings. He had contacts, he had influence, he had the ear of important people who could exert pressure. None more so than the prime minister. Of course the prime minister was no longer his chum, John Major, but that made little difference. In point of fact, he had close personal contact with the past three premiers.

Among the hand-written letters from Number 10 which I unearthed in his papers, there are three that stand out. One from Margaret Thatcher, 'Thank you so much for your kind letter about the recent leadership change. I do appreciate it....It has been a difficult time but I'm sure the decision I took was the best under the circumstances.' Denis Thatcher, let us not forget, was a keen cricket fan and he and Colin were good friends. The friendship with John Major was even closer. Evidently in response to a letter of congratulation on his election victory in 1992, Major had written, 'Thank you for your kind letter...Such support is heartwarming, especially in view of all the hard work that lies ahead.' And just to show that the colours of Kent embraced both blue and red, Colin had clearly been badgering the new Labour prime minister, Tony Blair, following his initiative in the House of Lords debate. Blair had written back, saying, 'Thank you for your letter seeking a meeting to discuss regenerating grass roots sport.'

* * * * *

I do not believe the meeting ever took place. Two months later, Colin had a major stroke and effectively, his public life came to an end. Not the least of the sadness of this untimely event was that, having tirelessly manoeuvred himself into a position where he could make a difference to the paucity of opportunities for sport for the young, his health, not his resolve let him down. It was nothing short of tragic.

The stroke was untimely in another distressing way, this time closer to home. With his two sons, Christopher and Graham, having finished their careers with Kent (the other son, Jeremy, had chosen to pursue a career in the City), the coast was clear for Colin to become president of his old club. Hitherto, he had always resisted requests to become Kent's president while his sons were still playing but now there was no excuse; he accepted, with alacrity, pleasure and modesty.

As with his presidency of MCC, there was a harmonious correlation in the date. It was the millennium year, 2000. He was equally pleased that 2000 had been earmarked by Kent for an appeal for youth cricket in the county. As usual, he sat down to work out a plan for how best to celebrate the special season. The centrepiece would be a President's Tent for each day of the match during Canterbury Week. On all four days, he invited about 70 people to lunch and to watch the game. One proud guest was his captain at Oxford, Alan Dowding. He remembers the occasion with great fondness. 'Colin looked fine. He stood up to welcome us all and spoke brilliantly, with no notes. He remembered everyone in the room and made reference to us all in his usual, wonderful, smiling, cheerful way. It is so sad to think that was the last time any of us saw him.'

That evening, Colin was struck down by a stroke. It was serious. At the hospital, the family gathered and while there, they decided the best way to proceed was for each one of the boys to take it in turns to host the remaining three days at Canterbury, while the other two remained by their father's bedside. That the lunches went ahead at all was a tribute to their emotional resilience; that the celebrations were a great success says a great deal about the Cowdrey tradition of courage, fortitude and tenacity in the face of ill fortune, leavened as always with a sprinkling of humour. The show must go on. Or, to put it another way, no matter what the score, how many wickets have gone down, you have to pick up your bat, put on your gloves and go out there to do battle. By all accounts, they carried it off with the same aplomb as their father would have done, while inside, their hearts were close to breaking.

There is a charming letter in Colin's files, a hastily scrawled missive on A4 paper, written by Carol to her father when she got back home after having attended the second of the three re-organised lunches. I quote from it, not sparing her blushes or her wrath at my temerity, but I hope she will forgive me. 'Darling Dad, Jay was amazing. Everybody thought he was brilliant. You would have been proud. If ever you have doubted in your life how much people like and admire you – never doubt it again...Chris had the same reaction yesterday and I'm sure Graham will tomorrow...You've given us all a great scare this week. We have been *so* delighted to see you fighting back. I love you to bits. C x'

She showed me a photo of all three occasions, with Chris, Jeremy (Jay) and Graham giving their speeches. 'Look at the boys,' she urged me. 'The strain is etched on their faces. How they managed is beyond me.'

But they did. It was the Cowdrey way. Just as it was the Cowdrey way to fight back. The family were in awe at how Colin battled to overcome the catastrophic effects of his stroke. He had regular physiotherapy, something he did not shirk, in an attempt to learn how to walk again but it was a huge struggle, one that he was never going to win. Chris remembers his father in some of these sessions 'where he would try to catch a tennis ball while walking slowly, which seemed to stimulate his mind and movement'. As you would expect, he reminded me, of someone who stood third in the list of all-time English catchers in Test cricket, below Cook and Strauss and equal with Botham, on 120.

'A week before Dad died,' Jeremy said, 'he got himself dressed up in his Kent tie and went to a pub supper with Carol and me. He walked very, very shakily into the pub. He was never going to be back to normal.' Nevertheless, Colin's thoughts, as usual, were with others, not his own predicament. There is a delightful telegram in his files, sent from the Cowdrey family. 'For the attention of Alec Stewart, c/o the England Team. Message: Our father was having his first food since the stroke. The nurse told him it was the day of your 100th Test. After a pause and with a mouthful of porridge, he said, *Send a fax... wish them luck!*'

Yet again, the letters poured in. To plagiarise Carol's words, if anybody doubted the affection and regard in which Colin was held throughout the cricketing world, both playing and spectating, never doubt it again, having read through the reams of goodwill. 'My dear Kipper, Glancing through the paper today, I came across a little snippet which, much to my alarm, stated that you had not been well... There is nothing in the world you HAVE to do. Not doing it will not change the world,' Frank Tyson, in Queensland. 'Dear Colin, I hear from your myriad offspring that you are out of hospital. Great news,' Mark Nicholas. 'My dear Kipper, Delighted to hear you continue to make progress,' Doug Insole. 'Just heard the news – you shouldn't be overdoing it,' Tom Graveney. 'I was sorry to hear you were admitted to hospital. From what I hear, you are on the mend. I trust it is so,' Alec Bedser. And many, many more.

The messages of hope, encouragement and good luck were to no avail. Colin died, at home, on 4 December 2000, aged just 67.

Epilogue

'Some journey, some life, some cover drive,
some friend.'

Inscription on Colin Cowdrey's gravestone.
Words by John Woodcock

M ARCH of 2001 had been unseasonably cold, with bands
of rain, sleet and snow periodically sweeping across the
country. However, Friday 30 March dawned sunny in
London; the air had turned mild, with a hint of spring dancing on
the light wind. County cricketers, who would be reporting back for
summer duty in just two days' time, allowed themselves to believe that
yes, the season was truly just around the corner. Some of them were
dressed in club blazer and tie, unfamiliar attire for a clan resolutely
informal off the field of play, as they fell in step, making their way
towards the sound of the pealing bells of Westminster Abbey.

What brought them to this place, beside the River Thames, a
stone's throw, or a jolly good heave to the wicket from third man, from
the seat of government? Their sense of the importance of the occasion
must have grown, as half-familiar figures seemed to be joining them,
clearly heading in the same direction. Other cricketers yes, but some
long since retired, as well as recognisable faces from other sports and
influential walks of life.

Was that Sobers, with that familiar rolling gait? Yes it was. Tom
Graveney, Ian Botham, Mike Gatting, Ted Dexter, Dickie Bird, Asif
Iqbal, John Reid from New Zealand, Ali Bacher, Brian Huggett the

golfer. And that looks like the whole of the Kent team that won the championship back in 1970. Michael Stoute and Walter Swinburn from the world of racing, Brian Rix, Ronnie Corbett, and what was William Hague doing here? And is that – it can't be – John Major? Well, well, well. They were aware that Colin Cowdrey knew lots of people but this was ridiculous.

The crowd, sorry, congregation, was enormous. Somebody said the old abbey could have been filled four times over. Just as well they had a pass. Nice of the Cowdreys to leave them tickets on the gate, sorry again, nice of them to send invitations to their father's memorial service. It could only be here, couldn't it, at the site of coronations and burials of kings and queens, that his life would be celebrated. Still, no less than the old boy deserved.

As the great and the good made their way up the aisle to take their seats, the hum of conversation, interspersed with the odd cry of recognition, overlay Albinoni's 'Adagio' on the organ. At once, the opening bars of the hymn 'Praise To The Lord The Almighty' rang out and everybody rose. This was no diffident congregation; voices soared. The bidding prayers were delivered by the Dean of Westminster. His final enjoinder said it all, 'Therefore let us remember Colin Cowdrey who by his life and his faith graced our nation.'

A frail, stooped figure made his unsteady way to the lectern but his firm diction belied his age. John Woodcock read the lesson, the famous one from Corinthians – 'Though I speak with the tongues of men and angels and have not charity, I am become as sounding brass, or a tinkling cymbal.' – as if he knew it by heart. 'When I was a child, I spake as a child, I understood as a child, I thought as a child but when I became a man, I put away childish things. For now we see through a glass darkly...now abideth faith, hope and charity, these three, but the greatest of these is charity.' You could almost sense everybody nodding inwardly. That was Colin all right.

The rousing hymn, 'Guide Me, O Thou Great Redeemer', deflected any such introspective thoughts. There was a rustle of expectation as Christopher Cowdrey walked briskly to the lectern to deliver the eulogy to his father. His reputation as a speaker went before him. He did not disappoint. The same ability to tell a story, to recount an anecdote, to make a point, to convey a truism, with a light, but never a frivolous, touch – so reminiscent of his father – was all there.

Some of the memories were well-known, such as the call-up at the age of 42 to Australia to face the fury of Lillee and Thomson, but lost nothing in the retelling. The story of the parental telling-off for poor work in the back of the car at prep school, which turned into a synopsis of the second headed goal of five Chris had scored that afternoon, brought audible gasps of laughter from his audience. Due recognition was given to special guests, among whom were representatives from all the Test-playing nations, the current captains of Homefield School, Tonbridge School and Oxford University, and all the Kent team who won the championship in 1970. 'My father would be proud that every part of his life is so well represented here,' including 'his beloved family and nine grandchildren'.

Another amusing story followed. When he was a young boy, Chris was taken to Lord's by Colin. 'This is the home of cricket,' his father told him, gesturing around the famous old ground. 'The home of MCC.' As a six-year-old, Chris was vaguely aware his father's initials were MCC and was secretly rather pleased that one day all this would be his.

He then went on to make mention of his father's celebrated habit of writing letters. 'Do not be surprised if each and every one of you has a card from him on your doorstep this afternoon, thanking you for coming.'

Of course, Chris continued, the family had to share Colin with the rest of the world, and there was no complaint about that, which was generous because, as we know, the family did miss him. The trouble was, as Chris pointed out, his father had one endearing fault. He could never say no. 'Was there a church fete he hadn't opened, a charity he hadn't supported or a school at which he hadn't spoken?' Sport had given him a position of privilege in life and he owed it to cricket to give a little bit back. Chris's final judgement was, 'He gave everything, and more.'

It was a masterful address from Colin's eldest son. Like one of his father's finest innings, it was perfectly pitched, beautifully timed, expertly crafted, a sparkling gem of a performance. Following John Barclay's reading of that delightful poem, *A Glorious Game We Say*, by William Douglas Home – 'Yes cricket's a glorious game, say we/ And cricket will live in eternity.' – the congregation were treated to a rendition of an excerpt from Arthur Sullivan's *Mikado*, with the lyrics specially adapted by Sir Tim Rice, a noted cricket lover and good friend of Colin's. One couplet in particular caught the ear:

'I used to think that sledging was a sport that needed snow.

But now I know it's something else, it really has to go.'

John Major was next in to bat, walking stiffly with that gammy leg of his towards the lectern. His tribute is reproduced in full at the front of this book. Suffice to say, according to those who were there, he spoke it even better than it reads.

That was it, more or less. The prayers were read, one by Colin's old compatriot, Rev. David Sheppard, the stirring hymn 'I Vow To Thee My Country' raised the roof and everybody retired to the strains of Widor's *Toccata* on the organ. Jeremy told me that the authorities at the abbey had been marvellous. 'They said we could organise it however we wanted. With one proviso, that the service did not exceed 60 minutes. We came in just under 59 minutes.' Colin would have been pleased at that. Just as he would have enjoyed the party later at the House of Lords.

As Garry Sobers had the first word at the front of this book, I give him the final words now.

'It was almost the perfect party. What would have made it perfect? Why, if Colin had been here of course.'